DATE DUE

AUG 0 6 2012	
MAR 1 9 2014	

THE WORLD THAT MADE NEW ORLEANS

FROM SPANISH SILVER TO CONGO SQUARE

Ned Sublette

Library of Congress Cataloging-in-Publication Data

Sublette, Ned, 1951–.

The world that made New Orleans : from Spanish silver to Congo Square /
Ned Sublette.

p.   cm.

Includes bibliographical references and index.

ISBN 978-1-55652-730-2 (cloth)

ISBN 978-1-55652-958-0 (paper)

1. New Orleans (La.) – Civilization.   2. New Orleans (La.) –History.   3. New
Orleans (La.) – Description and travel.   4. Louisiana – History – To
1803.   I. Title.

F379.N55S83   2008

976.3'35–dc22   2007031857

Jacket design: Monica Baziuk

Front cover photos: Twilight © Lee Tucker, (inset) Ned Sublette

Author photo: Alden Ford

Interior design: Pamela Juárez

pp. 47, 49, 70, 83, 84, 101, 108, 129, 159, 205, 256: New York Public Library

pp. 15, 51, 99: Department of Special Collections, University of Notre Dame Libraries

pp. 73, 249: Historic New Orleans Collection

pp. 277: Maryland Historical Society

pp. vi–vii, 278, 289, 300, 305, 307, 308, 309, 313: Ned Sublette

© 2008, 2009 by Ned Sublette

All rights reserved

Published by Lawrence Hill Books

An Imprint of Chicago Review Press, Incorporated

814 North Franklin Street

Chicago, Illinois 60610

ISBN 978-1-55652-730-2 (cloth)

ISBN 978-1-55652-958-0 (paper)

Printed in the United States of America

There is more gold to be gotten from men than from rivers.
—Bertolt Brecht, *Rise and Fall of the City of Mahagonny*

CONTENTS

St. Charles and Cadiz Streets,
New Orleans, February 2005.

THE SWAMP

1

ROCK THE CITY

"On sabbath evening," wrote a visitor to New Orleans in 1819, "the African slaves meet on the green, by the swamp, and rock the city with their Congo dances."[1]

Most of the United States was quiet on Sunday. In many parts of the rural, mostly Protestant nation, dancing was frowned on. But the mostly French-speaking, mostly Catholic, black-majority port city of New Orleans, proudly unassimilated into the English-speaking country that had annexed it, was rocking.

Jump forward 128 years, to Roy Brown's "Good Rockin' Tonight." If I had to name the first rock 'n' roll record, I would first say that there is no such thing, then I would pick "Good Rockin' Tonight." It was recorded at Cosimo Matassa's rudimentary studio on the edge of New Orleans's French Quarter: a microphone and a disc cutter, in the back room of a record store at Rampart and Dumaine.

Cosimo's place was catty-cornered from the legendary "green by the swamp," known in the old days as *Place Congo*, or Congo Square.

The distance between rocking the city in 1819 and "Good Rockin' Tonight" in 1947 was about a block.

This book is about how New Orleans got to 1819. It's not about music per se, but music will be a constant presence in it, the way it is in New Orleans.

When the United States took possession of the Louisiana Purchase in 1803, the city was an urban crossroads of languages, both spoken and musical, with a complex Afro-Louisianan culture already in existence. By the time

Louisiana became the eighteenth state in 1812, most of the elements that make New Orleans so visibly, and audibly, different from the rest of the country were already in place.

New Orleans was the product of complex struggles among competing international forces. It's easy to perceive New Orleans's apartness from the rest of the United States, and much writing about the city understandably treats it as an eccentric, peculiar place. But I prefer to see it in its wider context. A writer in 1812 called it "the great mart of all the wealth of the Western world."[2] By that time, New Orleans was a hub of commerce and communication that connected the Mississippi watershed, the Gulf Rim, the Atlantic seaboard, the Caribbean Rim, Western Europe (especially France and Spain), and various areas of West and central Africa.

New Orleans is an alternative American history all in itself. Different in everything, Louisiana had what amounted to three colonial eras in rapid succession: French, Spanish, Anglo-American. Moreover, each colonial power that ruled Louisiana was associated not only with a different European language, but with a different slave regime. Each change of flag brought new laws and customs, causing black New Orleans to develop differently according to the possibilities afforded it during each of the colonial periods, and each flag brought with it distinct black populations. The Bambara, the Bakongo, the Baptists—they came in different demographic waves, at different moments in history. Each new wave had to fit into, and became another layer in, the increasingly cosmopolitan African culture of New Orleans, which from the earliest days of slavery in Louisiana had its own personality.

Louisiana was founded as a French project, but the French colonization effort was halfhearted and brief, and the French king gave Louisiana away to Spain. A little more than forty years later, the still mostly French-speaking territory returned to French control—but only for twenty days, until Napoleon Bonaparte's governor could hand Louisiana over to the United States.

Spain held Louisiana for only about two generations—in theory, from 1762 to 1800; in practice, from 1769 to 1803. But this last third of the eighteenth century was a time of great change, encompassing the American, French, and Haitian revolutions. During this time, New Orleans began to be a port of importance, entering into its substantial ongoing relationship with Havana—a relationship that lasted more than 190 years. From the earliest days of New Orleans's commercialization as a port until the imposition of the U.S. embargo of Cuba by President Kennedy, New Orleans's constant trading partner was Havana, right across the Gulf of Mexico. The 1962 U.S. embargo of Cuba was also in effect an embargo of New Orleans, taking away a chunk of what had long been the city's core business and damaging the economy of New Orleans and the rest of the Gulf Coast. But not only that: with the embargo still in effect as of this writing, the more than forty years of communications blackout between New Orleans and Havana has clouded our memory of how important that link was, from Spanish colonial times though the 1950s.

Brief though it was, the Spanish period in New Orleans was crucial to the creation of Afro-Louisianan culture, and constitutes a singular moment in African American history. During the years when the Spanish governor of Louisiana reported to the Spanish captain general of Cuba, the rules in New Orleans regarding slaves were much like those in Havana. There was a large population of free people of color. Slaves were treated badly, but enslaved people had some liberties—most important, they had the right to purchase their freedom. That was more than black New Orleanians had before, and more than enslaved people in the United States would have.

In Cuba, where such a regime lasted through the entire experience of slavery, there is every indication that this greater degree of freedom within slavery was good for music. The big city of Havana, central to maritime commerce, took music in from all over, including from Louisiana, but radiated it out even more powerfully. As New Orleans grew, it would do the same, inhaling and exhaling music, up through the days of jazz, rhythm and blues, rock and roll, and the town's latter-day musical lingua franca, funk. Cities drive innovation, and New Orleans was *the* city of the antebellum South—a hot town where conditions existed for something new to appear, and a valve through which commerce and culture entered into and embarked from the United States.

Besides Cuba, there was another Antillean society whose legacy is essential to understanding New Orleans: the disappeared planter colony of Saint-Domingue, whose refugees transformed Cuba and Louisiana both. So did, from a distance, its black revolutionaries, who burned down the plantations of Saint-Domingue, forced the issue of emancipation, repelled the English, Spanish, and French armies, and created the Republic of Haiti, the second independent nation in the hemisphere. In the process, they reshaped the world's sugar and slavery businesses, and precipitated the bargain sale of Louisiana to the United States.

❧

To get around in New Orleans, you drive through history, navigating the dense web of references embedded in the street names. Lasalle. Iberville. Bienville. Orleans. Chartres. Poydras. Ulloa. Galvez. Miro. Carondelet. Claiborne. Lafitte. St. Louis. St. Charles. St. Claude. St. Bernard. Frenchmen. Names New Orleanians negotiate every day. The street map is a time capsule. Unpack all those names, and a lot of the city's history is right there.

Uptown, major thoroughfares are named for the big three of slave-owning presidents: Washington, Jefferson, and Jackson. The last president to own slaves while in office, Louisiana cotton planter Zachary Taylor, is commemorated by a street named General Taylor (pronounced something like *Jennatayla*), for his military leadership in the Mexican War, when he sent his troops down to New Orleans on steamboats.

You can even read history in the street names that aren't there. There's no Lincoln Street. Lincoln was considered the very devil when he ran for president in 1860, and wasn't even listed on the ballot in Louisiana, or anywhere in the South, because he was a threat to four billion dollars of human property—the total estimated on-paper value of slaves in the South. There's a Lincoln Avenue in the adjacent, unincorporated town of Metairie, but it's a double dead end, three blocks long.

Mystery, Music, and Pleasure are streets. Piety and Desire, without the latter of which Tennessee Williams would have had no streetcar, are a pair of one-way streets that run in contrary directions. A series of uptown streets dating from the 1830s commemorates Napoleon Bonaparte, who was the object of a considerable cult in Louisiana. Alongside the major thoroughfare named Napoleon, lesser streets celebrate the battles of his career: Valence, Jena, Milan (pronounced *Mylon*), Austerlitz, Marengo, Constantinople, Cadiz. This is a history that only commemorates victories, so there's no Moscow Street, no Waterloo, and certainly no Port-au-Prince. There is no Toussaint Louverture Avenue to honor the greatest black revolutionary leader in American history, betrayed and murdered by Napoleon.

For that matter, few New Orleans streets are named after black people. A stretch of Dryades Street (named to honor wood nymphs) was renamed Oretha Castle Haley Boulevard for the civil rights activist who died in 1987. A section of Melpomene (pronounced *Melpa-mean*)—just the part in the ghetto—was renamed Martin Luther King Boulevard while retaining its original name of the muse of tragedy spelled out on the sidewalk in chipped, gouged cornerstones. The entire length of the street wasn't renamed because it would have spoiled the set of nine parallel streets named for muses. ("We have no problems with Dr. King," said the president of the Coliseum Square

Association. "It's just that he wasn't a Greek muse.")[3] There is a corner where Martin Luther King meets Jefferson Davis.

In the city's antiquated architecture, slaves' handiwork is everywhere—in the grillwork, the tilework, the mortuary work, and the carpentry. One hundred fifty years ago, there were two dozen slave dealers in the vicinity of Gravier Street, with showrooms and slave jails. There are plenty of houses standing in New Orleans that are older than that—houses that were built by enslaved artisans, with the income from slaves' labor.

In New Orleans, you can easily see, and feel, that slavery wasn't so long ago.

2

THE GIFT OF THE RIVER

Mud, mud, mud.
　　—*Benjamin Henry Latrobe, describing New Orleans, 1819*[1]

*I*t was at a backyard Mardi Gras party where people kept falling out of their chairs.

Admittedly, there was drinking going on. But that wasn't the reason people were dropping onto the ground. Someone would shift their weight and suddenly a spindly, pointed, plastic chair leg would punch down, breaking through the soft, porous earth and penetrating the ground. The chair would tip over, dumping out its laughing, inebriated occupant.

New Orleans is not exactly built on land.

Thirty feet down there is not bedrock, but peat and clay. The water table is so high that the city has to bury its dead in aboveground tombs. The architect and engineer Benjamin Henry Latrobe, developing waterworks for the city in 1819, struck water not three feet down. There are vacant pockets underground where long-buried tree trunks and other organic material have rotted away. Many houses in the city sit on pilings that go fifty feet deep, or more; in the case of One Shell Square, at fifty-one stories the tallest building in Louisiana, they go two hundred feet deep.

The city is sinking. Some of New Orleans is subsiding a third of an inch or so a year. One of the worst-inundated sites of 2005, the Lakeview area, has sunk somewhere between ten to sixteen inches over the previous fifty years.[2] Not only that, the city is going south. Located on the hanging wall of a fault system, detached from the main continent, southeast Louisiana is sliding southward, away from North America, a few millimeters a year.[3]

And sea levels are rising.

∞

Louisiana is the nation's drainpipe. Approximately 41 percent of the runoff of the continental United States—water from as far away as New York State and Montana—flows down the Mississippi River past New Orleans on its way to the Gulf of Mexico.

After the Mississippi descends past New Orleans, it branches off into the delta, a maze of waterways and silt that becomes increasingly fractal.[4] Major Amos Stoddard noted in 1812 that "the Mississippi, near its confluence with the sea, is divided into five branches, and of course has its *embouchure* in the gulf by means of five mouths."[5]

There are delta regions all over the world, whose curious ecosystems figure in some of the oldest stories of civilization. "An incredible marshland, a tangled amphibious world, with floating islands of vegetation, muddy forests, fever-infested swamps and, living in this hostile environment, where wildlife thrives, a few wretched fishermen": that description of the delta in Romania where the Danube empties into the Black Sea could equally apply to the southern tip of Louisiana.[6] Statesmen of another time called the Mississippi "the American Nile"; upriver from New Orleans is the city of Memphis, formally incorporated in 1826 and named for the ancient Egyptian city.

Herodotus, the father of geography as well as of history, used the term "delta," deriving from the triangular letter of the Greek alphabet, to refer to the approximately triangular footprint of the fanning-out of the sedimentary deposit built up by the Nile as it approached the sea. "Anyone who sees Egypt," he wrote, "without having heard a word about it before, must perceive, if he has only common powers of observation, that [it] is an acquired country, the gift of the river."[7]

Lower Louisiana is a "gift of the river." Built up out of the Gulf of Mexico by the vast quantities of mud that the Mississippi River system carries, it's the geologically youngest part of the United States. As in other river deltas of the world, the area around the lower reaches of the Mississippi is mud—small grained, and, as a glance at southern Louisiana's riot of fast-growing flora can tell you, fertile.

There are no rocks in the soil of southern Louisiana, not "even a single pebble."[8] The river filters them out farther upstream. The filtering extends to the terrain of New Orleans: heavier grains of earth are closer to the river, so that the French Quarter has a coarser mud than the finer, slimier soil of what is known as Back of Town.

A traveler heading south to New Orleans in 1819 was surprised that plantations could be established on the unstable ground: "Early this morning we passed the thriving town of Baton-Rouge. . . . Not far from hence, the high lands or primitive soil terminates, beyond which, to the sea, the whole country is alluvial and marshy. Continued lines of settlements still present themselves on either bank, and cotton and sugar are the great articles of their agricultural opulence."[9] Even today, driving on the concrete ribbon of I-10 between Baton Rouge and New Orleans, it seems miraculous that they could run a highway over the slop.

Beyond New Orleans, the Mississippi River runs about ninety-five more miles, south by southeast, before it empties into the Gulf of Mexico. Obstructed by shifting sandbars, it has always been the least navigable part of the lower Mississippi. The Mississippi, which has changed its course various times over the millennia, took its present course in Louisiana perhaps eight hundred years ago, and the final fifty miles is geologically the newest of the new, built up only in that time. A glance at a satellite image of what geologists call the "alluvial birdfoot" of southernmost Louisiana makes clear that there is no exact demarcation where land ends and sea begins. What is called Plaquemines Parish is a strip thrown up by the Mississippi to either side that protrudes down into the Gulf of Mexico. Barely habitable, it has never been more than sparsely populated.

Old accounts refer to the town as the "Isle of Orleans." Built on the side of a natural levee of the Mississippi River, it pokes up out of a cypress swamp, surrounded by water and muck. Until the advent of electrical pumps in the 1890s made the swamp drainable, it slurped up to the edges of the city, constraining expansion that otherwise would have stretched outward from the crescent-shaped riverbend. Naturally fenced in, the town had a dense, urban character from the beginning. From the last years of the nineteenth century through the teens of the twentieth, New Orleans's push lakeward into drained swampland began a major new phase of the city's history that counterpoints the more famous notion of Storyville and coincided with the evolution of the musical practice that would come to be called jazz.

As long as there's commerce in North America, there'll have to be a port at the base of the Mississippi River. That crescent-shaped riverbend was a terrible place to build a town. But it was the least bad place in the swamp, and it was the spot that best connected the Mississippi River with the Gulf of Mexico. No place farther south on the river was usable, and any port farther north could be choked off by it. Whoever controlled that port possessed the key to the North American continent, which is why New Orleans was a primary target of Union forces in the Civil War, and why its capture in 1862 was a turning point for the fate of the Confederacy. It was a jump-off point for troops leaving for the Mexican War and the Spanish-American War, as well as for nineteenth-century filibustering expeditions against Cuba.

For that matter, the southern flank of the American Revolution was provided by Louisiana militias. Fighting under the Spanish flag, they checked British expansion into the Gulf region. A poem composed by, and printed at the expense of, Julien Poydras, a patriotic slave owner and leading citizen, attested to the bravery of the battalion of color in one of those battles. The military offered one of the best career paths open to a man of color, and New Orleans played a principal role in African American military history, continuing past the Civil War to the recruitment of buffalo soldiers in New Orleans, and beyond.

The city's maximum moment of military glory was the final action of the War of 1812. British troops invaded the area, fighting the Battle of New Orleans (more accurately, the Battle of Chalmette) in the first days of 1815. When the British hastily covered over their dead troops, the bodies oozed back up out of the mud: legs, arms, and other putrefying parts, reappearing as if in a nightmare. When they fled, the first rush of their retreat through the alligator-ridden morass churned up the mud, and those who followed were mired in it, sinking into the froth as they ran.

⁓

Set not only between, but also largely below, the Mississippi River and Lake Pontchartrain, New Orleans has often been described as a bowl set in water, though it might better be described as two bowls sitting side by side, separated by the Esplanade Ridge. That contour is not easily visible to the naked eye. New Orleans is not only the lowest elevated of any U.S. city, but also the flattest. When you read of higher or lower places in New Orleans, you should understand that these relative differences in elevation are almost imperceptible to anyone who has grown up where there are hills, though they make a lot of difference when it starts to rain.

As the world is now aware, New Orleans is ringed by levees that are supposed to keep water from spilling over into the bowl. The most desirable land is closest to the river, because it's the farthest above sea level. The lowest-lying part of town—some 15 percent of it—is more than ten feet below sea level.[10] None of it was below sea level in colonial times. Nor was it a bowl in those days; it was a gradual slope from the Mississippi River down to Lake Pontchartrain. The sinking is more recent, exacerbated by the lack of new sediment coming in because the levees keep it out, by drainage of the swamp, and by all the human activity on its paved surfaces.[11] Whether water rains down on New Orleans from the sky, seeps up from below, or, God forbid, overflows or crashes through the levees, every drop on the ground has to be "unwatered"—pumped out, uphill—or it just sits there, incubating mosquitoes.

In the twentieth century, builders began constructing houses in New Orleans over concrete slabs on the ground instead of the old way, raised up aboveground on pilings. But on August 29, 2005, when water rushed into the lower-lying land of the city, it tore houses off their slabs and covered the part of town that had been made habitable by pumping. The town was suddenly reduced to "the sliver by the river"—its old boundaries, the highest-elevated part. In effect, the swamp came back, smelling even worse than it did in the days when the little settlement of Nouvelle-Orléans dumped its raw sewage there.

As of this writing (August 2007), it's too soon to tell how the city will recover, and it's unclear whether there is sufficient protection against a future flood that might once again wreak havoc on the city. The French Quarter's still there, as are other historic neighborhoods. But what made New Orleans such an eloquent piece of living history wasn't only its elegant, termite-ridden housing stock. It was the people of the city, two-thirds of them people of color. The destruction of buildings in 2005 was fearful, but so was the loss of something intangible: African America took a terrible blow when the collective knowledge of black New Orleans was scattered to the four winds. Dispersing that population was like tearing up an encyclopedia in front of an electric fan. This book is dedicated to the people who are trying to put that book back together.

We've developed a curious American usage: when something's gone, we say, "it's history." New Orleans may or may not be history, but it still has a history. That history won't fit in a book this size. But let me see if I can at least sketch out my notion of the forces that shaped the city, and its highly musical culture.

I'm going to backtrack now, to well before the founding of the Louisiana colony, so that I can introduce my cast of political actors: Spain, France, and England, along with their respective New World colonies of Cuba, Saint-Domingue, and Virginia.

My story begins in 1492, in Roman Catholic Europe.

Four Spanish silver coins:

1. *ca. 1545*: A two-*real* silver coin from the Mexican mint, honoring Carlos V (Carolus) and Queen Johana.

2. *from sometime during the reign of Felipe II*: A one-*real* cob from the Mexican mint. Cobs were coins that were not flat and milled, but were irregularly shaped chunks of metal of the proper weight, stamped as coinage.

3. *1786*: A two-*real* piece from the Mexican mint, honoring Carlos III; in circulation during Estevan Miró's governorship of Louisiana.

4. *1793*: Its successor, from the mint at Lima, honoring Carlos IV, for whom St. Charles Street in New Orleans is named; in circulation during Baron Héctor Carondelet's governorship.

Source: Jordan, Louis (see Bibliography).

COLONIZATION

3

PIETY

Ya tan alto principio, en tal jornada,
os muestra el fin de vuestro santo celo
y anuncia al mundo, para más consuelo,
un monarca, un imperio, y una espada
Already so great a beginning, on such a journey,
reveals to you fulfillment of your holy belief
and announces to the world, to great relief,
one monarch, one empire, and one sword.
—Hernando de Acuña (1518–1580)
Sonnet to the King our Lord,
addressed to Felipe II of Spain

*L*a Española—the Spanish One—was the name Columbus gave to the second-largest of the Antillean islands when he "discovered" it on his first voyage. Today, the island is uneasily shared by the Dominican Republic and Haiti. To the Taínos, whom Columbus called *indios*, the island was *Quisqueya*, and *Ayiti* was their name for its mountainous part. But most of the Taínos on Quisqueya died within the first century of Spanish occupation, and the island was most commonly referred to by the name of its capital, Spain's first city in the New World: Santo Domingo.

At the time Santo Domingo was established, the one territory in Europe that might qualify as a nation-state by modern definition was the Ottoman Empire, which was Muslim. The militant Christian crusaders

Fernando and Isabel brought their kingdoms together in strategic mar-riage, but they were not monarchs of a united Spain, and their kingdoms had distinct laws and even languages. Fernando was king of Aragon, which included Cataluña and the Two Sicilies (present-day Naples and Sicily), while Isabel was queen of Castile, which included Andalucía and, once it was discovered, America.

The first European to sail along the Gulf Coast was the Spanish explorer Alonso Álvarez de Pineda, who sailed from Florida to Veracruz in 1519. From the amount of freshwater he found, he concluded that there was a sizable river nearby, which, unseen, he named Río de Espíritu Santo (Holy Spirit River). Had Spain not been stretched so thin, perhaps we would still call our great continental river Espíritu Santo instead of the Mississippi. But the Spanish had little interest in, or possibility of, settling the North American mainland, though in theory they had claimed all of it in 1492.

Before the Americas could be developed, Europe needed a money sup-ply. It might be said that Spain began to exist as a nation, if not officially then at least in practice, in 1497, when it established the silver *peso* (a word meaning weight), worth eight *reales* (royals), giving rise to the term "pieces of eight." Spain's urgent concern in the Americas was to rip out gold as fast as possible. At first, the conquistadores carted away treasure pillaged from the natives—altarpieces, jewelry, and the like.

As the Spanish established settlements in Nueva España (Mexico) and then in Peru, they began to operate silver mines. The flow of silver, modest at first, increased after 1535 and picked up further in the 1550s. After the appli-cation of the new quicksilver (mercury) refining process in 1557, it increased by a factor of ten, peaking perhaps in the first decade of the seventeenth century. After a mechanical method of minting coins was developed, the first mint opened in Mexico in 1535, and soon ten more were in operation.[1] As early as 1511, King Fernando was advised that one black could do the work of four Indians.[2] By the 1520s, Spanish colonists in the New World were clamor-ing for black slaves.

∞

The Caribbean Sea flows northward through the Yucatán Channel into the Gulf of Mexico in what becomes a "loop current" that winds into and around the Gulf. On its way out of the Gulf, the current flows past Havana, through the Straits of Florida, and into the Atlantic. There it becomes the Gulf Stream, the narrow, powerful current that carries ships to Europe—a river in the sea, as the saying went, that runs across the Atlantic almost directly from Havana to Seville.

Established in its present location on the Gulf of Mexico as of 1519, Havana boasted a deepwater bay at the end of a narrow, defensible channel. Havana's bay was the natural haven for the treasure from Mexico and Peru, and the port's location on the Gulf Stream made it the logical point of embarcation for Spain. The coins and ingots were transshipped to Havana, placed under heavy guard by a military garrison, and ultimately carried across the Atlantic in what by the 1560s became formalized as *la flota* (the fleet), a heavily escorted annual treasure convoy that excited delirious processions up to the House of Trade when it arrived in Seville.

It took months for all the fleet's ships to assemble in Havana before they could sail together for Seville in the spring. While they waited, there was the usual panoply of services on offer for the sailor: drinking, gambling, dancing, and fornicating. Havana was a rollicking good-times center from the sixteenth century on. Its permanent population at the time was probably under a thousand, but when the fleet was in town, the transient population could be a multiple of that. Spain became used to the rhythm: every year, for more than two centuries, the fleet brought fresh dance and music into southern Iberia from the Americas, via the hub of Havana.

Much of the money that arrived in Seville passed straight across the Mediterranean into the hands of the Spanish monarch's Genovese financiers, and continued on into the emerging trade networks of Europe. The injection of silver from the mines of the New World, which roughly tripled Europe's supply, created a new force field of European power that blew like a steady wind from west to east. Fernand Braudel concluded that much of the New World silver—perhaps a third or more—ended up in China, which sucked it up in exchange for the silks, spices, and other luxury goods the Europeans wanted. There it stayed, never to leave again.[3]

The deluge of silver from America coincided with the introduction of a heavy coin from the greatest European source of silver: the mines of Austria. First minted in 1512 in Bohemia's Joachimsthal, and taking its name from that region, the coin became known as the *thaler*. In the mouths of the Dutch merchants that became the *daalder*, and to the British it was the *dollar*. Within a century or so, the Spanish peso had become universally referred to in English as the "Spanish dollar," though in the Spanish world such a term was not used. Under various names in different territories, it was for centuries the closest thing the world had to a standard monetary unit.

⚮

King Fernando expired in 1516, having outlived Queen Isabel by twelve years. Their thrones passed to the sixteen-year-old French-speaking Charles of

Ghent, the Habsburg son of Fernando and Isabel's still-living daughter Juana la Loca (Juana the Mad, in whose honor Columbus had briefly named Cuba *Juana*). No one had envisioned that Charles would become King Carlos I, but the planned heirs had died, or had never been born. Officially, the son of the mad queen ruled together with his mother, who was locked away in a tower.

Carlos was the product of generations of strategic marriages that had already run to inbreeding, with disastrous consequences in generations to come. He inherited the kingdoms of each of his four grandparents, becoming ruler of a vast patchwork of societies, cultures, and languages. From Isabel he received the throne of Castile and its associated territories, including Spain's claim to the entire New World; from Fernando, that of Aragon and the Two Sicilies; and from his paternal grandmother Mary of Burgundy, the Low Countries (Belgium and the Netherlands), where he had grown up.

Then, in 1519, the quadruply fortunate Carlos inherited from his paternal Habsburg grandfather Maximilian the throne of the Holy Roman Empire. He became Holy Roman Emperor Carlos V, and incurred large debts bribing the seven noble electors who voted to confirm him in the title over other contenders (who included the Valois French king François I and even Henry VIII of England). As Holy Roman Emperor, Carlos V was defender of the faith, ruling over a mostly Germanic collection of territories (despite its name, the Holy Roman Empire did not include Rome). Coins struck with his likeness bore another of his titles: Carolus Caesarus (Carlos Caesar).

Carlos embarked on a costly quest that aimed at no less than unifying all of Christendom under one banner, then smiting the infidel of Islam and bringing together the world as one in God's kingdom on earth. Largely an absentee king of Castile and Aragon, he spent his thirty-nine-year reign as a central figure in wars that raged all over Europe, with France as his greatest enemy.

But there was also an enemy within his domains. A new, heretical religious current emerged in the Holy Roman Empire that was worried less about the Ottomans than about Rome. They saw the pope as the Antichrist, the priests as malevolent sorcerors, the Church a cesspool of corruption, the hagiography of saints a fraud, and the Bible a book to be read by the common man in his own language.

Martin Luther, a radical theology professor at the upstart university of Wittenberg, was not the first to break with the Church; the Hussites in Bohemia had done it a century previously. But his dramatic, public declarations started the mass movement that led to what historians call the Reformation, and the movement he began withstood all attempts to contain it.

Carlos burned the first martyrs of the new Lutheran movement at the stake in 1523 in the rich merchant city of Antwerp. As the schism deepened, it became identified with territorial struggle. The Lutherans promulgated the doctrine of *cuius regio, eius religio*, which Diarmid MacCulloch glosses as "where you come from decides your religion, and within that region no other can be tolerated."[4] It wasn't like *you* got to choose. The duty of the religious person was submission.

This territoriality of religion was to be carried over into the New World, where new colonies officially followed the religion of the mother country. After the first significant slave rebellion in the New World—in La Española in 1522, at the sugar plantation of Diego Colón (Christopher Columbus's son), during which Wolof slaves joined forces with Indians—Carlos forbade the importation of Wolofs specifically, of Muslim slaves in general, and, moreover, of all blacks raised in Islamized areas of Africa. The general disinclination of Spain to accept slaves from Islamized regions of Africa during the formative years of Hispano-American society had enormous consequences for the development of music in the New World.[5] Lutherans were also forbidden to come to the New World, as well as Jews. Catholic Spain wanted no troublemakers—not the ones they had spent almost eight centuries driving out of Iberia, and not the new dissidents that had appeared in the Holy Roman Empire.

Spain did not run its own slave ships from Africa, but relied on buying captives from Portuguese merchants. These slavers supplied the Spanish with captives that were already at least nominally Catholicized, from a region where Islam had never penetrated: Kongos and Angolans, often consolidated together in a single boat. By 1530, four to five thousand of them were being taken every year.[6]

⌘

The new evangelical movement—as of 1529 it would be called Protestantism—emphasized inner piety instead of outward ceremony. It flourished via a new medium that fostered private thought: the mechanically printed book. Publication of the Bible in the various languages of Europe occasioned the spread of literacy and scholarship and provided a vast market for the new printing industry, as heresy and the press fed each other.

The dour French Protestant reformer Jean Calvin fled Paris in 1533, ultimately arriving in Geneva. In the Germanic territories and Scandinavia, Lutheranism generally took hold; elsewhere, the Calvinists held sway. The two came into bitter conflict wherever they coincided. Rump factions and radical groups appeared, all of them as hated by the Lutherans and Calvinists as by the Catholics. Calvin had a favorite term of contempt for the freethinkers: *libertines*.[7]

The first monarch to leave the Catholic fold was Henry VIII, the Tudor king of England. Though he had supported the Catholic persecution of Lutherans, he broke with the Roman Church in 1534, naming himself head of the Church of England in order to divorce Carlos's aunt, Catherine of Aragon, who had failed to produce an heir to the throne. This new Anglican church was not Lutheran but retained the structure of Catholicism, with a hierarchy of bishops and a formal liturgy.

In France, Calvinism grew explosively during the 1550s. Beginning with small, clandestine groups, the movement encompassed some two million adherents by 1562. Its principal method of diffusion was song, and the vehicle was the Psalter, a book of the psalms translated into French. Though the psalms were sung antiphonally (leader-and-chorus) in ancient times, this new wave of congregational singing had been started by Luther, who reused beloved old tunes. The Calvinists went one better: they composed new tunes, printed in music notation above each of the texts. MacCulloch writes:

> The metrical psalm was the perfect vehicle for turning the Protestant message into a mass movement capable of embracing the illiterate alongside the literate. . . . The psalms were easily memorized, so that an incriminating printed text could rapidly be dispensed with. . . . The words of a particular psalm could be associated with a particular melody; even to hum the tune spoke of the words of the psalm behind it, and was an act of Protestant subversion. . . . The psalms could be sung in worship or in the market-place; instantly they marked out the singer as a Protestant, and equally instantly united a Protestant crowd in ecstatic companionship. . . . It was perhaps significant that one of the distinctive features of French Catholic persecution in the 1540s had been that those who were about to be burned had their tongues cut out first.[8]

By the late 1550s, those French Protestants who went to the stake singing were known as Huguenots, a name of uncertain derivation but possibly from the Dutch *huis genooten* ("house fellows," since they practiced their religion in private homes).

Ecstatic Protestant congregational singing would subsequently be carried over to the Anglo-American New World, where it was taken up by African Americans, whose music is so strongly marked by the heritage of church choir and sacred song, and who understood its power to unify a persecuted community.

Carlos V's son and successor Felipe (Philip) II, who took the throne in 1556, did not receive the title of Holy Roman Emperor—the Habsburg Empire had cleaved into Spanish and German parts by that point—but he became the first king of a politically united Spain. Felipe established Madrid as the seat of the court in 1561, though Seville, the Atlantic port city, remained the economic capital of Spain. In 1580, he became king of Portugal in addition to occupying the Spanish throne. The sixty years that followed marked the single period of history in which the entire Iberian Peninsula existed under a single crown. Felipe, who relocated to Lisbon for a few years, had all of Iberia's Atlantic coast and revenues from Portugal's African slave trade. Gold from Brazil's mines augmented the imperial glory of the Spanish crown.

At the peak of Spain's power, France was in no position to compete for empire in the New World, though French pirates and privateers plundered Spanish colonial ports and treasure ships. In sharp contrast to Iberia's monolithic Catholicism, France was consumed by war between Catholics and Huguenots during the last four decades of the sixteenth century, effectively collapsing as a nation and devolving into city-states. Two Catholic monarchs of France were assassinated, and thousands of common people were tortured and killed. In the St. Bartholomew's Eve massacre of August 24, 1572, some fifteen thousand Protestants were slaughtered in a single night on the orders of the French king Charles IX, following the advice of his mother, Catherine de Medici, and the killing continued across France through October. (For purposes of comparison, the feared Spanish Inquisition is believed to have executed some five thousand people during its centuries of existence.[9])

Felipe declared war on France in 1595, but he was thwarted by Henri IV, the first Bourbon king of France, who had converted to Catholicism in order to claim the throne. On April 30, 1598, Henri guaranteed freedom of religion for Protestants, supposedly forever, with his signing of the Edict of Nantes, which established Catholicism as the official state religion of France, but gave new civil guarantees to over a million Huguenots. France went back to work.

A weary Felipe died less than a year after finally making peace with France. His expenses had been even greater than the money he was receiving. Despite the fantastical flow of precious metal from the American mines, his son and successor, the less capable Felipe III, was reduced to issuing copper coinage for domestic use in 1605.

Spain's great imperial moment was at an end, even as its culture was flourishing. Europe's first great novel, *Don Quixote* by Miguel de Cervantes (who had been held by the Ottomans as a prisoner of war for five years), was translated and avidly read in France and England. Already bearing African influence acquired in the New World—an influence that came back, updated, via Havana every year—Spain's music and dance traveled upward through the Continent, across the Pyrenees and on past France, into the Protestant territories, and across the Mediterranean in a circuit with the highly musical cities of Italy. But Spain, bankrupt and distracted by war in Europe, made no attempt to develop its American colonies. Its interest was simply extraction, and its resources were focused on mining.

Spain never conquered the world with its army, but its coinage was everywhere. Spanish pesos were in use in the Philippines (the island territory in Asia, ruled by Spain and named for Felipe II) and in the merchant cities of China. But the American colonies were chronically short of hard currency. Existing only for the benefit of the mother countries, they were kept on a tight monetary leash and not supposed to develop their own commerce with each other. The colonists would have starved if they had followed the Europeans' rules. Almost everything they needed had to be imported. But they were only allowed to buy their supplies from vendors authorized by the *asiento*, a license the crown sold at a high price in order to regularize its unpredictable cash flow from the New World, so they were at the mercy of monopoly pricing and predatory lending.

With the Caribbean a "Spanish lake," as it was in the sixteenth century, the only ways for the other nations of Europe to participate in New World commerce were through contraband, which became a way of life for the colonies early on, and through piracy. The colonists developed methods of conducting local commerce by barter, and traded with forbidden ships that were floating bazaars.

Santo Domingo, the early center of Spanish colonial administration, withered from inattention and lack of support as the treasure port of Havana rose in importance. Contrabandists of various flags came to La Española's north coast, firing their cannons to alert the locals to come and trade. Buying up salted meat and hides, they drove up the price of beef in Santo Domingo. Worse, a cargo was intercepted of three hundred Bibles. *Lutheran* Bibles.[10] The archbishop was alarmed; no Protestants were permitted in the New World.

Madrid's response to loss of control over La Española was a spectacularly ill-advised order in 1605 to depopulate much of it, withdrawing the population to an area around the town of Santo Domingo. To achieve this, over a hundred recalcitrant colonists were hung, and homes and farms burned. The entire northern coast of the island, and all of the west, was left unoccupied.

The pirates moved in.

4

LOUIS, LOUIS

I am convinced that Sieur de La Salle's discovery is quite
useless.

—*Louis XIV, 1683*[1]

*J*acques Cartier claimed Canada as Nouvelle-France in 1536, but it was
only in 1608, with Samuel Champlain's establishment of Québec, that
French colonization of the New World began.

Québec is an Algonquin word meaning "narrowing," and the town is strategically located at the half-mile-wide mouth of the freshwater St. Lawrence
River, where it opens dramatically into the ten-mile-wide saltwater estuary
of the Gulf of St. Lawrence. Up the river, toward the southwest, the French
founded two other settlements: Trois Rivières (1634) and Ville Marie (or Montréal, in 1642). More than two thousand miles to the south, France established
settlements in 1635 on the islands of Guadeloupe and Martinique.

Meanwhile, Spain had given up control of the western third of La Española, which had become effectively independent. At the edge of the empire,
its society was free to the point of anarchy. The empty territory became populated by wild cattle, dogs, and men called *boucaniers* (or buccaneers, from
boucan, the brazier in which they cooked their food), who lived by hunting
the cattle and selling the hides to passing ships. This almost entirely male
society lived and worked in pairs, with the custom of inheritance upon death
for the surviving partner. The boucaniers, who lived lives of great hardship

but had no master, were freelance cousins of the French Canadian *coureurs de bois* and *voyageurs*, the later South American *gauchos*, the *vaqueros* of Mexico, and—the last to emerge—the cowboys of the North American West. The New World thus afforded to some a degree of freedom unknown in the Old, and complete slavery for others.

Off the north coast of the western territory of La Española, the small island of Tortuga became a haven for another kingless society: the freebooters, or filibusters (*flibustiers* in French, from the Dutch *flijboten*, or flyboats), better known as pirates. The emergence of nation-states saw piracy used practically as a military arm of the state: privateers were legalized pirates bearing letters of marque that allowed them to prey on merchant ships of enemy nations. The Spanish ships, groaning under the weight of so much silver, were their richest prizes.

Gradually, the pirates and boucaniers of the western part of La Española came under the control of the French. They became the vanguard colonists of a territory whose name was the French version of Santo Domingo: Saint-Domingue. As the French stabilized Saint-Domingue, it transitioned from piracy and cattle killing to agriculture. Its first crop was tobacco, the habit-forming aromatic weed that had been brought back to Europe from Cuba. By the 1640s the colony was beginning to thrive.

∞

After decades of war, Spain in 1609 signed the Twelve Years Truce—a peace compact bearing an expiration date—with its rebellious vassals in the northern Dutch regions, which now called themselves the United Provinces (the Netherlands). Hostilities between Spain and the United Provinces resumed on schedule with the expiration of the truce in 1621, but Spain had lost the Netherlands and would never regain them, nor would Spain ever fully regain its sense of empire.

The Dutch emerged as leaders of the seventeenth-century world economy. They were by far the most urbanized, and most tolerant, people of Europe. With their huge fleet of lightweight, high-capacity flyboats, their massive warehousing capacity, and sophisticated credit instruments, they built their empire carrying other nations' goods. In 1613, the Dutch established Nieuw Nederland, whose capital, Nieuw Amsterdam, was from the start the most urban of American cities. Polylingual, which is a good thing for towns that want to make money, Nieuw Amsterdam was also the most business minded, and the most tolerant of religion, complete with Jews both Ashkenazy and Sephardic.

Though not yet systematically engaged in the slave trade, Dutch privateers wound up dealing in slaves as part of their captured cargo. It was a
Dutch privateer who unexpectedly brought the first known slave ship to the
English colony of Virginia, in 1619.[2] Snatched from a Veracruz-bound ship
that had embarked at the Angolan port of Luanda, this cargo of "20. and odd
Negroes" quite possibly included people from up the African coast in Kongo
as well as those from Angola; the former would have spoken Kikongo, the
latter Kimbundu.[3]

It was probably in 1625 that Dutch privateers first brought captured Afri-
cans to Nieuw Nederland. The first two Africans in Nieuw Amsterdam whose
names we know were Simon Kongo and João de Angola, captured from the
Portuguese.[4] The Dutch became the second great power to emerge in the slave
trade after they seized the slave castle at Elmina (off the coast of modern-day
Ghana) from the Portuguese in 1637, and Luanda four years later. As Nieuw
Amsterdam's slave population grew, it was corporately owned by the Dutch
West India Company and had a number of legal rights, including the right to
marry, to bring legal action, and to testify against whites.[5]

Nieuw Amsterdam passed to English control, becoming New York in 1667
and definitively leaving Dutch possession as of 1674, traded for the plantation colony of Surinam. With its Dutch legacy giving it a different character
from other Anglo-American cities, New York became, and remained, the most
important North American business center.

The Dutch dominated trade in Europe and took over the Portuguese
trade routes in Asia. But they couldn't do that and also colonize America.
They tried. But no discontented masses of Dutchmen wanted to leave their
homes for the hazards of colonial life. Despite a doomed attempt to take over
Brazil, despite their control of Curaçao, Surinam, and a few smaller territories,
and though they were masters of the sea, the Dutch never became a power in
the Americas. However, they did much to stimulate colonial expansion.

In the 1640s, Dutch shippers brought the technology of sugar from the
northeast of Brazil to the English colony of Barbados. Since the Dutch controlled Elmina and Luanda, they were in a position to supply an Antillean
sugar plantation with slaves, then profit by shipping the product back to
Europe. Barbados, the Antillean island that sticks out the farthest east into
the Atlantic, is the easiest for traveling to and from Africa and Europe both.
In becoming the first slave-labor plantation empire of the Antilles, it under-
went rapid growth. The first New World colony with an African majority, it

had a population density four times that of England. Its sole product, sugar, was carried off to a distant market.[6] Barbadians were some of the first settlers of South Carolina, bringing their already "seasoned" English-speaking slaves with them.

Dutch privateers continued bringing to Virginia slaves diverted en route to the Spanish colonies. Some early Virginia planters went up to Dutch Manhattan to buy their slaves, while others bought from Barbados, making for a mix in Virginia of African and seasoned slaves. The Africans were cheaper, but the seasoned slaves were accustomed to the regimen, knew what was expected of them, could communicate, and survived better.

The earliest Africans in Virginia were not referred to as "slaves" but as "servants"; the difference between servants and slaves was codified in 1661.[7] Once there were second-generation domestic slaves, accustomed from birth to the conditions of Virginia, they were greatly preferable to indentured white immigrants, who died in large numbers after arrival. The native-born slaves were also considered more docile than the African-born, perhaps because they were already home; kidnapped Africans knew they would only return home when they died.

⌒∞⌒

The Canadian explorer Louis Joliet and the French missionary Jacques Marquette traveled in 1678 down the great central river of North America but turned back less than five hundred miles before reaching the Gulf of Mexico. Four years later, René-Robert Cavelier, Sieur de (lord of) La Salle, traveled across the Great Lakes, then went by canoe down the North American continent along the Illinois River and the Mississippi, arriving at the Gulf, claiming the entire Mississippi watershed for France as he did so. La Salle called the great river St. Louis, for Louis XIV. Though St. Louis ultimately became the name of a town on the river's banks, the name did not stick to the river permanently; it would be called by its Ojibwa name, the Mississippi. To the entire unexplored, unmapped territory drained by the great river, however far it might extend, La Salle gave the name La Louisiane.

By the time of La Salle's exploration, slave labor was already an integral part of the French colonial plantation economy. In March 1685, Louis XIV promulgated the Code Noir (Black Code), which established regulations for the treatment of slaves. The first of its fifty-nine regulations stated: "We enjoin all of our officers to chase from our islands all Jews who have established residence there. As with all declared enemies of Christianity, we command them to be gone within three months of the day of issuance of the present [edict], at the risk of confiscation of their persons and their goods." The second regulation required notification of authorities within eight days of purchase of a slave so that the slave could be baptized Roman Catholic, and the third stated: "We forbid any religion other than the Roman, Catholic, and Apostolic Faith from being practiced in public." The rest of the code dealt with such issues as the conditions under which slaves might be set free, what constituted appropriate conduct, a recital of the rights slaves had (very few, not including the right to own property or money), and under what conditions they should be whipped, branded, or have their ears cut off. In practice, the Code Noir was widely disregarded as soon as it was promulgated, and slave owners did what they wanted.

In October of that same year, as part of the same brutal policy that created the Code Noir, Louis revoked his grandfather's 1598 Edict of Nantes, removing civil guarantees for Protestants. This effectively declared the Huguenots' religion illegal, though by then they had enjoyed equality of opportunity for eighty-seven years.

It was late in the day for an act of intolerance of this magnitude. The seventeenth century in general had seen a rollback of Protestantism, as a Counter-Reformation reestablished Catholic power in many territories. The map was very largely Protestant north of the Pyrenees and the Alps, and Catholic below—a north-south divide that would be mirrored in the New World, which also divided into a largely Protestant north and a Catholic south. But there was a new current, especially in the more tolerant and affluent territories of the Netherlands and England. Fueled by disgust over decades of war, people were openly expressing skepticism about all religion, and demanding not merely tolerance, but religious liberty. Louis's action, all too reminiscent of Spain's expulsion of its Jews in 1492, was widely viewed as a great betrayal, and not only of the Protestants; their departure was a staggering blow for the French economy.

Huguenots' possessions were confiscated, and a number of them were broken on the wheel. A method of execution much employed by the French, it entailed breaking the victim's arms, legs, hips, and thighs, then leaving him stretched out face up on a cart wheel to die slowly in the sun. It was no crueler than other methods used in executions throughout Europe—tearing out entrails from a living victim, pulling apart limb from limb by horses, removing chunks of flesh with red-hot pincers, pouring molten lead into open wounds, flaying alive, boiling alive, slow roasting over a fire, water torture, and the ever-popular ritual of burning at the stake. Across Europe, the hanged—not hung by a quick drop-trap either, but a slow, dangling strangulation—were left on gibbets for crows to pick, set high on the hilltops where they could be seen from all around the surrounding countryside.

A number of Huguenots—conservatively estimated at two hundred thousand, though higher figures have been cited—fled France.[8] Among their ranks were many of the country's most productive and industrious people—artisans, craftsmen, and professional people. Some were quite wealthy. Various French cities became depopulated as the Huguenots fled in large numbers to resettle in England, Germany, Switzerland, and especially in the Netherlands. Many smuggled out their gold and silver with them, further depleting France's money supply.

The Huguenots' greatest expertise was in textiles, and they came to their new homes with skills and trade secrets. Some arrived bringing their looms, pointing the way to the coming Industrial Revolution, which would be based on textile production. The refugees produced silk brocades, satin, velvet, cambric, damask, lace, gloves, felt hats, and all sorts of linen, from fine cloth to thick sails. Two brothers brought to England the secret of taffeta sheen. Others improved England's technology for making fine white paper. They knew the art of spinning. They established bleachyards. They helped make linen Ireland's most important industry. There were glassmakers, jewelers, watchmakers, goldsmiths, and metalsmiths who made pins, scissors, and fine knives.[9] Others became pirates and slave traders.

In the aggressively pro-trade Netherlands, where some of the wealthiest Huguenot traders and merchants fled, Dutch towns competed with each other to attract the newcomers, offering what today we would call stimulus packages of such incentives as freedom from taxation for three years and interest-free loans.[10]

Some Huguenots made their way to the British colonies in North America. Among those refugees were two Soblet (Sublette) brothers, from one of whom this writer descends. Escaping via Amsterdam to London, the Soblets arrived in 1700 at the Huguenot settlement of Manikintown in the colony of Virginia, named for Elizabeth, the Virgin Queen of England. They had no interest in going to a territory named for Louis XIV, nor had they been invited.

⁕

Three years after he enraged Protestant Europe with his persecution of the Huguenots, Louis XIV in 1688 launched the next step in his campaign to conquer the world. Using the pretext of supporting his sister-in-law's dynastic claim of succession, he sent the largest army in Europe to invade the area of the river Rhine, a Protestant territory controlled by the Holy Roman Empire's Elector Palatinate, in what today is Germany.

Louis was resisted by a multinational alliance that included Spain, the Netherlands, Denmark, and the remnants of the Holy Roman Empire. This pan-European war is remembered under various names—the War of the Augsburg League, the War of the Palatinian Succession, and, retrospectively, the Nine Years War—but following the entry into the conflict of Willem (William) III of Orange, the Dutch king seated on the English throne, it became the War of the Grand Alliance. In the New World, where associated battles were fought, it was known as King William's War.

France had much greater wealth than England, and, at twenty million, a population more than three times as large. But England, besides having a greater navy, had a more modern political and economic structure than France. Physically passing around trunks of coins was too slow for the needs of commerce, so in 1694, the Bank of England was founded, creating an essential weapon that France did not have for managing the expenses of war: reliable paper money.

Louis XIV does not seem to have comprehended the new reality of oceanborne commerce. Like Madrid, Versailles was an inland capital, remote from the force that was remaking the European economy. Unlike Britain's broadbased taxation of consumer goods in her own thriving internal market, which brought in predictable revenues from diverse sources, the feudal French taxation system entailed the king squeezing nobles for money, who in turn squeezed those below them. Religious tolerance in Britain created a much wider talent pool for business and industry than in France, which had just finished expelling its most productive class. The British had a bank and a system of credit; the French did not.

The War of the Grand Alliance ended inconclusively, though Louis's aggression was blunted and France ended the war insolvent, yet again. Most of the captured territories were restored to their previous owners in 1697 by the Treaty of Ryswick. As part of that swap, the feeble Spanish king Carlos II formally conceded Saint-Domingue to France, making official what was already a fact on the ground. With France no longer at war, more plantations sprang up on Saint-Domingue, which was now well on its way to creating phenomenal wealth.

France's economy had been depleted by the War of the Grand Alliance. Now, with that war ended, it was time for France to make its move in the southern part of North America, where it hoped to duplicate Spain's success at finding precious metal and establish a new empire. In this vast, unexplored territory, there must be gold and silver.

Unfortunately, they began their search in a place where there were no rocks at all, let alone rocks of gold.

5

MARDI GRAS

Smoke my peace pipe, smoke it right.
—*Wilson Turbinton, a.k.a. Willie Tee*

*L*ouis Phélypaux, Comte de Pontchartrain, minister of the French navy, received the intelligence in 1698: the British were planning to establish a post at the mouth of the Mississippi. Fearing British control of the river and the Gulf, he sent Pierre Le Moyne, Sieur d'Iberville, down from Nouvelle-France (Canada) to discover where the Mississippi emptied into the sea and to establish a colony there.

Born near Montréal, Iberville was the third of fourteen children of Charles Le Moyne, who had come to Nouvelle-France at the age of fifteen, beginning as an indentured servant to the Jesuits. Le Moyne *père* learned the languages of the Huron and the Iroquois—Iberville grew up speaking them—and with time became a wealthy fur trader.

Iberville was considered a hero for his bravery during King William's War: he had taken a lead role in a massacre at Corlaer (Schenectady), looted furs from the English at Hudson Bay, and resold them for his own profit.[1] But he was Canadian and not French, so he was not rewarded by being entrusted with the governorship of Terre-Neuve (the English called it Newfoundland), which would have carried with it possibilities for the lucrative exploitation of his network of fur-trading contacts. As in other American colonies, those born in the New World were second-class citizens to those born in the European metropolis. Instead, Iberville accepted Pontchartrain's commission to sail for the Gulf of Mexico, taking with him his younger brother, Jean-Baptiste Le Moyne, Sieur de Bienville.

Controlling Louisiana might have been the key to taking over Spain's mines, but the French had no clue what overland distances might be involved to get there from the Mississippi. For all they knew, there was gold to be dug out of the Gulf Coast. The Spanish, meanwhile, were not even aware of Marquette and Joliet's expedition down the Mississippi and may not have known of La Salle's territorial claims.[2] But when they learned in 1698 that the French were sending a colonizing expedition, the Spanish in turn ordered the founding of a post at the Bay of Panzacola, later spelled *Pensacola*. (Possibly the Hispanicization of an Indian name, it means "Bellytail": *panza* = belly, *cola* = tail.)

Sailing from the French Atlantic port of Brest via Cap Français in Saint-Domingue, Iberville made his first mainland stop at Panzacola Bay, but finding it occupied by the Spanish, he continued west. On March 3, 1699, Iberville set up a campsite on the East Bank of the Mississippi River. It was the day known as Mardi Gras (Fat Tuesday), the day before Ash Wednesday, so Iberville gave the name Mardi Gras to a small "river" that emptied into the Mississippi, and named his campsite Pointe du Mardi Gras.

Iberville had been around Indians all his life and was comfortable with them. On March 20, he met with representatives of the Houma Indians, who greeted him with a ceremony in which they rubbed their bellies together. They smoked the calumet of peace, which caused Iberville some discomfort, as he did not use tobacco. The Houmas conducted him to their village, where, according to Iberville's journal:

> We were given a formal ball in the middle of the square, where the whole village had assembled.
>
> To the middle of the assembly were brought some drums and *chy-chycoucy*, which are gourds containing dry seeds, with sticks for handles. They make a little noise and help to mark the beat. A number of singers made their way there. Shortly afterwards came twenty young men, between twenty and thirty years old, and fifteen of the prettiest young girls, splendidly adorned in their style, all of them naked, wearing nothing except their *braguets*, over which they wore a kind of sash a foot wide, which was made of feathers or fur or hair, painted red, yellow, and white, their faces and bodies tattooed or painted various colors, and they carried in their hands feathers that they used as fans or to mark the time, some tufts of feathers being neatly braided into their hair.

The young men went naked, wearing only a girdle like the girls, which partly concealed them. They were prominently tattooed and their hair was well arranged with tufts of feathers. Several had kettles shaped like flattened plates, two or three together, tied to their girdles and hanging down to their knees, which made noise and helped to mark the beat. They danced in this way for three hours, appearing very merry and frolicksome.

When it got dark the chief lodged us in his hut or house, which he had had vacated. After we had eaten a supper of Indian-corn *sagamité*, a *flambeau* of canes fifteen feet long, bound together, as big around as two feet, was fetched, lighted, and set up in the middle. It burned at the top and gave sufficient light. All the young men of the village made their way there with their bows and arrows and headbreakers and war equipment along with a few women and girls. Here they began all over, and sang war dances up until midnight, which I found very pretty. . . .[3] [paragraphing added]

So it was that the first Louisiana colonist celebrated Mardi Gras, then during Lent, partied all day and into the night with splendidly adorned naked people, dancing to a beat.

⁂

Iberville built his first settlement to the east of the great river, at the place he called, not surprisingly, Bay St. Louis, near the place the Indians called Biloxi. With no potable water and no anchorage, it was a bad place for a settlement. Its sandy soil, hurricane-ravaged coastline, and low-lying, flood-prone land made it useless for agriculture. (In 1969 it took a shellacking from Camille, the hardest-blowing hurricane ever to hit the United States, and it was devastated by Katrina.)

"[Iberville's] colony consisted almost entirely of Canadians," wrote Antoine Simon Le Page du Pratz, a Dutchman who arrived in the colony at the age of twenty-three in 1718 and remained there until 1734.[4] His memoir, published in French in 1758, is an incomparable source of information about Louisiana in that era. In it, Le Page du Pratz describes Biloxi:

I never could guess the reason, why the principal settlement was made at this place, nor why the capital should be built at it; as nothing could be more repugnant to good sense; vessels not being able to come within four leagues of it; but what was worse, nothing could be brought from them, but by changing the boats three different times, from a smaller size to another still smaller; after which they had to go upwards of an hundred paces with small carts through the water to unload the least boats.

But what ought still to have been a greater discouragement against making a settlement at Biloxi, was, that the land is the most barren of any to be found thereabouts; being nothing but a fine sand, as white and shining as snow, on which no kind of greens can be raised; besides, the being extremely incommoded with rats, which swarm there in the sand, and at that time ate even the very stocks of the guns, the famine being there so very great, that more than five hundred people died of hunger; bread being very dear, and flesh-meat still more rare. There was nothing in plenty but fish, with which this place abounds.[5]

Iberville soon moved the settlement to Mobile Bay. In the meantime, he fulfilled Pontchartrain's charge to him to discover the mouth of the Mississippi—not an easy task, since where the Mississippi empties out into the sea, the river breaks up into multiple distributaries easily confused with blind bayous from the coast ("*bayouc*, a stream of dead water, with little or no observable current," wrote Le Page du Pratz).[6]

When these first French-speaking colonists arrived, there were already free blacks in the area. Iberville learned from a native informant of the existence of a community of black Spanish-speaking *cimarrones* (maroons), some ten days' travel to the west-northwest: "At this settlement there were only Negroes with their families. [The Indian informant] reports them to be rather numerous and leads us to believe that the Negroes at this settlement did not welcome any white Spaniard; and when white ones came, the blacks drove them off without speaking to them."[7]

Iberville also learned from the Indians about the overland portage trail connecting the Mississippi River to a sluggish finger of a stream that the French called Bayou St. Jean (St. John). From the southern shore of the lake that was at first called—what else?—Lake St. Louis, but better known as Lake Pontchartrain, the Bayou St. John protrudes south, into the swampy area that in the twentieth century, drained and populated, would be northeastern New Orleans.

In the classic Louisiana tradition of words not meaning what they mean elsewhere, Lake Pontchartrain is not really a lake, but a saline estuary. It opens at its eastern end into a channel called the Rigolets, and then into the smaller Lake Borgne (also a saltwater estuary, though with freshening influence from the Pearl River), and from there into the Gulf of Mexico. The water connection that could be made from Bayou St. John via Lake Pontchartrain all the way out to the Gulf was separated from the Mississippi by only a two-mile portage trail. The trail, which geologists call Esplanade Ridge and city maps today call Esplanade Avenue, provided the short overland connection between river and lake that ultimately would be a principal reason for siting New Orleans there. But Iberville did not think the Mississippi was fully navigable, so it fell to his brother Bienville to build on the site, nineteen years later. The area around the Bayou St. John was the first part of present-day New Orleans to be cleared, in 1708.

Meanwhile, the Canadian fur traders (the *coureurs du bois*, or *voyageurs*) were living the wild life. Quoting Jesuit missionaries, Carl A. Brasseaux writes that "when not engaged in fur trading, which actually occupied only a small portion of their time, hundreds of voyageurs annually devoted the bulk of their energies to travelling, 'drinking, gambling and lechery.'"[8] Many had gone native, taking Indian wives or even living in native communities. In the early days of the Louisiana colony, and possibly before, these Canadian trappers appeared down south. Some of them settled there, while others sold female Indian slaves to the French and Swiss soldiers in Louisiana, who for their part formed the only coherent labor force in the territory.[9] The first slaves to Europeans in Louisiana were thus Native American sex slaves. In 1704, a shipment of twenty-two French girls arrived in Louisiana, but they "failed to satisfy the garrison's need for women."[10]

Iberville presented the crown with a plan, never to be realized, that called for relocating the Indians into strategic hamlets and for combining French, Spanish, and Indian forces to attack the Carolina territory and wrest it from the English. The crown was stingy, because the crown was nearly broke, and the Le Moyne brothers had to develop the colony out of their own pocket, which they lined, in Gwendolyn Midlo Hall's words, "at the expense of the colonists, of France, and of any victims they might encounter."[11]

The Spanish chose not to try to evict Iberville's Louisiana colony, and were in any case in disarray. Since 1665, their king had been Carlos II, remembered as Carlos the Hexed (*El Hechizado*). Retarded, deaf, and epileptic, with an exaggeratedly long, thin face that may have been a result of the pituitary disorder called acromegaly, he was thought the victim of sorcery. He may have been, but this last monarch to be descended from Juana the Mad was also the product of inbreeding. He had ascended to the throne at the age of three; his Habsburg mother, Mariana of Austria, ran the weak Spanish government until she died in 1696. Carlos expired four years after her, without leaving an heir. His death in 1700 was a turning point in Spanish history: the

Habsburg line in Spain, which presided over the birth of the Spanish nation and founded great cities in the New World, was extinguished.

With the coronation of the French-speaking seventeen-year-old Philip Anjou as Felipe V, the Bourbon era in Spain began. The new monarch was both the great-grandson of Felipe IV of Spain and the grandson of Louis XIV. Once again, Louis XIV went to war, this time to defend Felipe's throne; in the alternative, the German branch of the Habsburg family, headed by Holy Roman Emperor Leopold I, would claim the Spanish throne from Austria, and the resulting empire surrounding Bourbon France would be a grave threat. By then, the idea of interterritorial royal dynasties with arcane succession rules was seeming increasingly ludicrous in the face of the real requirements of power and the emerging idea of the nation.

The economic impact of the New World colonies was already capable of fomenting major conflicts in Europe. England feared that the union of French and Spanish colonial power would force them out of the Antilles, and in 1701 the War of Spanish Succession began between France and England, each with various allies. Beginning only four years after the end of the last war, this one lasted twelve years, until 1713.

In France, the people went hungry at home and abroad, not for the first time. Fernand Braudel reckons that France experienced thirteen general famines in the sixteenth century, eleven in the seventeenth, and sixteen in the eighteenth, not counting hundreds of local famines.[12] The war so depleted France's treasury and credit that shipments to the colonies practically ceased. The French navy barely existed, so all available ships were pressed into service in the war.

The result was that the few Louisiana colonists lost all contact with France. In the first decade of the eighteenth century, they had to go native or starve. The colony actually disbanded on several occasions as residents went to live with the Indians, from whom they learned much about how to survive in the peculiar environment of Louisiana. After 1704, the next supply ship came in 1706, then 1708, then late 1711.

Iberville made only three expeditions to Louisiana, leaving the colony for the last time in 1702. In 1705, Louis XIV commissioned him to lead a wide-ranging assault, at the head of a large fleet divided in two independent squadrons, whose compound mission was to capture Barbados and Jamaica, drive out the English from South Carolina, and harass New York. By 1706, Iberville's command had gotten as far as sacking and pillaging the small island colony of Nevis after an extended siege of the British positions there, imprisoning the island's entire population of around 7,000, stealing 1,309 slaves, and carting off complete sugar mills. He resold the slaves for his own benefit in Saint-Domingue,[13] putting in at the grand bay in the central part of the colony. In commemoration of his visit, the town subsequently built there took the name Port-au-Prince, for one of Iberville's ships, *Le Prince*. Iberville proceeded on to Havana, where he fell ill, apparently with yellow fever, and died on shipboard. His body was interred in Havana's cathedral.

It fell to Bienville, Iberville's younger brother, to develop the Louisiana colony. He too was a profiteer, and lived luxuriously in the hard-pressed territory. Gwendolyn Midlo Hall, citing a letter from Antoine de la Mothe, Sieur de Cadillac, writes that in 1709 Bienville and Major Pierre d'Artaguette "sent a ship to St. Domingue for their own benefit, and at the expense of the king. The ship . . . stopped over in Havana, under the pretext of looking for powder, and embarked several slaves. This is the first documentary evidence of the entrance of black slaves into Louisiana."[14]

In a world of masters and servants, a clear hierarchy developed from the first generation in Louisiana.

❧

A French commoner who began his career in the New World as a privateer, the Sieur de Cadillac adopted his aristocratic-sounding identity in Québec on the occasion of his marriage. Returning to France, he successfully pitched to Jérôme Pontchartrain (Louis Pontchartrain's son, who had become Secretary of the Marine) the idea of establishing a Canadian settlement on the southwestern end of the Great Lakes to control the fur trade and establish a military presence.

Cadillac traveled voyageur-style, in twenty-five birchbark canoes, up the St. Lawrence with an entourage of one hundred soldiers and colonists. On a tongue of land between the western shore of Lake Erie and the southern shore of Lake Huron, he founded a new settlement, which he named Fort Pontchartrain d'Etroit. The name—*détroit*, or narrow passage—meant approximately the same thing as *québec*, narrowing.[15] It became the great American motor-and-music city of Detroit. Two centuries after the settlement's founding, Cadillac's name was a synonym for mass-produced luxury. He thus has the best name recognition today of any French colonist, and his memory resounds in countless song lyrics.

But Cadillac's colony was not productive for France. Fort Pontchartrain d'Etroit acquired high-quality furs, but the crooked Cadillac lined his own pockets by selling them to the English instead of shipping them back to France as he was supposed to. Unsuccessful in his attempt to be named Marquis of

Detroit, he was demoted by Pontchartrain to the position of governor of the wilderness colony of Louisiana.

If France was to retain the Louisiana Territory, the crown would have to look for a private financier. Cadillac returned to France, where he pitched the exploitation of Louisiana to the kingdom's wealthiest businessman, Antoine Crozat (whose less affluent brother, Pierre, maintained a salon of musicians and artists that included painter Antoine Watteau). There were silver and gold mines in Louisiana, Cadillac told Crozat, and . . . pearl fisheries![16] The last part was true, but the pearls were poor specimens. Crozat took the bait. On September 14, 1712, the king gave him an exclusive fifteen-year concession to develop Louisiana, making him financial administrator of the territory, with Cadillac as governor. The Canadian-born Bienville was relegated to second in command, to his great disgust.

Crozat and Cadillac were not interested in colonizing, but in discovering new sources of silver and gold. Refusing the counsel of Bienville, who knew the territory, Cadillac insisted on searching for precious metals. But there were none to be found, and Cadillac's tenure as governor was a disaster. Notwithstanding his previous boosterism, he described the colony in a 1713 letter to Pontchartrain as "an unhealthy country, without bread, without wine, without meat and without clothes."[17]

After twelve years of bloodshed, the War of Spanish Succession ended in 1713, with the Treaty of Utrecht. France was once again the loser. Though the British were unsuccessful in divesting Felipe V of the Spanish crown, and Spain remained Bourbon (at the beginning of the twenty-first century, its King Juan Carlos was a Bourbon), the magnitude of Britain's victory otherwise confirmed its position as the world's great sea power. The most valuable prize of the war's settlement for Britain, well outstripping the perceived value of receiving Nova Scotia and Newfoundland, was the coveted *asiento*—the exclusive right to sell slaves to Spain's colonies in the Americas. This brought a massive market for slaves, as well as contraband manufactured goods sneaked into Spanish colonial ports in large quantities via the slave ships. To use an overworked but apposite phrase, it was a license to print money. A fevered speculation in London wildly inflated the value of the South Sea Company, which ran the slave ships, and nearly bankrupted England when the bubble burst. Meanwhile, a mania for things French seized the Bourbon Spanish court, where the *contredanse* became the *contradanza*.

France did not go to war with Britain again for another thirty years. During that interval, Louisiana was colonized. In 1714, after receiving intelligence that the British might try to establish a settlement on the Gulf Coast, Cadillac sent Bienville's second in command, Louis Juchereau de St. Denis, Sieur de Beauport, to occupy the mainland. With advice from Bienville, St. Denis founded an inland post for trading with the Indians: Fort St.-Jean-Baptiste, located at the highest navigable point on the Red River, right at the site of the Natchitoches Indian village. (How St. Denis pronounced it, I don't know, but today, whatever its spelling might seem to imply, Natchitoches is pronounced *Nackatish*.) Above this new settlement, impeding the flow of the Red River and making it sluggish, yawned what would become known as the Great Raft—a 150-mile jumble of natural logjams that had been there since at least the fifteenth century.

Ten days after St. Denis's arrival, a Spanish patrol was surprised to find French there.[18] Interpreting the French moves in Louisiana as aggression, the Spanish began to occupy the territory, from which they had previously retreated for lack of any compelling reason to be there. The Natchitoches settlement thus triggered the Hispanicization of Texas. Twelve miles west of Natchitoches, the Spanish established Los Adaes, their first settlement in the Mississippi watershed, and the strip between the two settlements became the frontier between Spanish and French territory. The Spanish languished hundreds of miles from reinforcements, and, like the French, were vastly outnumbered by the Indians, so both sides were compelled to practice diplomacy with the indigenous people. The absurdity of colonial commerce was such that the two neighboring posts were not allowed to trade with each other.

Today, Natchitoches is a small, pretty college town. With its brick-paved Front Street along the Cane River Lake, it relies on its quaintness to be a tourist attraction. The town's original raison d'être vanished with the high water of 1832, after Henry Shreve altered the hydrodynamics of Louisiana with his massive engineering feats. Using his giant state-of-the-art "snagboats," which had previously removed obstacles from the Mississippi, Shreve dismantled the Great Raft above Natchitoches, causing the Red River to shift its channel five miles to the east, leaving behind a blind oxbow lake. Natchitoches lost its status as a river traffic town, and Shreve's Port, or Shreveport, became the region's big city.

As the locals never tire of reminding you, Natchitoches is four years older than New Orleans. But those four years were significant, because the year after Natchitoches was founded, King Louis XIV died.

6

THE DUKE OF ARKANSAS

Am I not well avenged on the French? I have ruined them and enriched foreigners, I have made their king my subject, the regent my crony, the great noblemen my clerks, their women my whores, and the first prince of the blood my carriage-hirer.

—*John Law, 1721*[1]

*L*ouis XIV died on September 1, 1715, ending a seventy-two-year reign that had long since outlived itself. His son was dead; his libertine grandson was on the throne of Spain. The heir to the French throne was a sickly five-year-old great-grandson. Until he attained his majority, a regency would have to govern in the name of the child Louis XV. The plum of regent went to Louis XIV's nephew: Philippe II, Duc d'Orléans.

Orléans's father, Philippe I, known to all as Monsieur, had been frequently humiliated by his brother the king, and derived great pleasure from shocking the court. Monsieur was flamingly homosexual, appearing in public on one occasion "in décolletage and earrings" to dance the minuet with his beautiful lover, Philippe de Lorraine-Armagnac.[2] Though Monsieur had managed to beget a son, in the street they said it was because he married a manly looking woman, who for her part described in a letter a variety of preferences of French nobles: "Some hate all women and only love men. Others like both men and women. Others like only boys of ten or eleven, others again young men of seventeen to twenty-five, and they are the most numerous."[3]

Atheistic and undisciplined, a notorious womanizer and drinker, the young Philippe indulged in a degree of dissolution only possible for aristocrats; in 1698 there were "1,226 servants and officers in the Orléans household."[4] But he was probably the best-educated young man anywhere. Orléans had studied mathematics with Joseph Saveur, France's most distinguished mathematician; set up his own chemistry laboratory with the German chemist Guillaume Homburg (which became the source of rumors that Orléans was an occult scientist crafting poisons for his enemies); and studied music composition with Marc-Antoine Charpentier.

He played instruments and sang motets. An opera he composed, titled *Penthée*, was performed at one of King Louis's galas at Versailles on August 9, 1704. Four days later, the Duke of Marlborough's cavalry destroyed the French army in the Battle of Blenheim, killing, wounding, or capturing some forty thousand soldiers. There was mourning, but the fete continued, with a fireworks display, on August 27.[5] Orléans proved a successful military leader the following year, in 1705, when he directed the siege of the Catalan citadel of Lérida.

Upon taking charge as regent in 1715, Orléans moved the court from Versailles back to Paris, which had the effect of revitalizing the arts there, and greatly inconvenienced the many hangers-on who had relocated from Paris to Versailles. He surrounded himself not with people of his own class, but with people who "shone by their wit or their depravity," in the words of his friend and exact contemporary, the Duc de Saint-Simon.[6] His preferred male companions were *roués*—disreputable young men—and his taste in women tended toward girls from the Opéra, who were not known for their chastity. "The Regency," writes Francine du Plessix Gray, "was the most dissolute period in French history and might well vie with the late Roman Empire as the most debauched era of Western civilization," though others award the palm to the reign of Louis XV, which followed.[7] Orléans's extreme fondness for his daughter, the Duchesse du Berry, gave rise to rumors of incest between them. She, for her part, took to going wherever she went accompanied by trumpeters and drummers, who heralded her arrival with fanfare.[8]

In the evening, Orléans held suppers for his friends. It was a time of great experimentation in food, the period in which France's reputation for haute cuisine began. Philippe applied the techniques of chemistry to the creation of new sauces; vegetables entered the menu.[9] Louis XIV had eaten in the time-honored manner, with his hands, forbidding those at his table to use forks.[10] But now, writes Saint-Simon, "All the utensils were of silver and the

Philippe II, Duc d'Orléans, Regent of France, debauched amateur composer, gourmet, and festive night owl, for whom New Orleans was named and for whose family Bourbon Street was named.

guests often joined the cooks to make experiments."[11] Philippe popularized the drinking of chocolate, a Mexican product that was already being grown in Saint-Domingue.

> At the beginning [the regent] rose early [wrote Saint-Simon], but gradually he grew more dilatory, then uncertain, or positively late, according to the time when he had gone to bed. At two or two-thirty in the afternoon all might come to see him drink chocolate, and he conversed with the assembled company. This lasted as long as he chose, but usually not more than half an hour. . . . After the Regency council, or about five o'clock if there were no meeting, he was done with work.[12]

Orléans's suppers became the subject of scandal, with orgiastic goings-on rumored to be taking place nightly amid excessive drunkenness. Given the excesses of the aristocrats of the era, it is hard to believe otherwise. But no one outside his clique knew what went on, because, wrote the Duc de Saint-Simon, who was never a guest at these events:

> As soon as supper-time arrived, the outer doors were bolted and barred so that, no matter what occurred, the Regent could not be disturbed. I

do not mean for private or family matters only, but in case of danger to the State, or to his own life; and the incarceration lasted all night and well into the following morning. The Regent thus wasted an infinity of time with his family, his diversions, and his debauchery.[13]

The town of New Orleans was named for him, and has tried to keep his customary hours ever since.

◦◎◦

During his short working day, Orléans tried to find an escape from the economic ruin his uncle had left behind. Before 1685, France had a positive balance of trade with Britain; now the money was flowing in the opposite direction. The War of the Spanish Succession had crushed a revival of France's trade that was getting under way in the four years of peace after the War of the Grand Alliance. Most of the war's costs had been financed with debt, and an attempt to introduce paper money during the war had only caused hyperinflation. England, not France, had the *asiento* to provide slaves to the Spanish territories. Money was scarce, commercial activity was at a standstill, land went uncultivated, buildings were deteriorating, workers were unemployed, peasants were in debt, and the crown was facing bankruptcy.

Into this dilemma came John Law, the son of a wealthy Edinburgh goldsmith, with a proposition. Goldsmiths were the precursors of bankers in seventeenth-century Britain; their notes were accepted in lieu of physical transfer of gold, and Law grew up observing the stimulating effect this had on commerce. A young womanizer, Law had in 1694 killed an older man in a duel over a woman; forced to flee to the Continent, he made his living as a professional gambler. The Duc de Saint-Simon wrote: "He was a schemer and a calculator, always balancing one thing against another, and extraordinarily knowledgeable and learned in such ways, the kind of man who, without ever cheating, continually won at cards by the consummate art (that seemed incredible to me) of his methods of play."[14] Gambling was a mania among the moneyed classes of the time, and Law probably was able to win consistently because he counted cards and accurately assessed risk when playing wealthy, inebriated opponents who trusted luck.

As Law gambled in the Netherlands, seeing nightly how quickly money wants to change hands, he studied the workings of the great Bank of Amsterdam and watched the actions of the banks of Genoa and Venice and the fledgling Bank of England. Law worked out a theory of banking, based on the idea that a banknote could change hands many times as fast as one transaction involving the physical transfer of gold or silver.

M.ᵣ JEAN LAW CON.ᵉʳ DU ROY EN TOUS CES CON.ˢ CONTROLEUR GNAL DES FINANCES an 1720.

John Law, a professional gambler turned economist whose Mississippi scheme privatized the French state, confiscated precious metals, replaced the money supply of France with paper backed by future earnings from Louisiana, impelled the building of New Orleans, sent shiploads of convicts and prostitutes to people the colony, and got the Duc d'Orléans to sign off on one of the biggest fiascos in economic history. He is depicted here as he looked in 1720.

Law thought it foolish to require a bank to issue only as many banknotes as it could pay out in silver or gold coins. With a stable political and financial structure, the notes would not be called in, and thus it was not necessary to back up but a fraction of the paper money with metal. The important thing was to have commerce, which meant having enough money available to conduct it with. He spent years attempting to get one European nation after another to let him start a bank. In December 1715, he wrote a letter to Orléans, whom he had known for two decades by then, that called to the new regent's attention how the Bank of England's powers of credit had been a major factor in England's triumph in the War of the Spanish Succession: "Before the introduction of credit the State which was richest in specie was the most powerful; now it is the one best served by its credit."[15]

Having a large, fast-circulating supply of trustworthy paper currency would expand commerce and bring prosperity, permanently. Not silver, but the real estate of France, would be security for the notes a new bank would issue. And with the territory of Louisiana factored in, which had not yet begun to produce anything—which, in fact, had as of yet only 215 French-speaking people in it, 160 of them soldiers—an enormous amount of money could be created.[16] The French were becoming addicted to tobacco, which they were buying from Virginia. Louisiana could grow tobacco for this expanding domestic market.

Orléans went for it. Crozat was relieved to be quit of the colony, giving up his rights to it after five years, during which he had lost some 1.2 million livres.[17] In August 1717, John Law's new Company of the West (*Compagnie d'Occident*) was given proprietary rights to Louisiana, whose chief export was buffalo hides, and Canada, whose chief export was beaver pelts.[18]

It was probably the following month that Law's company passed a resolution to establish New Orleans.[19] The city already existed on maps in France when Bienville began building it, probably sometime between March 15 and April 15, 1718,[20] using a work gang of fifty or so men to tear the thick growths of cypress out of the swamp. The site was the sloping northeastern side of the natural levee of the Mississippi River at the point where it takes a crescent-shaped bend, five and a half miles south of Lake Pontchartrain, at the best spot, imperfect though it was, for connecting the Mississippi River with the Gulf.

Natchitoches was an extension of the old Canadian way of doing things: a fur-trading post. But New Orleans was a visionary idea. Its strategic location made it the potential linchpin of commerce in the region, and the security gate to the interior.

The French would create the biggest circuit of waterborne commerce that the continent could offer, using two great river systems to outline an empire. Arriving in Canada from France, they would ascend the St. Lawrence River from Québec into the continent. From there, they would go overland to the Great Lakes, then, by any of several routes—most likely, by what became known as the Chicago Portage overland to the Illinois River—float all the way down the Mississippi River to the Gulf of Mexico, and from there, with a stop in Havana or Saint-Domingue, back to France.

To finance the money his bank printed, John Law issued fifty thousand shares in the Company of the West with a face value of one thousand *livres tournois* each. Law received the right to collect taxes and assumed the state's debt. Functions of the French state were privatized, assigned to Law one by one as he consolidated his position as head of a monopoly corporation. The French companies for foreign exploitation were folded into Law's company. In September 1718, it took over the tobacco monopoly. It controlled both ends of the French slave trade by taking over the Company of Senegal, which exported slaves from Africa, and the Company of Saint-Domingue, which supplied that plantation colony with slaves. In January 1719, Law's bank became the Banque Royale. Four months later, with the acquisition of the East India Company and the China Company, the Company of the West became the Company of the Indies.

By October 1719, with speculative frenzy at its peak, one-thousand-livre shares in the company were trading at ten thousand. The following year, with the merger of the Banque Royale and the Company of the Indies, the French

A one-hundred-livre note issued by John Law's bank.

government completed its spin-off into a single monster corporation, backed by the crown and headed by the Scotsman. Law was under pressure to get Louisiana producing, fast.

In the absence of treasure mines, this new paper money supply would have to be backed up with profits from trade and agriculture, and that meant colonization. Unfortunately, peopling the colony was a serious problem. The Mississippi had a terrible reputation. Few workers volunteered to come, though a few hundred colonists arrived to claim their promised land grants in 1718. Among them was Le Page du Pratz, whose account of the first leg of the crossing, from France to Saint-Domingue, with eight hundred colonists on three boats, gives a sense of what it took to travel by sail:

> We were two months in this passage to Cape François [sic]; both on account of the contrary winds we had on setting out, and of the calms, which are frequent in those seas: our vessel, besides, being clumsy and heavy, had some difficulty to keep up with the others; which, not to leave us behind, carried only their four greater sails, while we had out between seventeen and eighteen.[21]

They remained in Cap Français for fifteen days, where "six weeks before our arrival, fifteen hundred persons died of an epidemic distemper, called the Siam distemper" (yellow fever).[22] From Saint-Domingue it took them *three months* more—longer than the sailing time from France—to sail around Cuba and reach Louisiana's Dauphine Isle, near Mobile. He notes, "We had a prosperous voyage all along, and the more so, as no one died, or was even dangerously ill the whole time, for which we caused *Te Deum* solemnly to be sung."[23]

Bogus reports in the French press described New Orleans as "eight hundred handsome houses" instead of the true situation of "a hundred huts without much order."[24] Recruitment efforts failed. Cadillac, who had again returned to France, was briefly clapped in the Bastille by John Law for disparaging the official propaganda that claimed there were silver mines, and an emerald boulder, in the Mississippi. No one believed the portrayals of Louisiana as El Dorado. Nor would the crown pay people to emigrate; Louisiana was, and would be, chronically underfunded by the French. The Huguenots, who with their work ethic and artisanship might have successfully colonized Louisiana for the French, had been chased out of France two generations ago.

The French solution to underpopulation in Louisiana, previously used in Canada, was forced emigration, so the social condition of Louisiana was complicated by its conversion into a French penal colony in 1719 and 1720. Pushed by John Law, the gendarmes jumped at the chance to deport their undesirables, emptying French prisons and sweeping the streets. After a November 1718 ordinance to suppress vagabonds in France, the campaign quickly broadened. Prostitutes and female criminals (with the fleur-de-lis branded on their shoulders to mark them as under sentence for life) were rounded up for exile to Louisiana. Many of the deportees were salt bootleggers (salt was a royal monopoly), and the gendarmes rounded up tobacco smugglers, thieves, beggars, vagabonds, orphans, the unemployed, the incorrigible, the vicious, the depraved, the wrongly accused, and bystanders. People denounced their enemies, or their neighbors, in order to get rid of them. The *forcées* included "160 prostitutes and 96 teenaged *débauchées*, from Paris's La Salpêtrière house of correction for women; by 1721, this group had come to constitute 21 percent of the colony's female population."[25]

To say "Louisiana" in the France of 1719 was more or less the equivalent of saying "Siberia" in twentieth-century Russia. Forcibly wedded prisoner couples were marched across France through town after town on their way to the port, in a rolling caravan that served as a reminder that only the dregs of society went to Louisiana, and only in chains. Far more deportees were sent than survived; many died even before reaching the port of embarkation. In September 1719, 150 French girls rioted to avoid being carried from Paris to La Rochelle, there to cross the Atlantic. The guards shot six of them to death, and wounded a dozen more. The remainder were herded to La Rochelle, where they remained, ill clad and ill fed, through a freezing winter that many did not survive.[26] In January 1720, inmates at a French prison revolted, overpowering the guards and fleeing the prison, in terror of being sent to Louisiana.[27]

By April of that year, police in Paris were using press gangs, arresting beggars and the unemployed en masse, to come up with warm bodies to send to the Mississippi. "A wave of revulsion against 'Louisiana slavery' swept France, and in Paris people battled the *archers* in the streets."[28] The phrase "Louisiana slavery" was no exaggeration: in Louisiana, they were referred to as *esclaves*, and there is little to indicate that they were treated better than native slaves or, a little later, black slaves—though, unlike the blacks, their children were not born into slavery.[29] After the dragnet had become so broad as to sweep up business visitors to Paris, Orléans put a stop to the forced emigration policy. But it had done its damage: there was little voluntary emigration from France to the Louisiana colony after that.

Probably some seven thousand French were deported to the *Misicipy*, but with high mortality en route to embarcation, at sea, and after arriving, only some thirteen hundred of the forced emigrants arrived. Even so, that was a lot for a colony so thinly populated. Bienville concentrated them in New Orleans. By 1721 there were 178 of them left.[30]

Law did manage to entice a population of Germans to immigrate, and beginning in 1718, after suffering epidemics and starvation that reduced their numbers significantly (a 1722 census shows 330 Germans in Louisiana, though some 1,500 had embarked), they settled along the section of the Mississippi subsequently known as the German Coast, where they provided some stability to the region.[31]

The engineer Adrian de Pauger began drawing a street grid for New Orleans in 1721. A hurricane blew away most of the settlement of New Orleans on September 23, 1722, necessitating its rebuilding in any case. The lots in the rebuilt town—today the part known as the French Quarter, or Vieux Carré—were rectangular, with space behind the houses for gardens. Drainage canals divided the area into blocks, with a larger canal at the boundary that carried sewage in the direction of the lake and dumped it in the swamp.

The streets of this new capital of La Louisiane would have no Indian names like Natchitoches or Biloxi. They would bear the names of rich Parisians who would never cross the ocean to set foot in the pestilent colony, but who would hopefully patronize Law's enterprise. They were awarded duchies, with titles. Law, who never traveled to the New World, became the Duke of Arkansas.

Meanwhile, the Company of the Indies was in chaos. After Law printed a surfeit of paper money, he tried to forbid the French to use hard coin, and even sent gendarmes across France on a house-to-house confiscation of precious metals. Law's undoing was Louis François de Bourbon, the Prince de Conti, who called in his shares of the company, demanding hard coin for them. There was a run on Law's bank, and shares crashed. By September 1721 they sold at five hundred livres, one-twentieth of their peak value.

There is no John Law Street in New Orleans. After a six-month wild ride, the company went into bankruptcy, ruining numerous aristocrats and speculators, and even temporarily crippling the productivity of Saint-Domingue.

Louis XV was declared to have attained his majority at the age of thirteen, and was crowned king on February 15, 1723. The Duc d'Orléans died in December. A rumor—not true—ran through Paris that during the autopsy one of his Great Danes jumped up and began feasting on his heart.[32] Under Louis XV, the capital moved back to Versailles.

John Law became a gambler again, and died, ruined, in Venice in 1729. The failure of his experiment caused the French to shun paper money, with long-lasting consequences. Britain, whose economic and political systems were more developed than France's, weathered its own concurrent speculative disaster of the South Sea Company. But the Bank of France was not founded until 1800, 106 years after the founding of the Bank of England, and even then it was hobbled by onerous requirements to keep one-quarter of the face value of its notes on hand in specie. In the end, France never became a major industrial power. It was, and remains, famed for luxury goods, rather than mass-produced items for common people.

The "Mississippi bubble" of speculation that Law's scheme generated is one of the most famous disasters in European economic history, celebrated by Charles Mackay in his protosociological volume of 1841, *Extraordinary Popular Delusions and the Madness of Crowds*. Some have suggested that his plan might have worked, but that its execution was fatally flawed. For the economist Joseph Schumpeter, who saw history as tending toward the glory of capitalism, "[Law] worked out the economics of his projects with a brilliance and, yes, profundity which places him in the front ranks of monetary theorists of all times."[33] The Duc de Saint-Simon, who saw it all up close, tells us:

> [Law's] bank . . . would have been excellent in a republic or in a coun
> try such as England, where the people control the finances. Regarding
> the Mississippi, he was deceived, for he truly believed that there were
> rich possibilities in America. He argued like an Englishman, failing to
> understand how little suited our fickle nation was to great commercial

enterprises. Lack of experience, the greed of those eager to make vast fortunes without delay, the difficulty of working under an authoritarian government without firm principles, in which one minister's work might be totally destroyed by his successor, were all against him.[34]

A less generous way of looking at it would be that New Orleans was founded as a gambler's bluff. Quite naturally, many people in New Orleans, as in France, came to see paper money itself as a scam.

7

THE SENEGAMBIAN PERIOD

Here are the warrior men, the farmers,
They farm the rice, they farm the millet that we eat.
When it is hot, they await the rain
Witness, witness the warriors.

—*Youssou N'Dour*

Ⓝew Orleans was a dissolute town from the beginning.

The crooks and whores were unsuited by experience and temperament for artisanship or agriculture, but were well prepared to establish a culture of criminality and poverty. Carl A. Brasseaux writes: "Embracing the moral code forged in the wilderness by [the Canadian] *coureurs des bois*, Louisiana's independent, anticlerical, and hedonistic pioneers effectively resisted the limited moralizing influence of the Catholic clergy while creating a frontier society that reflected their newly acquired values. . . . These libertines . . . had a lasting impact on colonial Louisiana."[1] The word *libertine* comes from the same root word as *liberty*. Both concepts came into their own in eighteenth-century France. By this point libertinage had evolved from a Calvinist epithet for a religious freethinker into a term meaning more or less what it means now, with connotations of sexual license. Either was appropriate in frontier Louisiana, where there was much licentiousness and few bothered to go to church.

With such unpromising personnel, it seems unlikely that the colony would have survived at all had it not been for another group of forced emigrants who began arriving in numbers in 1719: African slaves.

From a cultural point of view, it might be appropriate to refer to the French period alternatively as the Senegambian period. The French kept careful records, so there is high-quality information about how many Africans were brought to the colony. Gwendolyn Midlo Hall makes the numbers available in *Africans in Colonial Louisiana*: during the period France governed Louisiana, a total of 5,951 Africans arrived on twenty-three slave ships. Surely there were undocumented importations as well, but it seems unlikely that the number of those was very great.

The first two slave ships arrived in 1719, and by 1721, seven had come. All but one had arrived by January 1731; the final one, a private venture by planters, brought 190 captives in 1743.[2] After that, no more Africans would come to Louisiana for over thirty years, with the single known exception of a slave ship captured from the British in 1758. For slave ships coming from Africa, the eager, affluent market of Saint-Domingue made unnecessary the impractical, longer trip past that colony on to impoverished Louisiana.

The first two slave ships to arrive in Louisiana were from Ouidah, on the so-called Slave Coast; by then under the control of the Dahomeyan empire, in what is now Benin, it was a slaving port whose captives included people from nearby Ardra. But the bulk of the captives brought to Louisiana—3,909, or about two-thirds of the total, on sixteen out of the twenty-three French slave ships, including the final ship of 1743—embarked from Senegal.

Of the seven non-Senegambian ships, six were from Ouidah, and one ship came from Cabinda (Angola). All the non-Senegambian ships, except for one of the ships from Ouidah, arrived by June 1721. The captives on these earliest ships suffered the highest mortality rates, not a few of them starving to death.[3] Two of the Ouidah cargoes were criticized by Bienville for being old and sick. The Cabinda cargo arrived sick, and had the misfortune to arrive during a period of famine; twenty-eight of the captives died after landing.[4] The *Africain*, which arrived on March 17, 1721, from Ouidah, had 180 captives out of 280 that had embarked; the *Duc de Maine*, arriving six days later, had 338 out of an original 394.[5] A November 1721 census found only 680 Africans in the colony.[6] But at that, the blacks seem to have survived in Louisiana better than the whites did.

Despite the many distinct African subgroups and languages that have been identified for every part of Africa and in the New World, the distribution of Africans in the Americas was not random. For obvious logistical reasons, there was a tendency for slaves from the northern reaches of slaving territory to be taken to the more northern parts of the New World (the British colonies), and for those from the south to be taken to South America (Brazil). This fact—mapped onto the general settlement of European Protestants in the northern part of the New World and Catholics in the South, with their different approaches to music and culture—determined much about how music evolved in the Americas.

It should be understood that when I speak of Senegambia or of Kongo in this volume I am speaking in general terms, as per John Thornton: "Using language, we can divide the parts of Atlantic Africa that participated in the slave trade into three culturally distinct zones, which can be further divided into seven subzones."[7] He identifies those three main zones as Upper Guinea, reaching from the Senegal River down to modern Liberia and speaking Mande, Wolof, and a diversity of other languages; Lower Guinea, reaching approximately from the western Ivory Coast to Cameroon and speaking languages of the Akan and Aja family; and the Angola coast, including the Ndongo (Ngola) and Kongo kingdoms, speaking Bantu languages.

French Louisiana took representatives of all three of these broadly defined regions, but not in equal proportion: Upper Guinea, represented by the Senegambians, dominated; Lower Guinea was a minority, with the ships from Ouidah; and there was one ship from the Angola coast.

༄

In 1725, when the town needed an executioner, it freed a black slave, one Louis Congo, who belonged to the Company of the Indies, to give him the post. He carried out sentence on white and black alike—not only executions, but lesser punishments, like flogging or collaring. Being free and feared was preferable to being a slave, and Louis Congo was able to negotiate to have his wife come live with him in his own house, as well as a ration of wine. Hall reproduces a list of prices paid to him: a hanging brought thirty livres, breaking on the wheel forty.[8]

Louis Congo: a prototypical New Orleanian name. The first name tells us the colony he was in. Pronounced French-style, "Louie," it remained a popular name in Louisiana for centuries (e.g., Louis Armstrong, as well as the singer billed as the "white Louis Armstrong," Sicilian American New Orleanian Louis Prima). Louis Congo's last name tells us he came to Louisiana on the one ship known to have arrived from Cabinda, Angola: *la Neréide*, which arrived in Biloxi in April 1721 with 294 slaves—181 men, 121 women, 37 boys, and 37 girls.[9]

It was common at the time for slaves to be given as a surname the name of their home nation (adopting the word *nation* for convenience while dissociating it from the European implications of the term) or port of embarcation. You can still find people with the last name "Sinegal" in Louisiana. During French Louisiana's few slave-importing years, the preponderance of slave ships arrived from Senegal, because Law's company had the exclusive concession to slave the territory. The Senegal River was navigable, and the French established a slave-trading post, Fort St. Joseph, upriver and well inland. There the French bought slaves that had been sold down the Niger River, so that captives came from many hundreds of miles inland, in sharp contradistinction to the coastal pattern of slaving that dominated elsewhere.[10] Meanwhile, the Segu rebellion in the region was generating captives. Philip D. Curtin writes that "from about 1700 to 1730, unusual numbers of slaves were sold down the trade routes toward the Senegambian coastal ports."[11] This coincides exactly with the French slave trade to Louisiana—1719–1731—and dovetails with what Hall tells us: that the largest number of early Afro-Louisianan men were Bambara, from what had in previous centuries been the Malian empire.

Though the Bambara were not Muslims, they had long been in contact with Islam, and their culture had a tradition of *jali*, or bards. They were Mande people, an ethnic grouping that also includes the Mandinga, the Mandinka, the Dyula, and others. Also coming from the Senegambia were Wolofs, the largest number of them women, so many Afro-Louisianans had Bambara fathers and Wolof mothers.[12] This collection of Africans in Louisiana was clearly a community, despite its enslaved status. By 1724, enough slaves had arrived that a *Code Noir de la Louisiane* was enacted, applying to the mainland the rules Louis XIV had promulgated in 1685 for the Indies, with fifty-five regulations for slave owners.

The Senegambians came from a culture of artisanship. Among them were goldsmiths and silversmiths, ironworkers and farmers. They were sophisticated: their African territory, directly to the south of the Sahara and long crisscrossed by trade routes, was a place where cultures met and interpenetrated one another. According to Hall, they knew how to work indigo, which grew wild in both the Senegambia and Louisiana, and which the Europeans did not know how to process into dye; it became an important crop in Louisiana.[13] At the request of the French colonial slave buyers, the first two slave ships to come to the colony brought hogsheads of rice seedlings from Africa, along with captives who knew how to cultivate it.[14] Rice became, and remains, a staple of the Louisiana diet. In other words, Africans brought not only necessary manual labor, but also came with knowledge, skills, and foods that were crucial to keeping the white settlers of Louisiana from starving.

The largest number of the early slaves brought to South Carolina—the major rice-growing area, with the largest concentration of blacks, in the English-speaking South at the time—were also Senegambian. "During the eighteenth century," writes Hall, "Greater Senegambians were more clustered in colonies that became part of the United States than anywhere else in the Americas."[15] One would suppose that the music of Africans in Louisiana during the French period bore a strong resemblance to the music of the Senegambia, the homeland of the majority of its people. It is worth noting the numerous correspondences between essential characteristics of African American music and those of that relatively arid, Islamized region of Africa. Very different from the communal, syllabic, highly polyrhythmic, drum-dominated music of the forested Kongo, this was a bardic, melismatic, swinging music, influenced by Koranic chanting, with a less polyrhythmic texture, favoring portable stringed instruments.[16] Fiddles came to French Louisiana from two directions: from Europe, but also from Africa, because the Senegambians had a bowed-instrument tradition, and had possibly had it as long as, or longer than, France. In the New World, the Senegambians' musical knowledge could be expressed on the European violin, as well as on the banjo, an instrument that derives from a Senegambian family of plucked instruments.

Firsthand documentation of the Afro-Louisianans' culture during that time is scarce. There is enough, however, to confirm what we might assume, that from the beginning they played their music and practiced their religion. Le Page du Pratz writes that the slaves

> are very superstitious, and are much attached to their prejudices, and little toys which they call *gris, gris*. It would be improper therefore to take them from them, or even speak of them to them; for they would believe themselves undone, if they were stripped of those trinkets.[17]

This documents that gris-gris—later an essential element of New Orleans voodoo, though that word does not appear in Le Page du Pratz—were part of black life in Louisiana from the beginning, arriving direct from Africa with the earliest captives. In present-day Haiti, where there is much vodou and little communication with New Orleans, the term *gris-gris* is, as far as I have been able to ascertain, unknown. Ina Fandrich gives a Mande derivation for the name:

gergerys, meaning "charm."[18] They were worn for protection in seventeenth-century Senegambia. William S. Simmons, who studied the Badyaranké people of Senegal, characterizes gris-gris as "Koranic amulets," made and sold by the people known as *marabouts*.[19] Islam has a long history in that region of Africa: the kingdom of Takrūr imposed Islamic law in the eleventh century, and the Almoravids, strict Muslims who in that century conquered Iberia, did so from a base in the Senegambia.[20] Generally, African Islam was a religion of the chiefs and merchants, while the common people continued practicing traditional religion, but over the centuries elements of the different beliefs mixed, in the process anthropologists call syncretization. The Bambara were not Muslim, but they knew how to make gris-gris.

Meanwhile, the first two ships from Ouidah had to have brought with them the religion of that region, which forms the core (though by no means the totality) of the religion known in Haiti as *vodou*. There are various records of "Ardra" people, who presumably arrived with the cargoes from nearby Ouidah. Ardra is the home of the *foddun*—the divine figures in their religious practice, specifically beings who descend from the twin divinity Mawu and Lisa—from whom the word variously spelled as *vodun*, *vodou*, *vaudoux*, *vodú*, and *voodoo* derives. Their music, as well as their spiritual practice, was quite different from that of the Bambara. (A nomenclatural note: the word *voodoo* does not refer to just any African religion. What they do in Havana today, for example, is not "voodoo." In this text I will use the word *voodoo* to denote the practice specific to New Orleans, as distinguished from *vodou*, which is how I spell the Domingan/Haitian practice.)

And there was that one ship from Cabinda on which, presumably, Louis Congo came. Hall notes that Louis Congo could sign his name, unusual for a black man in that place and time. But then, Kongo people had been (at least nominally) Christianized by the Portuguese over two centuries before, and some of them arrived in the New World knowing how to read and write—in Portuguese.

Black music in New Orleans at this time must have been strongly Senegambian flavored, and it will forever remain a tantalizing question how the music of the minority Ouidahns and Ardrans, and Angolans and Kongos, might have reinforced or opposed it. When a first-generation New Orleans culture was being defined, no one saw fit to write down much about the music of black people, so we have to draw inferences by listening to the most traditional music of the regions in Africa from which they came.

We know that Africans in Louisiana gathered regularly, in numbers, speaking their own languages. Moreover, "the labor statute for public works brought slaves from all along the river into New Orleans for periods of thirty days,"[21] so Africans from different farmholds were in contact with each other in an urban setting. An Afro-Louisianan culture quickly formed, with its character-istic music and its spiritual beliefs, though we can only make informed guesses as to what they might have been. This culture was further locked into place by thirty-five years of isolation, with only two shiploads of Africans known to have entered Louisiana between 1731 and 1766—the ship from Senegal in 1743 and the captured ship of 1758 with its cargo of 122 Angolans.

Before the Africans arrived, the colonists enslaved the natives, who knew how to deal with the peculiar local conditions. Le Page du Pratz describes buying a native slave before the arrival of African slave ships in the colony:

> A few days after my arrival I bought an Indian female slave of one of the inhabitants, in order to have a person who could dress our victuals. . . . As for my slave and me, we did not understand one another's language; but I made myself to be understood by signs, which these natives com-prehend very easily.[22]

One can imagine what those signs might have been. The enslaved Indian girl became his concubine, and, given the choice, chose to follow him rather than stay with her father when he relocated to Natchez. He does not refer to her by name; perhaps I am reading too much into it, but he seems to enjoy writing the words "my slave." Du Pratz recommended that Frenchmen learn the Indians' medicinal secrets, noting their skill in treating bullet wounds and that "disorders frequently accounted almost incurable, are, without any pain-ful operation, and in a short time, cured by physicians, natives of Louisiana."[23] He tells this story:

> It was almost night, when my slave perceived, within two yards of the fire, a young alligator, five feet long, which beheld the fire without moving. I was in the garden hard by, when she made me repeated signs to come to her; I ran with speed, and upon my arrival she shewed me the crocodile, without speaking to me; the little time that I examined it, I could see, its eyes were so fixed on the fire, that all our motions could not take them off. I ran to my cabin to look for my gun, as I am a pretty good marksman: but what was my surprize, when I came out, and saw the girl with a great stick in her hand attacking the monster! Seeing me arrive, she began to smile, and said many things, which I did not comprehend. But she made

me understand, by signs, that there was no occasion for a gun to kill such a beast; for the stick she shewed me was sufficient for the purpose.

The next day the former master of my slave came to ask me for some salad-plants; for I was the only one who had any garden-stuff, having taken care to preserve the seeds I had brought over with me. As he understood the language of the natives, I begged him to ask the girl why she had killed the alligator so rashly. He began to laugh, and told me that all new comers were afraid of those creatures, although they have no reason to be so: and that I ought not to be surprized at what the girl had done, because her nation inhabited the borders of a lake, which was full of those creatures; that the children, when they saw the young ones come on land, pursued them, and killed them, by the assistance of the people of the cabin, who made good cheer of them.[74]

As Africans came into the new environment, they too learned from the natives the arts of survival in the strange new swampland. When they escaped, they sometimes hid out with Indians, on occasion marrying into their society.

8

AN EAR FOR MUSICK

As late as the end of the seventeenth century, the belief was held by many, even in England, that the negro was not a man but a wild beast, marked by an intelligence hardly superior to that of a monkey, and with instincts and habits far more debased. He was considered to be stupid in mind, savage in manners, and brutal in his impulses.

—*Philip Alexander Bruce*, Economic History of Virginia, *1895*[1]

*O*ver a century after the Spanish established their first settlements in the Americas, the British brought Protestantism to the New World to stay.

Barbados's church was Anglican, as was Virginia's. But different colonies handled religious matters differently. The colony founded by the Quaker William Penn was tolerant. There was even a Catholic British colony, for a time: Lord Baltimore's Maryland, named for Henrietta Maria, the Catholic Queen Consort of England, was a place where Catholics could safely come when Oliver Cromwell was in power in England, though the Puritans later outlawed Catholicism there and burned the churches.

Virginia's official Anglican church practiced a Protestantized version of Catholicism, retaining the autocratic structure of a bishopric rather than a council of clerical and lay presbyters, with a formal liturgy performed by a highly professionalized clergy in solid, centrally located brick churches. A law, poorly enforced, required everyone to go to church at least once every four weeks or be fined.

Pilgrims, Puritans, Quakers, Anglicans—none of them thought the use of musical instruments in church proper (though there was always a liberal tide in the Anglican church that wanted to have an organ). Instruments in worship were associated with popery. When the young Thomas Jefferson was a student at William and Mary College, he practiced his violin three hours a day—which is to say, he probably played pretty well. He had his problems with the institution, though: "An establishment purely of the Church of England, the Visitors were required to be all of that Church; the Professors to subscribe its 39 Articles, its Students to learn its Catechism, and one of its fundamental objects was declared to be to raise up Ministers for that church."[2] We may owe our tradition of constitutionally guaranteed freedom of religion not only to the practices of Penn's colony, but also in part to Jefferson's and James Madison's uncomfortable experiences in Virginia of the Anglican church as a religion of state.

Religious dissenters from this official Christianity—first the Presbyterians, then the Methodists and Baptists—spread through the colonies. Their churches were humble wooden meetinghouses in no special location, their preachers were laymen, and their congregations were known for their seriousness of devotion. By the mid-1700s, during the period that has come to be called the Great Awakening, their influence had traveled down from New England to Virginia. Rhys Issac writes:

> Contemporaries were struck by the contrast between the challenging gaiety of traditional Virginia formal exchange and the solemn fellowship of the Baptists, who addressed each other as "Brother" and "Sister" and were perceived as "the most melancholy people" who "cannot meet a man upon the road, but they must ram a text of Scripture down his throat."[3]

Unlike Anglican slave owners, the evangelists were eager to convert slaves, who, in the English-speaking territories, were strictly forbidden to practice their ancestral religions. As the religion of the Bible was made available to the slaves, they made the most of it, performing it in their style, some certainly viewing Christianizing as a path to emancipation. And, as in Europe, it was diffused by singing. Unfortunately, we don't know what early black psalm singing sounded like, but a tantalizing, if vague, description comes from a pair of letters written in 1751 by a Presbyterian evangelist in Hanover, Virginia, asking for books:

Bibles, and *Watt's Psalms and Hymns* . . . I am the rather importunate for a good number of these, as I cannot but observe, that the Negroes, above all the Human Species that I ever knew, have an Ear for Musick, and a kind of extatic Delight in *Psalmody*; and there are no books they learn so soon, or take so much Pleasure in.

The reference to "Human Species" is telling: this evangelist at least saw blacks as human, though a different species. After receiving the books, he wrote:

The books were all very acceptable; but none more so than the *Psalms and Hymns*, which enabled them to gratify their peculiar taste for Psalmody. Sundry of them have lodged all night in my kitchen; and, sometimes, when I have awakened about two or three a-clock in the morning, a torrent of sacred harmony poured into my chamber, and carried my mind away to heaven. . . . In this seraphic exercise, some of them spend almost the whole night.[4]

These slaves could read. But as of 1740, a South Carolina law prohibited teaching slaves to read, and, though Protestantism was based on the idea of literacy, most black Protestants had to learn the Bible tales as oral folklore. They markedly preferred the stories of the Old Testament. Those long-ago Jews— Ezekiel who saw the wheel, Joshua who fit the battle of Jericho, Jonah in the whale, and the great conjurer-liberator Moses—became archetypal characters of African American spiritual life. Their stories were recounted in a style of preaching that was passionate, direct, and musical, with a sense of pitch and rhythm that would have been different than that of the whites—which is to say, maybe their psalmody was a little bit funky.

꿍

The first citation of the word *funk* in the *Oxford English Dictionary* comes from circa 1330, in the vague but perhaps self-explanatory phrase "not worth a fonk." By the following century, its use seems to have been established to mean a spark, a bit of fire: "Funke or lytylle fyyr, *igniculus, foculus*." In this sense it is related to the word *punk*, meaning the same thing, as well as *spunk*.

By the seventeenth century, *funk* had acquired another meaning: "a strong smell or stink." The first known instance of that comes from America, in a 1623 letter written from Virginia that complains of the smell during a transatlantic crossing: "Betwixt decks there can hardlie a man fetch his breath by reason there ariseth such a funke in the night that it causes putrefaction of bloud." While the inhumane conditions of slave ship travel are well known, this letter was not about a slave ship. Travel conditions in the early days of colonization were revolting, especially for the poor. Epidemics roared through the tightly packed ships during their weeks-long voyages, and the lack of cleanliness devastated passengers and crew alike. (Even on slave ships, the mortality rates of the crews at times exceeded those of the cargo.) There is a mention of a ship that arrived in Virginia on which 130 out of 180 people had died en route. The death rate among newcomers to the colony was frightful as well. One source asserts that in the first thirty years of the Virginia colony, one hundred thousand people died in the process of "seasoning."[5]

A dictionary from the year 1700 defines *funk* as "tobacco smoak," another bad smell, and one associated with a bit of fire. It appears that in the polyglot linguistic environment of early colonial slavery, a word was more likely to be taken up if it could be identified with a meaning in both European and African languages. Robert Farris Thompson identifies the word *funky* with the Kikongo *lufuki*, meaning strong body odor, a concept associated with hard work and spiritual power.[6] That's not incompatible with its emergence in Virginia, where there were Kongo slaves from early days, who would have sweated all day working on tobacco plantations. Tobacco and sweat are a strong combo. Those laborers must have been extra funky. Since the word *funk* was in use in Virginia as of 1623, we can pretty well assume it has been part of the African American vocabulary ever since. In New Orleans in the 1890s, when the legendary first jazzman (the closest we can come to naming such a figure, at any rate) Buddy Bolden sang his big hit "Funky Butt," a plea to open a window in a room full of unwashed people and tobacco smoke, he was using it in exactly that sense.

To judge from slave masters' complaints, the slaves' funk bothered them considerably. The funk had its own power. Funk was slave master repellent.

∞

In Europe, and among the Europhile class in America, the eighteenth century was a period of secularization. Many slave owners were not much concerned about their immortal souls burning in hell. But the Africans, who came from a deeply religious world, found something in common with those ruder white folk who were so serious about their spiritual practice.

In my book *Cuba and Its Music*, I discuss in some detail differences between Afro-Cuban and African American music, which I will not repeat here. But I would like to point out one major difference between the two that is not only musical but has much to do with poetics as well: the differences between the Bible-thumping sermonizing of the Protestant preacher and the mystical rituals of the Catholic priest. I cannot think of one Cuban song that quotes a Bible verse. Nor are there mentions in Cuba of Old Testament prophets, or references to sin and salvation. Nor is there any counterpart in Afro-Cuba to that archetypal African American practice of testifying, witnessing, and elaborating on Bible stories.

Slaves in officially Catholic Cuba were baptized but not catechized. Domestic slaves often attended mass as children, where they served as pillow-carriers for their mistresses and absorbed the Church's impressive forms of ritual without being trained in the associated doctrine. Afro-Cubans practiced their ancestral beliefs with the aid of diviners and problem-solvers who, like priests, were scholarly ritual experts that spoke in ancestral languages, drawing on a vast repertoire of African religious knowledge to perform elaborate procedures, communicating with pantheons of African spirits that the Cubans call *santos*. Through the much-discussed syncretization, they disguised their spirits with the images and attributes of Catholic saints, and adapted outward forms of the religion as necessary to make their traditions survive. Something like this process had already happened in Africa before the transatlantic slave trade began, most visibly in the Catholicized Kongo.

In Ardra and Ouidah, or Cuba or Saint-Domingue or Louisiana, where there were no evangelists, blacks danced their religion. But in Virginia—and Maryland and New England—people didn't dance in church, and, if they were devout, not in their private lives either. As the evangelists converted slaves, they convinced some of them to give up dancing. Not all black people, of course; still, the repudiation of dancing was "neither eccentric nor an isolated phenomenon, but widespread and quite general among both white and black converts to various evangelical sects."[7]

But that is not to say that black Protestants held still. On the Sea Islands of Carolina and Georgia, there were ringshouts, the sacred dance during which a circle of loud steppers expanded and contracted, singing to the rhythm they stomped. And there was ritual: the Baptists' ceremony of adult baptism by total immersion must have been meaningful to an African religious sensibility that had previously venerated riverine gods. When an English-speaking slave received the power of the Holy Spirit, it was not a very different phenomenon of spirit possession from the *lwa* in Haiti, or an *orisha* in Cuba, coming down to ride the believer's head. You can see it today when the spirit comes down at a gospel meeting.

Despite their discouragement of dancing, the evangelists never stamped out the kinetics of African culture. Black gesture—not only dance, but what we might now call body language—was a way of transmitting Africanness that lasted for generations in America after the ancestral languages had been replaced by English. For all the copying of black style by whites, black gesture is distinct from white gesture still. But the tension between the music of sin and the music of salvation—absent in Afro-Cuban music, the conflict exists in African American music to this day—played itself out over the issue of dancing.

Dancing was the principal entertainment all across Europe and America, and an important part of life on plantations throughout the New World. As a schism formed between white Protestants who did and didn't dance, the music for those who did was routinely provided by black musicians. Sawing the fiddle all night for a white people's dance was an important source of income for a musician, though, then as now, he would surely have complained about the low pay.

The musician's trade was not at all desirable for a white man, and certainly not an honorable one. But the small income it provided could make a crucial difference in the survival of a black man, who was born dishonored.

⊂∞⊃

With Africans, French, Germans, and indigenous people in Louisiana, there was surely plenty of music, though we don't know much about it. The priests had music at vespers and masses. On April 5, 1722, when the ship *Profond* arrived, "a *Te Deum* was sung to thank God for His help, for the colony was desperate for food." Another *Te Deum* was sung a week later to give thanks after news arrived of the twelve-year-old Louis XV's recovery of health.[8] In 1725 the Capuchin brothers established a school in New Orleans that included singing, and a choirmaster was hired.[9] The city was regulated by bells, and a fifer and a drummer were in residence in New Orleans by 1727.[10] Other military musicians probably were as well, but, even in Europe, the military band of the time was not as highly developed as it would become even fifty years later, as instrument technology improved and armies became more professional.

A 1727 map of the West Indies by London cartographer Herman Moll, on which shipping paths are visible: "A map of the West-Indies &c. with the adjacent countries: also ye trade winds, and ye several tracts made by ye galeons and flota from place to place."

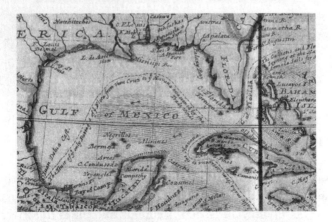

Detail of Moll's 1727 map. Natchitoches and Pensacola are represented; New Orleans, founded less than ten years before, is not.

In August 1727, some Ursuline nuns arrived in New Orleans, along with some Jesuit priests. The Ursulines had been handmaidens of French expansion since 1639, when two independent-minded sisters arrived in Québec to evangelize the natives. This new group of Ursulines came to Louisiana with support from the Company of the Indies. At first domiciled in Bienville's house, they moved to their own plantation, worked by their own slaves, just upriver of town, until their convent could be built. They worked in the military hospital and ran a girls' school.

Now that there were nuns, decent girls could be sent to Louisiana. As described in Charles Gayarré's *History of Louisiana* (published in French in New Orleans in 1846–47, and subsequently rewritten in English):

> In the beginning of 1728, there came a vessel of the company [of the Indies] with a considerable number of young girls who had not been taken, like their predecessors, from houses of correction. The company had given to each of them a casket containing some articles of dress. From that circumstance, they became known in the colony under the nickname of the "filles a la cassette," or "the casket girls." The Ursulines were requested to take care of them until they should be provided with suitable husbands. Subsequently, it became a matter of importance in the colony to derive one's origin from the *casket girls*, rather than from the *correction girls*.[11]

At least one of the Ursuline sisters was trained in music. "During Holy Week," writes Alfred Lemmon, "the nuns sang a *Tenebrae* service and a *miserere*, accompanied by musical instruments. On Easter Sunday, students sang four-part motets and a mass, also accompanied by instruments."[12] The consecration of their chapel in 1734 was accompanied by military music.[13]

The Ursulines' musical abilities are attested to by a manuscript handcopied in 1736 and presented to them in 1754. A partial copy of a series of volumes published in Paris in the 1730s, it consisted of 294 songs by French and Italian baroque composers of the bygone era of Louis XIV—Couperin, Lully, Marin Marais, Campra, and others. The songs of the manuscript were divided into two categories: songs of virtue and songs of vice. The texts of the songs about "Vices" were lettered in red ink. Though these were secular composers, the texts of the songs had been replaced by words extolling a Christian life. This practice, known as sacred parody, or contrafacta, turned "Happy lovers, how I envy / The favours with which love crowns your sighs" into "To virtue let us consecrate our lives / It is the glory and the sweetness of our days." [14] The girls who sang these sanitized lyrics were well aware of the original words, as Father Albert de Paris had earlier observed:

> There is a most regrettable consequence, which is that, in general, the original words under which these profane songs have become popular are disreputable, and these ideas are awakened when people sing them: often, indeed, they repeat the wicked words in order to get the singing under way, before turning to the proper words. [15]

A surprising word appears in the Ursulines' manuscript: *vaudeville*. The word is of uncertain derivation, though a frequent suggestion is *voix de ville*, voice of the town. In this context, the word referred to a song in free rhythm, though in France it was already being used in its theatrical sense. Thus the word *vaudeville* turns up in New Orleans not only long before it appears in the Anglo-American world, but thirty-eight years before New Orleans got its first theater.

There is a marvelous recording of music from the Ursulines' manuscript, performed by the French early music group Le Concert Lorrain. Listening to the first tune on the CD (the notation is pictured on the facing page), one notices that the two eighth notes in the last beat of measure two, as well as all the other eighth notes in the piece, are not played as even eighth notes, but as unequal ones, with the first note longer, perhaps twice as long, as the second. This is the Baroque practice known in France as *notes inégales*. It is also the standard performance practice of jazz, where—with the upbeats accented—it is known as swing.

In *Cuba and Its Music*, I speculated that the swing feel of jazz derives from a typical feel still easily audible in traditional music in the Senegambia and Mali today, and that New Orleans was a key point in its dissemination. To that I would like to add that there was a point of reinforcement between French New Orleans and Senegambian New Orleans: both sides played unequal eighth notes. If the Ursulines, who were educators, were teaching the musical practice of *notes inégales*, that only helped to establish it in an environment where white, free colored, and enslaved musicians all crossed paths. If I were to hypothesize a continuum between Afro-Baroque New Orleans and the jazz era, I would locate it in the playing of black violinists, who were likely playing along with the whites in French New Orleans, as they were in Martinique, Guadeloupe, and Saint-Domingue, to say nothing of Cuba. I would also note the sometimes extreme fondness for melisma in New Orleans

Page from the Ursuline manuscript. This song, about the vice of pride, has its text in red ink. It was sung by teenage girls, over strong propulsive bass lines, with lots of ornamentation in the accompaniment and uneven eighth notes.

(e.g., the ornamentation of Aaron Neville's singing or James Booker's piano playing), which is an attribute of both the French Baroque and the music of the Islamized Senegambia.

But in black New Orleans there were also drums, and in Louisiana as elsewhere, they implied revolt. There is no question that Africans gathered to drum and dance, in assemblies that were feared by the whites, who were always wary of an uprising. For Le Page du Pratz:

> nothing is more to be dreaded than to see the negroes assemble together on Sundays, since, under pretence of Calinda or the dance, they sometimes get together to the number of three or four hundred, and make a kind of Sabbath, which it is always prudent to avoid; for it is in those tumultuous meetings that they sell what they have stolen to one another, and commit many crimes. In these likewise they plot their rebellions.[16]

In this passage, Le Page du Pratz, who was in Louisiana from before the first arrival of African slave ships, is describing a Sunday dance-and-market gathering of several hundred blacks. Where did this happen?

From the beginning, blacks were segregated in New Orleans, quartered outside the city. One group of houses stood right outside the city's ramparts. Another, on the opposite side (the "west bank") of the Mississippi River, was a depot for quarantining newly arrived slaves, and the Law Company established a plantation there. That area, called Algiers, is the only place on that side of the river that is part of Orleans Parish today.

Perhaps Le Page du Pratz, writing years after the fact, was describing something he had seen happen at the Algiers plantation, after he became its manager. But it is also possible he was describing the gatherings held near the black residential area just outside the city—perhaps even in the place not yet known as Congo Square.

Le Page du Pratz's association of the *calinda* with slave revolt is significant. The calinda (also spelled *calenda*) was a transnational dance of this period. The first known mention of it dates to 1654. Père Jean-Baptiste Labat described it in Martinique in 1694.[17] If you wonder whether Africans communicated among themselves during slavery times, look at how dances traveled from port to port, for centuries. These transnational dances included, in the sixteenth and early seventeenth centuries, the *zarabanda* and the *chacona* (both of which crossed from the African New World via Havana into Spain, becoming the *sarabande* and the *chaconne*); in the seventeenth century, the calinda and the *bamboula*; and in the eighteenth or possibly earlier, the *chica*. (The string continued in the nineteenth century and into the twentieth with the *tango* and subsequently the *mambo*.)

The British colonies did not permit these dances, so the calinda and the bamboula did not flourish in the plantation societies of Virginia and Carolina. The British prohibited African languages, religions, and drums, along with the liberty of enslaved people to gather en masse publicly. When there is an account of a dance (what Anglo-American slave masters called a "frolic") in British North America, the instruments invariably mentioned are fiddle and/or banjo, instruments that were not loud enough to call across to the next plantation.

The banjo is an instrument of the same general family of instruments as the Arabic oud. Mentions of it appear under various related names (*banza*, *banjar*, etc.) from a number of colonies: Martinique in 1678, Jamaica in 1679 and 1739, Barbados in 1708, Maryland in 1754, and Saint-Domingue in 1797—but, significantly, not in Cuba, Spanish Santo Domingo, or Puerto

Rico, colonies to which the importation of Senegambians was forbidden in the days when the Afro-Spanish world was first being created, nor in New Orleans until 1819.[18] There are innumerable accounts like the one Nicholas Cresswell wrote of his visit to Virginia in 1774: "Sundays being the only days . . . [slaves] have to themselves, they generally meet together and amuse themselves with Dancing to the Banjo . . . a Gourd . . . with only four strings. . . . Some of them sing to it."[19] And anything could serve as a percussion instrument—a box, a bottle, a pair of spoons, the percussionist's own body. As long as it wasn't loud enough to transmit a message over distance.

The fiddle, whose African variant was likewise played by Senegambian musicians, was a central part of American popular musical life in the eighteenth and nineteenth centuries. That playing the fiddle was a way of earning money, or at least a drink, anywhere is attested to by how many times one reads, in those omnipresent runaway slave advertisements that began appearing as soon as there were newspapers in the colonies, of fugitive fiddlers absconding with an instrument. Other instruments are sometimes named, but fiddle was the most common. To cite but one example, Captain Joseph Hale in Newbury, Massachusetts, was willing to pay five pounds' reward in 1745 for the return of Cato, who "sometimes wears a black Wigg, has a smooth Face, a sly Look, took with him a Violin, and can play well thereon."[20]

⌒∞⌒

On November 29, 1729, angered by French attempts to take their lands, the Natchez Indians, in league with some slaves, attacked Fort Rosalie (better known as Natchez, founded in 1716). They massacred perhaps 250 whites (though Le Page du Pratz put the number at close to 700), burned the fort to the ground, and destroyed the tobacco works there. It was a serious blow to the company of the Indies' Louisiana project: perhaps a tenth of the French settlers in the colony died in the uprising. Some four hundred Natchez were sold into slavery in the West Indies as a result.

Then, in 1731, a conspiracy was broken up that may have involved as many as four hundred Bambara. Le Page du Pratz gives an account of his role in uncovering it, which, while self-serving and unsupported by documentation, is in Gwendolyn Midlo Hall's words, "perhaps not too much less authentic" than the documentary accounts:[21]

A female negroe receiving a violent blow from a French soldier for refusing to obey him, said in her passion, that the French should not long insult negroes. Some Frenchmen overhearing these threats, brought her before the Governor, who sent her to prison. The Judge Criminal not being able to draw any thing out of her, I told the Governor, who seemed to pay no great regard to her threats, that I was of opinion, that a man in liquor, and a woman in passion, generally speak truth. It is therefore highly probable, said I that there is some truth in what she said: and if so, there must be some conspiracy ready to break out, which cannot be formed without many negroes of the King's plantation being accomplices therein: and if there are any, I take upon me, said I, to find them out, and arrest them, if necessary, without any disorder or tumult.

The Governor and the whole Court approved of my reasons: I went that very evening to the camp of the negroes, and from hut to hut, till I saw a light. In this hut I heard them talking together of their scheme. One of them was my first commander and my confidant, which surprised me greatly; his name was Samba.

I speedily retired for fear of being discovered; and in two days after, eight negroes, who were at the head of the conspiracy, were separately arrested, unknown to each other, and clapt in irons without the least tumult.

The day after, they were put to the torture of burning matches, which, though several times repeated, could not bring them to make any confession. In the mean time I learnt that Samba had in his own country been at the head of the revolt by which the French lost Fort Arguin; and when it was recovered again by M. Perier de Salvert, one of the principal articles of the peace was, that this negro should be condemned to slavery in America: that Samba, on his passage, had laid a scheme to murder the crew, in order to become master of the ship; but that being discovered, he was put in irons, in which he continued till he landed in Louisiana.

I drew up a memorial of all this; which was read before Samba by the Judge Criminal; who, threatening him again with torture, told him, he had ever been a seditious fellow: upon which Samba directly owned all the circumstances of the conspiracy; and the rest being confronted with him, confessed also: after which, the eight negroes were condemned to be broke alive on the wheel, and the woman to be hanged before their eyes; which was accordingly done, and prevented the conspiracy from taking effect.[22]

The torture of being broken on the wheel was alive and well in the New World, only now it was being applied to rebellious Africans. By that time, blacks significantly outnumbered whites in Louisiana. As the Natchez upris-ing had demonstrated, and as the Haitian Revolution would demonstrate sixty years later, the Samba Bambara conspiracy, if indeed it existed, might conceivably have succeeded.

Though it is not known for certain, the executioner who broke the Bambara on the wheel and hanged the woman might well have been Louis Congo.[23] Shannon Lee Dawdy has written an intriguing article about this man; noting the opprobrium (and physical threats) directed at executioners, she writes: "The fact that being the executioner was the lowliest (and perhaps loneliest) position a free man could occupy meant that Louis Congo did not enjoy an elevated status among law-abiding free people."[24] I would add that having come on the sole ship from his homeland, on which, as a Kongo, he may have been a minority among Angolans, Louis Congo was a member of a minority group within Africans in Louisiana, a smaller group even than the people who came on the boats from Ouidah. Whether black or white, society in New Orleans seems always to have been characterized by rivalry among groups, and though we have no record of Louis Congo's thoughts, it is entirely possible that he didn't much mind breaking Bambara on the wheel.

The year of the alleged Bambara conspiracy, 1731, was also the year that saw the final bankruptcy of the Law Company, which in its ruin had outlived both John Law and the Duc d'Orléans. That was the end of slave shipments to Louisiana, and the end of the colonization effort. It was also the year of the publication in France of the Abbé Antoine-François Prevost's *Histoire du Chevalier des Grieux et Manon Lescaut*. The first widely successful French novel, its plot turned on forced emigration to Louisiana (though Prevost never traveled to the New World). Enormously popular, it was banned upon publication but circulated in numerous pirate editions. Its narrator is Des Grieux, a young man of noble birth who, though it is clear to the reader, is continually unaware of how he is being mistreated and cuckolded by his beloved Manon, a prostitute. He undergoes ever-deepening degradation on her behalf, throwing away his future and social standing for passion, and he ultimately follows her as she is deported to Louisiana in chains. She expires in his arms on the sands of Biloxi and is buried in the desert wastes. The book is wickedly humorous; part of its charm is that the reader is free to take it as a sentimental tragedy or a deeply cynical satire on a young man's self-absorption. Today, it is better known as an opera, having served as the basis of librettos for Daniel-François-Esprit Auber, Jules Massenet (who composed a sequel as well), and Giacomo Puccini, who launched his career with a *Manon Lescaut* in 1893, and as a 1974 ballet by Kenneth McMillan that is a standard of the London Royal Ballet repertoire.

After the Law Company's spectacular wipeout, Louisiana went back to being a royal colony. It was a loser, producing nothing of value. In December

1732, a ship arrived in New Orleans from France, loaded with flour. It could find no return cargo.[25] The plantation on the West Bank of the river became the property of King Louis XV, as did its slaves. Le Page du Pratz served as the plantation's manager for it, and, in the words of Shannon Lee Dawdy:

> Fancying himself an architect, Le Page du Pratz set about designing slave quarters for the King's Plantation. . . . Le Page du Pratz's design for a slave village resembles the neat, linear quarters that planters began to build somewhat later in Virginia and the Carolinas, including "Mulberry Row," designed by Jefferson at Monticello. Le Page du Pratz's decision to enclose the compound with a wall and locked gate, however, imposed an unusually strict control of slave movement within the plantation space.[26]

Segregated housing was already the rule. Security issues aside, Le Page du Pratz was bothered by the funk, which he ascribed not to slaves' living and working conditions but to a racial characteristic. He recommended remaining upwind when visiting the Negroes at their work, and his memoir advises building slave quarters with that consideration in mind:

> The negro camp ought to be inclosed all round with palisades, and to have a door to shut with a lock and key. The huts ought to be detached from each other, for fear of fire, and to be built in direct lines, both for the sake of neatness, and in order to know easily the hut of each negro. But that you may be as little incommoded as possible with their natural smell, you must have the precaution to place the negro camp to the north or north-east of your house, as the winds that blow from these quarters are not so warm as the others, and it is only when the negroes are warm that they send forth a disagreeable smell.[27]

As an economic elite emerged that could afford to keep domestic servants (and as those black servants began giving birth to lighter-skinned babies), more people of color began living in town. Meanwhile, by the 1730s, many of the forcibly married couples who had been dragooned from France to Louisiana had divorced. Over the decades, the few *forcées* who survived matured into senior delinquents and ran fencing operations outside of town that traded with slaves for stolen goods, making burglary a problem in New Orleans, not for the last time. They bartered with the Indians to sell them liquor and ran the prostitution business with an experienced eye.[28] A hospital for venereal disease was in operation by the end of the decade.

In 1732, as Louisiana reverted to being a royal colony, General James E. Oglethorpe, a veteran of the campaign against the Turks, was authorized to found Georgia as a refuge for the "worthy poor," the first new British North American colony in over fifty years. His colonists began arriving at the site of Savannah early the following year. It was a strategic move for Britain to control the region between Spanish Florida and prosperous South Carolina. Six years later, Spain and Britain began the War of Jenkins' Ear, fought over trade issues in the West Indies, with hostilities stretching from Georgia and Florida down to Havana, present-day Panamá, and Cartagena. The Southern colonists were aware of how vulnerable they were to slave rebellion, and Spanish subversion was suspected when "Angolan" slaves revolted at Stono in South Carolina. John Thornton believes that the rebels were former Kongo soldiers, who knew how to handle firearms from their days in Africa; they converged "dancing, singing and beating drums," according to an eyewitness account.[29]

The conflict between Spain and Britain was subsumed in 1742 into the War of the Austrian Succession, a complicated conflict involving the major powers of Europe. Known as King George's War in the New World, it entailed much privateering in the West Indies. By 1744, Britain and France had resumed their normal status of being at war with each other. With no new colonists, and no new slaves to do the work, and France once again tied up with war, the isolated Louisiana colony continued in its own already peculiar ways. Though there continued to be a French governor in Louisiana and the French flag continued to fly, power increasingly flowed into the private hands of the emerging economic elite, which came to control the Superior Council that regulated the town.[30]

The planters were Louisianans now. Of those who had come from France, few if any had been aristocrats. But many had come from Canada in the first place, and a new generation was emerging: the Creoles. This word, *Creole*, which has caused considerable confusion in referring to people in Louisiana, comes from the Portuguese and Spanish word *criar*, to raise (as in, to raise a child), and probably originated with the Portuguese, since they initiated the oceangoing slave trade. *Criollo, crioulo,* or *Creole* referred to a person born in the colonies, as opposed to a person born in Europe, with no implications for skin color. The word is used in Cape Verde; an archipelago of Atlantic islands three hundred miles off the coast of Senegal, it was uninhabited when the Portuguese established it as a shipping base in the fifteenth century. In Louisiana, the meaning of *Creole* varied with the era. At the time of statehood, the word was used to refer to those who were already present in Louisiana, whether of French, Spanish, or African descent; in speaking of the black community, the term came to imply lighter-skinned people, who often had French names.

In May 1743, the Canadian-born Pierre François de Rigaud, the Marquis of Vaudreuil, arrived as governor of the vast Louisiana Territory, and Bienville sailed for France (he would die twenty-five years later, in Paris). Vaudreuil was an astute officer who cultivated good relations with the Indians, forestalling through diplomacy a war with the Choctaws. A descendant of an old aristo-cratic family, the *beau Marquis* held court in the tiny frontier town of New Orleans as if it were Versailles. He gave state dinners on gold plates, sponsored musical dramas, and held grand balls for those who could afford to live such a life. With slaves to do the work, and winters that were short and relatively mild, those New Orleanians who were prosperous had ample time for leisure, something that became practically the stereotype of the New Orleans Creole in the nineteenth century.

Dancing was an essential social skill in this New Orleans. There was a French dancing master, Baby, but he was killed by Indians in 1748. "The fate of poor Baby must have caused great sorrow to the ladies of New Orleans," wrote nineteenth-century Louisiana historian Alcée Fortier. "Where did they find another master to teach them the minuet and the stately bows with which they were to salute the governor and his wife?"[31]

As was common throughout the colonial New World, a few people were accumulating wealth, and their power was growing. Meanwhile, the libertine population of New Orleans, from the wealthy few to the many poor, contin-ued celebrating with their dances, their masquerades, their drinking, their gambling, their fighting, and their couplings, especially during the Carnival season but also during a year-round schedule of festivals, parties, and balls. The great period of New Orleans' taverns had yet to begin; a 1746 regulation limited the number of *cabarets* (taverns) to six, not counting one canteen for the French troops and another for the Swiss.[32]

Vaudreuil remained as governor for ten years, then returned to Canada. As of February 1753, the governor was Louis Billouart, Chevalier de Kerlérec, a naval officer. Both men—Vaudreuil in Canada, Kerlérec in Louisiana—were about to have the great misfortune of being on the losing side of a very big war.

9

THE CABILDO

I was on board Genl. O'Reily's fleet when he ascended the Mississippi and took possession of New Orleans. Two hundred men, having the approbation of the country could have burned that fleet and defeated the expedition. The Mississippi is in no part one mile wide from the Balize upward, and in general but nine hundred yards. Its current is so rapid as to require, frequently, thirty days to ascend thirty leagues to New Orleans.

—*Letter from Colonel George Morgan*
to Don Diego de Gardoqui, August 20, 1789[1]

*T*he twenty-one-year-old George Washington started a world war. At least, the French said he started it.

If you looked at a French map of the North American mainland in the mid-eighteenth century, only the Atlantic coastal region and Hudson Bay were under British control, while the French territory reached all the way down from Canada to New Orleans and out to the Gulf below. But if you looked at a British map, Virginia and the Carolinas extended westward through the continent. The inevitable territorial confrontation materialized when a French force was sent north from Louisiana to establish forts in the largely unexplored upper Ohio Valley—that is, the far western reaches of what was then considered by the British to be Virginia—with the ultimate aim of connecting France's settlements at either end of the continent.

Under the command of Lieutenant Colonel Washington, the British sent out an expedition to expel the French interlopers. When Washington's forty men from the Virginia Regiment surprised a party of French on May 28, 1754, he rashly gave an order to fire, according to the French; the British said the French fired first. Not in doubt, however, is that Washington took the French commander Joseph Coulon, Sieur de Jumonville, prisoner, along with thirteen others. Unfortunately, the prisoners were murdered by Washington's Indian allies while in his custody. Realizing he had stirred up a hornet's nest, Washington retreated and hastily erected a fortification, which he named Fort Necessity.[2]

On July 3, a regiment of some six hundred French and one hundred Indians from the New Orleans, Natchitoches, Baton Rouge, and Opelousas posts took Washington's fort under the command of Jumonville's brother, capturing Washington in the process—the only time in his career he ever surrendered. Washington was forced to sign a statement in French, but since he did not read the language, he did not realize he had confessed to assassinating a diplomat, much less that his confession would be news in the excitable French press.

North Americans call the war that ensued the French and Indian War, but in the rest of the world it is usually remembered as the Seven Years War. Fought in a multicontinental theater that ranged from the Pacific to India to the Senegambian coast to the Caribbean to Canada, it was a contest between "Prussia, allied with Great Britain, Hanover, Brunswick and Hesse" and "Austria, most of the Holy Roman Empire, Russia and Sweden, all allied with France"[3]—to say nothing of the American Indian factions, some of whom were allied with Britain and some with France. Britain subsidized the winning campaigns of Frederick the Great of Prussia, while France went into its pockets for its allies. A number of territories changed hands as part of the war's resolution, among them Louisiana.

French mapmaker Jean-Baptiste Nolin's 1756 map, at the beginning of the Seven Years War, shows the French vision of their empire in the New World. The dispute over where the French drew their eastern frontier versus where the British drew their western frontier caused the first skirmish of a war that took on global dimensions.

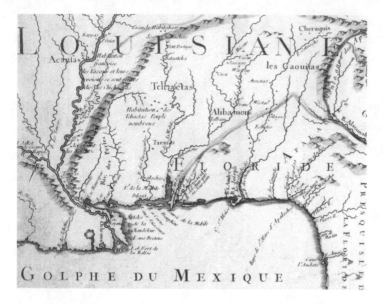

Detail of previous map. The political importance of the various tribes in the French and Indian War is reflected in their visibility on the map.

It would have been easy for a navy to plunder New Orleans, but none did, and no battles took place there during the French and Indian War. There was not much of value there. The French soldiers were "so given to 'unrestrained debaucheries of liquor and women'" that Governor Kerlérec "considered his garrison 'more dangerous to the colony than the enemy itself.'"[4] They avidly patronized the town's gambling dens. Thanks to the town's population of ne'er-do-wells, there were prostitutes, albeit sometimes syphilitic ones, to service the troops. The New Orleans hospital for venereal diseases, which had closed by 1740, reopened around 1756 after an epidemic arose among new recruits, many of whom had been exiled from France for misconduct.[5] Outside the city, in the swamps, blacks and Indians lived in marronage. The more brazen ones came into the city to steal: a member of the Superior Council complained in 1754 that maroon blacks were entering the city at night.[6]

Kerlérec, for his part, was alarmed. There were no fortresses in Louisiana, and no defenses to speak of. If the British attacked, his command would fall immediately. There was also considerable fear that the Cherokees, who were British allies, would make war on them, so the Creoles depended on alliances with other Indian groups for their defense. But by the end of his tenure, Kerlérec had earned a nickname from the Choctaws: *Chef Menteur*, or Chief Liar.

The name outlived him to become a part of local geography: a narrow water-way between Lake Pontchartrain and Lake Borgne is called the Chef Menteur Pass. Running over it is the Chef Menteur Highway, otherwise known as U.S. 90, which takes you through a neighborhood trashed by Katrina—the middle-class black residential neighborhood of New Orleans East—and on to Slidell.

Though the British did not attack New Orleans, they did blockade the Gulf of Mexico, cutting Louisiana off from France, on which the colony depended for its supplies. By 1759, the troops were on half rations, and France even authorized Kerlérec to trade with Mexico. No coin came in, and the colony's already discounted paper money lost more of its value. The merchants were hurting.

In 1760, the Marquis de Vaudreuil, the former governor of Louisiana who had become the French governor of Canada—the last one, as it turned out—surrendered to the British. France's claim to the continent had been demolished. With that, France's Native American allies lost their protection against the British, and from then on, the power of the indigenous people diminished steadily. Meanwhile, the British decisively defeated the French in India, beginning the era of India's colonial subjugation to Britain, now an imperial power with increasingly global reach. The cheap, brightly colored textiles exported from India to England changed British styles of dress and popularized the wearing of cotton fabrics.

By 1761, France had been beaten up and down the hemisphere, and no French supply ship had come to Louisiana in four years. That's when Carlos III, the Italian Bourbon who had become king of Spain in 1759, committed a grave political error. Spain had been sitting out the Seven Years War, but in 1761, at the instigation of Louis XV's prime minister Etienne-François, duc de Choiseul, Carlos agreed to reinstate the old family compact of mutual aid among Bourbons. Even though by then France had all but lost its war with Britain, Carlos promised—secretly, he thought—to enter the war on the side of France on May 1, 1762, if it should still be going on. When British intelligence learned about this, England seized the initiative and declared war on Spain on January 4, 1762.[7] Spain, an increasingly backward kingdom, was now at war with Britain—a wealthy country with a dynamic economy and the world's most advanced industry, largely self-sufficient in food, possessing the world's greatest navy, and which, moreover, had already won the war in Canada.

On March 5, 1762, the British invaded the nerve center of the Spanish empire in the Americas. Avoiding Havana Bay's formidable sea-facing defenses, they landed east of the city and seized Morro Castle by marching up from behind. Occupying Havana, they took the richest prize in the hemisphere, the 1762 silver fleet's entire cargo. The British held Havana for almost eleven months, without bothering to occupy the rest of the island. Their stay, while resented by the locals, was a boon to Havana's trading class, and the brief period of British occupation transformed the economy. The British scrapped restrictive laws that had required Cuba to trade only with Spain. They cranked up Cuba's sleepy sugar industry, bringing in approximately four thousand slaves, purchased from British dealers, to do the labor. Cuba had been importing slaves for over two centuries, and had a legal infrastructure for dealing with its slave population, but it had never seen Africans arrive on its shores at this pace. By the time Spain took Havana back, Cuba was on a different, and more independent, track, with an accelerated slave trade and an expanding economy. The emerging class of Cuban Creole planters wanted all the slaves they could get.

As compensation for Spain's losses, and to keep Britain from taking over Louisiana, Louis XV, prompted by Prime Minister Choiseul, made an unexpected and audacious move. He wrote to his cousin Carlos III on November 3, 1762, offering to give him the Louisiana Territory west of the Mississippi. Now that French hopes of controlling the North American continent had been dashed, it was no longer worth the expense. Carlos had no alternative but to take Louisiana, because he needed a buffer zone between the aggressive British colonists and his silver mines in New Spain (Mexico). The offer was accepted, despite the expense and the burden of governance it imposed, and Louisiana was to be turned over to the Spanish, though the French and Spanish cousin-monarchs kept the deal a secret between themselves.

Britain had trounced the Bourbons. After peace was finalized on February 10, 1763, France gave up its remaining claims on Britain's second choice, Canada. The first choice was Saint-Domingue, and there was even debate in Britain as to whether to take Canada or the small but lucrative island of Guadeloupe. But the British colonial sugar planters in Jamaica had sufficient financial clout and political power in London to keep that from happening, and even in defeat, France was determined to hold on to its most profitable colony. In their peace negotiations, the British required that Spain cede either their Florida territory or Puerto Rico in order to get Havana back. Spain unhesitatingly chose to surrender Florida. Among its many other provisions, the Treaty of Paris restored "the Havannah" to Spain, and Martinique and Guadeloupe to France. It also fixed the Mississippi River as the boundary between British and French territory. That French territory along the Mississippi was actually now Spanish territory, but France's cession of Louisiana to Spain a few months previously had not yet been made public, least of all to the Creoles of Louisiana. Britain came out of the deal in charge of the entire Gulf Coast east of New Orleans, a territory that included Pensacola, Mobile, and Baton Rouge. The boundary of West Florida now ran from the Mississippi to the Apalachicola River, with its capital at Pensacola; eastward from there, including the peninsula, the territory was known as East Florida.

In 1763, a complicated dispute between a group of Jesuits and their creditors regarding the Jesuits' extensive plantations in Martinique resulted in expulsion of the Jesuits from France, a move of political anticlericalism that was an early signpost on the way to the French Revolution. Thinking themselves still French, the Louisianans followed the lead of the French parliament, and that year, the Jesuits were booted out of Louisiana too, though the Ursuline sisters remained. The Jesuits' role in the colony's religious life was taken over by the more austere Capuchins, and their large plantation, across what is now Canal Street, became royal property, then was privatized to prosperous locals. Part of it ultimately became New Orleans's first suburb.

Also in 1763, attorney general Nicolas Chauvin de la Frenière complained to the Superior Council of New Orleans about the illicit tavern keepers outside the city who doubled as fences for stolen goods:

> The rear of the City is infested with numbers of men without occupation. The just and severe ordinances of our Kings have always provided for the expulsion [of such people] from the Cities. These people require constant attention and deserve the utmost severity. Most of them were brought here at the cost of the King and lodged and fed on the plantations at his expense. The object was to establish cultivators on a rich and fertile soil and to provide the City through these people with the necessities of life. Living here they defeat the consummation intended, they increase the cost of living, they are the first at the markets and are consumers instead of creators. To accelerate their earnings and to meet the expenses they incur, they adulterate the liquors they sell and expose the slaves to violent maladies. While furnishing drink they incite them to pilfer and to steal from the houses of their masters indiscriminately all they can find; the handkerchief, the towel and empty bottles, etc., all have a price and disappear in the traffic of these clandestine taverns. The negro drinks and loses his senses. He recognizes no restraint nor

the necessity of submission. He would not be violent if he did not find in these secret taverns the means to satisfy his brutal passions; what hidden pernicious disorders have resulted![8]

By this point, the Superior Council had no metropolitan power to back it up. France displayed complete indifference about the fate of its Louisiana colonists—they were mere colonials, after all. Only on April 21, 1764, more than eighteen months after secretly offering the colony to his Italian cousin in Madrid, did Louis XV send a letter of notification to the Louisiana governor of the transfer of sovereignty. By means of the first broadside printed in New Orleans, Louisianans found out, to their great unhappiness, that they were to become Spanish subjects. The Creoles sent a delegation headed by New Orleans's wealthiest merchant, Jean Milhet, to plead their case before Louis XV. "On his arrival in Paris, Milhet sought and located Bienville, who was then eighty-six years old and who was living miserably in a garret, and asked him to accompany the Louisiana delegation on its visit to the Prime Minister."[9] Choiseul received them and sent them on their way without a royal audience. Severed from the royal government, the local government in New Orleans began to feel a sense of its own sovereignty. Britain, which had been granted use of the Mississippi River, was by this time provisioning the Louisiana Creoles through smuggling.

France had been frightened by losing control of Martinique and Guadeloupe during the war, though it had regained them in the settlement. Saint-Domingue had not changed hands during the war and emerged effectively unscathed. It began an intense expansion, with slaves imported pell-mell. Now that France was at peace with Britain, it was determined to hold on to Saint-Domingue. "Versailles spent liberally to make [Saint-Domingue] more French," writes John Garrigus, "hiring more administrative personnel, building new urban infrastructure, establishing a colonial mail service, and installing the colony's first printing press. Private entrepreneurs matched the public outlay by building cafés and clubs."[10] A cultural life flowered. With the printing press came the colony's first newspaper, *La Gazette de Saint-Domingue*, in 1764.[11] Saint-Domingue threw off spectacular riches as the world eagerly consumed its accelerated output of sugar, coffee, indigo, tobacco, and cotton.

Spain waited more than three years to begin its occupation of *Luisiana*, choosing first to reestablish its control over Havana, where the king ordered the construction of the immense new fortification of San Carlos de la Cabaña, with room for one thousand troops, behind the Morro Castle. (Castle construction was an Italian industry, and Carlos, who had abdicated the throne of Sicily and Naples to become king of Spain, was much in favor of it.) Spain scrapped the *asiento* system of licensed monopoly vendors to the colonies, thus throwing open the door to free trade in slaves to Cuba, which powered the rapid expansion of Cuba's sugar industry.

Now that the British had taken over Mobile and Pensacola, implementing their much harsher laws for treatment of people of color in the process, Spain resettled its colonists from there to Cuba and other parts of the empire. The French colonists in Louisiana, however, did not resettle, but remained in Louisiana, where they would be an unending source of vexation for the incoming Spanish governor.

The idea of a territory changing national identities was nothing new to Europe, where for millennia cities had been swapped from empire to empire. The same town might be under one flag one year and another the next. Carlos V had ruled Amsterdam and Vienna, so why couldn't his admittedly less heroic latter-day counterpart take over little New Orleans?

Though Spain had a long colonial experience, it had never acquired another nation's colony before. Its other colonies had been created from scratch. Moreover, Spain's great colonial period had been the era of Habsburg crusaders. The Bourbon government employed a much more reasonable, even meeker, tone than that which had subjugated Mexico. Spain sent its top talent to serve as governors.

∽

Antonio de Ulloa y de la Torre Guiral was a distinguished man. In 1736, at the age of twenty, he had gone to Peru as one of two Spanish mathematicians attached to a French Academy of Sciences team that was engaged literally in geometry, taking measurements at the equator to determine whether the Earth's diameter was greater longitudinally or latitudinally.[12] He remained there for eight years, and subsequently published a lengthy, widely read account of his observations in the New World. A Sevillan who embodied the Enlightenment's belated appearance in Bourbon Spain, he was one of Spain's best-known scientists, in addition to being a naval officer and—the least successful part of his career—a colonial administrator. An astronomer, meteorologist, naturalist, mathematician, and author, he had accomplished the extraordinary feat of becoming a Fellow of the Royal Society of London after arriving in England as a prisoner of war captured at sea. From London he brought back to Spain its first scientific knowledge of electricity and magnetism. He was the first European to describe the properties of platinum. His *Voyage to South America*, published in 1748, had "provided Europeans with the first comprehensive and authoritative account of the region."[13]

In 1758, he returned to Peru, this time in charge of the quicksilver mine at Huancavélica—an important and highly paid post, as the mine was the only source in the hemisphere for mercury, which was essential for silver production. The mine's discovery in 1556 had begun the great era of cash flow to Spain. For two centuries, Indian laborers there had trod barefoot all day in vats of a toxic amalgam of crushed silver ore and mercury, chewing coca to keep themselves going. (In *Noticias americanas* of 1744—a scientific work, as such term would have been understood then, though its chapter headings are "Entertainment I," "Entertainment II," etc.—he describes meticulously the method of preparing and using coca, observing: "The Indians hold it in extremely high regard, and if they lacked it, they would not work enthusiastically.") Unfortunately, the administration of the mercury mine, like the colonial government in Peru, was corrupt, and Ulloa was unable to root out the corruption. The Spanish government lacked the ability to back him up, and ultimately pulled him out in what amounted to an admission of failure, returning him to Havana in 1765 before posting him to Louisiana the following year as the first Spanish governor of the colony. He arrived on March 5, 1766.[14]

Ulloa may have been chosen for the New Orleans post because of his experience dealing with the French: in addition to the time he spent working with the French scientists in Peru, he had lived in France for two years. But the French-speaking Louisiana colonists detested being Spanish subjects, and Ulloa's term as governor was ultimately a dismal failure. As had happened in Perú, the Spanish administration failed to provide him the necessary support.

Ulloa declined to take official possession of Louisiana until the Spanish government backed him up with troops or funds, neither of which were forthcoming. In September 1766 he went to the Balize, at the mouth of the Mississippi, and remained there until March, awaiting the arrival of his wealthy bride from Peru. In the absence of a show of force, the French-speaking Louisianans, several years adrift from any effective colonial government, became bolder in their opposition. Ulloa's greatest headache was the Superior Council, particularly its attorney general, Chauvin de la Frénière. The council continued to issue decrees, while French soldiers refused to serve under the Spanish flag. There were two governments, neither with authority. A glut of French paper money was trading at 50 percent of its face value, and the French colonists insisted it be redeemed by the Spanish at 100 percent.[15]

Not long after Ulloa arrived, he authorized the importation of new slaves, a priority for the Louisiana French. It had been decades since slave ships had come to Louisiana. Even without importation, slave numbers had increased somewhat (from 4,112 in 1731 to 5,552 the year Ulloa arrived),[16] but it was an aging population. The French laws remained in place, and Ulloa put a lax trade policy into effect, even allowing English dealers to sell slaves on credit.

But despite Ulloa's efforts to please them, the French-speaking merchants of Louisiana were horrified at being absorbed into the commercial straitjacket Spain imposed on its colonies, limiting markets for their products and fixing their prices. On March 23, 1768, complying with a royal decree, Ulloa was forced by Spain to implement commercial regulations to prohibit Louisiana from trading outside the Spanish empire, as all Spain's other colonies were also forbidden to do. Though the principal market for New Orleans's products had been Saint-Domingue, it was now forbidden to trade there. The Spanish territories, now Louisiana's only legal trading partners, were not greatly interested in buying Louisiana's timber, tobacco, and hides: people in Spain did not need fur coats. The Creoles of Louisiana were facing financial ruin.

Ulloa's enemies began plotting. The inflation the colony was experiencing was bad enough, but the ultimate insult was a royal decree that forbade, among other things, the importation of French wines into Louisiana.[17] Nothing was more likely to set a Frenchman's blood boiling than being forced to drink Spanish wine. But there were lots of other issues. Like what to do about a new contingent of people who had arrived.

⚬❦⚬

Arcadia was the name of an isolated region of Greece that became synonymous with pastoral paradise when Virgil imagined shepherds and nymphs gamboling through it in his *Eclogues*. *Acadie* was the name applied hopefully by the French to their Atlantic Canadian territory, presumably because it was settled by peasants. The British less preciously called it Nova Scotia (New Scotland). After the territory was ceded by France to Britain in 1713 following the War of the Spanish Succession, the descendants of the French Acadians remained there, but found themselves under a cloud of suspicion by the British minority, both for speaking French and for being Papists.

In 1755, emboldened by the presence of British troops as the French and Indian War got under way, the British governors of Massachusetts and Nova Scotia made a land grab. They expelled the Acadians, burning their houses and sending them into the flight remembered as *le grand dérangement*. Of the approximately twenty thousand Acadians living there at the time, some seven thousand were deported; the rest fled, many to nearby Île Royale (known to the British as Cape Breton, its fiddle music is distinctive to this day). Their confiscated lands wound up in the hands of speculators, who sold them to English-speaking settlers. Thus New England was purified of Catholics, with the eager participation of American colonial Protestants, who joined in their governors' persecution of the Acadians and stole their land. In 1758, after the British took the French fort at Louisbourg (built under the Regency in 1719, and named for the child Louis XV), there was a second massive deportation that removed the Acadians who had fled to Île Royale.[18] Some fled further into Canada; others went to France. But they were not "returning" to France, because the Acadians were not Frenchmen; they were Canadians, influenced by their contact with the Micmac Indians, whom they in turn had Catholicized.

Beginning around 1763, these Acadians came to Louisiana, where they would become known as Cajuns. Many of them recrossed the Atlantic Ocean from France, hoping to reunify their community. Ulloa encouraged them to immigrate to Louisiana from the places they had scattered to, but his real priority was establishing settlements at strategic locations to counter British power. When he attempted to dictate where the Acadians might settle, they became enraged.[19]

Anti-Spanish conspirators among the French told them that Ulloa had silver to redeem their worthless paper currency from Canada. The conspirators also stirred up German farmers in the area (who were there thanks to the legacy of a wave of immigration stimulated by John Law) by telling them that Ulloa would never pay for the farm products he had purchased from them. On October 28, 1768, about five hundred Acadians and Germans converged on New Orleans to demand money. With few Spanish troops to protect the governor, they were an insurgency to be reckoned with.

Ignoring a protest against their action by Charles Philippe Aubry, the French commander in Louisiana, the French Superior Council of New Orleans adopted an arrogantly worded resolution expelling Ulloa:

> [The council] enjoins Mr. Ulloa to quit the colony allowing him only the space of three days, either in the frigate of his Catholic Majesty in which he came, or in whatever vessel he shall think proper, and go and give an account of his conduct to his Catholic majesty.[20]

Ulloa sailed for Havana three days later, expecting to return with reinforcements. Encountering bad weather, his journey across the Gulf took three weeks. He never returned to New Orleans.

This unprecedented rebellion of French-speaking Louisiana Creoles prefigured the revolutionary struggles that would soon remake the Americas and Europe. The ultimate thrust of the Creoles' move would have logically been toward independence. They had overthrown Spanish colonial power, and in the process had defied the wishes of the French king, who had, after all, ceded the territory. But their victory was short-lived.

If the Creoles wouldn't cooperate with the scientist, they would feel the discipline of the warrior. In Ulloa's place, Spain sent its most powerful military figure, with orders to take definitive possession of Louisiana by a show of force and to punish the rebels. Spain had never responded to Ulloa's request for seven hundred troops, but on August 17, 1769, Alejandro O'Reilly, the Dublin-born inspector general of the Spanish army, arrived at the head of twelve ships.

The Irish, who viewed England as a Protestant slave master, had a tradition of sympathy for England's Catholic enemy, and a number of them found their way into positions of power in the Spanish-speaking world. Latin American history is dotted with their names: O'Reilly, O'Farrill, O'Neil, O'Higgins. Irish divinity students attended seminary in Spain, and Irish-born planters and merchants like Daniel Clark and Patricio Macnamara would become important men in Spanish Louisiana. O'Reilly's brief was to reorganize the Spanish defenses in the New World to match the new realities that the Seven Years War had created. He had recently come from Puerto Rico, where he created a disciplined militia and initiated a period of expansion that over the course of twenty years turned San Juan's sixteenth-century Morro Castle into the eighteenth-century fortress that still dominates the cityscape of Viejo San Juan. To put Louisiana right, he arrived with a force of 2,056 men (including 80 black and 80 mulatto members of the Cuban battalions) that outnumbered the approximately 1,800 white citizens of New Orleans.[21]

Four days after his arrival, a broadside announced that the ringleaders of the revolt against Ulloa would be punished. With no appeal, as wives and families wept, La Frénière and four other leading citizens of the town, ringleaders of the rebellion against Ulloa, were executed by a firing squad. The execution took place on the grounds of what later became the U.S. Mint, by Esplanade on the downriver edge of the old town. Rue des Françaises, or

Frenchmen Street, which begins there (now the major party-crawl strip of bohemian New Orleans), was named at the time of its construction in 1808 to commemorate the executed rebels (though La Frénière was not a Frenchman but a native-born Creole). Five other conspirators were sent to prison in Havana, and their property confiscated. The point was made: no one would treat the Spanish king's governor like that again.

O'Reilly expelled most of the foreign merchants from New Orleans, with the conspicuous exception of his friend from Havana, the Spanish-speaking Irishman Oliver Pollock, who had recently set up operations in town. Given free trade privileges, he provisioned both the garrison and the town with flour.

Though O'Reilly established Spain's command in no uncertain terms, the policies he and subsequent Spanish governors implemented were relatively progressive, at least by colonial standards. Abolishing the Superior Council, O'Reilly established a *cabildo*, or town council. The cabildo was one of Spain's fundamental institutions. New Orleanians don't worry much about what words mean elsewhere in the world, so in New Orleans, the word *cabildo* has come to refer to the *casa capitular*—the building that housed the cabildo—rather than to the cabildo itself. But while the cabildo was active, the word referred to the council that formalized the procedures necessary to the functioning of a city. Composed of powerful merchants and planters, it first met on December 1, 1769, and lasted thirty-four years. This significant step marked the formal incorporation of New Orleans.

One of the first things the cabildo did was require local property owners to put in and maintain sidewalks, called *banquetas*. The word was Frenchified to become *banquettes*, which, pronounced Anglostyle, *bang-kets*, is still what they are called in New Orleans. The banquettes were long overdue. Because of the lack of stone in the region, there was nothing to pave the streets with, so when it rained, all the streets turned into a muddy slough. Women who went to balls when the weather was wet slogged barefoot through the mud, which reeked from overflowing sewage and decomposing shellfish, while slaves carried their mistresses' dancing shoes and flambeaux, or torches, which both lit the way and kept the mosquitoes off.

Speaking of French words that aren't French, I have no documentation of when the word *lagniappe* first came into use in New Orleans, but it very likely was during the Spanish colonial era, and possibly even dates to the time of Ulloa. Lagniappe is something extra—the spoon bread the waiter brings you that you didn't order, the piece of candy for your kid at the hardware store. The word is used in New Orleans, and, in its Spanish form, throughout the Hispanic world. In Colombia, you might hear a salsa band's encore tune referred to as *la ñapa*. The word comes into Spanish from Quechua, the indigenous Andean language: *yapa*, hispanicized to *ñapa*, which, with the Spanish article, becomes *la ñapa*, which in Louisiana became creolized to *lagniappe*. It might have traveled from Peru to Louisiana any way that silver did.

During the years Spain held Louisiana, it established safety codes and taxes (inspecting chimneys three times a year and levying a chimney tax); built public works; lit the streets at night; drew up procedures for fighting fires; established standard weights and measures; regulated access to the levee and assumed responsibility for its maintenance; set licensing requirements for various professionals, including doctors; made carters responsible for filling in potholes; and generally tried to deal with the uncomfortable fact that the city had a Spanish government and a French-speaking people.

Throughout the New World, Spain established solid cities with strong governments, something it had learned the importance of during centuries of wars to expel the Muslims. This was in marked contrast to both France and Britain. When French Saint-Domingue was at its peak, with some half a million slaves at work, its largest city, Cap Français, had a population of only about twenty thousand. The British, for their part, developed hardworking agricultural colonies, but their urban planning tended to be laissez-faire, leaving cities to grow more or less by themselves. (The most dramatic example of this is the Indian city of Calcutta. Practically synonymous with urban squalor, under British rule it grew from a village to a chaotic, unplanned city right around this same time, in the second half of the eighteenth century.)

It was during Louisiana's time as a Spanish colony that New Orleans became a city. Its defense was supplied from the grand urban center of Havana, by then two and a half centuries old but still in the early stages of its great period of prosperity. At the time the New Orleans cabildo was established, the largest Anglo-American city south of Philadelphia was Charleston, with eleven thousand people. Later, during the brief existence of the Confederacy, when New Orleans was the largest city of the Southern slaveholders' nation, that was possible because it had been given the structure of a city by the Spanish. The Spanish emphasis on urban settlements supported a constraint imposed by nature: expansion away from the crescent-shaped bend in the river was blocked by the swamp.

An essential part of O'Reilly's theater of subduing the French citizenry with a massive show of force and establishing the sense of Spanish power was an impressive-sounding uniformed military band. It would have been composed at least of trumpets (which did not yet have valves and thus could not play scalar melodies), perhaps clarinets or oboes, certainly fifes, and lots of drums. The town awoke to reveille and went to sleep to taps; the town crier's proclamations were preceded by a trumpet call.[22] "There were regularly 100 drummers and fifers in New Orleans from 1770, though the number may have decreased by 1778," writes John Baron.[23] As time went by, the Spanish military musicians also entertained the population, giving not only parades but also concerts, and moonlighting at dances.

⁂

Each slave power imposed a different regime on its slaves. These differences were not only felt in the laws of the metropolis: each colonial regime was also affected by the amount of autonomy the local slave-owning colonists had. Though slavery was always an inhumane institution, there were degrees of oppressiveness to the different regimes. The British colonies of North America, where the planters had more control of the society than in other colonies, developed the harshest slave regime of the New World, and were the first to declare independence. The Spanish colonies, where imperial government was strongest and local power the least developed, had the least harsh slave regime—more humane or merely weaker, depending on the point of view—and were the last to become independent.

O'Reilly announced the imposition of Spanish law in place of French law. He banned the enslavement of Indians, and the regulations he implemented for African slaves were less harsh than those of the French Code Noir. There were four major differences under Spanish law:

(1) Slave owners did not need to obtain official permission to free their slaves. The Code Noir required the furnishing of official permission and just cause.

(2) Slaves could own property. The Code Noir specified that slaves could not own property, since everything belonged to the slave owner. Nor could slaves under the Code Noir have their own money, receive inheritances, or enter into contracts, all of which were permitted by the Spanish.

(3) Perhaps most important, like slaves in Cuba, slaves in Spanish New Orleans had the right of *coartación*—that is, the right to demand a contract to purchase their own freedom for an adjudicated amount. The owner was not allowed to refuse this right of self-purchase. Out of all the slaving territories of the New World, this practice was only implemented in Cuba, though O'Reilly made it applicable to Louisiana as well. Based on a survey of notarial documents, Hans W. Baade writes, "It seems reasonable to assume that considerably more than one thousand instruments of manumission were executed by

the New Orleans *escríbanos* [notaries] in the thirty-four years of direct Spanish rule."[24] The significance of freeing more than a thousand slaves becomes clear when one considers that the total population of New Orleans in 1791 was 4,897, including the military. Ingersoll gives a figure of 1,330 blacks who freed themselves through purchase during the Spanish years in Louisiana, plus another 160 slaves freed by free blacks, for a total of 1,490, peaking during the final years of the Spanish regime.[25] The effect this had on slave morale can be imagined, and the society of Cuba, so different in its relationships between "races" than the United States, testifies to it. Under a system with coartación, the slave had the hope of becoming free, whereas under the Anglo-American system, the slave had no hope that even his or her grandchildren would be free.

(4) There was an active judicial check on slave owner abuses, by means of a special court authorized to hear slave complaints and order the sale of a mistreated slave to a different master. Nothing like that had existed in French Louisiana.

In short, under Spanish law, the slave was treated more as a human being, albeit an enslaved one, than under French law. British law regarding slaves was even harsher than French law, and its most severe aspects would be further developed in the southern United States. It should be noted that slaves in Spanish Louisiana often had a better deal in theory than in practice, owing to the regimes maintained by the planters, who were, after all, accustomed to ignoring the Code Noir. Even so, Afro-Louisianans had more freedom during the territory's three-plus decades of Spanish rule than they had during the French colonial period, and more than black slaves had or would have anywhere else in the South at any time before emancipation. This degree of freedom, brief and limited though it was, has much to do with why the black community of New Orleans developed such a distinct cultural expression. Even the iron hand of the Southern slavers and the restrictions of Jim Crow couldn't completely efface the legacy of that era.

They could speak in their ancestral languages and play their drums: they had a past. With the right of self-purchase, they had a future. Enslaved people in English-speaking America were not permitted to have either one.

◦◦◦

O'Reilly's execution of the five "Frenchmen" by firing squad was the most respectful and least painful way to execute someone at that time; we have already seen what the French did to rebellious slaves. The executions earned the governor the sobriquet "Bloody O'Reilly," but the ones who hung that name on him were bloody as well. When the planters came to O'Reilly in February 1770, shortly before he left office, and asked for permission "to punish slaves as had been done in the French era (branding, hamstringing, and execution)," O'Reilly refused.[26]

O'Reilly remained in Louisiana only a short time before moving on, serving for ten months as the second of nine Spanish governors, but he transformed the territory. Although the large military force went back to Havana with him, a permanent Spanish garrison remained behind in New Orleans. O'Reilly placed Louisiana under the administration of the captaincy general of Cuba, so New Orleans became a political appendage of Havana. Along with this came a cash subsidy for the colony. The money came from Spain's silver mines, via Veracruz, but unfortunately for the Louisianans, the Mexican governor was relatively unconcerned about their fate. Moreover, the money, once it left Veracruz, had to travel via Havana, where the captain general of Cuba on occasion "borrowed" it.[27] Wars, blockades, and piracy all contributed to the uncertainty of its arrival at various times. But to the extent that the subsidy actually did arrive, it attracted commerce like a magnet.

O'Reilly's successor as governor was Luis de Unzaga y Amezaga, who governed from 1770 to 1777. By now the Spanish were definitively in charge, so rather than confront Unzaga, the colonists got better results by cutting him in on the action. The chief beneficiary was Gilbert Antoine de St. Maxent, a French-born trader who had become wealthy in the Indian fur trade and was one of the region's largest slaveholders.[28] Politically astute, he had learned how to get commercial favors from the French governor Kerlérec and had cooperated with both Ulloa and O'Reilly.[29] St. Maxent gave his daughter María Isabel to Unzaga in marriage, thus directly investing him in the prosperity of the French slaveholding community.[30] Unzaga generally gave the slaveholders what they wanted, and they began to feel more comfortable with their Spanish government.

The merchant Oliver Pollock had great influence with Unzaga, and in August 1776 they collaborated on a deal to supply Virginia with thousands of pounds of gunpowder to fire at the British, for which Unzaga was paid in Spanish dollars by the colony of Virginia, via Cádiz. On November 2, 1776, the Continental Congress of the United States passed a resolution authorizing the issuance of currency payable not in pounds and shillings, but in dollars and cents (*centavos*, the Spanish said). The peso, or Spanish dollar, was the direct model for the United States dollar, created to resemble it in value.[31]

This four-dollar bill, issued by the Treasury of Virginia in 1776, was payable in "Spanish milled dollars." It bears a law-and-order motto: Death to Counterfeit. Mexican silver dollars continued to be legal tender in the United States until 1857.

Unzaga was followed by the most famous of Louisiana's Spanish governors: the twenty-nine-year-old Bernardo de Gálvez, who took office on January 1, 1777. He had been an effective governor in New Spain (Mexico), and being the nephew of the minister of the Indies, he was well acquainted with the concept of nepotism.[32] Gálvez married a second St. Maxent daughter, receiving slaves as part of the dowry even as he acquired a family connection to the previous governor. During his governorship, Gálvez overtly promoted his father-in-law's interests, made all the easier by having his uncle to call on.

Gálvez implemented a decree authorizing the importation of slaves from the French Antilles, pleasing the planters greatly. He also intensified colonization efforts, bringing in, at the crown's expense, several hundred *isleños*, or Canary Islanders, who came in families. Isleños had done the hard work of settling rural Cuba, forming the basis of its peasantry. In Louisiana, they put down roots in the swamp country. There are still traces of this population in existence, who count as part of their heritage fragments of the grand oral literature of Spain.

Gálvez gave the Creoles of New Orleans something no one else had given them: military glory. He brought the French and Spanish as close together as they would ever get in Louisiana, by leading them into battle against the hated English.

❧

Though Spain's long-term plan was to integrate Louisiana into its colonial structure, it had to proceed differently than it did anywhere else. Even though Louis XV had cast the Louisianans off in a thoroughly humiliating manner, the bulk of the colony's population was resolutely French speaking and French identified. Spain behaved far more leniently with Louisiana than it did with any other colony, hoping that, in Arthur Whitaker's words, "what priest and soldier could not do might be accomplished by trade and toleration."[33] But nothing had served to make the French-speaking population feel loyalty to the king of Spain.

The Spanish period in New Orleans was a time of critical transition for Cuba, which was transforming from a royal shipping hub to a tapestry of sugar plantations. The cumbersome annual flotas, the treasure-bearing convoys, were in their final days. The last of them left Spain in 1777 and returned in June 1778 from Havana under the command of none other than Antonio de Ulloa, who boasted that this final cargo was the richest load of treasure the fleet had ever hauled.[34]

In 1778, Gálvez rebuilt the fort at the Bayou St. John (known as the "Spanish Fort," it's still there). He began building up a free black militia (which grew from 89 men to 469 by 1801)[35] and created an elite cavalry to entice the ruling class of the town to enlist.[36] He also offered incentives for slaves to fight. People of color had been a regular part of the city's defense, among their other duties providing personnel for maroon-hunting teams. But under Gálvez, they would see real combat.

Gálvez held off on his big move until after Ulloa had seen the final Spanish fleet safely across international waters back to Cádiz. Then, in 1779, in a carefully planned campaign, he headed a series of actions designed to check the growing British power in the Gulf of Mexico and help the American Revolution. Spain couldn't officially participate in the American Revolution without giving ideas to its own rebellious colonists, but with Gálvez's actions, what was, in effect, the southern flank of the American Revolution came from New Orleans, flying the Spanish flag.

Communication between Gálvez and the American revolutionaries, who did not speak Spanish, passed through Oliver Pollock, who served as translator. Louisiana militias, white and colored, fought alongside Spanish army regulars. Spanish New Orleans marched on British Baton Rouge, and Gálvez emerged victorious. In the battle, free colored and white militias executed a daring diversionary move to draw British fire while Gálvez constructed his emplacements. The glory of the victory was shared by the colored soldiers, who were awarded medals. The wealthy planter Julien Poydras was moved to compose and publish at his own expense an epic poem in praise of the heroism at Baton Rouge. One couplet reads:

La marche finissoit, par les Gens de couleur:
Vifs, ardens à donner, des marques de leur coeur.

which I translate as:

The march finished up, by the People of color:
Alert they were, burning to prove their bravery.

Troops marched into battle accompanied by drums, so this couplet makes
implicit reference to people of color playing them. It was with the Spanish that
the grand tradition began of New Orleanians of color playing in a military
band. Gálvez probably had the same battling drummers, along with troops
from Cuba (who would also have had musicians among them), with him when
he took Natchez. He took Mobile early the following year.

While Gálvez was off battling the British, reinforcements were sent in
from Havana to guard the Louisiana colony. Military men were not always
counted in the census, but they were there throughout the Spanish period,
especially in times of war. Some of the soldiers and sailors who came in were
criollos from Cuba, and some were musicians.

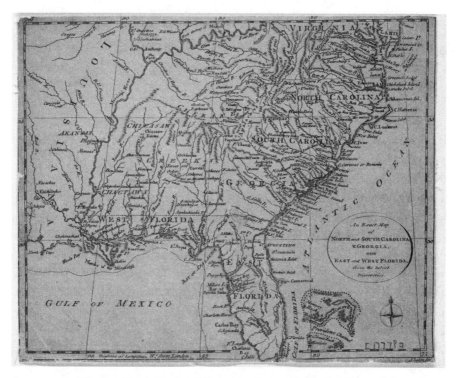

*An exact map of North and South Carolina & Georgia : with east and west Florida from the latest discov-
eries.* Published by John Lodge in 1778, this map shows the extent of West and East Florida, as well
as the extent of various Indian territories, and, more generally, the importance of rivers and port
towns as points of communication.

It was a prosperous time for whores and dance hall owners. Private dance halls for both whites and blacks were in existence in New Orleans by 1780 (and probably earlier), and musicians were needed to play in them.[37] Masked balls, providing leeway for license, were in vogue in much of Europe and the French and Spanish colonies; revelers wore their masks in the streets on their way to and from the dances. In February 1781, writes Kimberley Hanger:

> In an attempt to exercise some control over the multitude of troops, ships' crews, free blacks, and slaves who converged on New Orleans . . . the attorney general asked the cabildo to forbid *libres* and slaves from wearing masks and mimicking whites during the carnival season. With so many strangers in the city, officials found it difficult to identify the race of masked revelers.[38]

During this time, "intoxication seemed to prevail at all levels and among all classes of society," writes John G. Clark. "Among the troops stationed in Louisiana and West Florida, the immoderate use of alcohol was notorious. Colonel John Pope wrote that the 'inordinate use of Ardent Spirits and bad Wine' contributed to the poor health of the soldiers."[39]

The military men who crowded the town went to the dances. The French weren't the only ones mad for dancing: the Spanish had been dancing all up and down the New World since the sixteenth century, and the *criollos* were even more addicted than their metropolitan (Spanish-born) counterparts. The maritime traffic ensured that fashionable dances traveled from one New World seaport to another, up and down the hemisphere and to Spain and back, always laying up in the great center of Havana to wait for the boat. Now New Orleans was part of that dancing circuit, which, throughout the Spanish world, included black people, who set the styles.

After the interception of a document from Britain's King George III calling for an attack on New Orleans, Gálvez swiftly moved to put the town on a war footing. In March 1781, he began a two-month siege of Pensacola before successfully wresting it from the British, in an action partly financed by his father-in-law, St. Maxent, completing the Spanish conquest of West Florida. In victory, Gálvez announced that slave soldiers who had been seriously wounded would receive their freedom and one hundred pesos, and those lightly wounded would receive one hundred pesos and the right to buy their freedom at the low price of four hundred pesos.[40]

On October 30, 1781, Carlos III placed St. Maxent in charge of Indian affairs, which offered tremendous profitability for a trader of his experience. On March 1, the cabildo received a letter written by Gálvez from Havana designating Don Estevan Miró, a career military man, as acting governor during his absence. Gálvez went on to pay a state visit to Cap Français in Saint-Domingue. Unlike Louisiana or Cuba at the time, that colony had newspapers, and Port-au-Prince's *Affiches Américaines* reported that Gálvez's arrival was saluted by cannon in the harbor, and that he was feted with "military parades, a banquet, the illumination of government buildings, and a grand ball at the Salle de la Comédie that lasted until the early morning of the following day."[41]

Beginning with Ulloa, Spanish governors saw the military necessity of having forts and towns upriver. Attempting to stimulate colonization, they made land grants into Missouri. It appears that the social ambience of those upriver towns was a frontier version of what was going on in Louisiana, with endless balls and gambling on the part of white society, and continual cultural assertion on the part of the slaves.

"The slaves shall not be allowed to dance, either by day or night, in the village or elsewhere, without an express permission from their masters and the consent of this government," reads an edict of August 12, 1781, by Governor Francisco Cruzat at St. Louis, "and those who shall be arrested for failure to observe this order shall each receive in public fifty blows from the lash."[42] Three days later, Cruzat issued another order, this one concerned that "the savages, both free and slaves, and the negroes which belong to this post often dress themselves in barbarous fashion, adorning themselves with vermilion and many feathers which render them unrecognizable, especially in the woods." After this prohibition of blacks and Indians engaging in an activity that might be reminiscent of carnival masking, but which also had clear military implications as camouflage, the edict continues: "We enjoin the masters of said slaves to watch over their conduct, not only in this respect but as concerns the nocturnal assemblies which these colored people are accustomed to hold, but which for a very long time past have been forbidden."[43] The threat posed by nocturnal assemblies of slaves was only ten years away from reaching critical mass in Saint-Domingue.

If there's any doubt that there was a current of music flowing between New Orleans and Havana, consider that in 1783, Miró complained to Captain General José de Ezpeleta in Cuba that so many musicians had returned to Cuba with the troops, and went on to request trumpeters, clarinetists, and a director.[44] The soldiers' and sailors' tastes counted at the balls, the taverns, and the whorehouses, so it seems reasonable to think that the distinctive musical style of Havana, which had been developing as a rhythmic, creolized music for over 250 years by that point, in some way traveled to Louisiana with them. There were many dance forms in vogue, but the *contredanse*, or *contradanza*, was ubiquitous in Madrid and Paris, as well as in Cap Français, Havana, and New Orleans. Black musicians rhythmicized the contredanse, creating musical styles which evolved into the *habanera* (also known as *tango*) and, later, ragtime, as well as the *danza*, *danzón*, and ultimately the *danzón mambo* and its offspring the *cha-cha-chá*.

New Orleans marked the peace treaty between Spain and Britain in 1784 with three days of splendid ceremonies, and, though I know of no documentation of it, it's reasonable to assume that the fifes and drums, and perhaps clarinets, oboes, or (valveless) trumpets, of the *gens de couleur* participated. From that year also we have the first documentation of the existence of an organist at St. Louis Church.[45]

In 1785, Gálvez was promoted to viceroy of New Spain. Among the surviving documents of his authorship is *Ordenanzas para el Teatro de Comedias de México—Ordinances for the Mexican Comedy Theater*. That year, the Texas coastal island of Galveston was named for him. But he died suddenly after an illness in Mexico the following year, at the age of forty.

St. Maxent died in 1784. A partial inventory of his estate included, besides his home outside the city, 169 skilled adult slaves in fifty cabins, numerous cattle on various lands, and such items as a mahogany billiard table, nine full-length mirrors with gold-leaf frames, a clock with a bird that sang an aria, a library of forty-seven hundred books, and a clavichord.[46]

Did a slave—or a free person of color—ever get to play that clavichord? The identity of the first black keyboard player in New Orleans is unknown, as is the decade when such a person first existed. But it is well documented that everywhere Africans went, they learned to play European-style instruments as soon as they could get their hands on them. Louisiana was no different. But unlike in the English-speaking territories of the Atlantic seaboard, in Louisiana black people were permitted to play drums—not only military drums with sticks, but ancestral drums, making them talk with their hands.

The Spanish / Cuban period in New Orleans is one of the most important moments in African American history. For the intensity of its African culture and the relative freedom with which it was practiced, Spanish New Orleans was unique in North America. It must have rung from one end to the other with the music of its large black population, whose movement within the city was relatively free.

New Orleans, small as it was, was larger and wealthier than any other Spanish town in what is now the United States. It was part of the Spanish system of silver money, which, coming out of Mexico and Peru, ruled the hemisphere. And it was part of the Afro-Spanish system of rhythmic music, which, with Havana as its grand center, did the same.

10

THE KONGO PERIOD

An idea, a thought strikes a black man, and he immediately turns it into the subject of a song. . . . Three or four words that are repeated alternatively between the singer and the chorus sometimes form the entire poem. Five or six measures are all that is heard in the song. What is curious is that the same air, which is nothing but a continual repetition of the same sounds, keeps them busy, makes them work or dance for hours; it doesn't cause for them, or even for the whites, the tedious monotony that these repetitions might cause.
—*Abbé Guillaume-Thomas-François Raynal,*
Philosophic and Political History of European
Establishments and Commerce in the Two Indies, *1780*[1]

*U*nder the Spanish, Louisiana culture was transformed by the addition of significant numbers of new Africans, re-Africanizing the colony with the arrival of many different nationalities.

In 1782, the year Estevan Miró became acting governor, the Spanish scrapped import duties on slaves to their colonies, throwing open importation to slavers of different flags. Since there were no customs to collect, there was no need to keep records, so documentation of slave importation during this period is poor. But thousands were brought, and with them came a new wave of Africanization to the insular black communities of Louisiana, where only the older generation of slaves had been born in Africa and the rest were Creoles.

Exactly how many came is not known. The official count of slaves imported during the French period (5,951, plus the 1758 ship of 122 Angolan-embarked captives) might have been augmented by some undocumented trade, but likely not much. The numbers during the Spanish period are harder to get a handle on, but they are limited by the fact that the Spanish were actively slaving into Louisiana for only about two decades. Most scholars today believe that Philip Curtin's 1969 estimate of 28,300 slaves imported to Louisiana during the combined French and Spanish eras is too high.[2] Gwendolyn Midlo Hall's *Louisiana Slave Database* documents the presence in Louisiana of 16,089 people born in Africa, many of whom would have come in after the Louisiana Purchase, and necessarily leaving the number of undocumented to conjecture.[3] Even so, given that the population of New Orleans during the Spanish period was only a few thousand, the number of Africans that came in turned it into a much blacker town than any in British North America.

A wide variety of African ethnicities arrived simultaneously during the relatively brief period of Spanish slave importation, bringing different languages, religions, and drums, so a chaotic cultural flow happened quickly. But the largest single African group in Spanish New Orleans came from the Kongo-Angola region, the most heavily slaved territory in Africa and the one slaved for the longest period of time. "In the Spanish period [in Louisiana]," Gwendolyn Midlo Hall told me, "there's a continuous migration from the Bight of Benin . . . and there's a continuous migration from greater Senegambia, but there's an increased migration from the Kongo. . . . Shortly after the Spanish took over, it became heavily Kongo in New Orleans."[4]

The Kongos were taken in numbers to everywhere there were slaves, so it is not surprising that their influence is felt all over the hemisphere. Geographically ubiquitous, they were the strongest single influence on African culture in the New World. The largely uncomprehended legacy of the Kongo permeates the popular music the world listens to today. It is perhaps the strongest single link between the musics of Havana and New Orleans, which is to say, between Afro-Cuban and African American music, which are in other ways quite different.

The total number of slaves brought to colonial Louisiana from Africa was not large—certainly not by comparison with Cuba, which by the end of its slave trade in the 1860s had imported more Africans than all of English-speaking North America. Cuba at this time was in the first phase of sugar-powered economic growth, which would accelerate intensively in the first three decades of the nineteenth century. Its plantations expanded as rapidly as the slave labor force could increase. Whereas previously Cuba had a relatively small number of mostly domestic slaves, now thousands of captives fresh from Africa were brought to labor in Cuba at the field-and-mill complexes known as *ingenios*. Cuba's demand for slaves far outstripped Louisiana's. The French-speaking colony wasn't producing sugar yet, nor cotton, and no one knew that it would; its plantation crops were indigo and tobacco, the latter a specialty of Natchitoches.

If we wanted to be provocative, we could call the Spanish period of Louisiana the Cuban period, though Cuba was not yet a nation. Or, even more

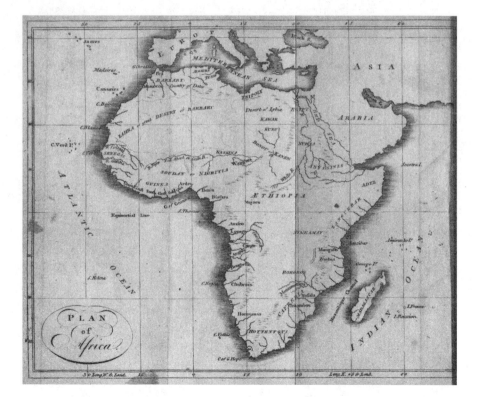

Plan of Africa, published in 1803. The most striking feature of this map is its lack of inland detail, while the coast is meticulously depicted. The first Africans to populate Louisiana—people from Senegal, Ardra/Ouidah, and Kongo/Angola—came from far-flung regions that had little contact with each other and were located at different latitudes, with distinct material environments and cultures.

to the point, the Kongo period. Cuba by that time had been home to Kongo people for some 250 years. To put it another way: one of the most important factors in the Cubanization of New Orleans was the Kongoization of the city, something that also established a continuity with the heavily Kongo black culture of Saint-Domingue.

In both Cuba and Louisiana, the Kongos coexisted with Catholicism. In the forest zone of Africa, where Islam had never penetrated, the Portuguese had converted the Kongos and the Angolans, or so they thought, though it might be more accurate to say they gave them a new set of structures and images. In the first half of the sixteenth century, the Kongo king Afonso I had, in theory, converted his people to Catholicism and erected churches in Kongo. A Portuguese-educated Kongo man was ordained a Roman Catholic bishop at the unusually early age of twenty-four in 1518.[5] In the New World, Kongos and Angolans were taken to every slave territory. To the Catholic territories, they brought an already syncretized religious practice. They were slaved for almost four centuries, until the last slave ship, carrying a cargo of Angolans, is believed to have landed in Cuba in 1873.[6]

If we want to have some idea of what Kongo culture in New Orleans might have been like, all we have to do today is visit Cuba (though such a visit is prohibited by U.S. law to most U.S. citizens). The island still lives and breathes explicitly African culture, and perhaps the most influential of those traditions is the Kongo religion, known in Cuba as *palo*.

The Kongo cross, showing intersection of the two worlds, disguised itself as the Christian crucifix. As you can see today in the practice of Cuban *paleros*, iron is a power element in Kongo thought. Blacksmiths, who knew the secret of working iron, had access to spiritual power; the black ironworkers who made crosses for tombs in the New Orleans cemeteries had a rich context in which to interpret the meaning. Those crosses, if you notice, aren't crucifixion crosses, with the crossbar chest high; they cross in the center.

Presumably something like the practices that might go on at a palero's house in Cuba today went on in Spanish New Orleans. For now it will suffice to quote something Robert Farris Thompson said to me:

We're not talking about a single little feeble thread coming from Kongo. We're talking about a coaxial cable, one that is most heavily associated with funerals. The Kongo idea of the funeral is send the dead off with a lot of music. You don't want them going sad to the other world. They might come back to haunt you. That's the rationale which, I would argue, was the secret rationale behind the jazz funeral in New Orleans.[7]

Something like that rationale was also well established in Iberia, where mourners danced at funerals. In Cuba, authorities repeatedly attempted, without much success, to ban the practice. We can't draw a complete, sharp picture of the history of the jazz funeral. But we know that the black funeral parade in New Orleans dates back at least to the Spanish period, when it was inscribed in a procession of the sort one might see all over the Catholic world. When black Protestants began to be buried in New Orleans in the nineteenth century, at some point they too began having processional funerals. After the step was taken of adding a brass band to the procession—and I can't put an exact date on when that happened—New Orleans musicians were on the road to something we could call jazz.

No other U.S. city has a tradition similar to the jazz funeral, but you can find cognates of the New Orleans funeral parade in the black urban neighborhoods of present-day Cuba and in Haiti. But then, no other U.S. city stops cold for Carnival, though it's celebrated from New Orleans all the way down the Antilles to Brazil.

Kongo culture was by no means the only African culture in Spanish Louisiana, nor was it even a majority, but it was the largest single group. Hall gives a chart breaking down slave ethnicities as inventoried on Louisiana estates. Though those inventoried were only a small portion of the actual numbers, the range of ethnicities given is telling, as in this breakdown from the 1790s:[8]

Ethnicity	Males	Females
Bamana	48	3
Chamba	46	17
Igbo	25	9
Kongo	119	41
Mandingo	70	23
Mina	69	11
Nago/Yoruba	38	17
Wolof	34	14
Total	449	135

In this sample, 160 out of 584 were Kongo, or about 26 percent, but there are seven other groups listed. Beyond this sample, it would be easy enough to list another dozen or more African groups that came to Louisiana during this time. Also worth noting is that the gender breakdown skews 78 percent men. This reflects the lesser desirability of women for hard agricultural plantation labor. The women went to the city, the men to the labor camp. Some men, particularly those who escaped, took up with Indian women, producing mixed black-Indian offspring that might be counted as black for purposes of continued enslavement.

A 1791 census gave the population of New Orleans as:

	White	Free people of color	Enslaved	Military
Male	1,153	324	871	381
Female	912	538	718	—
Total	2,065	862	1,589	381

Excluding the military, this made for a population of 2,065 whites and 2,451 people of color, though it should be understood that the "white" population included some people with ancestors of color. Broken down by gender, there were 2,348 men (plus the militia) versus 2,168 women—a female-heavy population, as frontier towns went.

Out on the plantations, the enslaved men largely had to do without women. But in the city, the large number of free women of color facilitated an easy availability of sex for white men that repeatedly astonished visitors, and fed directly into a trade of contractual concubinage. The practice was called *plaçage*—placing, as in placement of a woman with a male patron—and created a relatively prosperous, property-owning class of free women of color. With little else in the way of lucrative occupations available to them, they were trained from birth to the office. Gentlemen set them up in houses of their own, there to maintain long-term relationships that frequently involved multiple children.

And they owned slaves. Not only were free people of color frequently slave owners; on occasion, slaves in Spanish New Orleans owned slaves, whose labor they could appropriate toward purchasing their own freedom, or whose ownership they could trade as a partial payment on their own freedom.[9]

❧

Free black militia were put to work hunting down maroons. But there were outlaw maroon communities too big and too difficult for the militia to stop. Their depredations frightened plantation owners. The most troublesome, a band led by one Juan Maló, lived in the swamps, in a place only accessible by wading through chest-high water. He soon became known as San Maló, which was the name of a slave-trading port in France, but which in Spanish sounded very much like "Saint Evil." [10]

San Maló's gang was not made up of Africans; they were locally born Creoles and had a support network of family and other associates in town and on the plantations. Their growing maroon community attracted slaves who slipped away from nearby plantations into the swamp to join up with them. Not only their raids and banditry were worrisome: the Spanish became concerned that a general uprising involving maroons and slaves working together might be forthcoming. In spring 1784, a military expedition caught San Maló and seventeen others. The French would have put their heads on pikes, but the Spanish, after a trial, contented themselves with hanging four of them, including Maló, in the Plaza de Armas (present-day Jackson Square), on June 19, with most of the town in attendance. A week later, the commissioners wrote to the bishop of Havana that they thought "there were few slaves in the colony who were not directly or indirectly accomplices of San Maló." [11]

The following year a slave named Julia was said to have confessed to putting ground glass in her mistress's food. She was not punished with death, perhaps because her mistress did not die, but she was made an example of: an infantry guard marched her through town as she was whipped. The ambulatory spectacle was preceded by the town crier, who proclaimed in a loud voice, "This is the justice which the King our Lord commands and in his name Sr. Don Guido Dufossat, Alcalde in ordinary of this city and His Majesty's jurisdiction executes on this negress for having attempted to poison her mistress." [12] Her public march lasted until she had received two hundred lashes, at the end of which she was put in the stocks for two hours a day for eight days. [13]

In 1791, Miró closed the cabarets outside town because they had become hangouts for maroons, and a wave of arson followed. In July of that year, a group of Mina slaves was discovered conspiring at Pointe Coupée, up the river from New Orleans. African-born people, these Minas spoke their own language (Hall thinks they may have been Ewe speakers from the region of the Bight of Benin) and had a network of relationships with Minas in town. For recreation they even held their own Mina balls, probably since the mid-1770s. [14] The Mina conspiracy was apparently real, but it never resulted in action. The accused were taken to New Orleans and bound over for a lengthy trial, the progress of which was interrupted when Spain and France went to war in 1793.

⟨∾⊘∾⟩

Despite the tension, there was relative freedom for the slaves in Spanish New Orleans, where the life of a domestic slave resembled the life of a domestic slave in Havana. Slaves could maintain stable families, had Sundays and holidays off, and could shop in markets to buy goods for themselves, on their own. That degree of freedom was good for music, as it made attendance at dances easy. Festival days, such as January 6—known to the Spanish as Día de Reyes, or Kings' Day, and to the English as Epiphany—would have likely seen displays of Africanness (though I have no documentation of this). In Havana, Día de Reyes was the day on which the Africans could dress as they liked, in ancestral costume—to European eyes, a fantastical masquerade—and sing, drum, and dance in the street, to the annoyance and fear of the whites. That date is, as any New Orleanian can tell you, the traditional beginning of the Mardi Gras season.

One of the distinguishing features of Cuban society, as distinct from that of the southern United States, was its large number of free people of color. Some, the so-called *negros curros*, had emigrated from Spain, already free, in the sixteenth century. By the 1860s, with slavery still in effect, free people of color would be almost 40 percent of blacks in Cuba's central region.[15] They formed a black middle class and dominated the profession of music on the island.

In Louisiana, by 1805, the caste of free people of color was 33.5 percent of the African American population of New Orleans, and about 19 percent of the city overall; by comparison, in 1800, 98 percent of black people in the region from Kentucky and Tennessee southward into Louisiana were slaves.[16] Descendants of Louisiana's free people of color, some of them quite wealthy, persisted through the Civil War. (By 1810, after the arrival of a large wave of free people of color from Saint-Domingue, this class was 29 percent of the city's population.)[17] Though the number of free people of color in Louisiana was small by the time of the Civil War—18,647 by one count—it was by far the largest in the South.[18]

In Spanish Louisiana, free people of color were obliged to serve in the militia, constituting *batallones de pardos* (tan battalions) and *de morenos* (black battalions), organizations which also existed in Cuba. This meant that some people of color played wind instruments for drill, to say nothing of drums. It seems unlikely that they would not have moonlighted playing dances, as they did in Cuba.

And Cuba had its *cabildos*, a word that didn't only refer to the town government. Black people in Cuba had their own formally organized groups, called *cabildos de nación*. These had existed in Spain before 1492, when Seville was between 5 and 10 percent black, and they probably existed in sixteenth-century Cuba. They were mutual aid societies for Africans of the same places of origin and whomever else wished to affiliate with them. The Cuban cabildos de nación were concerned with such things as helping members with burial expenses, the proper care of the dead being a crucial aspect of African life. But they were also vehicles for the reassembly, preservation, and growth of African culture—best expressed in religion and music, each helping keep the other alive. Behind the doors of the black Cuban cabildos, the ancestral drums were played, the dances were danced, and the gods came down to ride believers' heads. There were many of these cabildos in Cuba, representing numerous ethnic and linguistic subaffiliations.

I have been to ceremonies or performances in Cuba representing five different (broadly defined) African groups—Congo, Carabalí, Arará, Gangá, and Yoruba—each with their own distinct drums, performed by practitioners of the respective religious traditions, and sung in African languages. This doesn't exist in the United States, where British colonial slave owners and their Anglo-American successors did their best to exterminate the drums, religions, and languages so that Africans could not communicate in secret (though it should be noted that there are isolated examples of African drums turning up in the South). The development of slap-dance, or "patting juba" (Kikongo *nzuba*),[19] with some of the same techniques as hand drumming, says much about the resilience of African American culture in the Anglo-American territories, but it also speaks to the encipherment that was necessary.

The one place where drumming and other direct manifestations of Africanness continued to be openly displayed in public, albeit on a limited basis—and it was the legacy of the Spanish period—was New Orleans. It would be a mistake to assume that New Orleans in the Spanish period was simply an extension of Cuba, though similarities between Havana and New Orleans—similarities which exist nowhere else in the southern United States—strongly suggest a cultural continuum. But the French slave-owning population was not keen on the Spanish way of doing things. They rebelled against coartación, and on occasion got governors to block it. The black population had their own thing going before the Spanish brought new slaves in.

There is no indication that the widespread Cuban institution of black cabildos de nación was copied in Louisiana, though it is possible that some historian may yet turn up some indication of such organizations. But free people of color in New Orleans created an organization in 1783 whose name is usually rendered in English as the Perseverance Benevolent and Mutual Aid Society. Even without claiming a direct lineage to the mutual aid societies of the late nineteenth century that spawned the jazz funeral and the second line, it is clear that the idea of such societies was already well established among free people of color in Cuba and Saint-Domingue, and existed in New Orleans as well.

And there was certainly drumming. All across Spanish America, including New Orleans, Sunday was the day for the slaves to dance. In Cuba, when they took a break at work, and on their day off on Sunday, drums would come out, and a circle would form. Many travelers to Cuba in the nineteenth century described such dances, and you might see something like a latter-day version of them when workingmen take a break in Cuba today.

In New Orleans, Africans gathered to drum and dance as soon as there were Africans in the colony and—unique in the United States—these gatherings continued at least until the 1840s. The takeover of New Orleans by the English-speaking Americans, with their much stricter racial laws, erased direct links to African culture that were clearly visible in the late eighteenth century.

Which brings me to the gumbo metaphor.

THE EIGHTEENTH-CENTURY
TANGO

pero si come harina y quimbombó
es congo de verdad

but if he eats flour and okra
he's a true Congo
—Jesús Alfonso (of Los Muñequitos de Matanzas)

*I*t's a matter of speculation exactly how the word *gumbo* came from
Angola into Louisiana to become the name of one of the most typical dishes of Louisiana cooking, but various opportunities for contact
existed. The word seems to have required no explanation in 1764, when runaway Mandingo women and Bambara slaves were cooking the dish in the
French Quarter, occasioning its first written mention in Louisiana.[1]

Travel writers were already thinking themselves witty in the nineteenth
century for calling New Orleans culture a gumbo. Nobody, it seems, can resist
it. A book about New Orleans will inevitably be reviewed as "a gumbo of a
book." The flood of 2005 was a "toxic gumbo." *Gumbo* is an album by Dr. John,
and it's the title of the first episode of Ken Burns's television history of jazz,
the part about New Orleans.

This kind of metaphor is hardly unique to Louisiana. To take the closest example at hand, Fernando Ortiz wrote of Cuban culture as an *ajiaco*, a stew. Or the idea of a music called *salsa*. The gumbo metaphor is generally invoked to imply that New Orleans was—to use another culinary metaphor, one that came into our lexicon through the Yiddish theater in New York—a melting pot. But that misrepresents gumbo.

Gumbo is not mush. Flavors and essences fuse, but you can tell whether you're biting into shrimp or sausage. Consigning the unknowable to gumbo when talking about music and history is too often a way of throwing up our hands and not inquiring further. There's a frustrating amount that we don't know—and a lot of myth, misinformation, and even disinformation—but Louisiana is not all that unknowable.

Nor is *gumbo* a vague way of saying multicultural. Its name tells us that it's of African descent.

The word *gumbo* means okra. It comes, the Oxford English Dictionary tells us, from *kingumbo*, which means okra, and is of Angolan origin. In Cuba, okra is universally known not by its Spanish name, *molondrón*, but as *quimbombó*: it's the same word as *kingumbo*.

The English word *okra*, which does not resemble the word *kingumbo* in the least, is also of African derivation, but from another part of Africa: it seems to be etymologically related to Accra, the capital of Ghana. The word *okra* seems to have first appeared in the New World in the British West Indies, in Jamaica, where the largest number of Africans were Akan. That there are two completely different African names for it in the New World tells you how basic that seedpod vegetable was to the diet of millions of Africans.

In Louisiana, gumbo means a stew served over rice (*yaya*, as in the title of Lyle Saxon's book *Gumbo Ya-Ya*). It's made with a roux, a flavorful base of flour carefully slow cooked with spices in butter or another fat or oil. You see this same idea in both French and African cooking. The idea of stirring the pot while standing for hours in front of the roux is fundamental to the gumbo metaphor, as when one of the Neville Brothers, in a radio interview on New Orleans's local-music station WWOZ, compared sharing the responsibilities of tracking an album to making gumbo: "We just take turns watching the roux." The flavors of a wide variety of ingredients blend in the roux, and that's a fair description of something that happened in New Orleans culture. But the gourmet gumbo you get at a fancy New Orleans restaurant today may not even include okra, and that puts it a long way

from the gumbo served to a traveler at this 1808 boardinghouse dinner in
Baton Rouge:

> The table was well covered with different made dishes, and a variety
> of vegetables, among which the most conspicuous, was a large dish of
> gumbo, served by the hostess at the head, which seemed to be a stand-
> ing dish, and much in repute, as almost every one was helped to it. It is
> made by boiling ocroc [okra] until it is tender, and seasoning it with a
> little bit of fat bacon. It then becomes so ropy and slimy as to make it
> difficult with either knife, spoon or fork, to carry it to the mouth, with-
> out the plate and mouth being connected by a long string, so that it is a
> most awkward dish to a stranger, who besides, seldom relishes it, but is a
> standing dish among the French creoles.[2]

This gumbo was an okra dish—a creolized African way of preparing
an African vegetable, cooked using local ingredients in a kitchen staffed by
slaves, who made it to suit the taste of, and served it to, their French-speaking
masters. The okra's gooey mucilage binds the whole dish together, and a binding together was happening in Afro-Louisianan culture. The percussive, syllabic music of the central Africans (Kongos and Angolans) had been laid
on top of the stringed-instrument, melismatic music of the Senegambians
(Bambara, Mandingo, Wolof)—to say nothing of the people that in Cuba
were called Arará (Fon speakers from Ouidah and Ardra), the people from
the Calabar region (Igbo, Efik), and all the other Africans who came during
the Spanish years.

⋙⋘

Right across Rampart Street from the French Quarter in present-day New
Orleans—that is, just outside the walls of the old city—is a place called Louis
Armstrong Park. To build it, beginning in the late 1960s, they ripped out nine
square blocks of the Tremé, the oldest African American residential district in
the United States. They tore out Economy Hall, where jazz was played when it
was being born, and the Gypsy Tea Room. They displaced some four hundred
families from their homes, and when they were done, they put up a statue of
Louis Armstrong.

It hasn't become a tourist magnet. Visitors generally prefer the vomitous
ambience of Bourbon Street, and Armstrong Park is locked up at night—and,
after the 2005 flood, during the day—because it's not safe to be there. But a

certain kind of visitor will make a pilgrimage to one part of the park, near the statue, by an old stand of trees, as if there were an invisible altar there.

It's the former site of Congo Square, sacred ground in the history of African America and legendary cornerstone of black New Orleans music. There is much myth and legend about New Orleans, but Congo Square was a real place. It was the only place in the antebellum United States where enslaved African Americans were allowed to hold public gatherings to dance, play ancestral drums, and sing in ancestral languages, albeit under police supervision. Those Sunday dances must have been avant-garde, if you will: a site not only of memory and tradition, but also of culturally encrypted communication, and a laboratory where a new musical and lyrical vocabulary evolved.

Besides being domestics, nannies, laundresses, seamstresses, and sex workers, black women in Louisiana from early in the French days peddled merchandise in the market, as women did in urban Africa. A slave who peddled had a great deal of autonomy, for a slave. She might even be able to rent a place to sleep, away from the household of the master. Slave women sold garden produce, meat, fish, and shellfish, as well as ready-to-eat food, alcohol, clothes, rugs, and other necessities.[3] Fine ladies did not go shopping in the market but sent their slaves instead, so slave women were not only the sellers, but also the buyers, though they had to please their mistresses in that capacity. In short, slave women had considerable control over an important sector of the local economy.

Beginning sometime in the period of French colonial rule, slaves attended two interpenetrating Sunday institutions: the market, and then the dance that took place there afterward, the one yielding to the other as the afternoon passed. These took place on the back side of the street grid, outside the city proper, at the place people began to call *Place Congo*, or in English, Congo Square. Gilbert C. Din and John E. Harkins write:

> Slaves in Louisiana generally had Sunday for themselves, and many of those living in the vicinity went to New Orleans to sell the products of their labor, work to earn money, purchase necessities at stores that eagerly sought their business, and generally enjoy themselves. . . . With increased economic activity and a larger population, markets flourished under the Spaniards. Congo Market at the rear of the city was principally for slaves and was used by a smaller number of free blacks. The Cabildo never sought to regulate it. About 15 years after the American takeover,

Benjamin Latrobe was astonished to see several hundred unsupervised blacks dancing in Congo Square. By then this custom was about three-quarters of a century old.[4]

That the Sunday dances were part of the local tradition was a crucial factor in their survival into the Anglo-American era. There was never any question whether there would be a dance on Sunday, because there had been a dance on Sunday in New Orleans as far back as anyone could remember. To this day, Sunday is the day for black street music in New Orleans, because it always has been. It's parade day, the way Monday is the day for red beans and rice.

If there's one thing everyone knows, or should know, about New Orleans music, it's Congo Square. Those Sunday gatherings in New Orleans were of unparalleled importance to the history of African American music—which is to say, the history of American music. Notwithstanding other places of importance, the musical concepts of Africa were more freely and more widely expressed in the dynamic, creative, violent city of New Orleans than anywhere else in the United States.

Various writers have stated that the Congo Square gatherings began during the American period. That does not appear to be correct, nor does it make sense. Though gatherings began at the place before Louisiana was a Spanish colony, the name likely wouldn't have appeared in the French days, for the simple reason that Kongo people came in numbers to New Orleans not during the French period, but during the Spanish.

As is often the case with New Orleans, there has been a great deal of vagueness and mystification about Congo Square. E. W. Kemble's frequently reprinted image of dancing there was made during Kemble's only visit to New Orleans in 1885, long after the dances had ceased, and was based on George Washington Cable's description of the dances; an anachronistic church spire is in the background.[5]

Now I must introduce a slight complication. There is a mention of *Place Congo* in a 1786 letter by Auxiliary Bishop Cyrillo Sieni, known in English as Cyril of Barcelona. A Spanish Capuchin friar, known for his rigidity, he denounced "the wicked custom of the negros, who, at the hour of Vespers, assemble in a green expanse called *Place Congo* to dance the bamboula and perform hideous gyrations."[6]

It is possible that several hundred people drumming, dancing, and singing across what is now Rampart Street would have disturbed vespers in the cathedral, six blocks over on the other side of town. But it seems more likely that the bishop was speaking of dances at the market right by the cathedral. This is what Kimberly Hanger, one of the scholars who has most studied Spanish New Orleans, believed: that the troublesome dancing was there, at the busy market of what the French called Place d'Armes, and what the Spanish called Plaza de Armas (since 1851 it's been called Jackson Square). If so, this reference to *Place Congo*—literally, "Congo Place"—was not to the spot that was later called Congo Square; it's being used as a term applied to a place where Africans gathered. In 1787 the city treasurer collected eighty-one pesos from *"las negras y otros individuos que venden en la Conga del mercado"*—the black women and other individuals who sell things in the Conga of the market. This would appear to refer to a section of the market where black vendors congregated, generically called *la Conga*.[7]

Was the bishop speaking of the main market at the Plaza de Armas, or the market commons at the more familiar location of Congo Square at Rampart and Orleans Streets? It's not clear. In the Spanish years, there would have been no reason for black dancing to have been restricted to one spot, as it later would be under the Anglo-Americans. There are eyewitness accounts of dancing on the levees. There was probably dancing wherever there was a market, dancing on the docks, dancing everywhere, like there was (and still is) in Cuba. None of which takes away from the importance of that spot across Rampart Street today remembered by the English name of Congo Square.

The slaves' gatherings in New Orleans were repeatedly noted by travelers. To see that many slaves assembling in public (albeit under the watchful eye of soldiers), let alone on Sunday, stood in sharp contrast to the southern United States. "There may nowhere assemble more than 7 male negro slaves," wrote Johann Schöpf of his travels through Charleston in 1784. "Their dances and other assemblies must stop at 10 o'clock in the evening. . . . The feast of the Sunday is strictly observed at Charleston. No shop may keep open; no sort of game or music is permitted, and during the church service watchmen go about who lay hold upon any one idling in the streets (any not on urgent business or visiting the sick), and compel him to turn aside into some church or pay 2 shillings 4 pence."[8]

Congo Square occupies a central place in the popular memory and imagination of New Orleans. At the core of it is the city's great musical riddle: what did it sound like? Since we don't have recordings, we don't exactly know. But we have some knowledge of the instruments that were played at Congo Square.

And I think I have a pretty good idea of at least one rhythm that was played there.

In February 2006, during a postflood visit, I went to the New Orleans Public Library to look at the cabildo minutes. I knew the page I was looking for; it would have taken years to examine all the minutes thoroughly from scratch. Mostly, I wanted to see these documents, of cardinal importance to the history of the city and the United States, with my own eyes and know they were safe.

To enter the library, I had to pass through a metal detector operated by beefy men whose T-shirts identified them as being employees of the Virginia-based private army Blackwater USA. They were very polite. Outside the library, I heard one of them tell a local who had engaged him in conversation that he had been in Afghanistan, Iraq, Bosnia, and Haiti. "Haiti was the worst," he said. I suppose library duty was a tad easier. The ground floor of the library was being used as a Federal Emergency Management Association (FEMA) resource center; apparently they were there to protect FEMA personnel from potential assaults by enraged citizens.

The cabildo minutes fill five fat volumes, having at some point been subjected to a standard library binding. The large sheets of thick, brown paper give off a strong sweet smell, like an aromatic wood. It is not quick work to decipher the flowing, curlicued ink script and enter into the period variants of spelling and usage. They were microfilmed some years back by the Mormons, who have a massive microfilm project. The Mormons didn't do a very good job, but in fairness, it would be hard to do a very good job. Back during the days of the WPA, someone seems to have thought it a good idea to affix Scotch tape all over the pages of the cabildo minutes. I don't know why, since the pages aren't torn. In some cases the tape has been laid down, not very carefully, over each line of text. On microfilm, the Scotch tape reads as a blotch. The pages have held their integrity just fine, but the tape is pulling up slowly from the page, and as it does, the ink beneath it blobs. The minutes are no longer completely legible, and are slowly becoming less so. In postapocalyptic New Orleans, this all seems like a metaphor for the vanity of man.

Nevertheless, inspecting the original, I went straight to, and could clearly make out, the reference I wanted, in Governor Estevan Miró's *Bando de Buen Gobierno* (*Edict of Good Government*) of June 2, 1786, a set of thirty-four orders for the colony. Apparently responding to Cyrillo's complaint about the *bamboula* being danced on the Sabbath, Governor Miró ordered that *los tangos, o bailes de negros* (the tangos, that is, the blacks' dances) be delayed until after vespers.

Los tangos, o bailes de negros. This is apparently the earliest written instance of the word *tango* anywhere. The word was surely being used in Cuba at that time, and probably long before that, but I know of no Cuban document in which it appears that early; for one thing, there was no popular press there yet. Robert Farris Thompson, who wrote a book on the African roots of tango without uncovering an earlier written instance of the word, traces *tango* to the Kikongo: it's "more than a word. It's a semantic spectrum. It's a semantic range. And on both sides of the Atlantic, it means a dance, a place of dance, the people who dance it, the beat of the dance, and many other things."[9]

So: the word *tango*, to describe black dancing in New Orleans. In 1786, a full century before the emergence in Argentina of the dance by that name. But not only that. It's being equated with dancing the bamboula. Cyrillo complained about the bamboula, so to please him, Governor Miró required the postponement of the tangos.

Hmmm.

◦◦◦

Forty-nine years after Governor Miró's edict, the word *tango* appeared in the first dictionary of Antillean Spanish, Esteban Pichardo's 1835 *Diccionario provincial de voces cubanas*, published in Havana, which defines it as "a meeting of *negros bozales* [blacks born in Africa] to dance to the sound of drums." Teodoro Díaz Fabelo's *Diccionario de la lengua conga residual en Cuba* (*Dictionary of the remnants of the Congo language in Cuba*), finished in the 1970s, notes that on February 23, 1841, in Havana's Teatro Tacón, "there was played and danced for the first time an African tango by an all-white company of Havaneros and Havaneras."[10]

As the nineteenth century progressed, the word *tango* implied a specific rhythmic cell, which Thompson identifies as the Kongo *mbila a makinu*, "the call to the dance."[11] It is also a familiar rhythm in Arabic music, and presumably was known in Muslim Spain. That rhythm was so identified with Havana that it became known elsewhere as *habanera*, branding it as Cuban everywhere it went. In the early decades of the twentieth century, the dance that traveled from Buenos Aires to Paris to sweep the world took its name from this underlying rhythm, which had traveled, somewhat indirectly, from Cuba to Argentina. When I say *tango* in this book, I am talking not about the Argentine dance of that name, but about the habanera/tango rhythm.

That rhythm is prominent in the music of the *tumba francesa* of eastern Cuba, which maintains folkloric traditions brought by Saint-Domingan exiles in 1803. There is a popular belief in Cuba, possibly true, that the addition of the tango to the contradanza, which had enormous consequences for the development of Cuban dance music, was popularized by refugees from Saint-Domingue in Oriente. On the other hand, that rhythm was surely in Cuba already. More likely, coming from black Saint-Domingue, that rhythm reen-countered itself as an already-established black Cuban tradition. Much the same process presumably happened in New Orleans, where the *tangos, o bailes de negros* were pounding in Governor Miró's day. While it can't be proved that that specific rhythmic cell was attached to the tangos that occupied Governor Miró's attention, it's not unreasonable to think it was.

That four-note habanera/tango rhythm is the signature Antillean beat to this day. It's a simple figure that can generate a thousand dances all by itself, depending on what drums, registers, pitches, or tense rests you assign to which of the notes, what tempo you play it, and how much you polyrhythmicize it by laying other, compatible rhythmic figures on top of it. It's the rhythm of the aria Bizet wrote for the cigarette-rolling Carmen to sing (though he lifted the melody from Basque composer Sebastián Yradier), and it's the defining rhythm of *reggaetón*. You can hear it in the contemporary music of Haiti, the Domini-can Republic, Jamaica, and Puerto Rico, to say nothing of the nineteenth-century Cuban contradanza. It's Jelly Roll Morton's oft-cited "Spanish tinge," it's the accompaniment figure to W. C. Handy's "St. Louis Blues," and you hear it from brass bands at a second line in New Orleans today. At half speed, with timpani or a drum set, it was a signature rhythm of the Brill Building song-writers, and it was the basic template of clean-studio 1980s corporate rock. You could write it as a dotted eighth, sixteenth, and two eighths. If you don't know what I'm talking about yet, it's the rhythm of the first four notes of the *Dragnet* theme. DOMM, DA DOM DOM.

It's the rhythm the right hand repeats throughout "La Bamboula (Danse des Nègres)," Op. 2, a piano piece composed in 1848 to international acclaim by the eighteen-year-old Domingan-descended New Orleanian piano prodigy Louis Moreau Gottschalk (1830–70). A stellar concert attraction of his time, and, in this writer's opinion, the most important nineteenth-century U.S. composer, Gottschalk's legacy is inexplicably neglected today in his home country. As a toddler, he lived briefly on Rampart Street, about a half mile down from Congo Square, at a time when the dances were still active, and he would have, like other New Orleanians in the old part of town, been familiar with the sound of the square. Some have suggested that Gottschalk was not trying to evoke the sound of Congo Square literally in the piece. But I think Gottschalk was telling us something: when they danced the bamboula at

Congo Square, they repeated that rhythm over and over, the way Gottschalk's piano piece does, the way reggaetón does today—and over that rhythm, they sang songs everyone knew.

Frederick Starr identifies the basis for the main theme of Gottschalk's "Bamboula" as a popular song of old Saint-Domingue, "Quan' patate la cuite," which Gottschalk learned from Sally, his black Domingan governess.[12] Was Gottschalk, a programmatic composer, drawing a sound portrait of a dance at Congo Square? And might he be inadvertently telling us that the singing, drumming, and dancing circles put popular melodies into their own rhythm and style? That is to say, were they doing what jazz musicians were doing fifty years later? The same thing I heard at a Haitian vodou ceremony in New Jersey in November 2006, when a group of women broke seamlessly into a seasonally appropriate chorus of "Jingle Bells" in Kreyol (complete with the "dashing through the snow" part), as the vodou drums continued slamming, before returning to songs of African origin?

If that is reading too much into it, another way of expressing it is that maybe the eighteen-year-old Gottschalk was simply playing his version of the dance music he was accustomed to hearing in New Orleans, in the days when the habanera was king and there were full dress balls even for Creole children, and everyone in town was familiar with the sound of Congo Square. But he didn't call his piece "La contredanse." He called it "La bamboula." However he did it, he came up with the perfect piece for his moment. It became a contest piece in Europe, and it should be known by every American piano student.

Gottschalk, who was a constant traveler, spoke French, English, and Spanish, and visited many of the Antillean islands, including, for extended stays, Cuba. The tango rhythm shows up in work after work of his. It's in the left hand in "Ojos Criollos (Danse Cubaine)," a piano piece he published in New Orleans in 1860, the last antebellum year. If you listen to "Ojos Criollos" today, it sounds like ragtime. But it's a *danse cubaine* that preceded the ragtime boom by thirty-five years, driven by that tango figure, now in the bass.

⌘

Miró forbade slaves from renting their own quarters in town and proprietors from renting rooms to them. He stipulated that a slave caught with a gun or a knife would be subject to two hundred lashes and three years of hard labor. He denounced merchants who slipped slaves that were not *bozales* (African born) into their cargoes, and he prohibited the importation of slaves from the French and British possessions: "Experience has shown that the admission of blacks born at the English or French Antilles is harmful to this province. It is necessary to erect a major barricade, and I order the merchants to cease introducing them." This marked a turning point in the Spanish importation of slaves; the direction had been toward liberalization of the slave trade, but now, in fear, it began to tighten. It was a standard practice to sell off troublesome slaves to neighboring territories, and Louisiana was concerned about the effect of Jamaican and Domingan evildoers arriving in their territory.

Miró also complained in the *Bando* about the idleness of mulatta and free quadroon women who, he asserted, subsisted from libertinage. In short, the fabled New Orleans was already present, and not so different from Havana. He went after their accessories, forbidding them to wear plumes in their hair and requiring women of color to wear *tignons*—head coverings, which the women turned into headdresses. Whatever its effect on modesty may or may not have been, the tignon established a sharply distinct look for females of each ethno-caste. White women were allowed to wear their hair free, whereas women who looked white but had "blood" were required to cover their heads. Seventy-five years after the establishment of New Orleans, with a substantial category of people in the city descended from both Africa and Europe, the difficulty of distinguishing "blacks" from "whites" had reached the point that a sumptuary law was thought necessary.

⌒∞⌒

The same institutions that gave Cuba an explicitly African heritage that remains vital today also operated for the four decades that New Orleans was Spanish. Those institutions were dismantled by the Anglo-Americans, causing black culture in Louisiana to evolve differently in response to harsh new conditions. But by then, the black people of Louisiana already had a culture quite unlike anything else in the United States.

Visitors to Cuba today are astounded when they encounter the contemporary vitality of the complex religious and musical tradition of the civilization of Oyó, brought by the people known in the nineteenth century as *Lucumí*, and known in more recent years as *Yoruba*. New Orleans seems to have been the one place in the United States where any discernible trace of the Lucumí/ Yoruba arrived; Hall puts them at 4 percent of Africans brought to Louisiana. This presence presumably derives from the slaving practices of the traders to Cuba, who started bringing small numbers of Lucumí captives in the 1780s, though the peak of Lucumí importation came later, after an Islamic jihad erupted and subsequently took down the Oyó empire in the 1820s and '30s. They were the last major African group to be brought to Cuba; by the time they were being slaved in numbers, export of Africans to English-speaking North America had largely ceased, so although they were numerous in nineteenth-century Cuba, they had little impact on African American culture. But the Lucumí did come, in small numbers at least, to New Orleans.

There must have been undocumented and unmeasurable contact between blacks in New Orleans and Havana, which at that time was larger than any city in British North America. Black stevedores worked the docks in both Havana and New Orleans, and sailors, some of them black, traveled back and forth as well. The flavor of the music on both sides of the Gulf must have been affected by that ongoing contact. Whatever the hip black dance of Havana was at the moment, it was likely being danced on the docks of New Orleans as well, if only by visiting habaneros.

There were plenty of opportunities for contact in the 1780s and '90s. During the French period, only six or so ships visited the port of New Orleans in a year, but in 1786, 113 ships left the port. In 1787, 41 ships out of 108 leaving New Orleans were bound for Havana; in 1798, it was 63 out of 102.[14]

❦

The street grid the French had laid out for New Orleans in 1721—later known as the French Quarter—was not yet fully populated when the French gave up Louisiana to the Spanish. It barely had any fortifications, and its buildings were made of the material that was there: wood. Southern Louisiana is geologically the opposite of Cuba, which thrust up out of the sea and sits on a cap of crumbly, porous limestone that served as a building material. In Louisiana there was no stone to quarry, but there was wood everywhere. Consequently, fire was a recurring problem. People without chimneys built fires on their dirt floors, an obvious safety problem in a city made of wood and *colombage* (plaster and straw between timbers).

On Good Friday, 1788, as the city was recovering from two hurricanes, an altar laden with candles set a house on Chartres Street afire while the owner was having dinner. The town's large bell, which should have warned the populace, was either not working or had been removed.[15] Nor were there buckets, or any kind of firefighting force. It was a windy day, and the flames blew from roof to roof.

About 80 percent of the wood-and-shingles town was incinerated. More than eight hundred buildings went up in smoke: residences, the cabildo, the military barracks, much of the armament that defended the city, the *calaboza* (jail, or calaboose), the cathedral, commercial warehouses, and much of the official archive of documents.

As the city began rebuilding, Governor Miró paid for balls and parties to keep morale up. News traveled slowly between the Old World and the New, so it wasn't until April 4, 1789, that the December 4 death of King Carlos III of Spain was announced to the New Orleans cabildo. A mourning period was declared in the city, which was still in the process of rebuilding from the fire. In May, as the Estates General in Paris were moving closer to the revolution that would erupt in the storming of the Bastille, the Louisiana colony celebrated the coronation of Carlos IV, the dead king's son, with the largest musical spectacle New Orleans had yet seen. The ruined town saw days of pageantry that included parades, military bands, and orchestral and choral performances.

In the aftermath of the fire, landowner Beltram Gravier began subdividing his property. Located on part of the former Jesuits' plantation, immediately upriver of what later became known as Canal Street, the area was then a ditch and a commons. This became New Orleans's first suburb, the Faubourg Ste. Marie (*fauxbourg*, literally, fake town). Later, anglicized to St. Mary, it would become the American sector (in other words, the part that wasn't the French Quarter), and in the antebellum years, it was the center of the slave trade. Now known as the Central Business District, or CBD, it still has a Gravier Street. A street was named to honor the new Spanish king Carlos IV: St. Charles, which, when extended later, became the great boulevard running uptown.[16] Since Carlos's profile was stamped on the coinage, one could almost say the street was named in honor of Spanish money.

New Orleans wasn't the only wooden city. Wood from Louisiana had been exported to build houses in Saint-Domingue, which had been deforested to clear room for plantations and to stoke the boilers of the sugar mills. John Vlach has argued that the classic shotgun house of New Orleans, a building style that spread to other parts of the Deep South, came to Louisiana from Saint-Domingue.[17] Those proto-shotguns of Saint-Domingue were built with cypress from Louisiana.

Unfortunately, cypress is highly flammable, and the houses in Saint-Domingue were about to burn down.

COMMISSION
CIVILE DE LA RÉPUBLIQUE.

Nous, ETIENNE POLVEREL & LEGER-FELICITÉ
SONTHONAX, Commissaires civils de la République,
délégués aux Iles françaises de l'Amérique sous le vent,
pour y rétablir l'ordre & la tranquillité publique.

PERMETTONS au Citoyen *Polez ha Cyen Savrie ez de*
eux enfans de s'embarquer pour *la Nouvelle Angleterre*
leur enjoignons de partir de la Colonie dans le délai
de *huit* jours, à dater de ce jour, à peine de nullité
du présent permis.

Cap, le *huit Juillet* 1793, l'an deuxième
de la République française.

Polverel   *Sonthonax*

Pour les Commissaires civils de la République

Pontteau
1er aux de la
Comité civil

Vû par moi Charles français Etot Consul de
la République française à Philadelphie le dix
Thermidor an 4e de la R. République Une et
Indivisible.

Pass, signed by Etienne Polverel
and Leger-Felicité Sonthonax,
Jacobin commissioners of Saint-
Domingue, to allow a refugee to
leave the island in 1793.

REVOLUTION

12

❦

DESIRE

The Creole loses sight of everything that is not part of satisfying his penchants, disdaining everything not marked with the seal of pleasure, giving himself up freely to the whirl that carries him along. Transported by his love of dance, music, parties, and everything that charms and entertains his delirium, he seems to live only for voluptuous pleasures.

How difficult it is for such dispositions not to become fatal in a place where the morals are perfect for encouraging them. How can a fiery temperament be tamed in a place where the class of numerous women who are the fruit of the mix of whites and slave women, is interested only in avenging, with the weapons of pleasure, the degradation to which they are condemned? Thus the passions deploy all their powers in the heart of the majority of the Creoles, and when finally the ice of old age arrives, it does not always extinguish desire, the cruellest of all passions.

One could truly say that everything combines to form an imperious character in the Creoles.

—*Moreau de St.-Méry*, "Of White Creoles," Description of the French Part of the Isle of Saint-Domingue (*1797*)

*S*ugar was practically a nation all its own, wherever in the hemisphere the plantations went up: Sugarland.

Most of North America lies too far north for cane sugar production, and thus never took part in the authoritarian, faux-aristocratic Sugarland culture. For most of the eighteenth century, it was believed that the growing season of southern Louisiana was too short to produce sugar, but Louisiana joined Sugarland in the 1790s, inheriting the capital-intensive, slave-hungry ways of its French Creole sibling, Saint-Domingue.

Sugar was the grand product of the centuries-old plantation system, which had moved westward by stages from the Levant, where sugar was grown in the twelfth century for sale to Europe. By comparison, the cotton plantation of the nineteenth-century U.S. South was a late-stage development. What Philip Curtin calls "the plantation complex" traveled across the Mediterranean to Cyprus, Sicily, and Iberia, on to the Canary and other Atlantic islands, and then across the Atlantic to Brazil. In the New World, plantations took on previously impossible dimensions through the use of industrial quantities of slave labor.[1]

Sugar is naturally suited for long-distance trade. Heavy and bulky, the cane is hard to harvest and transport, and must be processed quickly once it is cut. But after processing, reduced to about 5 percent of its previous volume, sugar is a compact, durable product that can be profitably transported across the world. It's not unlike the difference between the untransportable coca leaf and the highly transportable cocaine powder. All sugar colonies also produced molasses, which could be used to make rum. By the 1780s, according to one estimate, North America was importing some three million gallons of rum a year from the West Indies, in addition to the considerable amount the North Americans distilled themselves from imported molasses.[2]

Sugar required a big parcel of land, both to grow the cane and to harvest the wood necessary to fuel the boiling. But a sugar plantation was not only a farm. It was a factory, where cane was ground and either boiled into molasses or crystallized into raw sugar. Expensive, specialized equipment was required, along with a large number of laborers.

Sugar planters needed capital to run their industrialized agriculture, and their plantations were necessarily capitalist enterprises, though, as Curtin points out, they "also had certain features that can be called feudal"[3]—like, for example, the workers being slaves. While many of the elements of capitalism were present early on in the history of commerce, the word *capital* comes into use precisely in the era of the Antillean sugar plantations, with the publication of Turgot's *Reflections on the Formation and Distribution of Wealth* (1766, published in English in 1774).[4]

Other key works of philosophy, science, and economics appeared in that period, articulating, rightly or wrongly, courses of thought that still remain in the air. In 1775, Johan Friedrich Blumenbach's thesis *De generis humani varietate nativa* (*On the Natural Varieties of Mankind*) was a milestone of scientific racism that divided the human species into five "races": Caucasian, Mongolian, Malayan, Ethiopian, and American. By taking measurements of skulls, he determined that "Caucasians" had higher mental abilities and that "Ethiopians" were closer to apes. The following year, the Scottish economist Adam Smith's *An Inquiry into the Nature and Causes of the Wealth of Nations* famously proposed that markets function by means of a mystical "invisible hand," an idea still worshipped at the altar of marketplace ideology in our own time. In 1798, Thomas Robert Malthus's *An Essay on the Principle of Population* argued that population increases geometrically whereas food supply increases arithmetically, positing the division of society into a fortunate few versus a wretched mass, and celebrating the virtue of hard work.

None of these thinkers ever set foot on an Antillean plantation, though surely they consumed both coffee and sugar, all of which was grown by slaves. Each crop imposes its own dynamic on its workers, and the special needs of sugar cultivation, in the absence of any humanitarian impulse on the part of its growers, led to a particularly murderous form of slavery. Plantation workers had to be reckoned as part of the capital outlay—bought for this much, capable of producing that much, lasting for so long before they had to be replaced.

The sugar workforce was not self-reproducing. It was not deemed economical to bring women from Africa and keep them out of the workforce for long enough to give birth and nurse, then raise a child for years until he was old enough to do heavy labor. The invisible hand of the marketplace ordained that it was more profitable to bring male laborers from Africa, work them to death, and replace them with newcomers. It was helpful to think of them as being members of an inferior race.

Every dollar spent for workers' food was a dollar less of profit, so they were fed only the minimum necessary to keep them moving. They worked twenty hours a day in peak season. "How can we make a lot of sugar when we only work sixteen hours?" wrote Odelucq, business manager of the Gallifet plantation, south of Cap Français, in 1785.[5] A laborer might last ten years or so before expiring. But individual workers in the death camp of sugar were survived by their culture, which was constantly re-Africanized by fresh arriv-als. To that sugar plantation culture, the music of our hemisphere owes no small debt.

Once the cane was cut, quick and intensive labor was required at the plantation's mill before the cane went sour. It wouldn't have been necessary to work slaves to the edge of death and beyond if there were enough of them to do the work. But that would have necessitated feeding them during the dead time, when there was no work for them to do. To achieve maximum economy, sugar plantations in peak season exacted what amounted to more than a double shift of hard labor to do the grinding and boiling. After emanci-pation, when wage laborers were used, they simply remained unemployed and destitute during the part of the year when they were not needed.

A sugar plantation in Saint-Domingue might have three to four hun-dred slaves and as few as two or three whites. Terrified of being overrun, the overseers maintained iron discipline, using the whip as an integral part of the workday. But the punishment of slaves went beyond labor-force discipline. It was the era of the Enlightenment, but also of libertinage. The hyperbolic cruelties of the Marquis de Sade's writings were not mere fantasy in Saint-Domingue, where a rich woman could have her cook roasted alive in the oven if she was displeased. Every planter was a little king on whose goodwill everything depended. As was true in every slave territory, some slave owners were more humane than others; but there was nothing to restrain the more monstrous ones, who treated their property as they liked.

The common dream of white planters in Saint-Domingue was to retire wealthy in France. They were, in Franklin Knight's phrase, "psychological transients."[6] The contemporary observer Médéric Louis Elie Moreau de St.-Méry, describing the social milieu of the colony, wrote of "the general mania to speak of returning, or of passage to France. Everyone repeats that he is leaving *next year*."[7]

The big Antillean sugar plantations, with their large, brutalized popula-tions of male laboring slaves, were essential to the growth of wealthy nations in Europe. They were also the backdrop for slave uprisings, most spectacularly in Saint-Domingue.

⌒∞⌒

The most successful owners of Saint-Domingue plantations lived in high style in France, leaving their properties to be run by local managers. But it was frequently the case, in Saint-Domingue and elsewhere, that plantations were not all that profitable for their owners. The system was rigged against the colonial planters in favor of a handful of metropolitan merchants. "The planters," writes Braudel, "were caught up in a system of exchange which barred them from making any large-scale profits. . . . Most of the wealth produced in the [Saint-Domingue] colony went to swell the coffers of rich men in the home country. The planters made a profit of 8 to 10 percent at the very most."[8] Thomas Jefferson's complaint (and this *after* the American Revolution) that Virginia planters were "a species of property, annexed to certain mercantile houses in London" would have been endorsed by planters everywhere, who saw themselves as being in bondage.[9]

Despite the heavy capital outlay sugar required, France's financial institutions were late in developing. Often the planter's only source of credit was the French merchant, who could extract a margin from the planter in two ways: by buying the finished crop at a previously fixed price or by selling the planter his supplies, including slaves, at high prices. The merchant was in a position to offer take-it-or-leave-it terms.

The policy the French called the *exclusif* meant that Domingans were not supposed to trade with their neighbors in British Jamaica, or Spanish Cuba and Louisiana, but only with the French. Moreover, given the chronic and deliberately maintained shortage of money in the colonies, any clandestine trading that did go on most likely entailed barter. Bertrand de Molleville, the marine minister of France, described the advantages of having colonies in a speech to the National Assembly in December 1791—that is to say, in revolutionary France, more than two years after the fall of the Bastille:

Can we fail to see, that an obligation to sell their produce only to the members of the mother-country, and to buy of them alone every article they want, forms a double source of riches, of which the measure is immense? In short, the Colonies take from us all they want at such prices as we please to impose; they return us a sufficiency of their valuable produce, not only to serve the consumption of twenty-five millions of inhabitants, but to form a very great surplus, which we sell with profit to the nations who have no Colonies of their own.[10]

He was, it should be noted, speaking of profits that accrued to the French merchant, not to the Domingan grower who sold his product at a price determined in France. Not only economic control but also political control lay across the ocean. Heavily subject to influence peddling, the French court fixed the commercial terms under which the colonies were forced to operate. The fact that Saint-Domingue provisioned most of its food not from France but by clandestine trade with British North America was a perpetual sore spot in relations between colony and metropolis.

The *grands blancs* of Saint-Domingue were as frustrated by France's restrictions on their activities as the rebellious North American merchants and planters were by British restrictions and taxes. But the planters of Saint-Domingue got paid in another way: by having slaves, acquired in such quantities that they were not individuals but articles for consumption. The Creoles of Saint-Domingue never had to do anything for themselves or pay to have work done. Everything on their plantations, from construction to repair to blacksmithing, was done by people who didn't charge for their services, which lessened the need for cash. The fees charged by free people in the towns were kept down by the vast amount of slave labor that could perform the same trades. Even when teetering on the brink of insolvency, the gentlemen of Saint-Domingue enjoyed an aristocratic lifestyle that French nobles could not have.

"Everything lends to Saint-Domingue," wrote Moreau de St.-Méry, "a character of opulence that astonishes Europeans. The crowd of slaves that attends the orders and even the signals of a man, gives an air of grandeur to the one who commands them, who has the dignity of a rich man, with four times as many domestics as he needs."[11] As a planter approached a door, it was opened for him. His clothes appeared in the morning and were put on his body for him. His boots were pulled off his feet at night. His drinks were fetched and refreshed by people who had learned the hard way to anticipate their owner's wishes. The Creoles of Saint-Domingue were raised to this lifestyle from birth, in a climate of excess and indulgence. This was not so different, except perhaps in degree, from the way the gentlemen of property in Virginia lived. Johann Schöpf, who visited Virginia in 1784, observed that "if no impulse to political affairs arouses them from their inactivity, they spend their days in idleness or in such pleasures as a country-life affords. . . . They pass the greatest part of the summer on soft pallets, attended by one or several negroes to ward off the flies, light pipes, and proffer punch, sangry, toddy, or julap."[12]

Sex required only a come-hither gesture to initiate and was accomplished under the satisfying dynamic of master and slave. Moreau de St.-Méry writes:

> No despot ever had more assiduous homages nor more constant worshippers than the Creole child. Each slave is subject to the variations of his mood, and his childish piques often disturb the domestic peace, which at his unjust command falls victim to a will he does not yet know how to control.

Even in his games the Creole child is reduced to being nothing but a tyrant. Surrounded by little slaves who are condemned to flatter his caprices, and even more revolting, to forgo their own immaturity, he will not tolerate the least frustration. What he sees, he wants, what one shows him, he demands; and if fate should permit one of his little companions to resist him, he becomes irritated, everyone comes running at the sound of his cries, and those unfortunates whose color marks them for submission immediately learn that they are constrained to give way and perhaps even that there is punishment for the disobedient ones who do not yet have the instinct of servitude.

Yet these same acts of shameful despotism are the source of good fortune for certain slaves; because, if the Creole child shows favor to them, they are assured a better fate. And if the Creole adopts another child who grows up together with him, there will come a day when, according to the child's sex, the slave will be either the object or the minister of his pleasures and this high status will spare the slave, and other slaves he or she may want to protect, from the injustices of the master.[13]

The object or the minister of his pleasures. A concubine or a procurer. The children of Saint-Domingue were raised from the cradle with their future human sex toys close at hand. And protection "from the injustices of the master" was greatly to be desired. With the planters under the constant stress of finances, and living in fear of their own hordes of slaves, some of them seem to have indulged in torture and even murder not only for disciplinary purposes, but for fun. The Code Noir, which set limits to slave punishment, was rarely consulted in Saint-Domingue, where corporal punishment was the rule. I will spare the reader a catalog of depravities documented in the literature of the day; it should be enough to cite a letter of 1736 that mentions "burning a little powder in a nigger's ass," a practice that entailed stuffing a slave's anus with gunpowder, attaching a fuse, then igniting it.[14]

The Louisiana colonist and memoirist Le Page du Pratz was transparently referring to Saint-Domingue when he wrote: "A Christian is unworthy of that name when he punishes with cruelty, as is done to my knowledge in a certain colony, to such a degree that they entertain their guests with such spectacles, which have more of barbarity than humanity in them."[15] This from a man who entrapped, and reported without qualm the breaking on the wheel of, rebellious slaves in Louisiana.

Why wouldn't slave masters in Saint-Domingue have whipped their slaves? French schoolmasters—especially the Jesuits, who ran many of the schools—

whipped their students. Ritualistically, in front of the assembled student body, in a tableau which became a familiar pornographic image. "Among the most distinctive traits of Jesuit schools in 18th-century France," writes Francine du Plessix Gray in her biography of the Marquis Donatien-Alphonse de Sade, "were their emphasis on corporal punishment, their reputation for sodomy, and their tradition of staging lavish theatrical productions."[16] The most perfect theater for erotic torture was the colonies, especially Saint-Domingue, where some human beings had power over others that the Marquis de Sade could only dream of.

The French and their Creole descendants in Saint-Domingue brought the same artistry to torture that they did to staging masked balls or making cakes:

> "Slow punishments make a greater impression than quick or violent ones," wrote one wealthy plantation owner to his managers. Rather than "fifty lashes administered in five minutes," he recommended "twenty-five lashes of the whip administered in a quarter of an hour, interrupted at intervals to hear the cause which the unfortunates always plead in their defense, and resumed again, continuing in this fashion for two or three times," as being "far more likely to make an impression."[17]

Masters rarely did the whipping themselves, of course. There was a black overseer for that. Masters *watched*.

Which is not to say that slaves in Saint-Domingue didn't have fun, when they weren't being tortured or forced to work twenty-hour days. On Sundays they went into town to sell the produce they raised in garden plots. There were taverns, called *cabarets*, for them. And there was Carnival, when blacks and whites both celebrated. The slaves drank tafia—known in Spanish as *aguardiente* (literally, firewater), the raw, unrefined cane liquor that was abundant in the sugar colonies—and they dressed in costume, as they did everywhere Carnival was celebrated in the Afro-Atlantic world.

The theaters were an important part of the colony's intellectual life. Most of the planters expected to finish their days living in Parisian society, where they would need to be cosmopolitan and au courant. In competitive provincial high society, the aristocracy followed cultural news from Paris, perhaps the world's greatest music capital in the mid-eighteenth century. "The *querelle des Bouffons*"—the comic-opera war of the 1750s between the schools of romantic melodists, represented by Rousseau, and classicist harmonists, represented by Rameau—"would have an 'echo' in the salons of the planters," writes Alain Guédé.[18]

But the principal recreation was dancing, for black and white both. Planters were not, of course, accustomed to hiring labor; they owned it. When they needed to put together an orchestra to play at their balls, they looked to acquire slaves who could play instruments. There were professional white musicians, but more often black musicians, both free and enslaved, played at the balls as well as in theater orchestras. They knew how to make people dance: they played the contredanse their way, putting a little something extra in the rhythm, something the colonial dancers came to crave.[19] In Havana, something similar was going on, but Havana's fashions arrived from backward Madrid rather than trendsetting Paris.

In Saint-Domingue, the endless balls, which commenced in the playhouse when the evening's opera was over, provided an important extra source of income for the theaters. The best balls were, not surprisingly, those given by the mulatresses—the free women of color, who, like their counterparts in Cuba, gave balls to which admission was refused to men of color. On occasion they held transvestite balls. The regimental band entertained with concerts. And everyone, whatever their social status, loved the grand fireworks displays, given a safe distance away from the flammable wooden town.[20]

⤫

In the countryside, wrote one Domingan, "one can scarcely find one white for sixty blacks."[21] In the rugged hills, maroons lived in outlaw communities. Some had even been born in marronage, a counterculture that dated back to the days of the pirates of Tortuga. The best-known figure of this population was François Makandal, whose disciples believed he was able to shape-shift. Said to have had a Muslim background in Africa, he knew at least some Arabic vocabulary and something of traditional medicine. After losing one of his hands to the machinery at the sugar mill where he worked as a slave, he was given lighter duty. Escaping to the hills, he spent eighteen years as a maroon in the northern province, where he organized and trained a network of outlaws, over whom he maintained strict discipline and charismatic command. This network stretched throughout the northern province of Saint-Domingue and may have extended through the rest of the colony as well. Their grand plan was to poison the water supplies of Cap Français, all at the same time, in a coordinated action, followed by a general massacre.

Before their plan could be carried out, however, Makandal was apprehended at a *calenda*, his identity given away by his mangled hand. His trial
records have been preserved; in them he admitted to making *wanga*, spiritual
weapons. The word *wanga* derives from the Kikongo *nganga*, referring to the
packet or repository that is the center of practice, and in Haiti today survives
as the word for a ritual expert, *houngan*. In a scene as familiar to Haitians as
Joan of Arc's martyrdom is in France, Makandal was burned at the stake in
1758. The poisonings became less frequent after that but did not stop, and
continued to panic the colonial population. The terror was then transferred
onto the black population by the white masters in the form of interrogations
and executions, in an effort to root out the poisoners. This band of outlaws
formed the first important center of resistance to slavery, which would cul-
minate in the destruction of the French colony of Saint-Domingue and its
replacement by the Republic of Haiti.

The maroons' signature art of poisoning came to the colony from two
directions. France had a long tradition of nobles poisoning each other in inter-
necine rivalry; Catherine de Medici, from Machiavelli's hometown of Flor-
ence, brought the art to a high level in sixteenth-century France. But also in
Africa—especially in forested Africa, for obvious reasons—there was a sophisticated knowledge of how to use herbs, both to cure and to kill. In addition
to their traditional arsenal of venoms, the black poisoners of Saint-Domingue
apparently were able to procure French arsenic, used in small amounts in
pharmaceuticals of the day; Hillard d'Auberteuil described how a free person
of color in league with Makandal bought a quantity of it at an apothecary's
bankruptcy sale.[22] In other words, black outlaws in eighteenth-century Saint-
Domingue developed a clandestine distribution system for a poisonous drug.
And there was a war on illegal drugs: any slave caught with arsenic would be
put to death immediately.

The nineteenth-century Martinican historian Xavier Eyma wrote of poisonings on his island: "Rarely, in fact, was the poison applied with violence;
almost always, it proceeded by small doses. Death would come slowly, progres-
sively, with the alternatives of hope and of supreme agony. It was perhaps a
refinement of the cruelty, an atrocious game, that allowed the poisoner to
be present for the sufferings and the languishing of his victim."[23] Not only
whites were poisoned; slaves were poisoned by other blacks in a terrorist campaign against the plantations. Moreau de St.-Méry mentions a plantation in
Saint-Domingue where four hundred slaves were poisoned over a period of
twenty-five years. Cattle, oxen, and mules were poisoned. Midwives poisoned
white babies to keep the masters from having heirs, and they poisoned black

babies to liberate them from slavery at birth. Slaves committed suicide, certain they would return to Africa. The Igbo especially were known for this practice; on occasion all the Igbos on a plantation would get together and hang themselves.

∽∾

Dizzy with the profits from Saint-Domingue's agriculture, the French and their colonials imported so many African laborers that whites constituted less than 6 percent of the population in the island colony. There are different estimates of the population of Saint-Domingue on the eve of revolution, but they all skew approximately the same way: anywhere from 30,000 to 40,000 whites, 28,000–37,000 free people of color, and perhaps 450,000–500,000 slaves. Some researchers have suggested a higher number of slaves; it is likely that they were somewhat undercounted, as there was a small head tax for them imposed on their owners, but there seems to be something of a consensus around half a million. About two-thirds of the slaves had been born in Africa; in the years 1785–89 alone, 150,000 African captives were brought to the colony. None of the slaves, apparently, were of "mixed race." That such a large population of free people of color—approximately the same size as the white population—had been created in less than a century is an indicator of how commonly white men took up with women of color.

No comparably sized piece of West African ground had ever sustained anything approaching the population of Saint-Domingue. It was the densest concentration of Africans that had ever been assembled. In the growers' and merchants' haste to import volumes of slaves, people were grabbed wherever they could be obtained. Coming from diverse regions of Africa, these many slaves brought with them a wide range of knowledge and experience. Some were simple farmers from isolated forest patches; others were sophisticated urbanites from regions that had been commercial crossroads for centuries, if not millennia; still others had carried guns in organized African armies. Some were from the Islamized Senegambia, though they were not necessarily Muslims themselves, since Islam forbids selling other Muslims into slavery but allows selling infidels. Some—the largest single group—were from the Kongo, which had ostensibly been Catholicized but in practice had incorporated the symbols of Catholicism into its own ancient religion, a practice Kongos would follow all over the New World. Still others were from places where only traditional African religion had ever been practiced since the dawn of time. It presented a formidable new set of cultural issues to be negotiated in the slave barracks.

There might be slaves from a number of different African nations on any given plantation. They had to learn to work together under what was effectively military discipline, working in coordinated gangs and living together in a labor camp, their day regulated by bells, the movements of their work coordinated by rhythmic song. They developed a creolized New World religion—*vodou*, which, though it showed a dominant influence from the religion of Ardra (Dahomey) and the strong influence of Kongo, made a place for the various African traditions that informed it, at some point becoming a system of *nanchons* (nations). This was incorporated into a form which borrowed such elements of the Catholic ritual as the Africans cared to use. These nanchons retain distinct features into the present day, so that a houngan will keep both a *rada* and a *petro* altar in his house, embodying two different traditions that are seen as distinct components of a single practice.

Africans in Saint-Domingue had reached such a critical mass that they could formulate their own composite religious system to suit their needs. In Cuba today, the traditions have remained distinct, in spite of their frequent crossings with each other. In Brazil, there are various mixed traditions. But in present-day Haiti, there is an *e pluribus unum* of African religions, with room to accommodate the complexities of different traditions within the single system known as vodou.

Perhaps two-thirds of the whites of Saint-Domingue were concentrated in the colony's cities. Cap Français would have seemed like a provincial rat hole to most Parisians, but it was the closest thing to Parisian style in the still-raw New World. Though France had decrepit financial and social systems, the arts, sciences, technology, culture, and fashions of its elite were the envy of eighteenth-century Europe. The plantations of Saint-Domingue had the best agricultural equipment available. Small though they were, Cap Français and Port-au-Prince were both bigger towns than New Orleans, and Saint-Domingue had newspapers before Cuba or Louisiana did. The latest psychic fads came, too: colonists experimented with séances, spiritism, magnetism, and mesmerism, some elements of which found their way into the black spiritual world of Saint-Domingue as well.

Besides the numerous gambling dens, dancehalls, and brothels, there were cafés, cabarets, Masonic lodges, literature societies, and grand masked balls. Though Saint-Domingue was overwhelmingly a rural plantation society, there were playhouses in eight towns of Saint-Domingue. Provincial casts and touring companies entertained the urbanites of Saint-Domingue with Parisian *opéra bouffe*—comic opera, whose origins were in the Neapolitan *commedia del'arte*, though in Saint-Domingue a theater might have to make do with an orchestra of six players. . . . There were concerts by military bands and numerous balls. Port-au-Prince had three theater companies. . . . Shops sold sheet music and instruments.[24]

This world would burn to the ground.

&

The single most informative source about life in Saint-Domingue is the work of M. L. E. Moreau de St.-Méry, previously quoted in this chapter. Born in Martinique in 1750, the son of a magistrate who died young and left him penniless, Moreau went to Paris at the age of nineteen, where he became a gendarme and studied law. Arriving in Cap Français in 1772, he practiced law and began connecting with the city's elite via his enthusiastic participation in Freemasonry, becoming president of the Saint-Jean de Jérusalem écossaise (Scottish St. John of Jerusalem) lodge. In 1781, he married Louise-Catherine Milhet, a daughter of Jean Milhet, which made him a member of a family with heroic status in the French colonies. Milhet was the exiled New Orleans merchant who had traveled from New Orleans on a useless mission to plead Louisiana's case to France in 1765; one of the anti-Ulloa conspirators, he had served a prison sentence in Havana's Morro Castle. Moreau became connected socially through his wife's two well-married sisters, both of whose husbands were founding members of the Cercle des Philadelphes (Circle of Brotherly Love), a *société de pensée* of which Moreau became a member.

After practicing law in the colony for eight years, he was appointed a judge. Finding no single code that compiled French colonial law, he embarked on a project to create one. This was no mere technical matter. Having an independent, coherent body of law was essential if the colonists were to control their own destiny. All over the hemisphere, businessmen were yearning to be free of the trade restrictions imposed by the metropolis. The North American colonies had already rebelled, and were winning their independence.

Slavery had been a part of human history forever. Only at the time of massive sugar plantations in the Americas did a movement begin to eradicate slavery, an idea unthinkable before the mid-eighteenth century. The fever for abolition was growing in England and beginning to find adherents in France. To protect the institution of slavery that was essential to Antillean prosperity, it might soon be necessary to have a separate body of law for the colonies. Moreau's research led him to investigate the colonial archives of Saint-Domingue, Martinique, Guadeloupe, and St. Lucia, then to travel back to France to do archival work in Paris and Versailles, where his Masonic connections gave him entry to the highest levels of society. The first of the six volumes of his *Laws and Constitutions of the Leeward French Colonies in the Americas* was published in 1784. By then, he was the best-versed historian of the colony and the most knowledgeable scholar of colonial law. He returned to Saint-Domingue from Paris in 1787, where he made his only visits—brief ones—to the west and the south of Saint-Domingue. He returned to Paris, where through his Masonic connections he received a post at the new Musée de l'Homme and worked politically toward the establishment of an independent legislature for Saint-Domingue.

∽∾∾

Louis XVI's support with money, materiel, and manpower was decisive in the success of the American Revolution. It included, during the October 1779 siege of Savannah, the crucial participation of some 750 free colored troops from Saint-Domingue. In Haiti, it is generally believed that future leaders of the Haitian Revolution participated in that campaign. There is no documentation to support that belief, but there wouldn't be: virtually all governmental archives in Haiti were burned during the nineteenth and even the early twentieth century, leaving little primary historical documentation within the country. At Savannah, their opposition included black troops who had escaped from slavery to fight for the British, many of whom evacuated with the British when they left Georgia.[25] Some fled into Florida, where they lived in marronage among the Indians.[26]

In Europe, the outcome of the American Revolution was seen as a victory for France, which had sided with the Americans. But, ironically, Britain became more prosperous than ever after losing its North American colony, while France was destabilized. Against a backdrop of food shortages and riots at home, France's involvement in the American Revolution had been spectacularly costly and had done much to leave France, which still had no national bank, insolvent yet again. Moreover, the American struggle against Britain inspired France's wealthy colonial subjects to move toward independence.

In a move that would be Louis XVI's undoing, he called in 1788 for the first meeting in 175 years of the advisory body known as the Estates General, largely to discuss how to address the debts incurred in the American war. Moreau de St.-Méry was elected a representative. When the Estates General convened, representatives of the Domingan planters showed up uninvited, and Moreau made common cause with them.

The issue of slavery in the colonies was taken up at once. Saint-Domingue accounted for some 40 percent of French foreign trade,[27] thus making France's economy dependent on slave labor. As was the French metabolism: Saint-Domingue had pioneered the cultivation of coffee in the New World and was the world's leading producer of the tasty drug, which, thanks to its plentiful supply, had become available to the masses in France. The Société des Amis des Noirs, or Society of Friends of the Blacks, was founded in May 1788 and, inspired by British abolitionism, unsuccessfully lobbied and tried to build public support for the abolition of slavery. They were opposed and outmaneuvred by the Club Massiac, the pro-slavery planters' caucus, of which Moreau was an important member.

On June 20, 1789, the members of the Estates General, in a revolutionary move, declared themselves a National Assembly. The planters, who had been pushing for independence on the American model, suddenly found themselves enmeshed in a European revolution that might go against their interests if it led to the emancipation of their human property. Their ally Moreau de St.-Méry, defender of slavery against the Society of Friends of the Blacks, was a revolutionary, indeed a minor hero of the fall of the Bastille. On July 27, 1789, Moreau was elected vice president of the Paris Commune. As one of the Electors of Paris, he twice addressed Louis XVI.[28] For three days, he liked to recall, he was king of Paris.[29]

Suddenly, France was a nation, as per the Declaration of the Rights of Man and Citizen: "The source of all sovereignty resides in the nation." Not in the king, but in the nation. But did the nation include the colonies? Or the free people of color, or the slaves? Not all the revolutionaries in mother France assumed that *égalité* would apply to slaves overseas. For the planters, it meant something rather more like what we now call free trade.

The American Revolution was a political revolution, but not a social one—an independence movement for colonies tired of mercantile restrictions that left slavery not merely intact but strengthened, while establishing lasting political institutions. By contrast, the French Revolution changed society forever, but could not establish permanent political institutions. In the colony of Saint-Domingue, these two contradictory revolutionary impulses collided.

13

THE SINCEREST ATTACHMENT

Our politics for the next twenty years will consist in being afraid of the Jacobins, and what a fear! Every year we will believe ourselves on the verge of '93. You will understand, I hope, the things I will say at my receptions! It's beautiful! Anything that might diminish that fear a little will be seen as supremely moral in the eyes of the nobles and the religious.

—*Stendhal*, The Charterhouse of Parma

Though it took place on a small island remote from the centers of power, the Haitian Revolution was the most radical revolution of a revolutionary era. It aimed squarely at destroying slavery—even if the goal of full abolition, never before achieved and barely imagined, may not have been entirely clear to all the people engaged in the struggle. A violent response to the slave-powered plantation system that dominated the New World economy, it was the beginning of the end of black slavery in the hemisphere. The fury it unleashed lingers still. In Haiti today, vodouisants say that the spirits called up during that time were so powerful they haven't yet been able to get rid of them.

The conflict in Saint-Domingue was mind-numbingly complicated, involving all four social classes of the colony, who acted not together but antagonistically: (1) the *grands blancs*, or "big whites," the monied class of aristocrats, wealthy merchants, and planters; (2) the *petits blancs*, or "small whites," or, more simply, the common people, a category that included non-landowners from tradesmen to petty criminals; (3) the *gens de couleur*, or free people of color, who were generally the offspring of white men and women of color, or the descendants of such unions; and (4) slaves, by far the most numerous class.

To complicate the story further, the course of revolution was different in each of the three provinces of Saint-Domingue: the North, the West, and the South, which communicated with each other by sea.[1] The North, the richest territory, had the best sugar land and the colony's most important port, Cap Français, the "Paris of the Antilles." The misnamed West would have been more accurately called the Central province, since both the North and South extended farther west than it did; its major city, Port-au-Prince, was new, having been founded only in 1749. The South, the least developed, least populated, and most isolated of the three provinces, is a peninsula that sticks out westward into the Caribbean. Its port city of Jacmel (a Gallicization of the Taíno name of Yáquimo)[2] did much smuggling business with nearby Jamaica and eastern Cuba.

Beginning in 1788, on the eve of the French Revolution, the four social classes of Saint-Domingue fell into open rebellion against each other, one at a time, in a complex dance of death.[3] The first to revolt was the ruling class, the *grands blancs*, who had insisted on sending representatives to the meetings of the Estates General. The second group to rebel was the *petits blancs*; by 1790, feeling excluded from political power and antagonistic toward independence, they were practically in a state of civil war with the big whites.

The free people of color followed quickly. They had good reason for dissatisfaction: the period after the Seven Years War had seen a series of measures to limit their freedoms.[4] A color barrier had been erected and was being made more restrictive, with people of color in Saint-Domingue forbidden to practice a number of professions. They were seated separately at the theater, and as of 1773 were required to adopt African names. "Whites began to use the term 'affranchi,' meaning 'ex-slave,' to refer to all free coloreds, even though a substantial number had been born in freedom."[5]

Despite their social marginalization, the power of free people of color was increasing. Stewart King writes, "Free coloreds served as a small landholding class, filled the ranks of the peasantry, dominated urban small commerce and trades, and filled important roles in the colony's administration, especially in the area of security. The men generally had one of two career paths, and some did quite well, either in the military, or as planters."[6] King characterizes the free planters of color as tending to be conservative, risk averse, and concerned with planning for stability, as opposed to the more entrepreneurial, capitalistic, and profit-seeking military men.[7]

The vast undersupply of white women, and the common intention of male colonists to return wealthy to France and marry their way up in society, meant that, as Hillard d'Auberteuil noted in 1776, "marriages are rare in Saint-Domingue."[8] Concubinage was more convenient. As of April 5, 1778, French people were legally forbidden to marry people of color, though it sometimes happened anyway. Nor did slaves marry each other in the French colonies. In a colony chronically short of women, free women of color developed the profession of sexual consort, which, according to contemporary accounts, they raised to a high art form, entailing lucrative long-term concubinage with a single sugar daddy—the same institution of plaçage that became notorious in New Orleans. Be assured that these women practiced what Europeans called witchcraft, which everywhere finds a natural home in matters of love and sex. After all, they were professional enchantresses. For Moreau de St.-Méry, they were hypersexualized beings with spectacular style:

> The entire being of a Mulatress is given over to voluptuousness, and the fire of that Goddess burns in her heart, never to be extinguished during her life. . . . There is nothing that the most inflamed imagination could conceive, that she has not imagined, divined, done. . . .
>
> The Mulatresses' luxury is taken to the ultimate degree. . . . That luxury consists, almost entirely, of a single thing, clothing, since as a rule there is nothing simpler than the lodging of a Mulatress, which consists of one or at most two rooms. . . .
>
> Like all the Créoles, Mulatresses eat without having fixed hours for their meals, and they live with a remarkable frugality, which without doubt contributes to their youthfulness. . . . Everything is reserved for clothes. The most beautiful things that India produces, the most precious muslins, handkerchiefs, fabrics and cloths . . . rich lace, a multiplicity of jewelry, are employed in profusion; and the desire for those costly things is so insatiable, that one sees a great number of Mulatresses in Saint-Domingue who could wear completely different clothes every day of the year.[9]

The sexual fantasies of a slave owner, or the product of careful observation? Perhaps a bit of both. While his viewpoint was that of his gender, race, and class, Moreau was a meticulous observer, as demonstrated when he wrote about music and dance. The innumerable testimonies and complaints in Saint-Domingue, Havana, and New Orleans about free women of color living as concubines or shorter-term sex workers attest to the commonality of the practice. But it's also certain that such an occupation was by no means universal among free women of color and that many of them detested the stigma of being prostitutes. Kimberly S. Hanger has documented various legal cases in Spanish New Orleans occasioned by free women of color taking umbrage at being insulted this way.[10]

Unlike the white planters, the free people of color in Saint-Domingue had no dream of returning to France. They were already where they were going and were determined to make it work. Their economic success prompted their white competitors to promulgate a wave of laws to repress them. Their clout can be seen in a figure: they owned a significant portion—estimated by one scholar as high as 30 percent—of the colony's slaves.[11] Their demands did not include freedom for the slaves, but more freedom for themselves.

Vincent Ogé, a French-educated free mulatto son of a wealthy planter, pleaded his class's cause before France's National Assembly, to no avail. In frustration, Ogé led an armed revolt, bankrolled by British abolitionists and using arms purchased in the United States, in October 1790. It was brutally suppressed, and four months later, Ogé and coconspirator Jean-Baptiste Chavannes (who had advised making common cause with the slaves, something Ogé rejected) were broken on the wheel and their heads displayed on posts at the city gates, while nineteen other conspirators were hung. This was sensational news in France, where the hyperactive Parisian theater world mounted tragedies about Ogé.

In Saint-Domingue, each social group was thus making its own separate version of insurrection. Masters armed their slaves to fight on their behalf. But if slaves could fight, why shouldn't they fight against, rather than for, their masters? "Men are born and remain free and equal in rights" read the first article of the Declaration of the Rights of Man and Citizen. When those words reached Saint-Domingue, they caused a social earthquake. The Société des Amis des Noirs seemed very big and powerful when viewed from across the Atlantic; conservatives saw it as a British plot to undermine France. Pamphlets declaring all men equal clashed with the underlying principle of the slave-driven plantation economy that was the colony's entire livelihood, as well as with the second-class status and increasing repression of the free people of color.

During all this time the slaves had made no move. But when they did erupt, it was in a premeditated fashion that was organized according to military principles, African style.

⁓◈⁓

The revolt was preceded by a series of secret nighttime assemblies of slaves representing major plantations in the North. On August 14, 1791 (the usually cited date; Laurent Dubois suggests it may have been August 21),[12] the plan for a coordinated rebellion was finalized at an assembly attended by some two hundred delegates. Many of them were black overseers who drove the work gangs and were allowed to handle weapons. This meeting terminated with a vodou ceremony, said to have been presided over by the rebel leader Boukman Jetty (some sources say Dutty). The only contemporary account of the event, written in 1793–94 by Antoine Dalmas (who was not present) and published in 1814, describes it like this:

> Before executing their plan, they celebrated a kind of fête or sacrifice, in the middle of a wooded, uncultivated ground on the Choiseul plantation, called *Caïman* [Alligator], where the negroes assembled in very great number. A completely black pig, surrounded with fetishes, loaded down with offerings each more bizarre than the other, was the holocaust offered to the all-powerful genie of the black race. The religious ceremonies that the negroes practiced in cutting the pig's throat, the eagerness with which they drank the pig's blood, and their desire for the prize that each one wanted to possess, a kind of talisman, that, according to them, would render them invulnerable, all serve to characterize the African.[13]

Later accounts added that the ceremony had taken place during a violent storm with lightning, thunder, and fierce wind, as well as a speech that Boukman is said to have given, whose key phrase is known to Haitians today: *couté la libeté, qui palé coeur tous nous*—listen to liberty, speaking in all our hearts. Vodou provided a method of organization and a sustaining faith for the rebellion, and the ceremony at Bois Caïman (Alligator Woods) is the founding legend of the nation of Haiti.

Boukman is not a French name, nor is it African. The troublemaking slave Boukman is generally believed to have come from Jamaica. Saint-Domingans were not supposed to be importing Jamaican slaves, but, as Dubois points out, British traders would circumvent the *exclusif* and the shortage of hard coin by trading slaves to Domingan colonists. The exchange was usually for sugar (which Saint-Domingue produced cheaper than Jamaica, mainly because its food supplies were cheaper than the provisions Britain sold Jamaica) and coffee (of which Saint-Domingue was the world's leading exporter): "Among the slaves the Jamaicans sold this way were some they especially wished to get rid of because they were rebellious."[14]

On August 22, 1791, the slaves began burning and killing across the colony's northern province. By the next day, there were between one and two thousand rebel slaves in action. By the end of the month, there were fifteen thousand. By November, there may have been as many as eighty thousand. Whites were slaughtered, and the magnificent mansions and expensive agricultural facilities were reduced to smoke and ashes. The rebels, writes Carolyn Fick, "took care to destroy . . . not only the cane fields, but also the manufacturing installations, sugar mills, tools and other farm equipment, storage bins, and slave quarters; in short, every material manifestation of their existence under slavery and its means of exploitation."[15]

The ferocity of the massacre was astounding. Atrocities were described that have become a part of the standard lore, repeated in fearful tones throughout the hemisphere. White families slaughtered, white women raped on top of the bodies of their husbands, a carpenter placed on his boards and sawed in half. Did these things actually happen? The source of some of this seems to have been survivors' testimony as related by the planters' representatives to the French National Assembly, in a pamphlet widely read in France and quickly published in English in London, where it sold like hotcakes. "*Their standard was the body of a white infant impaled upon a stake*" (italics in original).[16] The baby on a pike also appears in a contemporary account published by the Jamaican planter Bryan Edwards.

That the carnage was cruel and widespread, even sadistic, there is no doubt, and sexual violation was ever a part of warfare, but perhaps some of the more symbolic atrocities were part of another phenomenon: the theatrically perfect image of creatively murdered babies seems to be an old part of arousing a populace to war. The grand example is perhaps the blood libel, the claim that Jews made their matzo from the blood of Christian babies.

Those murdered babies have traveled through history. In 1991, when President George H. W. Bush wanted to go to war against Saddam Hussein, the Kuwaiti government's U.S. public relations firm of Hill and Knowlton brought a teenage actress named "Nariyah," in reality the daughter of the Kuwaiti ambassador, to tell Congress and the media an entirely fabricated story of babies being yanked off respirators. People always seem ready to believe such things, as per New Orleans police chief Eddie Compass's flipped-out post-Katrina declaration on *The Oprah Winfrey Show* that babies were being raped in the Superdome.

Regardless of whether it actually existed or not, the white baby on a pike at the Gallifet plantation in Saint-Domingue became the slave owners' standard, part of the legend of the Saint-Domingue uprising. It was widely disseminated and framed the issue for contemporary observers as well as future historians. It resonated powerfully in the South as proof of the innate violence of the savage Negro.

The violence of the Haitian Revolution echoed the madness of the French Revolution, part of a well-documented history of French massacres and atrocities that goes back to the time of the Frankish king Clovis. On September 2, 1792, in an event remembered as the September Massacre, some twelve hundred prison inmates in Paris were murdered by a mob following the exhortations of Georges-Jacques Danton. As violence against royalists continued, Marie Antoinette's First Lady of the Bedchamber, the Princesse de Lamballe, was decapitated by a mob. The story was told and retold in greatly exaggerated detail, as in this 1908 biography, which I select for the pleasure of its prose style:

> Her head was carried in triumph through Paris on a pike, her heart upon another, her body dragged after: dancing crowds, shrieking "La Lamballe! La Lamballe!" surrounded it. M. de Lamotte, driving down a street, met the awful crowd, which stopped him, showed the ghastly trophy, and forced him to salute it. . . . The shop of a famous *perruquier* was passed, one who had often coiffed the Princesse in happier days, and some fiends in the mob shouted that he should dress the head again, and rouge the dead lips and cheeks, for they would carry their prize to Antoinette in her prison, and it was necessary she should recognise her friend. The wretched hairdresser was obliged to obey, and performed his task so well that the beautiful face was almost lifelike.

Though that story became part of the legend of the French Revolution, it appears that, decapitation apart perhaps, none of it actually happened. From there we pass to this fantastical, and clearly imaginary, vision of sexualized atrocity in Saint-Domingue conjured by a creole planter named Drouin de Bercy in a book he published in Paris in 1814:

> At Petite Ance, the inhabitants of the Cap [Français] delivered more than one hundred white women and maidens that were all nude, their feet in irons and in a posture that could not oppose any resistance to the lascivious lubricity of those monsters who fell on them by the thousands.[17]

This fantasy resonates through the ages, fueled by the belief that slavery as practiced by whites against blacks was a benign, even benevolent, institution, but were slavery to be practiced by blacks against whites, it would be a crime against nature. Whenever the point had to be made, whether in Saint-Domingue or in South Carolina, it was always, it seems, driven home with an image of sexual violation of white women by black men. Which was exactly the opposite of what went on, during the entire existence of the institution of slavery.

One aspect of the uprising dumbfounded the planters:

> Those slaves, who had been most kindly treated by their masters, were the very soul of the insurrection. It was *they* who betrayed and delivered those humane masters to the assassin's sword; it was they who seduced and stirred up to revolt the gangs disposed to fidelity; it was they who massacred all who refused to become their accomplices. What a lesson for the *Amis des Noirs!*[18]

The slaves who had been treated the least inhumanely were insufficiently grateful for the kindness which slavery had bestowed on them. According to the planters, the slaves were happy as could be before the Amis des Noirs started stirring up trouble. These planters pled their case to the National Assembly:

> Let any man, of feeling and information, compare the deplorable state of the negroes, in Africa, with the mild and comfortable lot they enjoy in our colonies; . . . let him recall the regulations which governed our negroes before they were seduced and alienated from us; provided against every want; supplied with accommodations, unknown in the greater part of the cottages of Europe; secure in the enjoyment of their properties; (*for, they had property, and it was sacred;*) nursed, in times of sickness, with an expence and an attention which may be sought in vain in the much-boasted hospitals of England: protected, respected, in the infirmities of old age; at ease in respect to their children, their families, and their affections; subjected to a labour calculated according to the strength of each individual. . . . The sincerest attachment connected the master and his slaves. We slept in security in the midst of men that were become our children, and many of us had neither locks nor bars to our houses.
>
> Not, Sirs, that we would disguise to you, that there did exist, among the planters, a very small number of hard and ferocious masters. But what was the lot of these wicked men? Blasted in their fame, detested by

men of character, outcasts of society, discredited in their business, they lived in disgrace and dishonour, and died in misery and despair.[19]

Which seems to boil down to: but we were so good to our slaves.

The slaves felt otherwise. The French soldiers were mystified by the slaves' readiness to die. But in Saint-Domingue and elsewhere, slaves had long committed suicide as a form of resistance, sure that they would return to Guinea. Fated to spend their lives in a prison camp, being systematically overworked to death, slaves on a sugar plantation were already *zombi*. That they would make ointments and cast spells to render themselves immune to bullets may have seemed absurd to the French; on the other hand, how else could a fighter with a machete bring himself to face a man with a gun? Moreover, the knowledge that the slaves would not yield was a tremendous psychological weapon that terrified the enemy. But the black soldiers did not rely solely on that; some of them made thick vests stuffed with cotton as body armor.[20] (Two decades later, the use of cotton breastworks was one of the famous features of the Battle of New Orleans, in which a number of Domingans of color participated.)

Saint-Domingue had had no major slave rebellion in the 1770s and 1780s. Boukman's uprising came as a shock, but not an unexpected one; the fear of slave rebellion was a constant dread throughout the history of the plantation complex in the hemisphere. The revolt in Saint-Domingue was not an anomaly as much as it was an apotheosis: the thing slave owners had been dreading all along actually happened. And could happen again, wherever there were plantations.

Refugees began leaving Saint-Domingue, as they would do in stages throughout the years that the conflict dragged on. Many of this first wave of emigrants—possibly as many as twenty thousand—went up the Atlantic seaboard to the new United States, telling their harrowing tales in the port towns of Savannah, Charleston, Norfolk, Baltimore, Philadelphia, New York, and Boston, among others.[21] A family of Huguenots who had settled in Saint-Domingue arrived as refugees in Princeton, New Jersey, in 1791: the Tulanes, whose son Paul, born there in 1801, would later endow New Orleans's university that bears his family's name.

Some refugees went to Louisiana, but it was not a first choice. It was harder to get across the Gulf of Mexico to New Orleans from Saint-Domingue than to go up the Atlantic seaboard (and it would have been harder to get back to Saint-Domingue when the revolution was put down, though that was not to happen). Besides, Louisiana was under the government of the unwelcoming Spanish, who prohibited the Domingans from entering with their slaves. Looking back at that era, Berquin-Duvallon wrote in 1803: "Without that rigorous intervention, they would have come in large numbers and established themselves [in New Orleans], bringing the remains of their ruined fortunes, if they could have come with those faithful domestics whom they would never have given up."[22]

Boukman was killed in November 1791, and his head displayed on a stake in the central plaza of Cap Français. His supporters celebrated his immortality, dancing a calenda in his honor that lasted three days. That same month, a gang of *petits blancs* burned and plundered two-thirds of the wooden city of Port-au-Prince, which went up in flames as easily as New Orleans had burned three years before.

The town of Cap Français escaped the torch, but only barely, remaining under French control until it too was invaded, in June 1793, and burned pursuant to a general massacre of the citizenry by three thousand invading slaves. It would take until January 1, 1804, for the Republic of Haiti to declare independence. But Saint-Domingue, the world's number-one producer of sugar, coffee, and indigo, fell abruptly from the international market in 1791, kicking the struts out of the French economy and creating a windfall for Cuba, where the sugar industry experienced phenomenal growth as it rushed to expand in order to take up the slack.[23]

∽∞∾

On January 21, 1793, as the revolution intensified in France, King Louis XVI went to the guillotine, as did thousands more during the Terror. Seizing the opportunity created by France's disarray, Britain and Spain made an unprecedented alliance. Both hoping to grab a piece of Saint-Domingue, they declared war on France, causing considerable tension in French-speaking, Spanish-ruled Louisiana. Britain declared war in February; with the exception of a short but significant, and tense, period of peace, it would remain at war with France for the next twenty-two years. In September, under the leadership of William Pitt, Britain sent an invasion to the French West Indies, hoping to reinstate slavery, take over the wealth of the Antilles, and smash French naval power. They were welcomed—invited, even—by many of the white planters, who had been making overtures to the British since well before Boukman's uprising, and who saw in them deliverance from the abolitionist revolutionaries. The British occupied all of the West, and much of the South, of Saint-Domingue.

The goal of the planters was free trade, achieved through independence from France. As with their counterparts in the American South, liberty for them meant the freedom to own slaves. For their part, the slaves expected to have a king; it was widely believed by them that the French king had authorized their emancipation, or, variously, decreed three free days a week, but that his desires had been thwarted by the slave masters and treacherous subalterns.

The French Revolution provided the ideological context within which a massive slave uprising became a full-scale revolution of its own. "The results of the American revolutions were, broadly speaking, countries carrying on much as before, only minus the political control of the British, Spanish, and Portuguese," writes Eric Hobsbawm.[24] Not so in the case of Saint-Domingue, which felt the gale force of social upheaval of the French Revolution.

In June 1793, the radical Jacobins came to power in France. That same month, black rebels, responding to a call from the Jacobin French commissioner in Saint-Domingue, Leger-Felicité Sonthonax, attacked Cap Français, burning the city in the process as thousands of whites fled for Baltimore. On August 29, Sonthonax proclaimed full emancipation of slaves in the North, effective immediately. This was an unprecedented and shocking step, and a daring tactic. With it, Sonthonax brought the slaves over to fight for revolutionary France against the white colonists, who wanted to keep them enslaved, and against their allies, the British.

In declaring emancipation, Sonthonax was responding to the slave rebellion, but also apparently acting on his own revolutionary principles. By doing so, he accomplished the French Revolution's most far-reaching, unprecedented, and infrequently noted achievement: full abolition of slavery. Immediately, with no period of transition, people who had been chattel property were suddenly full citizens, while people who had achieved great wealth by owning other people saw their fortunes turn to dust.

To much of the world, it seemed the French had gone mad in the name of reason. While their prosperity went up in smoke, they busied themselves with changing the calendar. On October 24, 1793, the Jacobin government of France adopted a new system in which years would be numbered with Roman numerals; year I began on the autumnal equinox of September 22, 1792. The twelve months were named not for the ancient gods of superstition, but for seasonal phenomena: April was Florial, July was Thermidor, et cetera. Months were divided into three ten-day weeks, with leap days to make up the discrepancy at year's end. The day was divided into ten hours, each consisting of one hundred minutes, each minute containing one hundred seconds. New decimal clocks were made.[25] The decimal day didn't catch on—though it drove such

French as were aware of clocks crazy until it was discontinued in 1795. The restructured calendar lasted for twelve years, until Bonaparte killed it.

On February 4, 1794, in Paris, the National Convention approved the abolition of slavery in all French territories, confirming Sonthonax's action. Sixty-nine years before Abraham Lincoln would issue his Emancipation Proclamation under the duress of war, the French revolutionaries issued theirs. It was unambiguous about the point the Founding Fathers of the United States had maintained a discreet silence on: "All men, without distinction of color, domiciled in the colonies, are French citizens, and they enjoy all rights assured under the Constitution."

In Paris, the abolition of slavery was celebrated by an event at the Temple of Reason,[26] formerly the Cathedral of Notre-Dame; the religious statuary had been smashed and replaced by likenesses of Rousseau, Voltaire, and Benjamin Franklin.

More slave owners fled Saint-Domingue.

✎

Born in Saint-Domingue of an African father, the freed slave Toussaint Bréda had been raised Catholic. He was about five feet two inches tall, and, unlike most blacks in the colony, he could read. He had come into contact with the work of the antislavery philosopher Abbé Raynal, along with other literature of the Enlightenment, and was a close-up observer of the revolutionary debate that occupied the whites. He was thus a participant in the European intellectual currents of his time, as well as heir to the African traditions brought to the island. Known for his upright moral character, he had helped his ex-master's family escape to the United States when the massacre of 1791 was unleashed. At the time of the revolution, he was a free man of color who had accumulated some money. He played a minor role in the 1791 revolt, serving under rebel general George Biassou. In 1793, already fifty years old, he came to prominence by forging a disciplined rebel army out of raw, poorly equipped slave troops, under the name he had adopted: Toussaint Louverture, "the

"Your most humble and obedient servant, Toussaint Louverture" in Louverture's hand, an example of fine penmanship and ironic language from the great revolutionary.

opening." At the head of six hundred men, he was commissioned a colonel by the Spanish.

The shifting alliances of the war were complicated: big whites, small whites, free coloreds, slaves, French, Spanish, and British. Toussaint, along with other slave leaders, fought under the banner of Spain, believing it their best hope for freedom. Accustomed through African tradition to monarchical government, they were perhaps more comfortable allying with the king of Spain than with a revolutionary nation that had killed its king. But after the National Assembly of France ratified Sonthonax's emancipation proclamation, Toussaint switched sides, swearing allegiance to France, and quickly gained in power, becoming the leader of the colony. The next seven years in Saint-Domingue is essentially the story of Toussaint in control, flying the French flag, trying to build a stable, emancipated, multiracial society, and repelling all invaders.

The southern United States was in a panic. The slaves of Saint-Domingue had risen up and killed not only their masters, but slavery itself. If the same thing had happened in the United States, we would never have had President Thomas Jefferson.

14

DANCE, BOATMAN, DANCE

In fixing the Unit of Money, these circumstances are of principal importance.

I. That it be of *convenient size* to be applied as a measure to the common money transactions of life.
II. That its parts and multiples be in *an easy proportion* to each other, so as to facilitate the money arithmetic.
III. That the Unit and its parts, or divisions, be *so nearly of the value of some of the known coins,* as that they may be of easy adoption for the people.

The Spanish Dollar seems to fulfill all these conditions.

—*Thomas Jefferson, 1784*

Prefiguring the increasingly heated disputes that would ultimately cause the nation to break in two, the first major sectional quarrel in the new United States was over New Orleans and the use of the Mississippi, in 1786.

The confederation that was the United States—as yet it had no president, no constitution, and a weak national government—tried negotiating for rights to use the Mississippi River. The Spanish offered them the use of the port of New Orleans, but not the right of navigation on the Mississippi. The specie-starved merchants of the northeast were eager to have access to the

port from the Gulf, but this arrangement would have frozen out the Southern states, whose agricultural products would not be able to move downriver.
This had the effect of setting the North and the South of the United States
in direct opposition. All eight Northern states backed the deal, but all five
Southern states rejected it; with one vote short of a two-thirds majority, it did
not pass.

In 1789, Spain permitted merchandise to come downriver to New Orleans,
but at a high tariff. Meanwhile, New Orleans was the destination for sailing
ships of "Private Adventurers from New-York, Philadelphia, and Baltimore
[who] carry on a tolerable Trade with this Place." So wrote John Pope, who
visited New Orleans in 1792, also noting that "they have an advance [profit]
of Cent per Cent on their goods, which are nevertheless cheaper than Spanish importations."[1]

Kentucky, carved out of Virginia and populated by Virginians, became a
state in 1792. The following year, Spain reduced the tariff for goods coming
down the river, and the year after that, forty-six boats floated down the Mississippi to New Orleans. The American downriver penetration of Louisiana
had begun. The largest number of boats started from Louisville (named for the
doomed Louis XVI, in honor of his aid to the American Revolution) down the
Ohio River, which empties into the Mississippi. Most were flatboats—essentially, big rafts with decks to provide some shade and protect the merchandise.
Fifteen feet wide and fifty to eighty feet long, requiring something like a five-
man crew, the larger ones could carry up to a hundred tons.[2] It was necessary
to sit as high in the water as possible, because the turbulent Mississippi was
full of sunken trees poking up underwater and vibrating with the current,
ready to punch a hole in the bottom of a boat.

Because there was no way to float upriver, flatboats were necessarily dis-
posable. After making the trip down to New Orleans, they were broken up
and sold for lumber, a practice that dated back to the earliest days of civilization, when boatmen descending the Tigris and the Euphrates in Mesopotamia
in animal-skin boats with wooden frameworks did much the same. There are
still houses standing in New Orleans made of the timber from flatboats. Much
of the wood also found its way into the banquettes, the wooden sidewalks of
New Orleans, which rotted away regularly and had to be maintained with
fresh boards.

It took about thirty-five days to walk back to Kentucky. Some of the
boatmen rode back on horses purchased in New Orleans. Others, especially if
they came from Pittsburgh, a couple thousand miles upriver, preferred to take
a boat to Philadelphia or Baltimore and come around by land; an 1804 French

traveler wrote that "they prefer this 20 or 30 day passage from New Orleans via one of these two ports and the 300 mile journey by land. This way is not so difficult as the route by land alone."[3]

In not a few cases, boatmen remained down South to try their luck. The continuing drain on skilled boatmen helped reinforce a certain amateurish quality to this small-scale enterpreneurship, in which a farmer might double as a boat captain and commodities merchant. Building a boat became an annual expense for a Kentucky farmer. After the advent of the steamboat, flatboat traffic actually increased: flatboats were still a practical method for getting goods downriver, but the steamboat made the return trip easier for the boatmen. Not a few slaves labored as boatmen as well; they, too, traveled down to New Orleans and back up, picking up information about the world while locked up for the night with someone else's slaves.

Unlike flatboats, keelboats could travel back upstream.[4] Lighter and smaller (fifteen to thirty tons), they had oars and were more maneuverable than flatboats, but much of the time going upstream, they had to be warped, cordelled, or bushwhacked. Warping was a laborious practice that entailed attaching a rope to an eye on the bow of the boat. The rope was then wrapped around a convenient tree by boatmen going ahead in a skiff, then pulled along by the boatmen, a thousand feet or so at a shot, then the process was repeated. Cordelling was similar to warping; the boat was towed along by boatmen walking on land, through whatever obstacles presented themselves. The third possibility, bushwhacking, meant grabbing overhanging branches and pulling the boat along. Edith McCall quotes from a history of St. Louis about the return trip from New Orleans, a distance of some 1,250 river miles: "Even with the assistance of sails, a keelboat could not make the ascent in less than 70 or 80 days."[5]

Besides flatboats and keelboats, there were heavy barges of approximately the same capacity as flatboats. Outfitted with sails, they could travel upstream, though they, too, often had to be warped, which required an enormous amount of manpower—as many as thirty to thirty-five boatmen; they could make only six to eight miles in a day. In 1808, the Yankee traveler Christian Schultz encountered a barge on the Mississippi that was proceeding upstream from New Orleans to Natchez. It had left New Orleans forty-two days previously, and had managed to go 165 miles upriver.[6]

It was the most grueling kind of work, and the boatmen who did it—those who were not slaves—were not the most refined sort of people. Kentucky was an almost entirely rural state at this time. Notorious in New Orleans for their crudeness, the "Kaintucks"—a name applied indiscriminately to Anglo-

Americans who came down the river—were the first Americans many of the Creoles saw, and the impression was not positive. Which is not to say that the Kaintucks didn't spend a fair amount of money drinking, playing cards, and whoring in the pleasure city of New Orleans. Many were green; it became something of a rite of passage for young men in Ohio, Illinois, Missouri, and Kentucky to go down the river on a flatboat.

⌘

After almost ten years of Governor Miró—nearly double the official five-year term—a new Spanish governor assumed command of Louisiana in December 1791: the Belgian-born François-Louis Héctor y Noyelles, Baron de Carondelet (whose name was, and is, pronounced not French style, *Carondelay*, but Spanish style, *Carondelett*).

Like Ulloa, the baron had previously been posted to Quito, and like Ulloa, he found himself in the delicate position of being a Spanish governor over a French-speaking people at a time of instability. Meanwhile, Saint-Domingue was on fire, with terrifying implications for slave owners everywhere.

Baron Carondelet took office at a time of great revolutionary enthusiasm. Though a number of French royalists escaped to Louisiana, there were also many in the colony who took pride in seeing France lead the nations of Europe in overthrowing the outdated system of monarchy, a system perfectly exemplified by the Spanish Bourbons. John Pope described a Good Friday procession in which "the Virgin-Mother was dress'd out a-la-mode de Paris, and traitor Judas, for political Reasons, appeared in the Regimental Uniform of a Spanish soldier."[7]

Unrest could conceivably come from two directions: from the Jacobins or from the Negroes, who might work together, as they had in Saint-Domingue. The importation of slaves from the French and British Antilles into Louisiana was already prohibited, but a wary Carondelet increased the penalties for importation on July 25, 1792. This also had the effect of closing Louisiana down to the larger part of refugee immigration from Saint-Domingue, because those who had the means to leave would not come unless they could bring their slaves, which were their wealth.

A group of Louisianans had petitioned the National Assembly of France for citizenship in the new French Republic in 1790. Now Carondelet required a loyalty oath to Spain for arrivals retroactive to that year, and booted out sixty-eight suspected Jacobins, including two respected merchants.[8] One of them, Charles de Pauw, went to Washington, where he spoke to the French minister to the United States, Citizen Edmond Genêt.

Excited by de Pauw's revolutionary zeal, and apparently acting on instructions from Paris, Genêt began a plot to revolutionize Louisiana. This was supported by an American plan for General George Rogers Clark, who had conquered Illinois during the Revolution and was the brother of William Clark (of the Lewis and Clark expedition), to go on an abortive mission to support a conjectured French uprising in Louisiana (a mission undertaken with the knowledge of Secretary of State Thomas Jefferson).

In early 1794, Genêt's Jacobin circle in Philadelphia published an inflammatory pamphlet that was smuggled into Louisiana; I quote a few excerpts, from Charles Gayarré's translation:

LIBERTY, EQUALITY

The Freemen of France to their brothers in Louisiana:
2d year of the French Republic.

The moment has arrived when despotism must disappear from the earth. France, having obtained her freedom, and constituted herself into a republic, after having made known to mankind their rights, after having achieved the most glorious victories over her enemies, is not satisfied with successes by which she alone would profit, but declares to all nations that she is ready to give her powerful assistance to those that may be disposed to follow her virtuous example.

Frenchmen of Louisiana, you still love your mother country; such a feeling is innate in your hearts. The French nation, knowing your sentiments, and indignant at seeing you the victims of the tyrants by whom you have been so long oppressed, can and will avenge your wrongs. A perjured king, prevaricating ministers, vile and insolent courtiers, who fattened on the labors of the people whose blood they sucked, have suffered the punishment due to their crimes. . . .

The hour has struck, Frenchmen of Louisiana; hasten to profit by the great lesson which you have received.

Now is the time to cease being the slaves of a government, to which you were shamefully sold; and no longer to be led on like a herd of cattle, by men who with one word can strip you of what you hold most dear—liberty and property.

The Spanish despotism has surpassed in atrocity and stupidity all the other despotisms that have ever been known. . . .

Compare with your situation that of your friends—the free Americans. Look at the province of Kentucky, deprived of outlets for its products, and yet, notwithstanding these obstacles, and merely through the genial influence of a free government, rapidly increasing its population and wealth, and already presaging a prosperity which causes the Spanish government to tremble. . . .

The peopling of Kentucky has been the work of a few years; your colony, although better situated, is daily losing its population, because it lacks liberty. . . .

Know ye, that your brethren the French, who have attacked with success the Spanish Government in Europe, will in a short time present themselves on your coasts with naval forces; that the republicans of the western portion of the United States are ready to come down the Ohio and Mississippi in company with a considerable number of French republicans, and to rush to your assistance under the banners of France and liberty; and that you have every assurance of success.[9]

As Jacobin clubs formed in various American cities, Carondelet found himself with insufficient Spanish soldiers to repel a French-manned local militia should it revolt. He appealed to the Spanish governor of Natchez, Manuel Gayoso de Lemos, who sent him some three hundred reinforcements. These were mostly English-speaking Americans who had become Spanish citizens; Natchez was a Tory town, where reactionaries had fled the American Revolution.

∽∾

The 1791 census of New Orleans indicated three professional violinists, one *músico* (musician), one *cantor* (singer, presumably for the church), and one *platicante* (a "talker," probably a declaimer). Which is not to say that those were the only musicians in town; dances would have been played by amateurs, or by moonlighting military bandsmen. The same census showed forty-eight people whose occupation was tavern keeper, with half those taverns on the strip along the river. We can figure that there was at least occasional dancing going on in those little taverns; probably it was much as it was in Cuba, where free men of color practiced an artisanal trade by day and supplemented their incomes playing for dances at night.

Now that New Orleans was a city, theater had become a regular part of its life. Productions had been going on sporadically in improvised playhouses since at least 1753, but on October 4, 1792, two Frenchmen opened the first permanent theater in New Orleans, on Calle San Pedro (St. Peter). The Spanish called it El Coliseo, though to French speakers it was Le Spectacle.

By 1793, it was employing quadroon actresses, probably refugees from Saint-Domingue, where the lively theater world had shut down almost immediately with the slave uprising.[10]

Few Domingan planters had chosen to relocate to New Orleans, in part because of the Spanish restrictions against bringing their slaves with them. Theatrical personnel, however, were not wealthy slave owners and thus had no impediment to going to New Orleans. Charleston found itself with Domingan players as well, but the resolutely French-speaking public of New Orleans offered a better audience.

Like Gálvez and Miró before him, Governor Carondelet took a personal interest in the arts. He saw the theater as important to the well-being of the city and, being what we would now call a micromanager, issued regulations detailing when the performance should begin (7:30), when it should end (9:30, in the summer), and how long the intermission should be (ten minutes if during one play, fifteen minutes if between two). His regulations remind us how much work was done by slaves:

> The actor or actress who is not ready to play his or her part shall pay a fine of $6 to the profit of the Royal Treasury and of the Public Works; that if the trouble is due to delay on the part of a workman, hairdresser, etc., he shall be punished with six days' imprisonment, or with a fine of $6 if he is a freeman.[11]

After Spain and France went to war in 1793, Carondelet prohibited the singing of Jacobin songs and the playing of "La Marsellaise" in the theater. But the freeing of the slaves by Sonthonax had considerably dampened Jacobin sentiment in New Orleans, since the prosperity of the town depended on slave labor. Carondelet did his best to keep the French happy by developing the colony economically as much as possible. Working to combat the seditious talk that was entering the town with every ship, he warned constantly of the danger of another Saint-Domingue-style uprising.

La Moniteur de la Louisiane, the first newspaper of New Orleans, appeared in 1794. It was published in French on the only printing press in town by Louis Duclot, a refugee from Saint-Domingue. Carondelet, who needed a political organ, supported its publication and seems to have had a heavy hand in its editorial content. *La Moniteur* published for twenty years and never had more than eighty subscribers. Issues are extremely rare today; the microfilms I have examined are illegible in many places. In an August 25, 1794, issue, an onomatopoetic Latin motto appears below the paper's name, expressing various timbres of rumor: "Bombalio, Clangor, Stridor, Tarantara, Murmur."

New Orleans slowly modernized as it rebuilt from the 1788 fire, though it kept encountering setbacks. In 1793, a yellow fever epidemic hit the city; it was believed to have come from Philadelphia, where it was believed in turn to have come from Saint-Domingue. (Yellow fever hit Philadelphia five summers in a row in the 1790s.) In August 1793, a hurricane damaged the crops. To improve the city's usefulness as a port, in 1794 Carondelet ordered a canal to be dug from the Bayou St. John to the city's ramparts, creating a drainage ditch and a water connection—albeit a slow, shallow one—from Lake Pontchartrain along the Esplanade Ridge portage trail that led to the Mississippi River. Meanwhile, he sent agents into Kentucky to cause trouble, and entered into a conspiracy, never brought to fruition, with the traitorous Colonel James Wilkinson to cause Kentucky to secede from the United States.

In May 1794, another of Carondelet's modernizations arrived, though it took until August to install: a street-lighting system, modeled on Havana's. Manufactured in Philadelphia, the eighty-seven lanterns burned bear oil and were kept lit by night watchmen, called *serenos*, who doubled as a street patrol.[12]

Two hurricanes hit the city in August. Then, on December 8, another catastrophic fire broke out. Even more costly than the previous one, it destroyed the city's entire supply of flour, and there was much looting. The fire damaged 212 buildings. That was fewer than the blaze of 1788, but it took out all the remaining French buildings save the Ursulines' convent (which still stands today, though modified from its original form—the only extant building in New Orleans from the French period). After this second fire, Carondelet's government enforced Spanish building codes that required the use of brick and gave incentives for Spanish-style tile roofs, making for sturdier structures. Now that New Orleans was becoming active as a port, building materials could be brought in. The French Quarter that so delighted travelers to New Orleans in the nineteenth century was called that because French was the language spoken by those who lived there. Some have suggested it should be called the Spanish Quarter, but only thirty-eight of the buildings in the neighborhood today date from the Spanish period.[13]

Relations between the Spanish and French continued to deteriorate. A renewed outbreak of insurrectionary fervor in 1795 saw alarming incidents of arson and civil unrest.

It was no longer possible to get aid from Gayoso de Lemos, [writes Ernest R. Liljegren] and Carondelet did not dare use his soldiers to coerce his subjects. Unchecked, the revolutionary movement approached anarchy; houses were set afire, and quite naturally there was considerable confusion. The mobs attracted to these fires were potentially very dangerous, but the officials were helpless. As there were not sufficient troops to patrol the streets at night, the best that the officials could do was to stay away from the scenes of disorder lest they precipitate a crisis or be assassinated.[14]

Two additional policemen were hired to watch for arson after a fire on May 26,[15] and all along, there was the constant fear that the slaves, inflamed by revolutionary bombalio, clangor, stridor, tarantara, or murmur, would one morning kill their masters.

⸙

Louisiana's agricultural economy crashed in the early 1790s. Spain, after encouraging the growth of a tobacco industry based at Natchitoches, had stopped purchasing the crop. Louisiana's other crop, indigo, was fading under competition from India, and in 1794, the indigo crop failed entirely, eaten by locusts and caterpillars. But two new crops appeared that would bring riches to Louisiana.

In 1793, Secretary of State Thomas Jefferson helped Eli Whitney get a patent for his new invention.[16] The cotton gin, which mechanically removed seeds from the cotton boll, made the cultivation of short-staple (green-seed) cotton in the Deep South practical. In doing so, it doomed generations of African Americans to slavery, an institution many people had hoped was fading. The burgeoning Industrial Revolution in Britain would consume all the cotton the South could grow. The new cotton industry quickly began to make planters rich, culminating in a boom in the 1850s.

Two years after the invention of the cotton gin, Louisiana discovered how to make sugar from local cane. Unlike the sugar-growing islands farther south, Louisiana freezes in the winter. It had long been thought that the seven months' growing season made sugar production unfeasible in Louisiana, since a crop of sugarcane requires some fifteen months of growth and several months of harvest. Louisiana cane juice had successfully been made into molasses, and into tafia. But in 1795, working with a Domingan sugar chemist, the planter Etienne de Boré produced granulated sugar from Louisiana cane.

In Charles Gayarré's telling: "Suddenly the sugar-maker cried out with exultation: 'It granulates!' and the crowd repeated: 'It granulates!'"[17] This bit of legend seems to have come from de Boré himself; a Creole from the Illinois territory of Louisiana, he was not a modest man, and ultimately became New Orleans's first mayor of the American years. The real story was likely less dramatic, resulting from intiatives that had been under way for a while. But de Boré's sugar crop was the famous one: after it brought him $12,000, sugar plantations sprang up along both sides of the Mississippi. By the following year there were ten sugar refineries in operation, as well as twelve distilleries producing tafia, which was abundantly available in the taverns of New Orleans.[18]

Not all sites in Louisiana were equally suitable for sugar. Owners of the most desirable land saw their value increase enormously. Only the wealthy could go into the business; the capital outlay and scale required for a profitable sugar plantation was much higher than for cotton. The abrupt disappearance of Saint-Domingue from the market had left an enormous void which even Jamaica and the fast-accelerating production of Cuba could not completely fill. A sugar aristocracy arose in southern Louisiana, as it had in other sugar colonies. Along the portion of the Mississippi known as the German Coast, some descendants of the Germans who had immigrated in the days of the Law Company became sugar planters, though by now many of them spoke a German-flavored French.

The planters even made money in the off-season from the part of their land that was unusable for sugar: the cypress swamps along their estates' back sides. To ship the sugar out, boxes were needed. Boxes made from the planters' cypress, fed into local lumber mills, supplied not only their own packaging needs but also were a good item of export to the sugar planters of Havana, whose territory had long since been deforested.[19]

More slaves were needed to do the murderous work of sugar, which they did for long hours, ill-clad, exposed to the damp, chilly weather of November and December. The ascent of cotton throughout the South drove the price of slaves up, because supply was tight: fearing the contagion of rebellion, slave importation from the Antilles had been prohibited.

In April 1795, with civic tensions running high in New Orleans, an extensive, well-planned conspiracy to execute a slave rebellion was uncovered at Pointe Coupée (Cut Point), located at a bend upriver from New Orleans. Though no transplanted Domingans participated in the conspiracy, the slaves who did participate were well aware of what had happened in Saint-

Domingue and knew that slavery had been repealed in the French territories.[20] As in Saint-Domingue, the slaves believed the same legend: the king had decreed that they should be freed, but the masters were refusing to declare emancipation.

The center of the conspiracy was the plantation of Julien Poydras, an old-school planter who continued to wear shoes with silver buckles when younger men had switched to shoelaces. His plantation was known for its relatively mild treatment of slaves; it was said that the whip never sounded there. But, as in Saint-Domingue, Poydras's slaves were ungrateful for the kindness of his slavery. The plot extended far beyond Pointe Coupée, all the way up to Natchitoches. Fifty-seven slaves and three whites, thought to be Jacobin rabble-rousers, were convicted. Under heavy pressure from the planters to make an example of the slaves, Carondelet reluctantly ordered a sentence to be carried out in the gruesome, theatrical French style. The twenty-three slaves who were sentenced to death were hung one at a time at various points along the river from Pointe Coupée to New Orleans. Their heads were cut off and nailed on posts, providing a cautionary display that continued for miles. This kind of punishment was not typical of the Spanish government of Louisiana, and Carondelet was later fined for not having gotten the permission of the captain general in Cuba to execute the slaves.[21]

On June 1, Carondelet, following instructions from Madrid, issued a new set of rules for quelling subversion and keeping peace. The welfare of agricultural slaves in Louisiana at this time was little different from the situation described by Major Stoddard in 1812: "The French and Spanish planters, in particular, treat their slaves with great rigor; and this has been uniformly the case from the first establishment of the colony. . . . These planters are extremely ignorant of agricultural pursuits, and of the quantum of labor in the power of a slave to perform in a given time. Few of them allow any clothing to their slaves, or any kind of food, except a small quantity of corn; and even this they are obliged to pound, or grind, while they ought to be at rest."[22] Carondelet issued new regulations requiring somewhat better treatment of slaves—now they would get a barrel of corn a month—apparently hoping to keep them content and thus prevent them from reaching the boiling point:

> Every Slave shall be allowed half an hour to rest at Breakfast, and two
> hours at Dinner time; They shall begin their work at break of day, and
> cease at the entrance of night.

> Every Sunday is their own day, but when the crops or other Business require it, their masters have a right to make them work on Sundays, paying them four rials per day, for the days work. . . .
>
> No person shall punish his Slave with more than Thirty Lashes at one time, under the Penalty of Fifty Dollars, but this punishment may be repeated, as the nature of the crime may require, leaving an interval of one day, between each punishment. . . .
>
> The intrigues, Plotts for running away, and excesses of other kinds committed by slaves generally take rise at their public meetings, and the intermixing of those belonging to different quarters, therefore no Inhabitant shall under the penalty of Ten Dollars, allow upon his Plantation, any Dances, or meetings whatsoever, of slaves belonging to other places. The Dances, and amusements of their own slaves, which shall take place upon Sunday only, shall always cease before night.
>
> No slave shall go beyond the limits of his master's Lands without a pass, under penalty of Twenty Lashes.[23]

With its clear connection to the ideology of Saint-Domingue, the Pointe Coupée conspiracy provoked a new repression on the part of Louisiana slave masters. On June 22, 1795, Carondelet prohibited all entry of slaves to Louisiana as long as the war between Spain and France continued. A month later, Spain made peace with France, so Carondelet issued another regulation to ban the practice.

The American, French, and Haitian revolutions greatly changed the way the usual territory swapping occurred as part of the peace negotiations. Spain had lost all aspirations for the Louisiana colony and began devising its exit strategy, though it would be eight years more before the Spanish colors were taken down. "As a colony, Louisiana was worse than useless to Spain," writes Arthur Whitaker, "but it was still valuable as a diplomatic pawn."[24]

The French wanted Louisiana back, but they were resisted by Spanish foreign minister Manuel Godoy, who controlled the slow-witted Carlos IV's foreign policy (and cuckolded him with the Spanish queen as well). Godoy played the game piece of Louisiana for Spain's advantage, giving France the Spanish part of Santo Domingo instead, which put France in charge of the entire island of La Española, at least in theory, though only a few French military men came to occupy Spanish Santo Domingo.

The United States would not remain a happy neighbor to Spanish Louisiana if its merchants did not have access to the port of New Orleans. Moreover, even as clandestine commerce, the American trade coming downriver was becoming essential to the city's economy. Godoy gave the Americans what they wanted with the Treaty of San Lorenzo of October 27, 1795: free use of the Mississippi and the right to deposit goods in New Orleans for transshipment. The treaty also gave the United States the Natchez Territory, which would be organized three years later into the Mississippi Territory (seized by Gálvez from the British during the American Revolution, it did not include the Mississippi coastal region, which was part of West Florida). That safely accomplished, the following year Godoy offered to trade Louisiana back to France—an offer that France, as of November 1795, under the control of the revolutionary directorate, refused; Spain's price was thought too high.[25] Though the deposit for U.S. goods at New Orleans would not be established until 1798, commerce was already on the upswing. There existed at last, in John G. Clark's words:

> that mobile population and potential source of capital which Spain was unable to provide herself. The sweep of Americans across the Appalachians, which appeared to the Spanish as a threat to New Spain, created the first productive hinterland for New Orleans and ultimately provided that population which would fill up the lands in and around Louisiana.[26]

At last the products of the Mississippi watershed began floating down to market. In the ten years following Kentucky statehood, as Anglo-Americans continued moving westward, an explosion of production and commerce redrew lines of political influence, expanding the power of the United States and dramatically increasing the affluence of New Orleans.

The United States had by then been clandestinely provisioning Louisiana for some time. Though Spanish rules prohibited trade with the Americans, flour shortages had repeatedly compelled the city to engage in illegal commerce with the North Americans. The flour was shipped first to Saint-Domingue, then traded on to New Orleans at a much higher price.

In 1796, New Orleans suffered its first major yellow fever epidemic. The cabildo intervened in the distribution of food "in an effort to stretch existing supplies of flour and rice . . . supervised experiments in which mixtures of rice and flour were baked into bread until an edible combination was finally hit upon."[27] With commerce open, American flour, sold direct down the river, dominated the market in New Orleans by 1801.

A flow in the contrary direction began as well. The United States did not have silver or gold mines, or a standard paper currency. Banks issued notes, the control of which occupied much of the U.S. presidents' energies. One of the great attractions of New Orleans was that Spain supplied it with specie, sinking an annual, albeit irregularly delivered, cash budget into Louisiana to maintain the colony. This coin consistently wound up in the hands of merchants, who ran a trade deficit with the outside world, and an increasing amount of that specie was passing into the United States.

Buyers in Spanish New Orleans paid for American products with Spanish silver dollars, which returned upstream with the boatmen. They in turn used the much-coveted specie to buy manufactured goods from the East. By 1802, writes Whitaker, "it was evident that the more produce the West sold down the river, the more goods it would buy over the mountains."[28] The silver Spanish dollars—not questionable, discountable, paper certificates from banks that might vanish, but hard coin—wound up in the port cities of the Middle Atlantic, who were thus linked by one remove to commerce with New Orleans.

⌁

The most celebrated actress of Saint-Domingue probably began performing in New Orleans in 1795. Mme. Marsan (players in that era were commonly referred to by their surname alone) likely sang in the May 22, 1796, performance of Jean-François Marmontel and André Grétry's one-act comic opera *Sylvain*, the first known performance of opera in New Orleans, though the Duke of Pontalba, who mentions it in a letter, indicates that it had been performed before.[29] (*Sylvain*, a repertory work from the prerevolutionary era, had premiered in Paris twenty-six years earlier.) The troupe consisted not of mere local tradesmen doubling as players, but of skilled, salaried professionals, several of whom had come from Saint-Domingue. They sang comic opera as readily as they played tragedy, and often did so in the same night. Quite possibly, enslaved musicians played in the orchestra, as some had done in Saint-Domingue.

But the money was in dancing, not theater, because New Orleans danced, and danced, and danced. In that same year, 1796, the cabildo opened a city-owned dance hall, assigning a concession to two businessmen, Santiago Bernardo Coquet and José Antonio Boniquet, who agreed to subsidize the theater as part of the deal. Dancing went from 7 P.M. until morning, with a five- or six-piece band, and I wish I knew exactly what instruments those bands consisted of. Dancing had heretofore been at private parties, or informally in taverns, or in the street, or wherever it could be done. Now there was a dance salon, complete with liquor and gambling. It was initially for whites, but soon Saturday was designated as colored night. Ostensibly for free people of color, the dances also attracted slaves, who had sufficient liberty in Spanish New

Orleans to get out to the dance hall on Saturday night, and who could earn their own money and dress well. These dances also attracted white men, lured by the availability of numerous women of color. Because all three of the city's skin-tone castes were present, the dances became known as "tricolor balls."

Relations between the new United States and France deteriorated, arriving at a state of undeclared hostility remembered in military histories as the Quasi War, whose most pressing cause was the damage done to American shipping by French privateers. When Manuel Gayoso de Lemos became governor of Louisiana and West Florida in 1797, he was obliged to prepare New Orleans against possible attack, even as the arrival of the all-important Spanish subsidy for the colony was delayed by the threat of piracy.[30]

Gayoso, the Portuguese-born former governor of Natchez, had trained under O'Reilly and advised both Carondelet and Miró. During his term as governor-general, writes Jack D. L. Holmes, "New Orleans society was already formed of the first families who could trace their forebears back to the early eighteenth-century French founders. It was a gay city, ready and eager at the first excuse to attend masked balls and operas. Theater seats were usually reserved for the first families, and even then they were difficult to obtain."[31]

Gayoso was both experienced and capable, but he died suddenly on July 18, 1799, probably a victim of that year's yellow fever epidemic. Upon his death, his position was divided between a civilian governor, the corrupt Nicolás María Vidal, and a military governor, Sebastián Calvo, better known as the Marqués de Casa Calvo, who had been present as an eighteen-year-old in O'Reilly's retinue at the taking of New Orleans by Spain in 1769 and the execution of the five "Frenchmen." The civilian and military governors did not get along, and they had a public rupture over the use of the theater. When they squabbled over the matter of a separate loge for Casa Calvo, Vidal settled the matter by ordering the theater to stop its gambling operations and its public balls for people of color. With its financial base undermined, the theater closed its doors after Mardi Gras, February 25, 1800, and remained shuttered until late 1801.

Vidal was replaced by the old, infirm, ineffective Manuel de Salcedo in August 1800. Dancing went on informally, and the large public gatherings of slaves continued. A visitor to the city in 1799, accustomed to a more sedate sabbath, was surprised to see, on a Sunday in New Orleans, "vast numbers of negro slaves, men, women, and children, assembled together on the levee, drumming, fifing, and dancing, in large rings."[32]

Napoleon Bonaparte, who had taken power in the coup d'etat of 18th Brumaire, revolutionary year VIII (November 11, 1799), quietly reopened stalled negotiations to reacquire Louisiana for France. Spain saw an opportunity to exchange Louisiana for something the Neapolitan-raised Carlos IV wanted: the Italian kingdom of Parma, which was controlled by Bonaparte. The Second Treaty of San Ildefonso, concluded between Spain and France on October 1, 1800, exchanged Louisiana for Italian territories, though Bonaparte was displeased because it did not also turn the Floridas over to him. Shortly thereafter, the African slave trade to Louisiana was reopened, though slaves from the Antilles were still prohibited. The Treaty of Aranjuez between Spain and France on March 21, 1801, further confirmed the retrocession of Louisiana. It was supposed to be secret, but word got out: at last Louisiana would return to its rightful place as a French territory. The preface of Louis-Narcisse Baudry des Lozières's travel narrative of Louisiana, published in Paris in 1802, began bluntly, "We are going to retake possession of Louisiana."[33]

Spain did not much care about the colony anymore. The governors were lame ducks. Law enforcement was lax. No matter who was ostensibly in charge, the Anglo-Americans would keep coming into the region. They could not be stopped. They were coming to make money.

15

Not Only as a Dance

We demand such hard work of black women, before and after their pregnancies, that their pregnancies do not come to term or the babies do not survive the childbirth. Sometimes one even sees mothers desperate as a result of punishments, who in the weakness of their state, at times, remove them from their cribs to smother them in their arms and sacrifice them with a madness mixed with vengeance and pity, to spare them the barbaric masters.

—*Abbé Guillaume-Thomas-François Raynal*, Philosophic and Political History of European Establishments and Commerce in the Two Indies, 1780[1]

Fleeing France one step ahead of the Jacobins' guillotine, the pro-slavery revolutionary Moreau de St.-Méry boarded a ship for New York. After a stormy 119-day crossing against headwinds, the ship arrived on March 8, 1794, in Norfolk, Virginia, where Moreau remained for two months.

He settled in Philadelphia. The largest city and the capital of the newly constituted United States was swarming with foreign diplomats and agents as well as with domestic intrigue. President George Washington wanted no political parties in the new republic, but two distinct factions had emerged, though in 1792 the "Republican" Party, insofar as it existed, consisted only of a few obstinate Virginia representatives. (These Republicans were the predecessors not of today's Republican Party, which was founded in 1854, but of the Democratic Party.)

The Federalists were the party of the American Revolution, but the Republicans came into existence after the earthquake of the French Revolution. By 1796, they were a force to be reckoned with. In the presidential election that year, in which Federalist John Adams defeated Republican Thomas Jefferson (neither man actively campaigned), the relationship of the United States and France was a burning issue. The Federalists (Washington, Adams, and the most extreme of them, Hamilton) thought the Republicans berserk French Jacobins, approximately the equivalent of calling them Communists; the Republicans (Jefferson, Madison, Monroe) thought the Federalists soft on Britain and yearning for a king. In 1803, Pierre Clement de Laussat, writing from Louisiana to his superior in France, matter-of-factly referred to the Republicans as "the French party" and Federalists as "the English party."

Taking advantage of his Masonic connections, Moreau became part of an exile community of Frenchmen and Domingans in Philadelphia. Its most illustrious member was his friend Charles Maurice de Talleyrand-Périgord, who scandalized the locals by walking arm in arm with his colored mistress in public.[2] Moreau opened Moreau de St.-Méry & Co., a bookstore at 85 South Front Street, which sold "books, stationery, engravings, mathematical instruments, maps, charts, and other," according to a 1795 catalog he published. The "other" category included a wide variety of hosiery and sundries, including condoms (the "French letters," used not for contraception but for protection against venereal disease, were not otherwise easily available in Philadelphia). For six months he published a daily newspaper in French.

Fortunately for posterity, he busied himself also with his great literary endeavor. He had spent years researching his wide-ranging work about Saint-Domingue, and by some miracle, the trunks containing his research materials, which he had feared lost, arrived in Philadelphia some months after he did. While Talleyrand was there, the two spent every evening conversing, and it was with Talleyrand's help that Moreau rounded up sufficient subscribers to print his masterwork, the *Topographical, physical, civil, political, and historical description of Saint-Domingue*. (I will refer to this work, from which I have already quoted, as *Description*.) Published by Moreau in Philadelphia in 1797 and 1798, it only covers the years up to 1789. There is little more than an acknowledgment of anything after that date. It provides a careful description of a world that had vanished forever.

Moreau's meticulous research and observations are coupled with a satiric prose style that spares no social group on the island. It's one of the masterpieces of the genre of exile literature, the predecessor of sentimental, longing-for-a-lost-land nostalgia voluminously expressed in postbellum Southern literature and, in our own time, from Cuban Miami. It should not be assumed that such works are backward looking; one is tempted to conclude that this genre as a whole seeks not merely to recall, but to reinstate. Moreau's expressed hope was that, as Laurent Dubois expressed it, "the details he provided might help in making the colony back into what it once had been."[3]

Before he published the *Description*, he produced several smaller monographs, intended to stimulate contributions for a never-published encyclopedia. One of these, written in 1789 and published by Moreau in Philadelphia in 1796, was a sixty-two-page monograph titled *Danse*. The first book published in the new United States about the art of dance, it was in French. Most of it concerns dancing in Saint-Domingue. It tells how the ruling class danced:

> Fashion rears its head as much in the outer reaches of the empire as in the [European] metropolis; that is to say, in the French colonies, for example, the minuet had its day, and then the contredanse with the rigaudon step [*contredanse à rigaudon*], or with the allemande step. For a while it was the [contredanse] *anglaise* that got all the votes; for a while one had to know how to waltz and execute *jetés-battus*, or give up the hope of figuring among dancers of high reputation. . . .
>
> One sometimes hears muttering about the short duration of the nights spent at the ball, and against the return of the sun that warns it is at last time to rest. During the period between one ball and the next there are frequent complaints about the long wait, which would be unbearable except for the work that goes into shining even more brilliantly in the next outfit.[4]

But much of Moreau's book on dance is about the slaves in Saint-Domingue. It is the most extended description of eighteenth-century black dancing that we have anywhere. Planters generally encouraged slave dancing on Sundays, holidays, or even at breaks, because they realized that dancing was important for—it is not an exaggeration to say—keeping the slaves alive. Not only because of the spiritual effect, but physiologically as well: dancing countered the strain on the body of the endless repetitive muscular motions of the slaves' labor. It is worth quoting Moreau on this at length:

Brought from all parts of Africa to our Colonies, where the climate is analogous to theirs, the blacks bring with them and conserve their penchant for dance, a penchant so powerful that even the negro most fatigued by work always finds the strength to dance and even to go to several places to satisfy that desire.

When the blacks want to dance, they set out two drums, that is, two barrels of unequal length, of which one end remains open, while the other is covered by a tightly stretched lamb skin. These drums (the shorter of which is called the *Bamboula*, because it is often made from a very large bamboo which has been dug out) resound under the fist blows and finger movements by each player straddling his drum. The larger drum is struck slowly, and the other very fast. This monotonous, low-pitched sound is accompanied by a number of small calabashes, containing pebbles and pierced on their long side by a long handle which serves to shake them with.

The *Banzas*, a sort of primitive guitar with four strings, joins the concert, the movements of which are regulated by the hand-clapping of negresses in a large circle. They form a chorus that responds to one or two principal female singers whose striking voices repeat or improvise a song.

A male and female dancer, or a number of dancing couples, leap forward to the middle of the space and begin to dance, always in couples. This dance rarely varies; it consists of a single strong step in which the dancer extends successively each foot and draws it back tapping several times rapidly the heel and toe on the ground, as in the *anglaise*. The dancer moves around the female dancer, who turns about and changes place with the dancer; that's all one perceives, except for the movement of the arms, which the dancer lowers and raises with his elbows fairly near his body and his hand practically closed; the lady holds both ends of a handkerchief which she waves. One who has not seen this dance would find it hard to believe how lively and animated it is, and how rigorously the measure is followed, which makes it graceful.

The dancers replace each other endlessly, and the negroes become so intoxicated with pleasure, that it is always necessary to force them to bring these balls, called *Calendas*, to an end. They take place in the middle of a field, on a smooth piece of land, so that the movement of the feet encounters no obstacle.[5]

Moreau's etymology of *Bamboula* is not to be taken seriously. Looking at a more likely source, we find one of the meanings given in Karl Laman's French-

Kikongo dictionary for *bambula* (accent on first syllable) is "to remember."[6] Singer-bandleader Ricardo Lemvo, a Kikongo speaker, tells me it means "to remind." Laman also tells us that *bula* means "town or village," as well as "to strike." When people played bamboula in the New World, they remembered their town or village by striking a drum.

Tracking etymologies of words that come into European languages from African languages is different from tracking, say, the collisions of French and German that went into English. However, when the same word is used to refer to a genre of music, its characteristic rhythm, the drum it's played on, the dance associated with it, and the party where it happens—without exhausting many more shades of meaning available to it—that clearly comes from African usage. In Cuba, for example, the word *conga* fits all of those descriptions, as well as referring to the Kongo. Bamboula, as Moreau de St.-Méry writes about it, is a drum, but if you ask a drummer in New Orleans today, it is a rhythm. At Congo Square, bamboula was the wicked dance that scandalized Cyrillo Sieni.

His mention of the *banzas* (banjo) is, to this writer's knowledge, the only mention of the instrument in Saint-Domingue. But that's not the only surprise in Moreau's little book on dance:

> In Saint Domingue . . . there has long been a genre of dance called *Vaudoux*, which requires two or four people, and which is characterized by movements in which the upper body, shoulders, and head move as if they were on springs. This dance also takes place with the drum, hand-clapping, and choral singing. I do not know the source of its name, but its effect on the blacks is such, that sometimes they dance it until they fall down fainting.[7]

So that in the first book on dancing published in the United States, we also find the first mention in print in the United States of vodou. Moreau speaks of vodou as a dance, which is consonant with present practice in Haiti today, where people do not speak of going to "ceremonies." They speak of going to a dance, and if you ask them what kind of dance, they will tell you: *danse lwa*. A spirit dance.

That Moreau is speaking of the religion that we know as vodou in Haiti today is unquestionable, because in his *Description*, published in 1797–98, he expands on it.[8] In a breathtaking understatement, he tells us that "it is not only as a dance that Vaudoux merits consideration." His remarks, which open out into an account of a ceremony apparently based on firsthand observation, are worth quoting in full. I yield the floor to Citizen Moreau de St.-Méry:

> According to the Arada negroes, who are the real sect-members of Vaudoux in the Colony, and who maintain its principles and rules, Vaudoux signifies an all-powerful, supernatural being, upon whom hang all the events which happen around the globe. In fact, this being is a non-venomous snake, a kind of grass snake, and it is under its auspices the believers assemble. Knowledge of the past, science of the present, and prescience of the future, all belong to this snake, who nevertheless will not communicate its power, or tell its will, except through the medium of a high priest chosen by the sect-members, and a negress, who has been elevated to the rank of high priestess by the love of the priest.
>
> These two ministers, who, it is said, are inspired by God . . . bear the pompous names of King and Queen, or the despotic names of master or mistress, or, finally, the touching titles of papa and mama. For their entire lives, they are the chiefs of the grand Vaudoux family, and they have the right to the unlimited respect of its members. . . .
>
> The real Vaudoux meeting . . . never takes place except secretly, when the night spreads its darkness, and in a closed place away from profane eyes. There, each initiate puts on a pair of sandals and places around his body a more or less considerable number of red handkerchiefs, or handkerchiefs in which that color predominates. The Vaudoux King has the most, and the most beautiful, handkerchiefs, and something all red winds around his brow to serve as his diadem. A sash, usually blue, proclaims his shining dignity.
>
> The Queen, dressed with simple luxury, shows also her predilection for the color red, most often in her sash or her waistband.
>
> The King and Queen take their places at one end of the room, near a kind of altar, on which is a cage in which the snake is kept, and where every affiliate can see it through the bars of the cage.
>
> Once they have determined that no one has entered the cell out of mere curiosity, they begin the ceremony of adoration of the snake, with professions of loyalty to its cult, and submission to all that it might require. Between the hands of the King and Queen, each one renews his oath of secrecy, which is the basis of the group, and this is accompanied by the most horrible things that delirium could imagine, in order to render it all more imposing.

When the Vaudoux sect-members are thus ready to receive the impressions that the King and Queen will share with them, the latter adopt the affectionate tone of a sensitive father and mother. . . .

Then the crowd scatters, and each one according to his need, and according to his seniority in the sect, goes to implore the Vaudoux. Most ask it for the ability to direct the spirit of their masters; but this is not enough, one asks for money, another the gift of pleasing a woman who ignores him; this one wants to get an unfaithful mistress back, that one asks for healing, or a prolonged life. After them, an old woman wants to conjure God to stop the contempt of one whose youthful happiness she wants to enjoy. A young girl asks for eternal love, or makes wishes dictated by her hatred of a rival. Another wish is made not out of passion but for the success of a crime, not always successfully disguised.

During each of these invocations, the Vaudoux King collects himself; the Spirit agitates in him. Suddenly he takes the cage containing the snake, places it on the ground, and makes the Vaudoux Queen stand on it. Once the sacred asylum is under her feet, having become a pythoness, she is penetrated by God, she shakes, her whole body goes into convulsions, and the oracle speaks through her mouth. . . .

Sometimes a vessel filled with the still-hot blood of a goat is used to seal the lips of those in attendance, who promise to die rather than reveal anything, and even to kill anyone else who forgets what has solemnly been sworn.

After that, the dance of the Vaudoux begins.

If there is a new initiate, this work is for his admission. The Vaudoux King traces a large circle with a blacking substance, and places the initiate within it. Into the initiate's hand he puts a packet composed of herbs, animal hair, bits of horn, and other disgusting things. Striking the candidate lightly on the head with a little wooden stick, he intones an African song, repeated in a chorus by those around the circle; now the initiate begins to tremble and dance; which is called to *mount Vaudoux*. If the excesses of the trance make him leave the circle, the song stops at once, and the King and Queen turn their backs, to cast out the evil omen. The dancer revives, re-enters the circle, becomes agitated again, limps, and finally goes into such convulsions that the Vaudoux King orders him to stop, striking him gently on the head with the stick or wand, or even with a cow's tendon if he thinks it appropriate. He is led to the altar to take an oath, and from that moment on, he belongs to the sect.

When the ceremony is finished, the King puts his hand or his foot on the snake's cage, and soon he is possessed. He communicates this to the Queen, and through her the commotion expands outward in a circle, and everyone begins to make movements, in which the upper part of the body, the head and shoulders, seem to dislocate. The Queen above all is prey to the most violent agitations; from time to time she goes up to seek a new charm from the Vaudoux serpent; she shakes the serpent's cage, and the little bells with which it is adorned, have the effect of deranging the madness further, as the delirium keeps growing. It is further augmented by the unsparing use of strong liquor, which helps to keep them going in the drunkenness of their imagination. Fainting and swooning occur in some, and a kind of fury in others, but in everyone there is a nervous trembling, which they do not seem to be able to master. They spin around endlessly. And among them are some who, in the course of the bacchanal, tear their clothes and bite their own flesh; others, who are no more than deprived of their senses and have merely fallen down in place, are transported, always still dancing, into an adjoining room, where in the darkness a disgusting prostitution holds sway over the most hideous empire. Finally, exhaustion brings an end to these reason-afflicting scenes, but upon recovering there is much concern about fixing the time of the next meeting.

It is very natural to think that Vaudoux owes its origin to the serpent cult, to which the people of Juida are particularly devoted, and which, it is said, originated in the kingdom of Ardra, also on the Slave Coast. . . .

What is very real and at the same time very remarkable in Vaudoux, is that kind of magnetic compulsion of the assembled group, to dance to the point of losing their senses. They are well protected in that respect, because Whites found spying on the mysteries of the sect . . . have sometimes themselves started to dance, and have consented to pay the Vaudoux Queen to put an end to this punishment. I cannot fail to observe that never has any policeman who has sworn war on Vaudoux not felt the power that forces him to dance, and that has saved the dancers from the need to take flight.

Doubtless in order to quiet the alarms that the mysterious cult of Vaudoux causes in the Colony, they pretend to dance it in public, to the noise of the drums and with handclaps; they even follow this with a dinner, where people eat nothing but chicken. But I assure you that this is merely one more calculated evasion of the magistrates' vigilance, the better to assure the success of their dark, secret meetings, which are not for amusement or pleasure. . . .

One would not believe the degree to which the Vaudoux chiefs keep the other sect-members dependent on them. Any of the members would prefer anything to the evils with which they are threatened if they fail to go to the assemblies regularly, and do not blindly do what the Vaudoux require of them.[9]

The fearful meaning of all this for whites was clear: there was a system of social organization going full tilt within the black world of Saint-Domingue, existing beyond the whites' abilities to control their slaves' thoughts and actions. In a footnote, Moreau gives the text of the above-mentioned "African song":

Eh! Eh! Bomba, hen! Hen!
Canga bafio té
Canga moune dé lé
Canga do ki la
Canga li

This hymn was apparently the big hit of the Haitian Revolution. It was noted, in a slightly different form, by a nun of the Cap Français Order of Notre Dame, who heard her vodou-practicing female students singing it, and claimed to have heard it again when the convent was assaulted by Boukman himself.[10] Moreau does not seem to have known the meaning of the words, which are Kikongo, though his transcription is good enough to decode its essence. To break it down:

Bomba is a word with many possible meanings, found in various contexts in Antillean popular music today. It is the name of the principal form of Afro–Puerto Rican music, which seems to have derived at least in part from music brought by refugees from Saint-Domingue. John Jantzen glosses the word as "serpent" or "rainbow spirit"; it could also be *mbumba*, the dead.[11] There is also the possibility that it might have been an untranslatable flavor word, like ¡olé! or ¡sabor!, and it probably did have something of that function. I might add that aeeeeee, ¡bomba!—a very similar phrase to the first line of this song—is the flavor catchphrase dropped into virtually every hit tune that the chart-topping Dominican merengue group Los Hermanos Rosario had in the 1990s.

Canga means to seal, arrest, impede.

Moune dé lé—the Cubans spell it *mundele*, meaning "white man," a word known in both the Congo and Carabalí languages of Cuba. It shows up in the

1930s in Arsenio Rodríguez's "Bruca Manigua," a landmark in Cuban popular song that complains in *bozal* language about the mistreatment of an African-born man by white slave owners.

Bafiote, meaning "abuse," is another word that appears in both "Bruca Manigua" and in this eighteenth-century Haitian revolutionary song. Carolyn Fick thinks it is a reference to the Fioti, a coastal slave-trading people. These interpretations are not mutually exclusive.

Do ki—that would be *ndoki*, which has a couple of possible glosses. Its meaning is sometimes glossed as a malicious charm. Perhaps more in keeping with the way African religion operates is Teodoro Díaz Fabelo's interpretation, in which the *ndoki* is neither evil nor good, but is the commanding spirit of the *nganga*—the iron pot containing human remains, animal parts, plant materials, and earth that is central to the practice of the *palero*, the Kongo-Cuban ritual expert. The ndoki, says Díaz Fabelo, can work for benevolence or harm, as directed by the palero.[12] The ndoki is an agent that causes action. As part of spirit technology, it was an essential part of warfare.

Wyatt McGaffey, queried by Fandrich, glossed the lyric as:

Eh! Eh! Bomba, hen! Hen!
Seize the blacks
Seize the whites
Seize the witches!
Seize him/her![13]

In Kongo, and possibly in eighteenth-century Saint-Domingue, these ngangas were not iron pots but more portable packets, which had to be tied up. Jantzen, queried by Fick, suggests "tie up" as a translation for *canga*, which might be interpreted in light of that practice: not tying up their bodies with rope, but tying up their power with stronger power.

Informed by these authorities, I might make another stab at translating this eighteenth-century war song:

Eh! Eh! Power of the dead, hen! Hen!
Tie up the abusers!
Tie up the whites!
Tie up the action spirit!
Tie them up!

Alfred Métraux, in his 1959 study of vodou, writes:

Analysed in the light of our present knowledge, the words of Moreau de Saint-Méry allow no room for doubt that there existed in Saint-Domingue, towards the end of the eighteenth century, rites and practices which have scarcely changed up to modern times. The authority of the priest, his dress, the importance of trance, signs drawn on the ground are familiar now as then. Moreau de Saint-Méry, however, was wrong in setting down this religion as a simple ophiolatry. Today also, the devotees of Voodoo worship Damballah-wèdo, the serpent-god, one of the divinities of the Dahomey mythology, but he is far from being the only great "Voodoo." . . . Although it is not normal practice now to represent Damballah-wèdo by living serpents, it must have been otherwise in the time of Moreau de Saint-Méry.[14]

But there was also another time and place where live snakes were commonly used in voodoo ceremonies: nineteenth-century New Orleans.

∽

Not content with introducing post-revolutionary Francophone Philadelphia to the concept of vodou, Moreau de St.-Méry described another dance:

[The Vaudoux] is nothing, if we compare it to Dance of Don Pèdre, another black dance, known . . . since 1768. Don Pèdre was the name of a negro of Spanish origin, from the Petit-Goave section, who by his bold character and certain superstitious practices had acquired, among the negroes, such a great reputation that he was denounced to justice as a leader of alarming projects.

The dance that bears his name consists, like the Vaudoux, of extremely vigorous movements of the head and shoulders; but this agitation is extremely violent, and to heighten it further, the blacks drink tafia [eau-de-vie] mixed with finely ground gunpowder.[15] The effect of this drink, driven and augmented by their movements, has a great influence over their entire being, so that they enter into a frenzy, with real convulsions. They dance seized with horrible contortions, they dance until they fall into a kind of epilepsy that knocks them down, in a state resembling approaching death.

It was necessary to prohibit severely the dance of Don Pèdre, because it caused great disorders and awakened ideas contrary to public peace. Maybe through electrical effect, the spectators themselves partook of this inebriation, and instead of ceasing their chants when the frenzy breaks out, they would redouble the volume of their voices, push the tempo, and accelerate the crisis in which to a degree they participate. How bizarre is man! In what excesses does he seek pleasure![16]

Moreau could only see this in hedonistic terms: pleasure seeking. But he gives us a full description of violent spirit possession and a mention of Don Pedro, who is well known in Haitian folklore today. The two best-known branches (there are others) of contemporary vodou are *rara* (from Arada) and *petro* (or *petwo*). The latter's rites are generally more violent and unpredictable than the former; according to tradition, its name comes from the name Don Pedro. Some writers have seen in Boukman's black-pig ceremony the outline of a petro ritual.

Moreau describes yet another dance, the *chica*, which he ascribes to the Congos of Saint-Domingue, noting that it was performed throughout the Antilles and the Spanish American continent. This is, then, a late eighteenth-century description of a transnational dance that developed in different ways in different countries. Some variant of it would very likely have been danced in black New Orleans. A sexually mimetic pursuit-and-capture dance, Moreau's description sounds like the dance that became known as *guaguancó* in Cuba and in Brazil as the belly-to-belly *umbigada*. Moreau found it arousing. A modern reader may be amused by the euphemism the "lower part of the kidneys":

> The art of the female dancer, who holds the corners of a handkerchief or the two borders of her apron, consists mainly in agitating the lower part of the kidneys, while keeping the rest of the body strictly immobilized. A male dancer approaches while she is in motion, and throws himself at her suddenly, almost touching her, withdrawing, and throwing himself at her again, while seeming to entreat her to yield with him to the spell that controls them. . . .
>
> There is nothing lascivious that such a tableau cannot offer, nothing voluptuous that is not depicted. It is a kind of struggle where all the ruses of love, and all the means of triumph, are put into action: fear, hope, disdain, tenderness, caprice, pleasure, denial, delirium, flight, intoxication, humiliation. . . .
>
> I will not try to express the impression that might be produced by viewing a Chica danced with all the precision of which the dancers are capable. There is no point of view that it does not animate, no point of

sensibility that it does not move, no point of imagination that it does not fire; it would make the decrepit feel alive.[17]

Deploying yet another standard trope of French libertinism, Moreau adds that "even nuns would perform in their convent courtyard, publicly executing the voluptuous steps of the Chica." In Moreau's *Description*, there is much more about music, dance, and ritual, at all levels of society. He describes funeral customs, as well as the *zombi* and the *loup-garou*. This paragraph leaps out:

> The domestic negroes, imitators of the Whites whom they love to mimic, dance minuets and contredanses, and it is a spectacle that would crack up the most serious face, that of one of their balls, or the bizarreness of their European trappings, given a sometimes grotesque character.[18]

Mimicry or mockery? Moreau's pejorative construction and dismissive judgment of this spectacle notwithstanding, it's an interesting description. He is clearly describing a scene that can still be seen in eastern Cuba, in the black antiquarian societies known as *tumba francesa*, of which there are three known to exist today. I have seen all three perform; they are jewels of living Afro-Franco-Cuban heritage and a fascinating living monument to the artistic tradition of the Saint-Domingan diaspora. If you are a connoisseur of Cuban folklore, you have probably seen groups whose performance tradition is straight out of the nineteenth century. That's rare enough. But this is out of the late *eighteenth* century. In these groups, the dance repertoire includes a version of contredanse, in a stylized wardrobe resembling the upper-class French dress of the day—set to an accompaniment of strictly African drumming.

We would expect that the Domingan diaspora that came to New Orleans brought some version of tumba francesa, though it did not survive in its historic form as it did in Cuba (I will discuss this in more detail). We know that black people performed the contredanse in New Orleans; a visitor's observation from March 3, 1808, notes black people breaking up into two groups—one to dance the bamboula, the other the contredanse.[19] Here we have present in New Orleans the same two dances that Moreau had observed in Saint-Domingue twenty years previous.

The tumba francesa of eastern Cuba also has a dance called *frenté*, danced with kerchiefs by a solo male dancer whose fancy steps are in rhythmic duet with a drummer sitting on top of his drum. I will have more to say about this, but it is enough for now to note that the drums that lay down the rhythm behind the soloist are called *bulá*. Recalling that *ba-* is a pluralizing prefix in Kikongo: *ba-bulá*. Or, as Fernando Ortiz wrote it in Cuba: *bambulá*.

Moreau cast a disparaging eye on what he saw as the blacks' ineptness in imitating whites, whereas more sympathetic commentators today read the style of contredanse as done by the tumba francesa societies in Cuba as mocking the whites' style. That same impulse—borrowing the dance gestures and forms of high society—can be seen in the later cakewalk of the United States and has attracted the same ambivalent commentary. But I think it's simple enough: the people appropriated for their own amusement something that was at hand.

By the time Moreau published his monograph on dance, the Terror had subsided in Paris, and was replaced by dancing mania. "A survivor of the Terror wrote about the summer and autumn months that followed it," writes Francine du Plessix Gray, "[that] 'hardly had the scaffolds been taken down, with the draining well still showing its gaping mouths to frightened passersby . . . and the ground still soaked with the human blood poured over it, when public dances began to be organized all over the capital.' . . . In the 1794–95 season alone, six hundred forty-four public dance halls were opened in [Paris]."[20]

Moreau left his American exile, returning to France on August 24, 1798, and worked his way back into Parisian society. His good friend Talleyrand, now the French foreign minister, had almost brought France to war with the United States in the so-called XYZ affair, and was instrumental in the coup that brought Bonaparte to power. A new French constitution, the second in five years, separated the legal system of France from that of its colonies, providing what Moreau de St.-Méry and the Club Massiac had advocated: distinct laws for each colony, paving the way to reinstate slavery in the Antilles. Bonaparte appointed pro-slavery administrators to his ministry, including Moreau de St.-Méry.

With the Jacobins gone, postrevolutionary France now had a solidly proslavery regime once again. The postrevolutionary United States was divided on the subject. Its president, John Adams, was a New Englander who detested slavery. But Adams would not be president much longer.

16

BONAPARTE'S RETREAT

The constitution you made, while including many good
things, contains some that are contrary to the dignity and
sovereignty of the French people, of which Saint-Domingue
forms only a portion.

> —*First Consul Napoleon Bonaparte's letter of
> November 18, 1801, to Citizen General
> Toussaint Louverture, carried by General Leclerc*

As the United States struggled to take shape in the 1790s, it was
in the context of the life-or-death struggle going on next door in
Saint-Domingue.

Newspapers, proliferating in the United States and worldwide, carried
the latest urgent news of the colony. People in the northern United States,
as well as both masters and slaves in the South, were aware that the rebels of
Saint-Domingue were a living example of slave insurrection. In 1797, Charles-
tonians were unnerved by the uncovering of a plot by "French negroes" to
murder them leaving church on Christmas Day.[1] This fear would never go
away. The possibility of a massive uprising in the southern United States
seemed very real, though it never occurred.

The disappearance of Saint-Domingue from agricultural markets impelled
a frantic restructuring of the international sugar business. It created bonanzas
in Cuba and Jamaica, where new acreage was planted as fast as equipment and
slaves could be acquired to work it.

The British remained as invaders in parts of Saint-Domingue until 1798, when they signed a nonaggression pact and withdrew, having lost tens of thousands of men in the course of losing a second major war in the New World. Toussaint Louverture, who, together with yellow fever, had defeated them, had to get the economy of Saint-Domingue functioning again. He set out to return the colony to viability as an agricultural producer.

But sugar is not the kind of work anyone does voluntarily. Attempts to induce ex-slaves to man the plantations produced poor results. The slaves had previously known a world where there were two kinds of people: those driven by the whip until they were worked to death, and those who did little or no work at all. Hard work in the sugar mill was not of much interest to them. Louverture modified the *fermage* system previously used by Sonthonax, using military coercion to force ex-slaves back into plantation labor, with a rudimentary form of socialism to distribute the proceeds. He even invited white planters back, to get the economy on its feet.

War continued in Saint-Domingue, with a bitter struggle between troops in the South led by André Rigaud versus Louverture's troops in the North and West. Rigaud represented the mulatto elite, which had never made common cause with the slaves and was being supported by the French in a divide-and-conquer policy; the division between mulatto elite and black mass was to become permanent in Haitian politics.

Louverture had shown himself to be an astute statesman. At a time when France and the United States had barely escaped going to war with each other, Louverture cut his own trade deal with the Adams administration, as well as with Britain—a move tantamount to declaring independence. The United States sold Louverture weapons, and the U.S. Navy helped Louverture by blockading ports of the southern province. Rigaud was decisively defeated in a brutal battle at Jacmel in July 1800; an American warship assisted Louverture in that battle, firing on Rigaud's forts from the sea—the first military intervention by the United States in the affairs of another country. In late December 1800, ostensibly in the name of France but actually on his own initiative, Louverture sent ten thousand troops into Spanish-speaking Santo Domingo, fearing that it represented a security risk for the reintroduction of slavery. After taking possession in January 1801, he was in active control of the entire island of La Española.

In Virginia, some six hundred people were involved in the conspiracy of Gabriel, carefully planned for the capital city of Richmond on August 30, 1800. Gabriel, a blacksmith, had made swords out of farm scythes, and intended to capture the militia's arms, stored in the state capitol. There was no well-armed militia in the region; the slave uprising might very well have succeeded had two would-be participants not lost their nerve and tipped off the authorities. Twenty-seven of Gabriel's conspirators were executed, and a number of others sold to foreign buyers.

The revelation that a Saint-Domingue-style rebellion had nearly occurred in Virginia was terrifying news that spread like wildfire among fearful whites.

∞

On March 4, 1801, Thomas Jefferson became president of the United States in an election decided by the House of Representatives that Jefferson called "the Revolution of 1800." With Jefferson's victory, the Republicans became a permanent part of the political landscape; it was the first peaceful transfer of governmental power to an opposition in modern history.

A hero to Southern planters, Jefferson was literally elected by the slaveholders, since his electoral majority over Adams consisted of the extra weighting given the Southern states under the three-fifths clause. A slave was three-fifths of a person, at least for purposes of electoral arithmetic. To accommodate the South and balance its political power with that of the North, the U.S. Constitution incorporated the notorious three-fifths clause, which gave states extra congressional representation and electoral votes based on an arbitrarily weighted 60 percent of their slave population—a population that was not allowed to vote. The clause in effect allowed slave owners extra votes in proportion to their wealth, to the great outrage of Northern merchants, whose wealth was not invested in human beings.

For that matter, few Americans were eligible to vote: only two states, Rhode Island and Virginia, provided for direct popular election of presidential electors.[2] The young republic was a long way from being a democracy. The president was chosen by the political class, which in the South was entirely composed of slave owners. Newspapers were highly partisan and played an essential role in the politics of the day; in the South they were also an essential part of commerce in slaves. Slave owners exerted a disproportionate control over American politics, as they would up through the Civil War.[3]

It would be an oversimplification of the complex political situation of the time to reduce Jefferson to being simply the pro-slavery candidate. But among all the things Jefferson was, he *was* the pro-slavery candidate. Thomas Jefferson wasn't afraid of much, but he was afraid of slave rebellion, and he was thoroughly hostile to Louverture. Like his constituents, Jefferson believed that it was necessary to "confine the plague to the island." Louverture, who had defeated all foreign invaders, had practically achieved independence from France. But at the peak of his success, his alliance with the United States disappeared overnight.

Four months into Jefferson's presidency, in July 1801, Jefferson was visited by Louis André Pichon, Napoleon Bonaparte's minister to Washington, who broached the possibility of an armed French intervention in Saint-Domingue. Pichon reported Jefferson's words back to Paris: "Nothing would be more simple than to furnish your army and your fleet with everything and to starve out Toussaint."[4]

This was a dramatic reversal of U.S. policy toward Saint-Domingue.

Bonaparte was not pleased by Louverture's independent diplomatic initiatives. His campaign to reclaim Saint-Domingue for slavery was already in motion, but the last straw came in October 1801 when he received the constitution Louverture had drawn up for Saint-Domingue. It specified that Saint-Domingue was part of the French empire, that slavery was forever abolished, and that Louverture would be governor-general for life.[5] The following month, Bonaparte dispatched an army of experienced troops to Saint-Domingue—the largest military force that had yet crossed the Atlantic—under the command of his brother-in-law, General Victor-Emmanuel Charles Leclerc.

Greenlighted by Jefferson, Bonaparte ignited a new, even bloodier, phase of the conflict in Saint-Domingue. He destroyed the possibility, assiduously cultivated by Toussaint Louverture, of whites and blacks being able to live together in the colony.

Bonaparte planned to reinstall slavery in the French Antilles, and with it, resume large-scale plantation agriculture in the West Indies. Laurent Dubois sees a

> failure of imagination that made it impossible for Bonaparte and his government to accept the remarkable and promising reconfiguration of empire being offered up to them. . . . [Bonaparte] did not take into consideration the dramatic transformations that had taken place in the Caribbean during the previous decade. A lack of political imagination—one tied both to racism and to a misunderstanding of the situation on the ground in the Caribbean—prevented decision-makers in Paris [from seeing] that France's best hope of channeling emancipation into a reconstitution of export-oriented plantation economy in fact lay in collaboration with Louverture's regime.[6]

The agricultural production of the Antillean colonies that Bonaparte planned to re-enslave would be dedicated entirely to export. However, Pichon did not inform Jefferson that their provisions—foodstuffs, timber, hides—were to be supplied from the French territory of Louisiana.

At the time, Jefferson was not aware of the secret Treaty of San Ildefonso that retroceded Louisiana to France. Once he realized the extent of Bonaparte's determination to establish not merely an Antillean but a mainland empire, his enthusiasm for the French mission flagged. Jefferson knew full well that his constituents would never stand for having Bonaparte in control of New Orleans, which had rapidly become essential to U.S. commerce. Speaking of the possibility of the transfer of territory, he wrote on April 18, 1802, to Robert Livingston, his minister to France: "There is on the globe one single spot, the possessor of which is our natural and habitual enemy. It is New Orleans, through which the produce of three-eighths of our territory must pass to market. . . . The day that France takes possession of N. Orleans fixes the sentence which is to restrain her forever. . . . From that moment we must marry ourselves to the British fleet and nation." These were dramatic words from a man so anglophobic.

⁂

By fall 1801, Bonaparte was moving toward peace negotiations with the British. The March 25, 1802, Peace of Amiens would only be a short respite in a twenty-two-year war, but, in it, Britain formally recognized the French Republic, and moreover, at last gave up the claim to the throne of France it had asserted since the fourteenth century. As usual, territory-swapping accompanied this settlement and included the British acquisition of Trinidad and the return of Martinique to France. With Spain no longer needed as an ally, Bonaparte flagrantly ignored the terms of their treaty and simply insisted that Louisiana be turned over to him—never mind the Italian part of the deal—humiliating the Spanish king in the process.

Had France and Britain been at war, Bonaparte could not have sent a large force into the Caribbean without encountering massive resistance, but the Peace of Amiens removed that obstacle. Technically, sending the French army to Saint-Domingue was not an invasion; it was French territory. He did not declare that his intention was to reinstate slavery. But the ex-slaves of Saint-Domingue were not fooled, and Louverture did not cooperate.

Bonaparte's instructions to Leclerc were to subdue Saint-Domingue in six weeks, send Louverture and the black generals back to France, then proceed to New Orleans. But Leclerc's troops never made it to Louisiana. Toussaint was in Santo Domingo when they arrived at the bay of Cap Français on January 26, 1802. General Henri Christophe, who was in charge of the city, refused to surrender to them. When the French began to disembark,

Christophe burned Cap Français on his own initiative and retreated to the countryside with his men.

In the end, Jefferson opted for a somewhat improvised policy of neutrality. Leclerc arrived in Saint-Domingue to find American merchants there. Jefferson refused to support a French call for a trade embargo of the territory, but also indicated he would not interfere with the French if they chose to implement a blockade.

Bonaparte then sent Antoine Richepence in May 1802 as the head of an invasion to Guadeloupe, where slaves had been emancipated along with those of Saint-Domingue in 1794. People who had been made citizens eight years previously, who were practicing professions and buying houses, were turned back into chattel slaves. Richepence executed or deported perhaps ten thousand people, a tenth of the population.[7] The example of Guadeloupe galvanized the free citizens of Saint-Domingue, and you can bet the slaves of Louisiana heard about it, too.

Tricking Louverture into coming to a meeting, Leclerc's men kidnapped him in June 1802 and took him in chains to France, where in April of the following year he died of hunger and exposure in a dungeon in the Jura Mountains.

In Louverture's absence, one of his former generals, Jean-Jacques Dessalines, who had fought for the French, gradually emerged as the leader of the blacks. Known for his cruelty, he consolidated his position by killing independent black leaders and vodouisants, whom he saw as a potential threat to his power. Leclerc, meanwhile, concluded that the only hope for pacifying the country was to embark on a campaign of genocide in order to begin the plantation system anew with fresh, docile slaves. His army slaughtered entire villages in an attempt to annihilate the population of the island, and even killed entire units of black troops loyal to France. But the resistance of the black Domingans was ferocious, and, as had happened to the British, French soldiers and sailors died of yellow fever even faster than they could be killed in battle.

The French spent twenty-one fatal months in Saint-Domingue. General Leclerc died from yellow fever there on November 2, 1802. He was replaced by the second in command, Donatien-Marie-Joseph de Vimeur, Vicomte de Rochambeau, whose father, the French general Jean-Baptiste-Donatien de Vimeur, Comte de Rochambeau, had played a critical role in the American Revolution. To replace the many dead troops, Rochambeau received twenty thousand replacements.[8] The Cuban plantocracy collaborated with Rochambeau at first, but by January 1803 they refused to render further aid, perhaps because of the benefits to them if Saint-Domingue, their former fierce competitor, never recovered.

Bonaparte and Talleyrand justified their actions to the world as a case of civilization standing up to barbarity. Rochambeau imported Cuban bloodhounds trained to tear out the entrails of the rebels they caught, though most of the dogs were ultimately eaten by desperate French soldiers. Meanwhile, certain that the primitive *noirs* could never withstand the full power of the French army, planters had returned to Saint-Domingue from exile in order to reoccupy at the earliest possible moment the lands of which they saw themselves as rightful owners. There is an eyewitness account of this migration by a U.S. writer, a memoir in the form of an epistolary novel:

> We arrived safely here, my dear friend, after a passage of forty days, during which I suffered horribly from sea-sickness, heat and confinement; but the society of my fellow-passengers was so agreeable that I often forgot the inconvenience to which I was exposed. It consisted of five or six French families who, having left St. Domingo at the beginning of the revolution, were now returning full of joy at the idea of again possessing the estates from which they had been driven by their revolted slaves.[9]

The book's full title is *Secret history; or, The horrors of St. Domingo, in a series of letters, written by a lady at Cape Francois, to Colonel Burr, late vice-president of the United States, principally during the command of General Rochambeau*. A former mistress of Aaron Burr, Leonora Sansay (writing under the pen name of Mary Hassall) was married to a Domingan plantation owner and returned with him to Saint-Domingue during this period. While the principal characters of her narrative are fictional, she was an eyewitness to the period she describes. Some of it is so sensational that, were she describing events anywhere else, one might think it lurid fantasy, but in the garden of atrocity that was Saint-Domingue, I leave it to the reader to wonder if something like this actually happened:

> Every inhabitant lived on his estate like a Sovereign ruling his slaves with despotic sway, enjoying all that luxury could invent, or fortune procure. The pleasures of the table were carried to the last degree of refinement. Gaming knew no bounds, and libertinism, called love, was without restraint. The Creole is generous, hospitable, magnificent, but vain, inconstant, and incapable of serious application; and in this abode of pleasure and luxurious ease vices have reigned at which humanity

must shudder. The jealousy of the women was often terrible in its consequences. One lady, who had a beautiful negro girl continually about her
person, thought she saw some symptoms of *tendresse* in the eyes of her
husband, and all the furies of jealousy seized her soul. She ordered one
of her slaves to cut off the head of the unfortunate victim, which was
instantly done. At dinner her husband said he felt no disposition to eat,
to which his wife, with the air of a demon, replied, perhaps I can give you
something that will excite your appetite; it has at least had that effect
before. She rose and drew from a closet the head of Coomba. The husband, shocked beyond expression, left the house and sailed immediately
for France, in order never again to behold such a monster.[10]

Parts of Sansay's narrative read much like the nostalgia for antebellum
bliss that the American South produced in quantity after the Civil War:

The place is tranquil. The arrival of General Rochambeau seems to
have spread terror among the negroes. I wish they were reduced to order
that I might see the so much vaunted habitations where I should repose
beneath the shade of orange groves; walk on carpets of rose leaves and
frenchipone; be fanned to sleep by silent slaves; or have my feet tickled
into extacy by the soft hand of a female attendant.

Such were the pleasures of the Creole ladies whose time was divided
between the bath, the table, the toilette and the lover.

What a delightful existence! thus to pass away life in the arms of
voluptuous indolence; to wander over flowery fields of unfading verdure,
or through forests of majestic palm-trees, sit by a fountain bursting from
a savage rock frequented only by the cooing dove, and indulge in these
enchanting solitudes all the reveries of an exalted imagination.

But the moment of enjoying these pleasures is, I fear, far distant.[11]

As the massacres continued, so did the festivities. Sansay gives an account
of a grand ball on board the secure location of a ship:

The ball announced by the admiral exceeded all expectations and we
are still all extacy. Boats, covered with carpets, conveyed the company
from the shore to the vessel, which was anchored about half a mile from
the land, and on entering the ball room a fairy palace presented itself
to the view. The decks were floored in; a roof of canvas was suspended
over the whole length of the vessel, which reached the floor on each

side, and formed a beautiful apartment. Innumerable lustres of chrystal
and wreaths of natural flowers ornamented the ceiling; and rose and
orange-trees, in full blossom, ranged round the room, filled the air with
fragrance. The seats were elevated, and separated from the part appropriated to dancing, by a light balustrade. A gallery for the musicians
was placed round the main-mast, and the whole presented to the eye an
elegant salon, raised by magic in a wilderness of sweets. . . .

Nothing is heard of but balls and parties. Monsieur D'Or gives a
concert every Thursday; the General in chief every Sunday: so that from
having had no amusement we are in danger of falling into the other
extreme, and of being satiated with pleasure.

The Negroes remain pretty tranquil in this quarter; but at Port-au-
Prince, and in its neighbourhood, they have been very troublesome.[12]

"Troublesome" might be understood as a euphemism for rivers of blood.

❧

On October 16, 1802, the cantankerous Juan Buenaventura Morales, Spanish
intendant of Louisiana, closed the American deposit at New Orleans—the
place where merchants placed their goods for transshipment—to new goods.
Citing as his reason that the Peace of Amiens no longer required tolerating
the commerce of neutrals, he acted without instruction from Spain and over
the objections of the governor.

He had done the one thing that might have caused the Anglo-American
settlers of the hinterlands to form an army and march down. "If New Orleans
has been peopled and has acquired importance and capital," wrote Laussat in
a letter of April 18, 1803, "it is due neither to Spain nor to the Louisianans
properly so-called. It is due to three hundred thousand planters who in twenty
years have swarmed over the eastern plains of the Mississippi, and have cultivated them, and who have no other outlet than this river and no other port
than New Orleans."[13] Jefferson had to placate the furious westerners: with the
North and South effectively functioning in balanced blocs, the western states
of Kentucky and Tennessee (and soon Ohio), though sparsely populated, had
two senators each and were what we now call swing states. To demonstrate his
resolve, Jefferson dispatched James Monroe as special envoy to Paris, where
he would join Livingston (who spoke no French) with instructions to try to
obtain New Orleans and West Florida.

Bonaparte cut his losses in the face of catastrophe. In April 1803, the
French minister François Barbé-Marbois astounded Livingston by offering to sell

to the United States all of the vast Louisiana Territory, which France had yet to take possession of. Livingston hurriedly dispatched the news to Washington before his unwanted colleague Monroe could arrive. The Americans, hoping only for New Orleans and West Florida, had never dreamed they would take all of Louisiana. (And, indeed, the deal did not include West Florida, though after the fact the Americans tried to claim that too.) Livingston and Monroe signed the deal for the Louisiana Purchase on May 2, 1803, less than a month after the offer was tendered (and less time than it took for a message to travel across the Atlantic and be answered), at the bargain price of sixty million francs, about fifteen million dollars. The French governor Pierre Clement de Laussat, who had arrived in Louisiana in March to take charge of the colony but had still not done so, learned about the pending transfer in August.

In July, Britain had imposed a naval blockade on Saint-Domingue. As the slaughter mounted, many of the remaining colonists, both white and free colored, fled once again, wherever they could go, taking their slaves with them when possible. They were ferried out, in many cases, on the boats of privateers, who essentially constituted a freelance naval force in the region and were experienced blockade-runners. Others took to the sea on boats that were little better than rafts.

Most of the Domingan refugees—perhaps thirty thousand or so, though some estimates are lower—went right across the water to eastern Cuba, primarily to Santiago (if embarking from the West or South) and secondarily to Baracoa (if from the North). Some traveled on—Leonora Sansay went on to Jamaica, per the dateline of the last letter in her book—but more stayed in Cuba. This exodus, which would continue on to Louisiana in 1809 after expulsion of the *franceses* from Cuba, had a major cultural impact throughout the Antilles. It is not too much to say that it was one of the generative explosions of popular music in the hemispheree.

The Domingans transformed the economy and the society of eastern Cuba with their superior agricultural technology, business skills, and highly developed arts, most especially including both white and black music and dancing. The whites brought an ideal of refined, luxurious living, as well as reactionary political views and a well-developed aesthetic of slave torture. The blacks brought their creolized but still recently African culture, which included sophisticated knowledge of war technique and revolutionary ideology and, as such, was central to creating a culture in eastern Cuba that would repeatedly erupt in revolution. Both groups were intensely social.

It had been a condition of Spain's retrocession of Louisiana that the territory would remain with France. Too bad. Word that Louisiana was to be sold to the United States didn't reach the street in New Orleans until November. The Louisianans, who thought they were going to become French citizens, were stunned to learn they were to become Americans instead.

Bonaparte, ever the strategist, knew very well the sale's consequences. It was his best defense against the power of Britain. The acquisition roughly doubled the size of the United States, though France never precisely defined the territory it was purporting to sell. To Robert Livingston's inquiry about its boundaries, Talleyrand merely responded, "I can give you no direction. You have made a noble bargain for yourselves and I suppose you will make the most of it."[14]

Rochambeau capitulated after the Battle of Vertières on November 18. Fleeing the island, he and his remaining troops were taken prisoner by the British navy, carried back to London, and imprisoned. Out of forty-three thousand French troops sent to Saint-Domingue, only eight thousand had survived.

∽◌∾

Nothing in the U.S. Constitution provided for acquisition of territory, and Jefferson, who had been a strict constructionist, greatly exceeded his authority, and contradicted his own firmly expressed principles, in taking advantage of the unexpected opportunity to annex Louisiana. Over opposition from New Englanders in both houses of Congress, the treaty was approved.

The French governor Laussat formally took possession of Louisiana from Casa Calvo and the doddering Salcedo on November 30. The colony he received was greatly transformed from the one Louis XV had turned over to Spain. New Orleans was a prosperous city that was fast becoming a major port. Though no white person thought of this as a virtue, the town had become a bulwark of black culture, with a population of free people of color that had grown from 99 in 1769 to 1,355 in 1803.[15] Laussat closed down the town's one theater on December 12, condemning the building as unsafe. Eight days later, he turned the Louisiana Territory over to Thomas Jefferson's twenty-eight-year-old appointee, William Charles Cole Claiborne, and General James Wilkinson.

Wilkinson, whose shady history in the city went back to the days of Governor Miró when he had turned up posing as a merchant, and who would soon be part of Aaron Burr's treasonous conspiracy to establish an independent republic in the west, was disturbed to see armed, uniformed free blacks in New Orleans. Claiborne, fearing a colored riot at the time of transfer, requested that Jefferson send "four or five thousand stand of arms," together with ammunition.[16]

In December 1803, with a sense of urgency and considerable confusion, Congress began considering a bill to establish a temporary government in Louisiana. The Americans, who saw the Creoles as children unprepared for the complexities of liberty, did not give them a voice in the government. Claiborne and the other territorial officers were Jefferson's appointees, and all power was theirs. Now Louisiana was a colony of the United States—in many ways, of Virginia. France had sold out Louisiana for the second time, leaving it without even a theater.

In admitting the Louisiana Territory, Congress established the division of Louisiana into two parts. The new Territory of Louisiana—everything from present-day Arkansas north—had its capital at the strategic upriver port of St. Louis (nine blocks long from north to south, it was now the westernmost city under U.S. control).[17] The southern part of the Louisiana Purchase—the part that was soon to become the state of Louisiana—became the Territory of Orleans.

Spain was outraged, and its diplomats protested in both Paris and Washington. The Spanish governor Casa Calvo remained in town, with a garrison of fifty soldiers, ultimately departing for Texas the following year. The United States quickly began claiming it had bought West Florida too, and by 1819 it had leveraged its Louisiana territorial claim to include the northern reach of the continent, all the way out to Oregon (though the southern extension, from Texas to California, would have to wait).

◦≫◦

Before Aaron Burr killed him in a duel, Alexander Hamilton had wanted to take Louisiana and the Floridas from Spain by force of arms and hoped to lead the invading army personally. He then planned to continue on to Mexico and Peru, to take over the silver mines, which would have made his bank into a world monetary power.

The annexation of the enormous Louisiana Territory, through purchase rather than Hamiltonian conquest, is frequently referred to as the great achievement of Thomas Jefferson's presidency, though alas, he got no silver mines with it. But Louisiana's price in blood had already been paid by the slaves of Saint-Domingue, whose victory forced Bonaparte's hand to sell the Louisiana Territory to Jefferson, and it would be paid again by future generations of slaves in the southern United States.

On January 1, 1804, just twelve days after the transfer of Louisiana, Saint-Domingue officially vanished, never to return. Proudly adopting an aboriginal name for the land, the Republic of Haiti came into being, with Jean-Jacques

Dessalines, whose title was General in Chief of the Indigenous Army, at its head. It became the second independent nation in the hemisphere, after the first and only victorious slave rebellion.

On April 28, Dessalines ordered death for the French remaining in Haiti. He went through the country from village to village to supervise the extermination personally, slaughtering hundreds at a time and sparing only a few. This massacre of whites, the final spasm of a cycle of atrocities, antagonized the world. Britain, the world's leading financial power, broke off negotiations for a treaty. Pro-slavery voices in the United States, dominant in the nation's politics until the Civil War, routinely used it as a cautionary example that blacks could not live together freely with whites.

In his earlier position as secretary of state, Thomas Jefferson had argued in favor of recognition of revolutionary France, in spite of the Terror. But as president, he refused to recognize Haiti. Though U.S. merchants continued to trade with the new nation for a time, the United States imposed a commercial blockade against Haiti in 1806 that lasted four years. After the trade embargo ended, Haiti traded with New Orleans, but the United States did not recognize the nation until 1862, when Abraham Lincoln recognized Haiti and Liberia at the same time, in hopeless pursuit of a longtime vision that saw both of them as possible places to which the black population might be deported in a projected—to use an anachronistic but accurate term—ethnic cleansing of the United States.

⟨∞⟩

The French Revolution is taught in history courses as a fundamental event in shaping the modern world, but, despite its substantial impact, the Haitian Revolution has been treated as a footnote. Adolphe Thiers's ten-volume history of the French Revolution, first published in 1832, contains only one index entry for Saint-Domingue, which leads to a two-page discussion that does not mention Toussaint Louverture.[18] In 1938, the Trinidadian scholar C. L. R. James published *The Black Jacobins*, still one of the best books on the Haitian Revolution, which treated the two revolutions as intimately connected parts of the same phenomenon, and argued for the insertion of the Haitian Revolution, and the figure of Louverture, into the world historical narrative.

Haiti was central to every major event in the hemisphere at the time, most especially to the Louisiana Purchase. Slavery continued in the southern United States for more than seventy years after Boukman's ceremony at Bois Caïman, and longer still in Cuba and Brazil. But the Haitian Revolution was the turning point. It made clear what the stakes of slavery were, and it put fear into the heart of the slave power. The desire to prevent "another St. Domingo" drove U.S. policy from then on, and was one of the main factors in the banning of the slave trade to the United States at the earliest date the Constitution allowed. It made the slave owners of the South more outspoken in defense of their beleaguered system. The widely trumpeted spectacles of Negro savagery, as it was portrayed in the press, intimidated abolitionist voices for a time. It blunted the ambitions of European colonial powers in the New World, and in doing so changed the relationship between Europe and America. Britain, inflamed by the loss of so many men, was forced to adopt a new perspective on the potential cost of defending slavery, and restricted the flow of slaves to her new acquisition of Trinidad, which had been poised to receive as many as a million Africans.

Those economies that were deeply dependent on slave labor—the agricultural economies of Brazil, the Antilles, and the Southern United States—became more militantly defensive of the institution and, especially in the case of the United States, became harsher, even paranoid, in their treatment of slaves. In economies that were moving toward industry—the Northern United States and Britain—the idea of being out of the slavery business gained in popularity. In Britain, and subsequently in the Northern United States, the abolitionist movement gathered force.

In the South, the importation of Africans was looking less and less attractive from the point of view of security. It was safer to buy domestically raised slaves, who were not only already acculturated and English speaking, but were, it was thought, less savage. Virginia's economy, meanwhile, was slumping from the poor performance of its tobacco industry and its surplus of slaves, whose maintenance costs were straining slave owners' purses.

Despite the lack of silver mines, there were ways to extract money from Louisiana. For Virginia, it was more profitable that the new Deep South buy its slaves domestically, rather than importing them from Africa.

~≈ PURCHASE ≈~

17

AN ADDITION TO CAPITAL

To be consistent with existing and probably unalterable prejudices in the United States, the freed blacks [in case of abolition] ought to be permanently removed beyond the region occupied by, or allotted to, the white population. The objections to a thorough incorporation of the two people, are, with most of the whites, insuperable. . . . If the blacks, strongly marked as they are by physical and lasting peculiarities, be retained amid the whites, under the degrading privation of equal rights, political or social, they must always be dissatisfied with their condition, as a change only from one to another species of oppression; always secretly confederating against the ruling and privileged class; and always uncontrolled by some of the most cogent motives to moral and respectable conduct. The character of the free blacks even where their legal condition is least affected by their color, seems to put these truths beyond question.

—*James Madison, letter of June 15, 1819*

Nowhere do the best and worst of American history collide more violently than in the figure of the man who annexed Louisiana.

Thomas Jefferson was arguably the most influential politician in American history. Though he never set foot in Louisiana, no one had more influence over the course the territory would take. Despite his occasionally

expressed misgivings about the institution of chattel slavery, Jefferson's annexation of Louisiana to the United States made him a key figure in American
slavery's expansion on a previously undreamed-of scale. That created a major
industry of traffic in domestically raised humans, which was not an unin-
tended consequence of territorial expansion but an obvious outcome, devoutly
desired by Jefferson's constituents.

By focusing on Jefferson as he looked from the perspective of slavery, it may
be objected that I am presenting a one-sided vision of a complex man. To which
I say, there are hundreds of books that extol his achievements, and his face is
carved into a mountainside in South Dakota. His virtues are well known.

Americans honor him for many things, including his contribution to our
tradition of freedom of—or if you prefer, freedom from—religion, as well as
for the appending of a bill of rights to the Constitution, a document largely
drafted by Jefferson's protégé James Madison, which Jefferson thought unsat-
isfactory. But then, there were those people who, according to the laws of
his place, his time, and his revolution, he owned. However much Jefferson
bewailed slavery, it was at the core of his identity. Nor was being a slave master merely his private business; the contradictions of his political philosophy
stemmed from it, and those contradictions were disastrous for the nation,
flowing right into civil war.

Until fairly recently, American historiography has been one-sided in the
other direction, tending to make excuses for Jefferson's actions and attitudes
regarding slavery: he was a prisoner of his time; a conflicted, even tragic, figure; tormented by the contradictions, et cetera. If one does not make those
excuses, the picture is not a pretty one. Jefferson disseminated blatantly rac-
ist ideas, and as a politician, he fought to secure the grand expansion of the
institution of slavery.

The only book Jefferson published, *Notes on the State of Virginia* (1784),
appeared in a French translation during the five years (1784–89) he spent in
France as a diplomat for the new United States. It gave him the reputation in
Europe of being a great thinker. His notorious explication of the differences
between "races" as expressed in the *Notes* is worth reading if one is to get a
sense of what was behind the conviction that "all men are created equal." This
is what the French learned from Jefferson:

Deep rooted prejudices entertained by the whites; ten thousand recollec-
tions, by the blacks, of the injuries they have sustained; new provocations;
the real distinctions which nature has made; and many other circum-

stances, will divide us into parties, and produce convulsions which will probably never end but in the extermination of the one or the other race.

It is worth noting this. In the years preceding the Haitian Revolution, this influential American politician in philosopher's robes was publishing in France his forecast of "convulsions which will probably never end but in the extermination of the one or the other race." When Jefferson heard of Toussaint Louverture's abduction by the French in 1802, he predicted that "a war of extermination will ensue." He had been predicting such a thing since *Notes on the State of Virginia*; between the influence of that book, and his thumbs-up to Napoleon to invade Saint-Domingue, he had done his part to turn his frightful vision of race war to the death into a self-fulfilling prophecy.

Moreover, one of those races was funky:

To these objections, which are political, may be added others, which are physical and moral. The first difference which strikes us is that of colour. . . . And is this difference of no importance? Is it not the foundation of a greater or less share of beauty in the two races? Are not the fine mixtures of red and white, the expressions of every passion by greater or less suffusions of colour in the one, preferable to that eternal monotony, which reigns in the countenances, that immoveable veil of black which covers all the emotions of the other race?

Add to these, flowing hair, a more elegant symmetry of form, their own judgment in favour of the whites, declared by their preference of them, as uniformly as is the preference of the Oran-ootan for the black women over those of his own species. The circumstance of superior beauty, is thought worthy of attention in the propagation of our horses, dogs, and other domestic animals; why not in that of man? Besides those of colour, figure, and hair, there are other physical distinctions proving a difference of race. They have less hair on the face and body. They secrete less by the kidnies, and more by the glands of the skin, which gives them a very strong and disagreeable odour. This greater degree of transpiration renders them more tolerant of heat, and less so of cold, than the whites. . . .

They seem to require less sleep. A black, after hard labour through the day, will be induced by the slightest amusements to sit up till midnight, or later, though knowing he must be out with the first dawn of the morning. They are at least as brave, and more adventuresome. But this may perhaps proceed from a want of forethought, which prevents their seeing a danger till it be present. When present, they do not go through it with more coolness or steadiness than the whites.

They are more ardent after their female: but love seems with them to be more an eager desire, than a tender delicate mixture of sentiment and sensation. Their griefs are transient. Those numberless afflictions, which render it doubtful whether heaven has given life to us in mercy or in wrath, are less felt, and sooner forgotten with them. In general, their existence appears to participate more of sensation than reflection. To this must be ascribed their disposition to sleep when abstracted from their diversions, and unemployed in labour. An animal whose body is at rest, and who does not reflect, must be disposed to sleep of course. Comparing them by their faculties of memory, reason, and imagination, it appears to me, that in memory they are equal to the whites; in reason much inferior, as I think one could scarcely be found capable of tracing and comprehending the investigations of Euclid; and that in imagination they are dull, tasteless, and anomalous. [paragraphing added]

The eighteenth-century prose style aside, there is not much in this passage that a latter-day Ku Klux Klan member, or my first-grade teacher in Natchitoches, would have disagreed with. Nor is there much to suggest that Jefferson's opinion had changed by the time of his death forty years later, though Jefferson lived to regret having written it, since his archenemies the Hamiltonians had much fun mocking the "secrete less by the kidneys" passage. It is perhaps too easy to point out that if Jefferson had had to labor as hard as a slave did, he too might have had "a very strong and disagreeable odour." (If this seems like a curious echo of Le Page du Pratz's previously cited complaint about black peoples' "natural smell," Shannon Lee Dawdy points out that Jefferson owned a rare first English-language edition of Le Page du Pratz's book, and recommended it to Lewis and Clark.)[1] Jefferson was in a sense a forward thinker; this proto-eugenicist discourse was ahead of the curve of scientific racism, which would not bloom into full flower until after Darwin.

⁙

In 1789, Jefferson traveled daily from Paris to Versailles for the meetings of the Estates General and was a secret collaborator in the French Revolution on the side of the moderates, advising the Marquis de Lafayette on the drafting of the Declaration of the Rights of Man and Citizen, which took the Declaration of Independence as a point of departure. He was present in Paris during the fall of the Bastille on July 14, 1789, six weeks after the inauguration of George

Washington. In an autobiographical text written thirty-two years later, Jefferson squarely laid the blame for the French Revolution not on a conjuncture of historical forces, but on a woman: Marie Antoinette. Jefferson, who found French women shockingly opinionated and forward, opined that had Louis XVI been left to himself,

> he would have willingly acquiesced in whatever [the Estates General] should devise as best for the nation. . . . But he had a Queen of absolute sway over his weak mind, and timid virtue; and of a character the reverse of his in all points. . . . *I have ever believed that had there been no queen, there would have been no revolution.* No force would have been provoked nor exercised. The king would have gone hand in hand with the wisdom of his sounder counsellors, who, guided by the increased lights of the age, wished only, with the same pace, to advance the principles of their social institution.[2] [emphasis added]

When Jefferson returned to Virginia with his daughters Martha and Maria (also known as Patsy and Polly), sailing from England for Norfolk on October 23, 1789, he brought with him a fine harpsichord for Patsy, made to his specifications in London by Jacob Kirckman, with British music historian and keyboardist Charles Burney acting as a go-between. The age of revolutions was also the age of transition from harpsichord to the pianoforte. Which is to say, it was the age of the crescendo, a startling musical device made famous in the 1760s by orchestra composers in Mannheim, Germany. As the name *pianoforte* implied, the instrument could be played loud or soft, unlike the harpsichord. Trying to forestall their coming obsolescence, harpsichord makers met the competition with what are now called "bells and whistles." Gadget fancier that Jefferson was, he bought the most complicated harpsichord possible. It had two ranks of keys and a "Venetian swell," a modification consisting of a set of Venetian blind–type louvers over the strings which, when pedal operated, gave the effect of a crescendo. To Kirckman's disgust, Jefferson also insisted on a new mechanical fad called a "Celestina stop," a rotating silk-thread bow that pulled a bowed-string sound out of the harpsichord, at the cost of gunking up the mechanisms with resin and detuning the strings.[3]

Along with the harpsichord, Jefferson brought back to Virginia with him a huge cargo that included, besides many books, a large shipment of fine wines, "Parmesan cheese, raisins, vinegar, oil, macaroni, kitchen furniture, books, a bust of Lafayette and a pedestal for it, mattresses and two bedsteads, a guitar, pictures, a clock, servants' clothes, chariot, phaeton, models of various machines, . . . and plaster busts of John Paul Jones destined for various American patriots."[4] Even on the ship, he found it hard to contain his chronic "acquisitive streak," and he asked the captain to procure him two mahogany tables like the one on shipboard.[5]

And he brought back another precious possession: the slave girl Sally Hemings. "Mighty near white," with "long, straight hair down her back,"[6] she had traveled to Paris as Polly's servant, and was now, according to her son Madison's later testimony, returning to Virginia pregnant by Jefferson. She was sixteen, or perhaps seventeen; Jefferson was forty-five.

There are people who indignantly claim that it is not true that Sally Hemings became pregnant by Jefferson in Paris. I don't know. Nobody else does either, not 100 percent, for sure. But there's circumstantial evidence, as well as the late-in-life assertion of Madison Hemings, to suggest that the well-known story of a long-term Jefferson-Hemings sexual relationship is true.[7] The denials of it that I have read—intense in their indignation and aggressively dismissive of the motivations of the questioners—assume that Jefferson must be presumed morally incapable of siring Sally's four children unless there is forensic evidence to prove otherwise.

The story is lurid, but hardly uncommon in eighteenth-century Virginia. Sally Hemings's mother Betty had been the legal property of Sally's father, the slave trader John Wayles; Jefferson married Wayles's daughter Martha. Wayles had some kind of conjugal relationship with Betty Hemings, within which he fathered the slave girl Sally, who was thus Martha's half sister by a different mother. Sally and Martha would have looked much alike, but Sally was twenty-five years younger and, being of one-quarter African descent, she was a slave—the daughter of a slave concubine, raised with a thorough knowledge of the role. She was one of 135 people Jefferson inherited title to from Wayles. With her came a complex set of family interrelationships among the enslaved Hemingses and the free Wayleses and Jeffersons, as well as Wayles's debts, from which Jefferson never extricated himself.[8]

Martha Wayles Jefferson suffered seven pregnancies with only two children surviving during her ten years of marriage, and died in childbirth in 1782. One might have thought Jefferson would have refrained from inseminating his wife to death, but then, Jefferson was not known for his self-control. He never remarried, but, so it would appear, went into clandestine concubinage with Sally and continued his inseminative streak with her.

To judge by the reference to the "Oran-ootan," Jefferson might have preferred not to mate with a black woman. But Sally Hemings wasn't funky, nor did she look black. She was three-quarters white. Having grown up in the house, her English would have been relatively genteel, unlike that of a field slave, though she would not have received any formal instruction. It is likely that she never learned to write—one more enslaved American who left no direct record of her thoughts.

Few issues in American history are more controversial. Needless to say, official history long treated the tale of Sally and Master Tom as a distasteful poison-pen rumor drummed up by conniving Federalists and believed by gullible Negroes. But the first published novel by an African American, the autodidactic, ex-slave William Wells Brown's *Clotel, or, The President's Daughter* (1853), was a historical novel about the subject. (Its first edition, published in London, used Jefferson's name; subsequent American editions were more circumspect.)[9]

Some distinguished historians—I will take Douglass Adair, editor of the *William and Mary Quarterly* and author of *The Intellectual Origins of Jeffersonian Democracy* (1943), as a good example—sputtered themselves blue in the face at this "libel" (Adair's word) of their hero. In an unfinished but influential essay published posthumously after Adair shot himself one afternoon in 1968, he said outright: it was a lie. The real father of Sally's children was . . . Jefferson's nephew Peter Carr. Moreover, it couldn't be true, because . . . well, it just couldn't be. Adair proposed what was in effect the standard rape-trial defense: she's a slut, she's lying, how dare you suggest that this honorable man would do such a terrible thing?

Why not? In England, in France, and especially in Virginia, aristocrats consorting with servants—a word that in the mouths of polite Southerners meant household slaves—was hardly uncommon. It seems strange to think that Jefferson wouldn't have been comforting himself with *someone* all those years after his wife died, when he had a pretty slave girl at hand who had been raised to the office of concubine.

Joshua D. Rothman notes that in 1796,

> French visitors noted evidence of sex across the color line on Jefferson's resident plantation. The Duc de La Rouchefoucauld-Lincourt mentioned "particularly at Mr. Jefferson's" slaves who had "neither in their color nor features a single trace of their origin, but they are sons of slave mothers and consequently slaves." The Comte de Volney, also traveling during the summer of 1796, similarly noted slaves at Monticello "as white as I am."[10]

Jefferson owned one of the largest tracts of land in Virginia, and his domain was made up of eleven different farms—not just a single patch of land—spread out over a broad area, so visitors probably would not have encountered the field slaves' cabins. It is likely, however, that guests at Monticello would have been most exposed to the house slaves, most prominently, the Hemingses.

Such forensic evidence as does exist is consistent with, though does not prove, Jefferson's having been the father of Sally's youngest child. A November 1998 article in *Nature* magazine summarized DNA tests that showed, in the authors' words, that "the simplest and most probable explanations for our molecular findings are that Thomas Jefferson, rather than one of the Carr brothers, was the father of Eston Hemings Jefferson [the last of Sally's children]." After that, the naysayers were reduced to pointing out that it *could* have been another male in the Jefferson family line, without offering any further evidence in that direction, assuming the burden of proof must fall away from Jefferson's paternity.[11] However, these findings reinforce circumstantial evidence such as the fact that all of Sally's pregnancies were conceived when Jefferson was present at Monticello (and none during his long absences), not to mention the fact of her children being freed upon his death (though the other slaves were sold), to say nothing of the oral tradition of Sally's family. And perhaps the most obvious factor: Jefferson was the big man on his plantation, and Sally was his prize property.

I can't claim to shed any light on the forensics of an issue which is as much a Rorschach blot as it is anything else. For me, the question the Jefferson / Hemings story brings up is not whether he fathered her children, but why did American historians kick and scream so hard for so long that this couldn't possibly be true? Of course it could be true. Whether Jefferson exercised his option or not, he could have sex with Sally Hemings whenever he wanted. The matter of her consent was irrelevant, because she could not refuse.

Because *that's* what slavery was.

When you have the legal authority to own another person, and not only another person, but their issue, and their issue's issue, and the right to sell your ownership to anyone else, who does the actual inseminating to produce the issue is a lesser matter. Even the word *rape*, increasingly used by a new generation of historians to refer to sex between slave owners and slaves, seems inadequate to describe the violation entailed. No one denies that, whoever sired them, Sally Hemings's children, as well as any children her children might have, and their children after them, belonged to Master Tom or whomever he might have sold or willed them to, the same way he might have done with horses.

Nor would such children have received more than a bare minimum of education. Jefferson, being somewhat liberal on the subject, was in favor of teaching slaves to read, but not to write—the two were taught separately in those days—because if they could write, they could forge passes to leave the plantation. Jefferson's slave boys didn't go to school, but went to work in his nailery. Setting a model for how manufacturing might have been accomplished in the slaveholding South had it developed, Jefferson was for a time one of the largest domestic producers of nails, in a home-based factory at Monticello, making him both an industrial and agricultural exploiter of slave labor.

No, we don't know absolutely for certain if Master Tom did impregnate Sally or not. If the matter were tried in a court of law, with a presumption of innocence and an expensive law firm to defend Jefferson (which is how a number of mainstream American historians seem to have seen their role in this case), we might have to let him off the hook for lack of definitive proof. On the other hand, if he were a poor man with substantial circumstantial evidence against him and a public defender, he'd accept a plea bargain, the way some 95 percent of criminal cases in the United States are resolved now, and get off with a guilty plea and a reduced sentence.

But then, no one has accused Jefferson of a crime. After all, you can do with your property as you like.

In Jefferson's autobiography, written near the end of his days in 1821, he stated clearly what he considered the necessary terms of emancipation:

> the freedom of all born after a certain day, and deportation at a proper age. But it was found that the public mind would not yet bear the proposition, nor will it bear it even at this day. Yet the day is not distant when it must bear and adopt it, or worse will follow. Nothing is more certainly written in the book of fate than that these people are to be free. Nor is it less certain that the two races, equally free, cannot live in the same government. Nature, habit, opinion has drawn indelible lines of distinction between them. It is still in our power to direct the process of emancipation and deportation peaceably and in such slow degree as that the evil will wear off insensibly, and their place be pari passu filled up by free white laborers.

This summed up a typical attitude of the day: the British were to blame for having imposed these troublesome people on us, and since they cannot live together with us, we must cope as best we can with the cursed legacy of slavery until that happy day when we can at last deport them all. Up through and including Lincoln, American politicians nursed a fantasy of repatriating blacks to Africa.

But they weren't going anywhere. They were essential. Slavery was the economic engine that drove an ever-expanding prosperity unprecedented in the history of the world. Two truths were held to be self-evident: Negroes, more physically resistant than whites, were needed to do labor that would kill a white man, and the two "races" could not live together under conditions of social equality because a race war to the death would result. Since deportation was impractical, emancipation was impossible.

Thomas Jefferson—amateur violinist, revolutionary, politician, farmer, nail manufacturer, architect, philosopher, Jefferson Davis's namesake, and grandfather of the Confederacy's minister of war (George Wythe Randolph, Patsy's son, born at Monticello in 1818)—owned over six hundred other people during his lifetime, between one and two hundred of them at any one time, including four who were probably his own children.[12] He lived his entire life dependent on the income from slave labor.

As was the norm for planters, Jefferson was both insolvent and fabulously wealthy. He was not a man to deny himself anything. Monticello was proof of that. When he remodeled Monticello, he mortgaged his slaves to cover the expenses. That was a common enough practice; plantation owners lived in constant debt, and their most visible asset was not their land—there was plenty of that to be had, and, especially in Virginia, the land might well be played out. Their best, and most liquid, asset was their Negroes, who formed the basis of their credit.

If you were ever skeptical that all the darkies were a-weepin' because massa was in the cold, cold ground, consider that the death of a master meant the piecemeal sale and separation of families and community to pay the debts run up during the master's extravagant life. That the sale happened after the slave owner's death meant he would be spared from having to face directly the human consequences of his financial position. This is exactly what happened after Jefferson's death in 1826, when his slaves—significantly, minus seven descended from Betty Hemings—paid for his lifelong acquisitive streak by being sold at auction for the benefit of creditors.

Jefferson was not a speculator in slaves, but, like other large slave owners, he sold slaves to raise cash when he needed to. Slaves formed a substantial amount of his net worth, so he was not disinterested in the price they brought. As a high-ranking government official, and ultimately as president, he was in a position to take measures that would enhance their value.

Compared with the living testimony of the example of Jefferson's life, and his consequential actions as a politician, his protestations about the eventual inevitability of the end of slavery add up to little. His presidency not only did nothing to make emancipation closer. Its monumental accomplishment was to extend the reach of the slave power.

Jefferson famously wrote in a letter, "I consider a woman who brings a child every two years as more profitable than the best man of the farm. What she produces is an addition to capital, while his labors disappear in mere consumption."[13] This is one of those felicitous confluences of source and vocabulary: Thomas Jefferson, with all he symbolizes for American history, referring to slave children with that trendy buzzword *capital*, recently popularized by the French. Capital is meaningless if it is not being put to work. Capital has to be lent, invested, mortgaged, its services rented, its ownership traded.

The interests of capital were spectacularly served by having a separate slave caste. Though this caste was generally easily distinguishable by its dark skin, its boundaries had to be rigidly policed if the value of human property was to be maintained. In the Anglo-American slave regime, if you were born to an enslaved woman, you were a slave, period, and your grandchildren would be slaves too. What emerged from a slave's womb was the next best thing to, and the thing most easily converted to, specie. Slaves were a self-reproducing perpetual annuity, the best life insurance possible for a family. The best dowry a woman could bring to a marriage was a Sally Hemings.

Such was the slave regime that Jefferson bequeathed Louisiana.

∽

With Jefferson at the helm, Napoleon Bonaparte's discarding of Louisiana led to the vast expansion of the uniquely perverse institution of American slavery, presided over by the master of Monticello. For the black people of Virginia, who were nearly half the state's population, the legacy of Jefferson's presidency was atrociously cruel. They or their loved ones were taken from their homes and families to be turned into money down South.

New Orleans was on its way to becoming the largest slave market in the United States.

18

THE SLAVE-BREEDING INDUSTRY

Some of the most awful scenes of cruelty are constantly taking place in the middle states of the Union. . . . We have
in the United States slave-breeding states . . . where men,
women, and children are reared for the market, just as
horses, sheep, and swine are raised for the market. Slave-
rearing is there looked upon as a legitimate trade; the law
sanctions it, public opinion upholds it, the church does not
condemn it. It goes on in all its bloody horrors, sustained by
the auctioneer's block.

—*Frederick Douglass, speaking in England, 1846*[1]

Slavery in the United States differed in essential ways from slavery in
the rest of the hemisphere.

In terms of material standard of living [writes David Brion Davis], the
slaves in the nineteenth-century American South were clearly far better
off than most slaves and forced labor in history; yet they were victims of
one of the most oppressive slave systems ever known in terms of the rate of
manumission, racial discrimination, and psychological oppression. . . .[2]

It would seem hard for a form of slavery to have been more oppressive
than that of the Cuban sugar plantation, where men were worked to death
in ten years or so. But even sugar slaves had at least some hope that, if they

survived, they might be able to buy their way into the large class of free blacks that populated the island. And slaves in Cuba had their own religions practiced in their own languages, and dances, and music. By contrast, slaves in the United States had lost their ancestral vocabulary, and were raised from birth to have no past and no future, as members of an eternally subjugated caste whose great-grandchildren would be born into slavery.

With the U.S. territory more than doubled by the Louisiana Purchase, there was such an abundance of land that it was worth little. But since there was an acute shortage of labor to develop the newly annexed land, the value of Southerners' human capital increased enormously.

A slave's labor did not just consist of bending a strong back, but of using his or her skills and intelligence. Johann Schöpf observed on his 1784 visit to South Carolina that

> the gentlemen in the country have among their Negroes as the Russian nobility among the serfs, the most necessary handicrafts-men, cobblers, tailors, carpenters, smiths, and the like, whose work they command at the smallest possible price or for nothing almost. There is hardly any trade or craft which has not been learned and is not carried on by negroes, partly free, partly slave; the latter are hired out by their owners for day's wages.[3]

Such a situation had the effect of depressing the wages of white craftsmen and preventing the formation of a Southern middle class, which never developed in any sizable way before the Civil War. But as a member of the superior race, even the poorest cracker could feel a caste, though not a class, solidarity with the wealthiest planter. (I use the word "cracker" advisedly; Schöpf notes that it was what the backwoodsmen of South Carolina were called, because of the noise their whips made when they drove their teams into town.)[4]

Slaves were phenomenal generators of wealth for their owners. As with all assets, slaves came with costs and risks, to say nothing of the numerous drawbacks entailed by the uncomfortable fact that they were, for all slave owners attempted to deny it, people. But you don't get a better deal than being able to appropriate 100 percent of the value of someone's labor—except by being able to have exclusive rights to all of that person's descendants' labor in perpetuity, and Southern slave owners claimed that too.

The reproductive abilities of enslaved people alone could increase a planter's worth by 5 percent a year. Slaves were triply valuable: they were not merely laborers, but salable merchandise; and not merely merchandise, but the best collateral. They could be rented out as farmworkers, industrial workers, sex workers, craftsmen, or servants. A slave's work created a revenue stream with which to pay a mortgage, at the same time that his or her person could be pledged as security on that mortgage. Since enslaved people were commonly mortgaged, they were a fundamental element of the banking system. In the event of a default, they could be liquidated at auction on short notice, as the market was always strong. It is not quite accurate to say they were money, because money is a medium of exchange. But slaves even approached that function, through their not uncommon use as barter. In a cash-starved South, they were the next best thing to money.

The United States had no gold or silver mines. There was an inadequate supply of hard coin, and there was especially little of it in the South. Such precious metal as there was, was in the hands of New England and New York merchants, who by the 1810s were running a trade deficit with China, exporting specie in exchange for luxury goods.[5] Southerners, who tended to see banking as a Northern conspiracy, were suspicious—not without reason—of banknotes and the banks that issued them. Many saw bankers as gamblers and crooks who took in real money, in the form of coins, and handed out play money, in the form of bills that might trade at a discount in the next city or state, or be totally worthless if the bank failed, either through force of circumstances or plundering by its directors. Banknotes were most easily usable as money with other customers of the same bank, with obvious complications for any but local commerce. Paper money was distrusted, and used as a last resort. Slave traders paid cash for their purchases.

As the most widely read magazine in the antebellum South, *DeBow's Review*, published in New Orleans, would put it: "[Slaves are] the first use for savings, and the negro purchased is the last possession to be parted with. If a woman, her children become heirlooms and make the nucleus of an estate."[6] But they were not only table silver to be passed down: they also were the prime indicator of social status, the most conspicuous wealth a family could have. Of course, a slave might die or escape, occasioning a total loss of the investment; for this reason, larger fortunes were better able to manage the risks of slave owning than small farmholds, and over the decades of slavery in the United States, slaveholding became concentrated into increasingly wealthier hands.

This chapter takes place rather out of chronology, because it discusses something already active in the 1790s that developed through the time of the Civil War. Historians usually call it the interstate slave trade. Beginning as a way of selling off surplus labor, it grew, and was maintained, through what can accurately be called a slave-breeding industry.

The child's version of U.S. history, at least as this writer absorbed it in school, did a very poor job explaining slavery, and certainly never mentioned this aspect of it. Partly that's because slavery is not a subject fit for children. It's embarrassing to have to explain what it consisted of. It gets into things we would prefer children not know about—middle-aged men fornicating with adolescent girls, women used for breeding purposes, children sired and sold, black men dehumanized, and families routinely shattered.

❦

Virginia's peak of prosperity was in the years 1710–70. During that time, it grew tobacco, which sold at a handsome price. The slave labor it employed cost as little as labor could possibly cost. But the soil played out, and the war for independence played havoc with agriculture and markets. With abundant land to raise food on and relatively mild physical conditions, together with the fact that Virginia was not growing the murderous crop of sugar, the slave population reproduced itself at high rates. Each new slave born was another mouth to feed. Freeing them seemed out of the question to slave owners, because then they would have to live with uncontrolled Negroes in their midst, and besides, slaves were supposed to be assets.

By the 1790s, there were no slaves in Massachusetts or Vermont. But down South, Virginia, Maryland, and Delaware were net exporters of *people*, sold for cash to the new market emerging further south. "From the beginning of agriculture [in Virginia] in the seventeenth century," writes Hugh Thomas, "propietors on tobacco plantations had . . . increased their stock of labor from home-bred slaves without excessive recourse to the international market. By 1800, slaves on some plantations were being deliberately bred there for sale."[7]

The African slave trade to the thirteen colonies effectively stopped with the Revolutionary War. Some African trade began again with American independence, but by the time Georgia shut its trade down in 1798, no state allowed the importation of slaves. Nor had importation been constant: South Carolina had a prohibitive tax on importation for much of the 1740s.

The U.S. Constitution was not so indelicate as to use the words *slave* or *slavery*. Dr. Benjamin Rush, a signer of the Declaration of Independence, cofounder of the Pennsylvania Society for the Abolition of Slavery, and a close friend of John Adams, wrote: "No mention was made of *negroes* or *slaves* in this constitution, only because it was thought the very words would contaminate the glorious fabric of American liberty and government."[8] But through euphemisms, the Constitution included the notorious three-fifths clause.

Nothing in the Constitution provided for the abolition of slavery, or of commerce in slaves. When the Constitution was being debated, no one knew that Eli Whitney was about to invent the cotton gin (though some forward-looking Southerners were trying to find someone who could create such a machine), nor did anyone know that the Louisiana Territory would become part of the United States. Nor did the Northerners fully comprehend how emotionally attached Southerners were to owning slaves. In the South it was widely believed that the Constitution protected the institution of slavery, and that Virginia, Maryland, the Carolinas, and Georgia had entered into a union with the others on the basis of that understanding.

The three-fifths clause in the Constitution acknowledged slavery as a fact in the United States, albeit euphemistically. The Constitution also had a fugitive slave provision, and it provided that the federal government could not prohibit, or lay prohibitive taxes on, the international slave trade, until 1808, as spelled out in Article 1, Section 9, Clause 1, of the U.S. Constitution:

> The Migration or Importation of such Persons as any of the States now existing shall think proper to admit, shall not be prohibited by the Congress prior to the Year one thousand eight hundred and eight, but a Tax or duty may be imposed on such Importation, not exceeding ten dollars for each Person.

Hoping that slavery was on its way to gradual extinction, the Northerners ceded the issue to the Southerners, who had to deal with the matter directly. John Adams said as much during the Missouri controversy in 1821, when he and Thomas Jefferson were both old men. Jefferson, like most Virginians, was in favor of extending slavery to the new state of Missouri, part of the Louisiana Territory that Jefferson had acquired. Adams wrote to Jefferson:

> Slavery in this Country I have seen hanging over it like a black cloud for half a century. I might probably say I had seen Armies of Negroes marching and countermarching in the air, shining in Armour. I have been so terrified with this Phenomenon that I constantly said in former times to the Southern Gentlemen, I cannot comprehend this object. I must leave it to you. I will vote for forcing no measure against your judgments.[9]

Admitting a new slave territory to the delicate balance was a touchy matter. At the time of the Louisiana Purchase, South Carolina favored an open African slave trade, whereas Virginia, possessing a surplus black labor force, was against it. But Virginia was a powerful state politically, home to four of the first five U.S. presidents—George Washington, Thomas Jefferson, and future presidents James Madison and James Monroe, who were protégés of Jefferson. The city of Washington, the nation's capital as of 1800, was located adjacent to Virginia on a site carved out of Maryland that was still an Indian village in 1775, after a deal cut by Jefferson and Alexander Hamilton over dinner. Now, operating out of Washington, the Virginians (and their Kentucky relatives) had taken control of New Orleans.

W. C. C. Claiborne, Jefferson's trusted subaltern, was a Virginian. In Louisiana he had to negotiate with a foreign legal system, a cantankerous French-speaking population, and an economy heavily dependent on sugar, a crop that ate slaves alive and required their frequent replacement. The grueling peak-season workday killed laborers within a few years and left female workers too feeble to reproduce. New slaves had to be imported continually to keep the sugar-mill labor force from dying out. Like slaves on the sugar plantations of the Antilles, and unlike the rest of the United States where sugar was not raised, the sugar slaves of southern Louisiana had negative birthrates for as long as slavery lasted.[10] The sugar plantations of southern Louisiana needed to refresh their slave population with new workers—one could say, new victims—constantly. Though sugar was mostly cultivated in one region of the country—Louisiana—it consumed a disproportionate number of black laborers.

In response to the transfer of Louisiana to the United States, South Carolina reopened its African slave trade at the end of 1803. The move caused anger in much of the rest of the country, both from those who thought slavery immoral and from those who thought there were too many black people in North America already (the two categories overlapped considerably). These new African kidnap victims, many of them Kongo,[11] were not by and large destined for plantations in South Carolina. They were to be sold to the new cotton planters of the Deep South, and to the sugar planters of Louisiana, who were clamoring for labor. These much cheaper imports badly damaged the Virginia trade in domestically raised slaves, causing considerable bad blood between the two states. Virginia, however, was the more politically powerful of the two.

Congress had never sought to regulate slavery, nor had the Southerners wanted it to: if it could regulate, it could prohibit. But making some determination about how slavery would be handled in the new territory was unavoidable. To the anger of the Louisiana planters, Congress prohibited the importation of slaves to both of the new territories that the Louisiana Purchase had been carved into, and both parts were prohibited from engaging in domestic or foreign slave trade. Planters hurriedly began importing slaves before the cutoff date and preparing a political response.

"The importation of negroes [to Louisiana] is abolished point blank," wrote Laussat in a letter of April 7, 1804. "The present inhabitant of Lower Louisiana could not have been attacked in a more vulnerable spot." In Louisiana, slaves were legally classed as immovable property—that is, as real estate, because land was only worth something if there were hands to work it. A sugar plantation would be sold complete with its slaves, which were as essential as the boiler. The European metropoles had insisted on forcing one-sided trade terms on their colonies, ultimately provoking the colonial merchant classes to foment revolution. Now the Virginians were in a position to deny the Louisiana Territory free trade in slaves, imposing a monopoly at higher prices.

On November 1, 1805, domestic slave trade to the Territory of Orleans was authorized; but the foreign slave trade to Louisiana would never again be legal. Prohibiting the foreign trade to the new Louisiana Territory may have had the outward appearance of a humanitarian gesture, but it was nothing of the sort. It was protectionism. One motive, certainly, was keeping the South free from contamination by black revolutionary thought that might enter without prophylactic measures—not only from Haiti, but also from Africa, where there were organized, gun-toting black armies and where, in some parts, a centuries-long wave of Islamic jihad roiled. Fear of murderous foreign Negroes played well with the general population. But more to the point, by keeping the cheaper African imports out, prices for domestically born slaves stayed high. The new Deep South territory—beginning to bloom white with cotton and, in Louisiana, green with sugarcane—was a bonanza for the old Upper South.

New Orleans was beginning its career as a destination city for immigrants to the New World. Already one of the most demographically diverse cities in the Americas, it was becoming more so. Anglo-Americans began moving in, and they were allowed to bring slaves with them. But Domingan refugees were not allowed to come in from foreign territories with their slaves, nor were Louisiana Creoles allowed to run their own ships to Africa or import slaves freely from dealers in Havana who did. They saw having to buy English-speaking slaves from Anglo-Americans as discriminatory against them. The great answer to all this—at least as a stopgap measure—was the clandestine commerce in slaves being carried on by privateers, who did a land-office business intercepting slave ships bound for Cuba and diverting the prizes to Louisiana.

On the earliest permissible date as per the Constitution, January 1, 1808—one of the most important dates in American history—all importation of slaves from abroad became prohibited by the federal Slave Trade Act of 1807. The United States followed the lead of Britain, which banned the trade that year. In practice, only South Carolina was actively in the trade by then; in the four-year period between South Carolina's reopening of the trade and federal prohibition of it, 39,075 captive Africans were imported.[12] This figure represented perhaps 8 percent of the total slaves trafficked to North America during the entire slave trade (figuring that number at half a million), and a much larger percentage of the number brought legally to the political entity of the United States of America, since the overwhelming majority of the North American slave trade took place to the thirteen British colonies, before the United States existed as such.

Why was the slave trade banned at the earliest constitutionally allowable moment? In large measure, because South Carolina's massive importations of slaves from Africa had ruined the market for Virginia-bred slaves. But the prohibition was packaged as anti-terrorism, and sold as keeping out the fiends who had burned down Saint-Domingue. Over the fifty-five years that elapsed between that date and the Emancipation Proclamation, prices for domestically bred slaves rose, and rose again, until they became a great speculative bubble.

Slaves were shipped down the Mississippi on flatboats and marched south in coffles. By the 1820s, they were coming south on ships from the Atlantic seaboard. More slave ships came to New Orleans from the east coast of the United States than had ever come there from Africa. Coming from many disparate and increasingly long-ago African cultural backgrounds, these English-speaking African Americans arrived into the well-established, unique cultural matrix of Afro-Louisiana.

∽∞∾

Anglo-American North America took only a small number of the slaves brought to the Americas, maybe 5 or 6 percent. About half a million Africans were abducted to the territory that would become the United States, but by the time of the Civil War there were some four million slaves. How did half a million become four million? The term historians have used is "natural increase." But the increase was not only natural, it was industrial. No slave owner, large or small, could afford to be ignorant of the fact that breeding slaves was a business, as per an 1818 letter written by a young Mississippian to his uncle in Louisiana: "For a young man just commencing in life the best stock in which he can invest capital is, I think, Negro stock. . . . Negroes will yield a much larger income than any Bank dividends."[13]

In North America, which at the time of the American Revolution had the highest living standard in the world thanks to the richness and abundance of its land, and where sugar was not an important crop (except in Louisiana, after 1795), it was possible to create a domestic slave-raising business. In the burgeoning merchant empire of the United States, slaves became a larger business even than cotton, more valuable than land. A commonly cited figure by ex-Confederates after the Civil War for their collective losses in slave property was $4 billion, which probably figures four million people at $1,000 a head.

This was an innovation of U.S. entrepreneurship. No comparable business existed elsewhere in the hemisphere. The only other place where something similar happened, though on a lesser scale, was in Brazil, later, when a domestic trade sprang up after the British cut off slave importation from Africa to Brazil in 1850. But Virginia and Maryland were well along with the business of the interstate slave trade by the 1790s.

Even for a miserable field slave, there were degrees of comfort. The most desirable situation was to be in an established, stable plantation, with a family and a community. That was almost to be a serf, who at least had the advantage of being attached to his land. James Sidbury writes:

> Enslaved people had been planting roots in Virginia and Maryland for better than a century prior to the advent of the interstate slave trade. During that time they had forged plantation communities with a distinctive culture. They had battled their masters over the terms under which they were forced to work, over their customary rights to food and leisure, and over numerous other issues. . . . The experience of being ripped out of a deeply rooted community and culture to be forcibly transported and sold into a frontier setting peopled not only by unknown white people but by blacks from Africa and the Gullah coast of South Carolina must have been a disruptive experience analogous, though not equal, to that of Africans sold into the Atlantic trade.[14]

With the opening of the Louisiana Territory, the growth of sugar, the invention of the cotton gin, and the cessation of the African slave trade, there came into existence a practically unlimited new market for slaves. Breeding, both of humans and animals, was a near obsession for planters, who, from the early days, fancied themselves well-bred aristocrats. Steven Deyle, in his study of the domestic slave trade, cites a Virginia slave-sale advertisement from 1769 that mentioned "breeding ability."[15] The trade commonly employed such terms: breeding Negroes, breeding slaves, breeding wench. Along with this came animal breeders' lingo: bucks, bitches.

Bernhard, Duke of Saxe-Weimar Eisenach, who traveled the United States in 1825–26, wrote:

> As the import of Negro slaves by sea has been abolished by Congress, having been declared an act of sea-piracy, a new type of internal American trade has evolved. Many owners of slaves in the states of Maryland and Virginia have established true—pardon this distasteful word, but I do not have a better word to describe this beastly business!—slave stud-farms, from which the plantation owners in Louisiana, Mississippi, and other southern states fill their requirement for these articles, whose price grows daily.[16]

There has been some argument over whether there actually existed large specialized slave-raising farms in the South, as enshrined in the popular twentieth-century imagination through the now out-of-print, onetime mega-bestselling novel *Mandingo* and its lurid sequels. Though there is anecdotal evidence that suggests they might have existed, much has been made of the lack of documentation for the existence of such farms. No one seems to have come up with a set of account books, for example. Most scholars seem to think they did not exist, and certainly not on a grand scale.

A farm purely given to slave-breeding without another product would presumably have been unprofitable, because compared to animal husbandry—which it would have been viewed as—it took too many years to raise children to maturity. Slaves were never left idle, so they would have done profitable labor as they matured. The farm, then, would have had to have another crop besides slaves, and would likely have preferred to have been identified by that crop rather than as a supplier to slave traders. I will not join that argument here, except to note that in the absence of documentary evidence, debating the existence of large people-raising farms is almost beside the point, because—

Every farm with slaves was a slave-breeding farm.

Raising slaves was mostly a cottage industry, a basic profit center of every small farm and plantation. Of this there is ample documentation. As Deyle points out, the birth of white babies was recorded in a Bible, but the birth of black babies was recorded in a ledger.[17] *Every* slave child born was, as Jefferson put it, an addition to capital.

The Kentuckian Henry Clay noted in an 1829 address that "nowhere in the farming portion of the United States would slave labor be generally employed, if the proprietor were not tempted to raise slaves by the high price of the Southern market, which keeps it [the price] up in his own."[18] The high price of slaves did not necessarily benefit the small farmer, or the Deep Southern planter; it benefited the seller of slaves, which is to say it accrued to the benefit of Virginia, the founder of the domestic trade. But then, almost every slave owner at some point bought or sold, so all of them participated in the trade to some degree, and since the price of slaves directly affected a farmer's well-being, it was an object of constant attention. The price climbed, steadily if not always smoothly, from the 1790s through the 1850s. By the beginning of the Civil War, the book value of the slaves held in the South was seven times the total amount of currency in circulation in the United States.[19]

In 1852, British traveler Edward Sullivan observed that

> One of the striking features in slavery to an Englishman is the perfectly cold-blooded manner in which it is treated and talked of by the press and individuals. In Virginia, where they breed slaves largely, the business is carried on as systematically, and they take as much pains to keep up a good breeding stock (drafting the weak and sickly ones), as they do for south-downs or short-horns in England. The slave-dealers know the men that raise the best stock, and they go down and buy at their fairs as our horse-dealers do in the north of England.[20]

For poorer whites, who hoped to ascend the social ladder, there was a single essential step: you joined the ownership society by purchasing your first slave. A young man would be well advised to build his fortune by saving up enough to buy a young female—except for fancy girls, they were cheaper than males—receive 100 percent of the profit of her labor, breed her himself, then sell the lighter-skinned children. It was a very good deal for the owner, and it allowed him to talk auction prices and trade tips with the other gentry in the only club that mattered in the South: the slave owner's club.

If you had a few slaves, and you were unlucky in cards, you could settle up your gambling debts by signing over somebody's son or daughter—maybe even your own. The depth of the degradation that slavery and its associated trade imposed over every aspect of society has, needless to say, not been a point of great pride for historical writers about the South, and one does not read much about it. A significant exception was Frederic Bancroft's 1931 work *Slave Trading in the Old South*, which addressed a near-total gap in the embarrassed historiography. It was the product of a life's work; Bancroft was born in 1860, and his research entailed speaking with people who remembered, and participated in, the slave trade. His work is extensively sourced with references from the antebellum popular press. He recounts high points of a debate in the Virginia legislature of 1831–32 about the abolition of slavery: "The antagonists agreed on two important facts—that slave-rearing was a common means of profit and that traders and other buyers annually took thousands of Virginia slaves to distant states."[21]

Walter Johnson writes, "As much as anything else in the years leading up to the Civil War, the planters of the Chesapeake were slave farmers who held onto their wealth and status by supplying the cotton boom with the offspring of slaves."[22]

This was all very well known to the world. In one of a series of articles about the American Civil War that he published in Vienna's *Die Presse*, Karl Marx wrote on October 25, 1861, of

> the rapid transformation of states like Maryland and Virginia, which formerly employed slaves on the production of export articles, into states which raised slaves in order to export these slaves into the deep South. Even in South Carolina, where the slaves form four-sevenths of the population, the cultivation of cotton has for years been almost completely stationary in consequence of the exhaustion of the soil. Indeed, by force of circumstances South Carolina is already transformed in part into a slave-raising state, since it already sells slaves to the states of the extreme South and Southwest for four million dollars yearly. As soon as this point is reached, the acquisition of new Territories becomes necessary, in order that one section of the slaveholders may equip new, fertile landed estates with slaves and in order that by this means a new market for slave-raising, therefore for the sale of slaves, may be created for the section left behind it. It is, for example, indubitable that without the acquisition of Louisiana, Missouri and Arkansas by the United States, slavery in Virginia and Maryland would long ago have been wiped out.[23]

Though Marx was not the first to observe that the slavery industry needed to expand in order to survive, the behavior of the South, which was willing to go to war in order to have new western territories to sell its slaves into, helped him confirm his observation that capitalism requires an expanding market. Nor did it escape Marx's notice that much of what little factory work there was in the antebellum South was done by slaves, with obvious consequences for the situation of free laborers. Perhaps Marx read *De Bow's Southern and Western Review*, the largest-circulating Southern magazine, founded in 1846 under the name *Commercial Journal of the South and West*. A business journal that aggressively championed the expansion of slavery (as per its title, with the words "Southern and Western"), it promoted a vision of an industrialized economy that would use slave labor in factories and railway construction.

In the pages of *De Bow's*, one could even read a principled defense of having sex with slave women, as in this excerpt from 1850:

> It is mostly the warm passions of youth which give rise to licentious intercourse. But I do not hesitate to say, that the intercourse which takes place with enslaved females is less depraving in its effects than when it is carried on with females of their own caste. In the first place, as like attracts like, that which is unlike repels; and though the strength of passion be sufficient to overcome the repulsion, still the attraction is less. He feels that he is connecting himself with one of an inferior and servile caste, and that there is something of degradation in the act. The intercourse is generally casual; he does not make her habitually an associate, and is less likely to receive any taint from her habits and manners.[24]

It is rare to read *any* defense of sexual intercourse outside of wedlock from that period of American history. But at some point, slave owners had passed the point of trying to deny it, and reached the point of simply saying: yes, we have sex with slave women, but that's not such a bad thing.

Basic to all this was children sold away from mothers, mothers sold away from fathers, brothers sold away from sisters. The desperate plea from a just-sold slave to the purchaser to purchase also a child, parent, grandparent, uncle, aunt, husband, wife, sweetheart, was a normal part of the theater of the slave auction. Slave owners were well aware that black families were potential centers of resistance. Breaking up the families and communities of the slaves was of a piece with destroying the language, religion, and drum. In Africa, where the ancestors are the gods, to take away one's family is not only to take away one's survival but one's soul. But then, agricultural slaves were not expected to have souls, especially since they were considered by so many slave owners to be less than fully human. Southern slavery was designed to make slaves not merely into conscript laborers, but to turn them into nonpeople, with no identity and no history.

The slave-breeding industry encouraged sexual license in black people, for which they were then blamed. Enslaved women were to fornicate, and fornicate more, to produce as many fatherless children for sale as possible, while enslaved men were displaced from their functions of father and provider. But the practice of slave-breeding more thoroughly corrupted the morals of the white men involved. Robert Sutcliff, visiting Virginia in 1804, wrote that "many [slave owners] paid no more regard to selling their own children, by their female slaves or even their brothers and sisters, in the same line, than they would do to the disposal of a cow or a horse, or any other property in the brute creation. To so low a degree of degradation does the system of negro slavery sink the white inhabitants, who are unhappily engaged in it."[25]

Whatever else slavery was, it was a system of sexual privilege. Owners could participate freely in the slave-breeding process, whether as actors or voyeurs. There is ample evidence that this privilege was extensively exercised by Southern slave owners. When the South went to war to defend the institution of slavery, it was, inescapably, defending the privilege of forced concubinage. Perhaps, beyond purely economic considerations, part of the irrational intensity of the South's defense of slavery came from the strength of slave owners' attachment to that privilege.

∽∾

The domestic slave trade was well under way at the time of the American occupation of New Orleans. Allied with the Irish-born merchant and U.S. consul Daniel Clark, the firm of Chew & Relf was already in business by 1803; among the other goods it handled, the firm sold slaves at auction. But it took until the mid-1820s or so, when slave ships from the Atlantic seaboard began arriving in numbers, for New Orleans to become the capital of slave sales, and it remained the greatest market right up until the Northerners stopped it.

The most commonly cited estimate is that a million people were taken by force from the Upper South to the Deep South, some two-thirds of them by traders. Perhaps double that number of slaves were sold in local transactions, to neighbors and other nearby purchasers, but I am focusing here on the interstate trade, because it was a major industry for New Orleans, and greatly affected the demographics and culture of the city.[26] Tourists who came to see the nation's capital, and European diplomats on visits of state, beheld the coffles that trudged through the streets of Washington, D.C., a regional distribution center for slave exports from parts of Virginia and Maryland.

The ships were headed for New Orleans, with Baltimore an important port of embarcation, while the coffles had Natchez as a frequent destination, though that city banished the sales to the Forks of the Road, outside of town. Sometimes when a coffle set off on its weeks-long march at twenty or twenty-five miles a day, its departure was heralded by a small band of musicians. The coffles were themselves a formative moment in American music, because as they went along on their long forced march, yoked together, the people in the coffles sang. Often, the drivers required them to sing. Bancroft writes:

> Music was the favorite distraction on the march as well as in the slave pens. There was rarely a numerous group of negroes without a violin, a guitar, a banjo, an accordion, mouthorgans or jewsharps. At the head of a coffle of about 70 met on the highway near Paris, Kentucky, in the 'twenties, were two slaves vigorously sawing their violins. . . . The gangs were encouraged to march through villages and towns, singing in melodious, plaintive chorus, while whoever had a musical instrument lustily played it.[27]

People from different parts of the South, descending from different parts of Africa, who had been consolidated together in the traders' slave jails that were a common feature of Southern hotels, hit a march tempo together, swapping songs and stories, harmonizing in their shackles as they went along.

Peter Bruner, who published a narrative of his childhod days as a slave in 1850s Virginia, recalled

> The slave traders would buy the slaves at market and take them down the river on a boat. Then he would tell them to start up a song, and then I would hear them begin to sing:
>
> O come and let us go where pleasure never dies,
> Jesus my all to Heaven is gone,
> He who I fix my hopes upon.
> His track I see and I'll pursue
> The narrow road till him I view.
> Oh come and let us go,
> Oh come and let us go where pleasure never dies.

Some of them seemed very much distressed because they had to leave their children and mothers and friends behind. Those that refused to sing they would throw that big whip in among them and make them sing. Then they would take them to Lexington where they owned a trading yard and put them in there and feed them well before the slave trader came from New Orleans to buy them, just the same as horse purchasers came from Richmond and Cincinnati to purchase horses at Oxford. After they remained in the trading yard for 3 or 4 weeks they would ship them to New Orleans.[28]

This was a slave, recounting a song he had heard other slaves sing, a song that then traveled down to New Orleans. Imagine the volume of communication that must have passed through the dense confines of the slave jails of New Orleans merchants.

The brutality of the business did not only manifest itself in the separation of families. The interstate slave trade made the Deep South into a penal colony for the Upper South, where problem slaves could easily be disposed of. Being sent to Louisiana was particularly feared by slaves elsewhere because of the notorious mortality at its sugar plantations. It was a punishment for the stubborn and the vicious.

The interstate slave trade created a collateral business: the abduction of free blacks from the North, who were then sold down South. This possibility was a constant source of fear for Northern blacks. One of the best-known cases was that of Solomon Northup, kidnapped in 1841 from his New York hometown of Saratoga Springs. Sold and resold, he wound up on a sugar plantation on the Red River of Louisiana. After finally managing to smuggle out a letter to his family, he was freed, and in 1853 published *Twelve Years a Slave*, a narrative of his experiences. Northup was a fiddler, and in his memoir he gives an account of playing in the house of a planter who had bought him in part because the trader had advertised his musical abilities:

Frequently I was called into the house to play before the family, mistress being passionately fond of music.

All of us would be assembled in the large room of the great house, whenever Epps came home in one of his dancing moods. No matter how worn out and tired we were, there must be a general dance. When properly stationed on the floor, I would strike up a tune.

"Dance, you d—d niggers, dance," Epps would shout.

Then there must be no halting or delay, no slow or languid movements; all must be brisk, and lively, and alert. "Up and down, heel and toe, and away we go," was the order of the hour. Epps's portly form mingled with those of his dusky slaves, moving rapidly through all the mazes of the dance.

Usually his whip was in his hand, ready to fall about the ears of the presumptuous thrall who dared to rest a moment, or even stop to catch his breath. When he was himself exhausted, there would be a brief cessation, but it would be very brief. With a slash, and crack, and flourish of the whip, he would shout again, "Dance, niggers, dance," and away they would go once more, pell-mell, while I, spurred by an occasional sharp touch of the lash, sat in a corner, extracting from my violin a marvelous quick-stepping tune. The mistress often upbraided him, declaring she would return to her father's house at Cheneyville; nevertheless, there were times she could not restrain a burst of laughter, on witnessing his uproarious pranks. Frequently, we were thus detained until almost morning. Bent with excessive toil—actually suffering for a little refreshing rest, and feeling rather as if we could cast ourselves upon the earth and weep, many a night in the house of Edwin Epps have his unhappy slaves been made to dance and laugh.[29]

Uncle Tom's Cabin, in which the saintly title character was sold downriver from Kentucky to a Red River sugar plantation, perhaps somewhere near Natchitoches, smacked the United States between the eyes with a two-by-four in 1852, and was known to even more people in its myriad theatrical adaptations than in its original form as a bestselling novel.[30] It was followed by a wave of white-composed popular songs still familiar today, most memorably those of Stephen Foster, that told of the tragic separations occasioned by the traffic that carried loved ones for sale from the Upper South to the Deep South. Despite their chilling narratives, these songs became sentimental favorites—golden oldies, if you will—to subsequent generations that do not seem to have given a thought to the lyrics beyond a generalized sense of antebellum nostalgia.

In "My Old Kentucky Home," a Stephen Foster song of 1853 that became the official state song of Kentucky in 1928, the reference to "sugar-canes" might pass for exotic color now, but at the time, it was understood to mean a death sentence in a Louisiana labor camp:

The head must bow, and the back will have to bend,
Wherever the darkey may go;
A few more days, and the trouble all will end,
In the field where the sugar-canes grow.
A few days for to tote the weary load,—
No matter, 't will never be light;
A few more days till we totter on the road:—
Then my old Kentucky home, good-night!

A hit song of 1856 by a white man in Ohio, Benjamin Hanby, was based on a story told him by Joseph Shelby, who had escaped from slavery:

Oh, my poor Nellie Gray, they have taken you away
And I'll never see my darling, anymore.
I'm sittin' by the river and a weepin' all the day
For you've gone from the old Kentucky shore.

When I learned this song as a child in Natchitoches, in a segregated, whites-only grade school, it seemed like the saddest song I'd ever heard. The teacher never mentioned, and at the age of eight, I didn't realize, that the song was about slaves. Let alone what it meant that it was about a female slave.

⌘

Backroom disrobing of the merchandise for as thorough an examination as necessary was an indispensable part of the ritual of auctioning slaves. Already in 1784, Schöpf observed that in North Carolina "if negresses are put up [for auction], scandalous and indecent questions and jests are permitted."[31] Fifty-nine years later, a British visitor to New Orleans observed that "when a woman is sold, [the auctioneer] usually puts his audience in a good humor by a few indecent jokes."[32]

The market term for young, light-skinned sex slaves was *fancy girls*. It was the most notorious, and the most profitable, segment of the slave trade. The lighter skinned they were, the more money they were likely to bring. Edward Sullivan noted in 1852 that in New Orleans, "a handsome quadroon could not be bought for less than one thousand or fifteen hundred dollars! though the market is well supplied at that price."[33] A quadroon technically was a person of one-fourth black ancestry, but the word was generically used to mean white-looking women of color. One fancy girl was knocked down for $7,000 in 1837, and another, in 1841, for $8,000; at that time, the mean price for slaves was somewhere around $700.

The place where you would see the kind of adventurous, affluent man who would openly buy an expensive quadroon sex slave at auction was New Orleans, the largest market for fancy girls by a factor of ten or more. Gamblers, who were a professional class in New Orleans, were frequent buyers, doubling as pimps. (The number-two market for fancy girls was another gamblers' town, the horse-racing capital of Lexington.) If you ate at a boardinghouse in New Orleans, your dinner would be cooked by a slave and perhaps brought to you by a slave, rented out by the slave owner to the boardinghouse owner. If you visited a brothel after dinner, you might be serviced by a slave. If you wanted to spend the money, they might have one with blond hair and blue eyes.

With each passing generation, an ever-lighter-skinned caste of sex slaves was being bred. Had slavery continued, this population would presumably have continued to expand.

c○○ɔ

Slave trading forged deep commercial links between the Upper South and the Deep South, with their mutually dependent exports of slaves and cotton, respectively. It virtually created the white South as an entity, one whose self-awareness led it to declare itself a nation and challenge the North for control of the continent as the nation expanded westward. It bound the Upper and Lower South into a common destiny based on the economy of slavery, and ultimately pushed them to secede from the United States together.

The interstate slave trade was a central part of the formation of U.S. culture. The churning of the black population through steady forced migration made African American culture more homogeneous, creating a kind of network of cultural unity all across African America that is still palpable. This culture was less explicitly, and more implicitly, African, defining new ways to be musically black in the absence of ancestral languages, religions, and drums.[34]

In this context, New Orleans takes on extra significance. Wherever in the country black people were, there was a sense of a knit-together culture that would later constitute a powerful national market for music. But New

Orleans was different. Its connection to Africa was more recent, and it had, by Southern standards, an enormous community of free people of color, as well as a legacy of greater relative freedom for the enslaved. With its heterogeneous population, its more or less open practice of African-derived religion, and its Sunday dances at Congo Square, to say nothing of the urbanness and density of its black population at a time when the United States was overwhelmingly rural, it represented an alternative path of development for African American culture.

As the enslaved population of the United States increased, New Orleans was both beacon and central node in an African American communication system that spread across thousands of miles.

19

THE FRENCH QUARTER

Time appears here only made to be lavished in amusement. Is the uncertainty of human life so great in this climate as to leave no leisure for anything beyond dissipation? The only serious pursuit appears to be the amassing and spending of that wealth which is wrung from the luckless toil of so many unfortunate Africans, doomed to an endless task, which is even entailed upon their posterity.

—*Thomas Nuttall, a visitor to Louisiana in 1820*[1]

At a ball in New Orleans in 1802, the ex-governor Vidal's son insisted on dancing "English contredanses," which were easier, or perhaps simply more to his taste, than the French ones. When the young Vidal pushed his privilege too far, an angry shouting match ensued between his entourage and the French:

—*Contredanse anglaise!*

—*Contredanse française!*

The military guard, supporting Vidal, unsheathed their bayonets, rifles, and sabers and were at the point of opening fire on the dancers, who were armed with épées and ballroom furniture. The Americans, says an 1803 account of the incident, remained neutral, and, while the French and Spanish men were confronting each other, they took advantage of the situation to slip away with the women.[2] Ultimately the situation was defused, and the French contredanse won the night.

During Laussat's ephemeral three-week governorship of Louisiana, he presided over a number of celebratory balls. (His diary entry for January 3, 1804, begins, "Yet another ball!")[3] Laussat's letters to his superiors are wonderfully informative, as, for instance, in the following excerpt, in which we see the United States' characteristic lack of comprehension of other languages already in full antidiplomatic effect:

> It was scarcely possible for the government of the United States to begin worse [he wrote in a letter of April 7, 1804], and scarcely could it have sent two men (Messrs. Claiborne, as governor, and Wilkinson, as general) less suited to win their hearts. The first, with charming private qualities, has few means and great awkwardness, and is extremely below his place. The second, already known here for a long time under ugly reports, is an illogical fellow, full of queer whims, and often drunk, who has been guilty of innumerable silly inconsistencies. Neither one understands a word of French or Spanish.

Playing out national rivalries over contredanses seems to have been frequent in New Orleans at that time. In spite of the similarity of the names, the *contredanse anglaise* and the *contredanse française* were quite different, and incompatible. In the former, the English "country dance," men and women separated in two long facing lines, and the music played was perhaps a reel. The *contredanse française*, also known as the *quadrille*, was danced in squares of four couples, with music that in New Orleans very possibly already had the flavor of the tango rhythm. Laussat described in his memoir what happened five nights later:

> An unfortunate germ of trouble erupted, at an ordinary public ball, between the French and the Anglo-Americans.
> Two contredanses, one French, the other English, were formed at the same moment. An American, taking offense, raised his walking stick at a fiddler. Big commotion. Claiborne stayed quiet. [Daniel] Clark roused him from inaction. Claiborne could not explain himself, he appeared embarrassed, weak, he yielded, then forced himself to reassert authority. He finally used more persuasion than rigor against the American, who was a simple surgeon attached to the troops. The French contredanse began again. The American interrupted it a second time with an English contredanse and put himself in place to dance; someone cried out: *If the women have a drop of French blood in their veins, they will not dance.* Quickly, all the women left the hall.

The Marqués de Casa Calvo, who was present playing cards, laughed up his sleeve. He had gumbo served to two or three women, who had taken refuge at his side, and maliciously continued his game.

Claiborne spoke to me about it. *There you have it*, I answered him, *an image of the feelings which animate them. Be careful that they do not clash over matters more grave and more important.* [italic in original][4]

Another entry in Laussat's diary tells of a brawl that broke out at a ball, with General Wilkinson present, when dancers tampered with the city-mandated rotation of two rounds of French contredanse, one round of English contredanse, and one round of waltz, at which the Spanish speakers excelled.[5]

There was considerable worry in Francophone quarters that the Americans would close down the balls, but Claiborne reassured the anxious Creoles that dancing would continue unabated. The shuttered theater was repaired and reopened, probably in late November or possibly early December 1803, with a cast of Domingan refugees.[6] In a letter dated January 31, Claiborne apologized to James Madison for "calling your attention to the balls of New Orleans, but I do assure you, sir, they occupy much of the public mind."[7] The problem of how to comprehend, and what to do with, New Orleans was already bedeviling Washington. In the Spanish empire, New Orleans had been *el norte*; now it was the American South. And it was the Wild West. The French-speaking Wild West.

The worry that black Jacobin terrorists from the West Indies would enter Louisiana was constant. Claiborne ordered all incoming ships containing people of color to be searched downriver from New Orleans, at the Balize, to make sure no disruptive elements were among them.[8] On July 12, he wrote to Madison again, assuring him that there was little possibility of uprising at present, but that "at some future period, this quarter of the Union must (I fear) experience in some degree, the misfortunes of St. Domingo."[9] Domingan refugees continued to come in; in 1803 and 1804, nearly a thousand of them arrived from Jamaica, many of whom had been there since 1798.[10] A letter written by a Domingan coffee planter in New Orleans in 1804 described his situation as he saw it:

Thrown upon Cuba with only a few domestics as my only resource [he had twelve], uncertain that I would keep them, seeing how easily Negroes here leave their masters, the cost of living, as miserable as it seems, is very expensive. Rent is sky-high due to the number of refugees. In a word, everything here leads me to look at other countries to find a more convenient place to live. I thought I saw in Louisiana the place that would offer the most advantages to a poor colonist forced to flee, because, first of all, they speak the same language. What's left of our Negroes is worth a lot more money, and they are more easily rented. Moreover, one finds there the same habits, as well as Frenchmen who know more or less who you are, either personally or by reputation, and who share more or less the same culture.[11]

Pierre-Louis Berquin-Duvallon, a Domingan who visited New Orleans in 1800–01 and didn't think much of it, described the city as a haven of depravity and dancing:

At the corners of almost all the cross streets of the city, and its suburbs, are to be seen nothing but taverns, which are open at all hours. There the *canaille*, white and black, free and slave, mingled indiscriminately, go to bear the fruit of their swindlings, and to gorge themselves with strong drink. And not far from the taverns are dark bawdy houses and dirty smoking houses, where the father on one side, and the son on the other, go, openly and without any embarrassment, as well as without shame, to give themselves to their passion for play, and to squander their moderate resources; or else to revel and dance indiscriminately and all night, with a lot of men and women of saffron color, or quite black, either free or slave.[12]

In the winter, he observed:

passion [for dancing] is at its height. Then, they dance in town, they dance in the country, they dance everywhere, if not with much grace, at least with great ardor; and the fiddlers are then always kept busy. For the rest, there is no variety in those amusements. There is the eternal contredanse, which is given without ceasing, although it is true some different forms are adapted to it, but at bottom it is always the same.[13]

On December 31, 1804, Claiborne wrote to Secretary of State James Madison that "winter amusements have commenced for several weeks; the two descriptions of citizens meet frequently at the theater, balls, and other places of amusement."[14] There had, needless to say, been unauthorized dances going on all the time. Throughout the Spanish era, colors and classes had mixed, especially in private homes, sometimes without masks, and sometimes—especially during Carnival season—with masks, which allowed inhibitions to relax even more.

Berquin-Duvallon wrote of "the famous house of Coquet, located near the center of the city, where all those sleazy goings-on [tripotage] take place in public."[15] The one place in New Orleans where dances were given legally for people of color was Bernardo Coquet's ballroom on St. Philip Street, which had, moreover, an authorized monopoly on them.[16] In 1805, Coquet moved his dances to a place by Bayou St. John, called the Tivoli—which was, not coincidentally the name of the new barrio the Domingans had built in Santiago de Cuba. Coquet leased his ballroom in town to Auguste Tessier, a Domingan who had previously directed the theater in Kingston, Jamaica; Tessier renamed it the Salle Chinois. In November of that year, Tessier began a new vogue by importing a Domingan tradition that was much like a similar one in Havana: dances for free women of color and white men. In Saint-Domingue, these were known as *redoutes*; in Cuba, they were *bailes de cuna* (cradle dances); in New Orleans, they were called quadroon balls. By 1808, Coquet had quadroon balls on Wednesdays and Saturdays, while a competitor had them on Tuesdays and Fridays.[17]

Imagine the competition among those women to be the most perfectly accessorized. Imagine the waves of fashion that rolled through that dance hall. Every belle employed a team in professions dominated by free women of color: laundresses, seamstresses, hatmakers, hairdressers, supported by the economy of concubinage. These beauty workers also entered into the houses of white women, where they made connections among the house's staff and learned secrets.

Contracts of plaçage typically resulted in the rental or purchase of a house, and free women of color became players in the town's real estate market. A sense of the gender and property distribution of the free colored community can be seen by looking at the 496 private claims for property damage resulting from the fire of 1788: 51 of the claimants were free women of color, versus only 21 free men of color.[18]

As the city prospered, music flourished. Henry Kmen writes: "Before the end of 1805 there were about fifteen public ballrooms. The next ten years brought close to fifteen more, and thereafter for twenty years additional ones appeared at a rate exceeding one each year. No fewer than thirty new dance locations opened for business between 1836 and 1841! Even a public bath house boasted its own ballroom."[19]

The first known performance of opera in American-period New Orleans took place on or around June 5, 1805: *Les visitandines*, an irreverent comic opera about nuns, popular in France, which scandalized the Ursuline sisters and caused them to complain to Claiborne.[20] "In 1806," writes Kmen, "Governor Claiborne wrote Henry Dearborn that the Fourth of July had been celebrated with a parade, a night at the theater, and a ball—a trilogy that foreshadowed the future development of music in the city."[21] In January 1807, after a military band played waltzes at a grand ball, waltzing to a band became the rage,[22] though military bands had long played for dances in Spanish New Orleans. (It should be recalled that trumpets did not have valves until the 1830s, so these were woodwind-dominated bands.) New Orleans was probably already moving toward a kind of ensemble that would dominate Antillean music in the nineteenth century and into the early days of the twentieth: dance bands with strings, winds, brass, and percussion.

Also in 1807, the St. Philip Street Theater opened, seating seven hundred, joining the St. Peter Street Theater. With fewer than ten thousand people, New Orleans had two theaters, both presenting work in French.

As the town became a primary immigration destination for Europeans, two well-established camps emerged. The French-speaking Catholics (and some Spanish-speaking ones) observed one set of rules and conventions, the English-speaking Protestants another. There were also a significant number of free, French-speaking (and some Spanish-speaking) Catholic blacks, who in many cases practiced creolized (or possibly not so creolized) versions of a variety of African religions. Then, slowly at first, there came the English-speaking Protestant blacks praising Jesus, born into a society that intended to keep all blacks as slaves unto eternity.

As Protestants died, they were buried in a separate section of the cemetery. Louisiana's first Protestant church, established in 1805, prohibited black worshippers.[23] Meanwhile, upriver, after more than a century of African American participation in Protestantism, a new, syncretized way of performing religion was erupting.

The camp meeting, or revival, made room in American Protestantism for the trance and spirit possession basic to African religion. In what came to be called the Second Great Awakening, in August 1801, in Bourbon County in western Kentucky, the spirit came down at the legendary Cane Ridge camp meeting. Between twenty to thirty thousand people, mostly from Kentucky, Tennessee, and southern Ohio, are estimated to have attended. Ministers preached day and night from Friday until Wednesday. Seized by "the jerks," hundreds of people at a time fell on the ground in a religious frenzy. In various accounts of camp meetings of the early nineteenth century, the writers stress the participation of both black and white people. Robert Sutcliff, observing an 1805 Methodist camp meeting in Pennsylvania attended by an estimated five thousand people, at which the preachers' "language and gestures were generally violent," noted that "I observed that a great number of negro families attended; and many of them in handsome carriages."[24]

A census of New Orleans at this time counted 3,551 whites, 1,566 free people of color, and 3,105 slaves.[25] It was, as it would be until the 1830s (and again, beginning in the 1970s) a black-majority city. But the new American slave laws were more severe. Now the reality of an American regime came crashing in on New Orleans's people of color, a community which boasted the first African American licensed physician, Santiago Derom (James Durham), who had previously been a slave to two different doctors and had learned medicine from them.[26]

The white planters were displeased at the rapidly increasing number of free people of color in Louisiana, and in 1806 the first popularly elected territorial legislature repealed the Spanish law of coartación, which had given enslaved people the right to purchase their own freedom. The new law limited, though did not completely deny, the right of black common-law wives and mixed-race children to claim the master's inheritance. Masters who wished to free slaves now had to certify that the slave "was not collateral to a debt"—their function in the banking system trumping other considerations—"and was at least thirty years old."[27] The legislature also prohibited the entry of free people of color from Haiti. New restrictions were added in 1807, and in 1808 it became mandatory for free people of color to be denoted as such in official documents, using abbreviations such as HLC (*homme libre de couleur*).

A police force was formed in 1805. At first peopled by volunteers, it took shape as a city guard. It developed along the lines of other Southern police organizations and unlike Northern ones: not so much a system of beat cops as a small military unit, prone to street-sweeping squad operations. Wearing uniforms, carrying swords, and generally moving in a group, they aimed not so much at suppressing street crime as controlling the slave population.[28]

Saint-Domingue had disappeared, never to return, but there was a Domingan diaspora, most numerously in Cuba.

Some of the 1803 Domingan refugees to Cuba went to Havana or other destinations on the island, but most of them stayed in Oriente, as the eastern part of Cuba is known. There they went about setting themselves up in business once again, having lost their lands and, in many cases, their most valuable property, their slaves. Some arrived with money, but more often refugees had to recapitalize. Some worked their way up, serving as managers, at which they outstripped the locals. Others raised money in a way that harkened back to the founding of Saint-Domingue: the Oriental ports of Santiago and Baracoa became centers of piracy, playing havoc with shipping and slaving in the region. Many of the French military men who found themselves idle and penniless in Cuba were eager participants in this trade.

By 1806 or so, the French influence in eastern Cuba had reached a peak. Perhaps thirty thousand refugees—whites, free people of color, and slaves—had come in, at a time when the population of Santiago de Cuba was some ten thousand people. Possessing greater entrepreneurial and technical skills than the locals, the new arrivals built coffee plantations up in the mountains, where the land had previously been thought unusable. They built grand estates there, with billiard rooms, libraries, and dance salons. (Traces of these *cafetales* are still visible in the mountains of eastern Cuba.)

In Cuba, the Domingans mounted theatrical performances in French. They established Cuba's first Masonic lodges, which would play a vital role in the Cuban wars for independence later in the century. The Domingans' sway in Oriente was such that there were rumors that they might do what they had done on La Española, and take over one side of the country for France. A sense of the state of mind at the time can be gleaned from a British account, *Present State of the Spanish Colonies*, published in 1810:

> [The Domingans'] habitual industry soon changed the face of the country [Cuba]; many were already in possession of two and three hundred Blacks, which raised the country to a state of affluence, consistency, and power, which it had never before attained in the hands of the Spaniards.
>
> Though so well settled, they were ever restless and devising plots, and drew up in a body long memorials which were transmitted to the emperor, soliciting that half of the island of Cuba, by a line drawn from Trinidad to Baracoa, might be ceded and confirmed in the right

of the French, together with the whole of Puerto Rico, where others of their settlers had also formed establishments. Active agents were sent to Paris, provided with funds raised from the subscriptions of both parties, who were directed to make the obtaining of this cession a common cause.[29]

The crisis came in 1808. In March, Carlos IV of Spain abdicated the throne to his son, Fernando VII. Bonaparte refused to accept the father's resignation and summoned both of the royals to Bayonne in France, where both resigned the Spanish crown on May 6. The following month, Napoleon's brother Joseph Bonaparte was made king of Spain. Eighteen thousand French troops were already in Spain, on the pretext of transiting to Portugal.

Annulling the central Spanish government had the effect of empowering provincial Spanish authorities, each of which formed a provincial junta and fielded its own army. Together they formed a *junta central*, with representation from overseas colonies. A unicameral parliament was convened at Cádiz; with Madrid in the hands of the occupiers, Seville became the de facto capital of Spain. It was a revolutionary moment: the word *guerrilla* entered the Spanish vocabulary at this time. As Karl Marx described it in an article published in the New York *Daily Tribune* of October 20, 1859:

> The division of power among the provincial juntas had saved Spain from the first shock of the French invasion under Napoleon, not only by multiplying the resources of the country, but also by putting the invader at a loss for a mark whereat to strike; the French being quite amazed at the discovery that the center of Spanish resistance was nowhere and everywhere.[30]

The Spanish ruling class genuflected to Bonaparte, so a popular movement in Spain organized resistance to the occupiers without the support of an established army, the nobility, or the church. The British made unprecedented common cause with the Spanish resistance, sending men down to Iberia to fight, Protestants and Catholics together, against the French. The removal of the royal family emboldened Spain's overseas colonies to move toward independence. Each colony was now on its own; by 1810, independence movements were stirring in Argentina, Venezuela, Nueva Granada (Colombia), and Mexico, and by 1825 only Cuba and Puerto Rico would remain under the Spanish flag. (The Portuguese Braganza royal family decamped to Brazil, which in 1822 became the Brazilian empire, under a Brazilian monarchy that was independent of Europe.)

MONI TEUR
DE LA LOUISIANE.

PUBLIÉ PAR J. B. L. S. FONTAIN, RUE ROYALE, N°. 19.

A la Nouvelle-Orléans. SAMEDI 22 JUILLET DÉCEMBRE 1809. (N°. 947.)

Issue #947 of the *Moniteur de la Louisiane* from July 22, 1809, not long after the Domingan migration from Cuba began, carrying war news from Europe.

When news of Joseph Bonaparte's installation on the Spanish throne arrived in Cuba on July 17, 1808, via an article published in a Jamaican newspaper, Cuba declared itself loyal to Fernando, the Spanish king.[31] The following week, a declaration of war on France by the Suprema Junta de Sevilla arrived in Havana, calling for hostile actions against all French nationals and property. French-speaking people in Cuba found themselves the objects of suspicion and threats.

Cuba's captain general, the Marqués de Someruelos, does not seem to have been tempted when, in December of that year, Jefferson dispatched General James Wilkinson to Havana to discuss the possibility of the United States purchasing the island—the first of many such offers, which, if accepted, would have united Charleston, Havana, and New Orleans under one slave-owning flag.

In Cuba, an expulsion order was issued on March 12, 1809, against "French nationals"—people who had not taken an oath of allegiance to Spain or married Spanish citizens. Displaced for a second time, a new Domingan diaspora began, this time from eastern Cuba to Louisiana.

New Orleans had Spanish-speaking Havana as an ongoing partner in the Gulf of Mexico. But with the arrival of the 1809 migration, the city was overwhelmed by an influx of French-speaking people coming from Santiago de Cuba—that is, from the Caribbean.

⚬⚬⚬

By no means did all the Domingans in Cuba emigrate. Many took loyalty oaths, or were married, or were well connected and able to pull strings. Some modified their last names to make them sound more Spanish. But the hardest core of French speakers was uprooted from Cuba, where they would otherwise have continued to amass economic, political, and social power, and would have made Cuban history very different. Instead, they were transplanted to New Orleans, which was ultimately the destination city for the largest number of refugees from the Haitian Revolution. New Orleans, not Santiago, wound up with a French-language opera company.

In the early days of the nineteenth century, New Orleans was the most diverse town in the South by far; as the decades passed, it became a primary immigration destination, though always a distant second to New York. Three and a half decades before the massive immigration of Irish fleeing the potato famine, the first known celebration of St. Patrick's Day in New Orleans was in 1809, though there may have been one earlier, since the Catholic Irish had been welcome in New Orleans during the Spanish period.

The first boatload of Domingan refugees from Cuba arrived in New Orleans on May 12, 1809, bringing with them their possessions—most conspicuously, their slaves. The United States had a problem with that: the importation of slaves was expressly prohibited as of January 1, 1808. For many of the slave owners, who had been dispossessed not once but twice, their slaves were their only capital. If they were not to become a drag on the public purse, they had to be allowed to keep their possessions, or so went the argument. For the time being, the slaves were not allowed to disembark, but were forced to remain on the ships, which were impounded.

Helping the refugees was a popular cause in New Orleans, and Governor Claiborne, who had married a French Creole woman, had a political imperative to please the community. On May 15, he "forwarded to Washington a petition in which citizens of New Orleans asked the federal government not to apply the law of 1808 to the slaves brought in by refugees from Cuba."[32] On June 28, 1809, debate was taken up in Congress, and a bill passed, allowing the refugees to import their slaves upon posting a bond, and letting the slaves out of their impoundments.

New Orleans received, then, the *last slaves to be legally imported* into the United States. It is possible that some of these slaves had been born in Africa. In any case, representing a more recent descent from Africa than the English-speaking slaves being trafficked down from the Upper South, they provided yet one more essential cultural connection that made New Orleans different from everywhere else in North America.

The bulk of the migration came between October and December. One ship of refugees came from Havana, but all the rest embarked from the eastern ports of Santiago de Cuba or Baracoa. There were perhaps sixty ships in all. On January 18, 1810, New Orleans mayor James Mather published a report giving the number of arrivals, reprinted in the *Moniteur*. This table[33] summarizes it:

	Men 15+	Women 15+	Children	Total
Whites	1,373	703	655	2,731
FPC	428	1,377	1,297	3,102
Slaves	962	1,330	934	3,226
Total	2,763	3,410	2,886	9,059

That is, 30 percent whites, 34 percent free people of color, 36 percent slaves. About a third, a third, and a third. But look at the gender balance. White men outnumbered white women almost two to one, while free women of color outnumbered free men of color by more than three to one. Almost exactly as many white men as free women of color and almost exactly as many white men as slave women. White men were bringing their mistresses, both free and slave, and families were bringing their female domestics. (I have never been able to find any gender data on the original 1803 Domingan migration to Cuba: one wonders if the balance might also have been similar, especially since men were less readily allowed to leave Saint-Domingue than women and children.)

Free men of color over fifteen years of age were not welcome in Louisiana, and many of those who arrived did not remain. "We have at this time a much greater proportion of that kind of population than comports with our interests," wrote Governor Claiborne.[34] Some continued north, or west: Spanish-speaking Texas was free territory and would be until the Virginia-born Stephen Austin and his associates reinstated slavery there in 1836 after winning independence from Mexico.

More arrivals of this three-tiered diaspora in early 1810 brought the total number of émigrés to more than ten thousand, approximately doubling the population of New Orleans within a few months. Many people in New Orleans today speak of the "Haitians" who came to the city. In fact, very few Haitians came to New Orleans, because the Republic of Haiti didn't exist yet when the people who came to New Orleans left Saint-Domingue. (This is why I speak of "Domingans" rather than "Haitians" in referring to people who left La Española prior to January 1, 1804.) All three of the groups that came in 1809–10—white, mulatto, and black—had spending six years in Cuba in common; the youngest of them had been born there. Within the city, it's safe to say that no aspect of New Orleans culture remained untouched by their influence.

Everywhere they went, whether up the Atlantic seaboard or down the Antilles, Domingans left an imprint. In New Orleans, they dominated the profession of law, assuring a future role for themselves by seeing to it that the authoritative version of the law of Louisiana was written in French rather than English, and according to Roman legal code rather than common law.[35] (Louisiana state law is not, as is commonly believed, "based on the Napoleonic code," but on a legal corpus cobbled together out of existing Spanish and French colonial law.) Domingans ran the newspaper business in New Orleans for decades, and were effectively the inventors of the profession of journalism there. Both Domingan whites and free people of color in New Orleans were, writes Nathalie Dessens, "politically aware, civically active, and ideo-logically influential."[36] There were merchants, bakers, skilled tradesmen of all sorts, fencing and dance instructors, and a piano tuner.[37] Louisiana's ornate, rhythmic piano tradition was probably under way already, and by the 1840s would produce the United States's first great concert pianist, the Domingan-descended, New Orleans–born Louis Moreau Gottschalk.

The whites were militantly against the foolishness of abolition, and favored harsh repressive measures against slaves. They hated Spain with a vengeance; the Spanish were disparaged and their role in local history mini-mized. The creation myth of this new community was the violent destruction by savages of the paradise of old Saint-Domingue. Their collective memory reinforced a fear of the horrors of slave uprising. Grandmothers frightened children with tales of fiendish Negroes massacring noble whites and loyal servants. These tales, exaggerated in the retelling, grew into received wisdom. After Gottschalk visited eastern Cuba in 1853, he was inspired to write in his memoirs:

The name of St. Domingo, seemed to speak to my imagination by recall-ing to me the bloody episodes of the insurrection, so closely associated with my childhood memories. When very young, I was never tired of hearing my grandmother relate the terrible strife which our family, like all the rest of the colonists, had to sustain at this epoch. . . .

I again found myself before the large fireplace of our dwelling on the street "des Ramparts" at New Orleans, where in the evening, squatting on the matting, the negroes, myself, and the children of the house formed a circle around my grandmother, and listened, by the trembling fire on the hearth, under the coals of which Sally, the old negress, baked her sweet potatoes, to the recital of this terrible negro insurrection. It was the same old Sally who, while listening all the time, spoke in a low voice to a portrait of Napoleon hung above the fireplace, and which she obstinately believed was bewitched because it seemed to look at her, in every corner of the room, wherever she might be. We cast fearful glances under the old bed . . . and drew closer together by creeping the one between the other, while my grandmother continued. . . . Sometimes Sally interrupted the narrative of my grandmother to exorcise a "zombi," of which, she said, she felt the impure breath on her face. We narrowed our circle, shivering with fright, around my grandmother, who, after crossing herself and scolding Sally, took up her story where she had left off.[38]

One of the most enduring stereotypes of New Orleans is as a place of ghosts and other malevolent spirits, an image to some degree defined by Lafcadio Hearn, who, in the words of S. Frederick Starr, "invented" New Orleans as a literary construct while working as a journalist in the city in the late nineteenth century (and then went on to similarly "invent" Japan).[39] The Gothic quality that Hearn found in the city derived not only from New Orleans's status as a slave market where black bodies, and those said to bear the taint of blackness, were bought and sold. The ghost that haunted New Orleans was the ghost of Saint-Domingue.

cᴑᴑᴑ

Early in 1810, the Territory of Orleans returned the bonds that the Domingan newcomers had posted for their slaves, and allowed them to sell (or mortgage) their slaves freely in the market. With prices for slaves healthy, and plots of land available, slave owners had collateral and a place to establish themselves.

The Domingans arrived as the city was expanding, and their housing needs fueled a real estate boom. The land upriver of the old town continued to develop into suburbs. Immediately downriver of Esplanade, the twenty-year-old Bernard Marigny began to create the Faubourg Marigny on the grounds of his former plantation in 1805. Marigny, a descendant of one of the colony's first families, had inherited some four million dollars and was the richest man in Louisiana. The neighborhood, today a treasure of Creole architecture, still bears his name (pronounced MER-rany). Marigny's legacy is of particular importance to the poetics of everyday New Orleans because he named so many of the streets downtown. Names like *Rue des Françoises*, *Champs-Elysées*, and *Rue de Craps* sounded grander in French, perhaps, but they stand out in English as well: Frenchmen Street, Elysian Fields, Craps Street. The last was named for the dice game, introduced to North America by Marigny. To lesser streets he gave names like Peace, Victory, Abundance, Poets, Love, Music, Bagatelle, and Spain—all in French, of course.

Marigny's community was not part of New Orleans, but a separate municipality. When the Marigny became politically unified with New Orleans in 1852, the names running upriver-downriver disappeared, replaced by the names of the French Quarter streets of which they had become extensions, so Rue de Craps became Burgundy, the name by which it is still known.[40]

Plan of the City and Suburbs of New Orleans, from an actual survey made in 1815. Around the map are engravings depicting public buildings of the city, prominently including the two theaters. The title panel depicts an allegorical, finely dressed Indian with a bejeweled woman nursing a child, on the West Bank, framing a view of the busy river port. The axis of alignment of this map is not north/south, as shown by the tilted compass, but according to the street grid of the French Quarter, the only rectangular section of the city. To the right of the French Quarter is Bernard Marigny's suburb; to the left, the American sector. Behind the Quarter (upward on the map) is the Faubourg Tremé, which as of the time of survey had only one named street—the one christened for its developer, St. Claude.

There was another housing option as well: Carondelet's canal to Bayou St. John had made the land of French planter Claude Tremé accessible, just to the north (lakeside) of the city and adjacent to Congo Square. Tremé had married a property-owning, manumitted woman of color named Julie Moreau (Moró) and subdivided the plantation land she owned, along with other land he acquired, to make the neighborhood. In 1812 the Faubourg Tremé was incorporated, and became a neighborhood for free people of color. Despite repeated insults to its architectural integrity from the 1960s on by the building of Louis Armstrong Park, the construction of I-10 literally over the neighborhood (popularly known as the "Claiborne bridge," though it's an overpass, not a bridge), and the floodwaters of 2005, the Tremé still exists. It has a street called St. Claude, for Claude Tremé, just as Bernard Marigny had one named St. Bernard.

The entry of the Domingan refugees, which made English speakers a much smaller proportion of the town's population, exposed Claiborne to Anglophone hostility. Supporting the refugees being thrown out of Cuba was a popular cause in Creole New Orleans, but many Anglo-Americans in Louisiana saw the new arrivals as Bonapartists, and were not kindly disposed toward their local "French" sponsors in any case. The newly independent United States had almost gone to war with France over the issue of piracy between 1798 and 1800, and the increasing "French" piracy in the Caribbean and the Gulf did little to win the Anglos' sympathies.

This influx of Domingans entered an increasingly cosmopolitan city that was booming with trade, at a turning point in its history. American capital was pouring in, and there was Spanish silver. The hinterlands that drained into Louisiana were accelerating their production of everything it was possible to make in, or extract from, the vast, unexploited continent. Products were

PLAN
of the City and Suburbs of
NEW ORLEANS

MISSISSIPPI

arriving by flatboats, which were stacked three deep along the levee, and by oceangoing ship. The pilferage alone from all this cargo was enough to make New Orleans a sumptuously appointed place.

Before the Domingan influx, in 1806, Thomas Ashe described the occupational panorama of commercial New Orleans:

> The trade of the city is conducted, for the most part, by four classes of men. Virginians and Kentuckyans reign over the brokerage and commission business; the Scotch and Irish absorb all the respectable commerse of exportation and immigration; the French keep magazines and stores; and the Spaniards do all the small retail of grocers' shops, cabarets, and lowest order of drinking-houses. People of colour, and free negroes, also keep inferior shops, and sell goods and fruits.[41]

Ashe's observation that low-down taverns were controlled by Spaniards—which might well have included what today we would call Cubans, since Cubans were not recognized as a separate nationality at the time—suggests that when it came to street-level music in the New Orleans of 1806, the "Spanish tinge"—most prominently, that tango rhythm—was in effect. Spanish had been a minority language in Spanish-ruled New Orleans, but even after the end of the Spanish colony, a permanent community of Spanish speakers remained. "Many Negroes speak three languages," an 1834 visitor to the city observed, "in such a manner as to defy you to tell which one of the three is their vernacular."[42]

A contemporary reader might easily miss the reference to the "brokerage and commission" business that Ashe tells us was dominated by Virginians and Kentuckians and that was distinguished from the "respectable commerse of exportation and immigration" of the Scotch and Irish. At the time, Virginians and Kentuckians were exporting domestically raised slaves for sale down South, and South Carolina was legally importing Africans for the same purpose. While brokers and commission merchants might handle any number of goods, the term *broker* was the polite way to say *slave trader*. According to Frederic Bancroft:

> The words *trader* and *negro-trader* had come to be shunned, except colloquially: as the business increased, the precise designation was avoided. Most of the men dealing in slaves advertised as "brokers, auctioneers, and commission agents." . . . Their business cards daily appeared in the

newspapers along with those of lawyers and physicians and the advertisements of merchants and of various kinds of enterprises.[43]

The "brokers" in New Orleans were doing a rip-roaring business. By the 1850s, there would be two dozen of them in the vicinity of Gravier Street, complete with showrooms where people to be sold were displayed in windows, and slave jails to warehouse their merchandise. (Such jails were also a feature of the hospitality business in the South, since a traveler would necessarily need to lock his Negroes up at night.)

Most slaves were disposed of at private sale, not by auction. But the numerous slave auctions in New Orleans were a popular theatrical event, conducted bilingually with auctioneers who could chant: *Deux! Two! Deux medie! Two-n-a half!*

The French Creoles, who valued wealth, leisure, and bloodlines, remained in their traditional city, while the new English-speaking arrivals, whom the Creoles saw as culturally cruder, settled on the upriver side of the old town, above present-day Canal Street. Around each of the populations, black neighborhoods grew, because New Orleans depended in every era on cheap—or free—black labor. By 1836 the incompatibility between the Creoles and the Americans had increased to the point that the city broke off into separate municipalities, with distinct governments, which, in the words of one writer, "practically established Canal Street and Esplanade Avenue into national boundary lines."[44]

⁗⁙⁗

The cleared swamp that is New Orleans can be a beautiful place to live. Trees, bushes, flowers, grasses, and plants of all descriptions grow as fast as they can be cut back. But throughout the nineteenth century, yellow fever raged every summer in the hot months, its cause unknown. People of means evacuated the city seasonally.

Meanwhile, the city's sewage was carried through the streets in open gutters to the swamp, where it festered. With the levee on one side and a morass of cypress swamps on the other that was "at all seasons totally impassable,"[45] the town's air seems to have had a perpetually fetid character. To compensate for the stink, residents planted sweet aromatic plants. Orange and fig trees were brought from Provence.

Only up on the levee was there a breeze and a breath of fresh air. Ships laid out boards so passengers could step off the boat onto it. Gentlemen retired there after work. This respite was not available to the respectable white women of New Orleans, who didn't go on the levee.[46] But it was a principal market for the free colored courtesan class, whose manners were beyond reproach. As Ashe tells us:

> The Levée at sun-set, is the principal market for all this traffic *de coeur*. There all the beauties assemble, and there all those who need the kind companion, joyfully repair: all walk up and down for a considerable time, or sit under orange-trees occasionally, with the objects of their separate choice. Such an expression of reserve, morals and decency reign over the women of every sort, that a stranger passes and repasses, before he can assume sufficiently to tell the one he admires the most *qu'elle est belle comme une ange*, and so forth. . . . Some mothers now, on becoming acquainted with the English timidity, begin to alter their line of conduct, and suffer their daughters to remove their veil *en passant un Anglois*, or flirt their fan, or drop a handkerchief, which they receive with such gracious accents of gratitude, that a conversation may easily succeed.
>
> The mothers always regulate the terms and make the bargain. The terms allowed the parents are generally fifty dollars a month; during which time the lover has the exclusive right to the house, where fruit, coffee, and refreshments may at any time be had, or where he may entirely live with the utmost safety and tranquility. Many do live in this manner, notwithstanding which, I have never heard a complaint against these interesting females.[47]

And that was *before* the influx of Domingans in 1809–10, who brought with them a number of members of that class. Because of the previously cited gender imbalance in favor of females among people of color in that migration, the new influx, besides doubling the size of New Orleans, skewed further the gender balance of the city. The courtesan's trade became even more competitive. Lower-priced sex workers prowled dockside, where the sailors and passengers were.

The arrival of thousands of Domingans to the small city of New Orleans, which had been a provincial outpost of Spain and a satellite of Havana for forty years, seemed to fulfill the Creoles' longtime dream of making New Orleans into a "French" city. But it happened when Louisiana was already a U.S. territory. The mass immigration retarded the Americanization of New Orleans for perhaps two generations, reinforcing the critical mass of French speakers in the city. The impact of the white Domingan immigrants on the politics of the town might be compared to that of the Cuban immigration to Miami in the years following 1959: ultrareactionary ex-plantation owners and the lesser members of their society, escaping a radical left-wing Antillean revolution, refusing to assimilate and insisting on speaking their natal language, transforming the city through their numbers, spinning nostalgic yarns about their lost paradise, becoming a magnet for reunification of families across a wide diaspora, forming strong civic networks to struggle with English speakers for control of the commerce of the town, extending their influence far beyond the bounds of the city where they were concentrated, and, in the process, helping to push the political environment of the region, and the entire country, to the right.

The Domingan-Cuban influx was a transforming moment for New Orleans history, but it was not the beginning of New Orleans culture. New Orleans was older than Port-au-Prince, and Louisiana society was already unique, with a well-defined language, music, cuisine, and personality. Nor was it the first time Domingan culture had been felt in New Orleans, given the longtime relation between the places.

The arrival of so many people of color—two-thirds of the immigrants, summing the castes of free mulattoes and black slaves—confirmed New Orleans as a black town. In the 1810 census, 37 percent of the approximately seventeen thousand residents were white; the rest were free people of color or slaves. No other U.S. city came close to that. It was one thing to have large numbers of black people on isolated plantations, but this was the city, where enslaved people enjoyed access to the streets along with a unique population of free people of color. Moreover, the artificial boundaries of race are easier to police in the country than in the city. Thus an urbanized population of color was interacting in the public spaces of the city, and intermingling with the whites, like nowhere else in the South. The three-caste system, broadly shared by both French and Spanish colonial society, was strongly reinforced by the Domingan migration of 1809–10. Domingan free people of color intermarried with the Louisiana Creoles of color, both French and Spanish speaking, promoting a social dynamic in New Orleans more like that which existed in Havana than anywhere in the Southern United States. Moreover, the incoming slaves had experienced the cabildo system of Cuba, in which they were allowed to maintain their own cultural associations. Some of them were relatively cosmopolitan, having lived in Africa, French Saint-Domingue, Spanish Cuba, and now the United States. Some had been to France in their capacity as personal servants.

The idea of blacks from Saint-Domingue entering Louisiana was viewed by Anglo-Americans with horror. There was a general fear that they would bring with them their black Jacobinage and sow the seeds of rebellion. And, indeed, the largest slave rebellion in U.S. history occurred the following year in the Territory of Orleans, on January 8, 1811, when the slave Charles Deslondes, together with others, began an insurrection some thirty-six miles northwest of New Orleans on the German Coast. It has frequently been written that Deslondes was born in Saint-Domingue, but Gwendolyn Midlo Hall is emphatic that he was Louisiana born.[48] The insurgents marched downriver, some five hundred strong, burning plantations as they went, killing two people in the process, and reportedly shouting, "On to Orleans!" A force of troops from the U.S. Army, which happened to be in the vicinity, together with local militiamen and civilians, attacked the rebels and massacred them on January 10, a task facilitated by the slaves' lack of heavy armament. Sixty-six rebels were killed by troops on the spot, and seventeen were reported missing.

Trials were held promptly, at which twenty-one people were sentenced to death. They were shot, then decapitated. As had been done after the Pointe Coupée conspiracy in 1795, in an anachronistic display of French-style exemplary punishment, their heads were placed on pikes along the highway.[49]

Among those who helped repress Deslondes's uprising were free men of color. As a class they were under tremendous suspicion, being seen by whites as likely to be the leaders of slave troops if a Saint-Domingue-style uprising were to be attempted in Louisiana. They were eager to prove their loyalty.

⌇

The first steamboat arrived in the thriving port of New Orleans in September 1811 after a two-week trip down from Pittsburgh. It was early in the steamboat's history, and to ride on one, with explosion-prone boilers over an uncleared Mississippi River, was a true adventure. The boat that arrived did not attempt to go back upriver, but six years later, Henry Shreve would manage to take a steamboat from New Orleans up to Louisville in only twenty-four days.[50]

Great prosperity was around the corner. As settlers came in, cattle were brought up from the Spanish territories. *Vacheries*, or ranches, appeared, and the practice of cattle raising subsequently crossed west from Louisiana into Texas.[51] Louisiana's population in 1810 was approximately 76,000, the vast majority of it in the delta region. That was more than double its population twenty-five years earlier of 37,000. By 1820, it would double again, to 154,000.[52]

On April 30, 1812, after repeated petitions by its residents to Washington, six weeks before the United States declared war on Britain, Louisiana became a state. Claiborne, who had supported the Domingan immigrants and was rewarded with their votes, was elected the first governor, and Julien Poydras became president of the state senate.

A Virginian, James Madison, was president of the United States. The Virginians had come into Louisiana and used a combination of political clout and popular fear of slave rebellion to dominate the slave-importing business. The response on the part of those frozen out of the trade—the Creoles—was to develop a black market based on smuggling, an art at which the Domingans were skilled.

During the fifteen years or so after the Americans took over Louisiana, thousands of slaves were sneaked in. Some were resold from Cuba, and others were hijacked on their way there. Few of them had made more than a pit stop on the way from Africa.

By the time of Louisiana's statehood, New Orleans was a center of what one could accurately call organized crime. It trafficked in luxury goods, consumer items, and people.

BARGAINLAND

Donde hay música, no puede haber cosa mala.
Where there is music, there can't be anything bad
going on.

—*Sancho Panza*[1]

In theory, privateers only operated during wartime. But there was always war going on somewhere nearby.

Royal authority made privateers (also known as corsairs) distinct from common pirates, who were stateless. Privateers' ships were legal enterprises, complete with syndicates of investors, operating legitimately under the flag granting them their letter of marque and sailing freely in and out of that country's ports. They were expected to seize their cargo politely, and to treat passengers and crew of the unlucky ship according to civilized norms. The crews of the ships they boarded rarely resisted; their lives were more valuable to them than the merchant's cargo they were carrying. The privateers were supposed to return the booty to their national havens, where they would in theory pay duties on it. In practice, smuggling was as much a part of the privateers' trade as seizing cargo.

With the upheaval of 1791 in Saint-Domingue, a new era of privateering began. In the Napoleonic era, Bonaparte, whose strength was on land and not at sea, granted letters of marque freely. Most of the (frequent) boarding of, and theft of the cargo aboard, merchant ships in the early nineteenth-century Caribbean and Gulf was in the hands of privateers rather than pirates, though there were also unlicensed pirates operating at this time—most notably, until 1809, exiled Domingans based in eastern Cuba. In practice there was often little difference between the legal and illegal plunderers. Both needed the same kinds of support systems on land. For that matter, there was not always that much ethical difference between privateers and "legitimate" merchants, if both were selling slaves.

Though the United States had a far smaller navy than the big European powers, American merchant shipping was becoming an industry of global importance. But it was under attack, caught between Britain and France, who were at war with each other, and both of whom denied the rights of neutrals to trade with hostiles. Protecting U.S. merchant ships became a prime national security goal. President Jefferson used the navy to go after the Barbary pirates off the coast of North Africa (as per "The Marines' Hymn": "to the shores of Tripoli"). In 1807, responding to attacks on U.S. ships, he tried to avoid war with Britain by resorting to commercial sanctions: he imposed an embargo on *all* oceangoing commerce, which almost destroyed American trade, and made him unpopular. In New Orleans, whose economy was dependent on shipping, the French Creole merchants saw their business crippled.

An enormous business in smuggling appeared all around the nation's ports, but it had a considerable head start in the Gulf of Mexico. Sugar and cotton producers were desperate, both to get their goods to market and to acquire more slaves. Meanwhile, the British seized French ships and American ones both, ultimately leading to the War of 1812.

In 1808, Jefferson authorized Commander David Porter to go after pirates in the Gulf, but Porter soon realized he was overwhelmed: the coastline was dotted with little havens for ships. The great center where sailors congregated and goods were best disposed of was the merchant city of New Orleans, which offered customers, whores, and tafia aplenty. In 1809, the U.S. Non-Intercourse Act reauthorized trade with Spain but reaffirmed the embargo of commerce with France and Britain, just in time for the wave of Domingans from Santiago and Baracoa to arrive in Louisiana. As had been the case with the escape from Saint-Domingue to Cuba, the flotilla that brought the refugees to New Orleans was not any national navy; many of the ships belonged to privateers.

In April 1810, as the big migration from eastern Cuba to Louisiana was winding down, Thomas Robertson, a U.S. official in Louisiana, complained of the presence of "desperadoes from St. Yago de Cuba accustomed to piracies and connected with the parties who furnish them with every facility to escape forfeitures or punishment."[2] The Domingan pirates who had established themselves in Cuba were now welcome in Creole New Orleans, where they were seen both as an assertion of power against the Anglo-Americans and as a necessary source of all sorts of goods, especially cheap slaves.

Planters in both Cuba and Louisiana were expanding their sugar acreage as fast as they could. But Louisiana was prohibited from having African slaves, whereas Cuba was entering its peak period of slave traffic—the first three decades of the nineteenth century. With miles of Louisiana coastline unpoliceable, and a vast fleet of privateers looking for prizes, this meant that many ships bearing Africans for Cuba were taken at sea and the human cargoes diverted. This, then, was the last big wave of Africans entering the United States throughout the 1810s: the clandestine, undocumented arrival into Louisiana of thousands originally destined for Cuba.

Many were taken to the sugar plantations of Louisiana to be worked to death, while others wound up in New Orleans. No other U.S. city experienced anything comparable at this time. New Orleans was, yet again, more African than any other town in North America.

⌑

In the second part of *Don Quixote*, the bumbling sidekick Sancho Panza is made governor of an island with the mock-heroic name of *Barataria*. The Spanish word for "cheap" is *barato*, so you could translate *Barataria* as Bargainland. The name was perhaps, says Cervantes's narrator, "because of how cheaply its government had been given to him" (*por el barato con que se le había dado el gobierno*). A more exquisite metaphor for Louisiana in Jean Lafitte's day would be hard to imagine.

Poking fun at the pomposity of their Spanish rulers, the French Creoles gave the name Barataria to the fifteen-mile-long bay on the southwestern Louisiana coast, around the birdfoot from New Orleans. With two barrier islands in front of it, Grand Isle and Grand Terre, the Bay of Barataria could only be entered by the quarter-mile-wide Barataria Pass. It was the region's most perfect natural spot for defense of a privateers' haven, especially once artillery had been set up at the entrances. The brothers Jean and Pierre Lafitte (sometimes spelled Laffite, with other variants) began operations there, and by 1811 Jean Lafitte was Louisiana's best-known privateer, at the head of a self-styled independent kingdom in the swamp.

It has often been written that the Lafittes were born in Port-au-Prince, but William C. Davis, who wrote an extensively sourced biography of them, believes they were French, from Bordeaux, and emigrated to Saint-Domingue. From there they moved on to Cuba in 1803, then to Louisiana, perhaps in

1809 with the big migration, possibly participating in the organization of the flotillas that brought refugees to Louisiana.[3] Spain was headless in 1809, and Spanish ships were easy prey.

In New Orleans, where only about an eighth of the population was Anglo-American, the Lafittes had enormous popular support in the Creole community. The Baratarian enterprise was a major regional employer, providing work for possibly thousands of sailors as well as all manner of support personnel. A large portion of Creole New Orleans collaborated in its business. When the privateers would be hauled into court, often the judges would simply let them go. You might see Jean Lafitte, a dapper, well-mannered Frenchman, at one of Coquet's quadroon balls.

Writing of a later era, the organized-crime specialist Selwyn Raab calls New Orleans "Cosa Nostra's Plymouth Rock" in the United States.[4] The first known establishment of the Sicilian secret society in the United States was operating in New Orleans as early as 1869 and the first public mention of the word *Mafia* in the United States was there, in 1890.[5] But eight decades before that, the Lafittes were operating a massive cut-rate hot-goods operation. Then and now, organized crime relies on corrupting officials, and the Lafittes found they could influence customs collectors as well as judges.

Barataria was the perfect base from which to attack Spanish shipping, and the privateers' business improved further with the first stirrings of independence in the Spanish colonies. One of the first places to declare independence was West Florida (the coastal region stretching from the east side of the Mississippi River to Pensacola), which enjoyed a brief month as an independent republic in 1810. But a major boost to the Baratarians' fortunes came when the heavily fortified port town of Cartagena, Colombia, rose up in rebellion. After declaring independence on November 11, 1811, the Cartagenans offered the Baratarians letters of marque to supplement their French ones. This gave them a second base from which to operate and a port they could legally take their Spanish prizes into, though it was often easier and cheaper to double-cross their Colombian sponsors by taking the prizes over to Barataria. The Baratarians operated with this second base in Cartagena for four years, during which time Spanish shipping hemorrhaged its riches into the underground economies of Louisiana and Colombia. There was a wide-open, active smuggling corridor between Cartagena and New Orleans, and two different directions from which to prey on Spanish vessels.

Jean Lafitte supervised the sea operations of their privateering fleet, while his brother Pierre did business in town, maintaining a retail outlet for their plundered goods on Chartres Street. The Lafittes had benefited enormously from Jefferson's ill-advised blockade of all foreign commerce, and in 1812, when the United States went to war against Britain, new opportunities opened up. The Lafittes were becoming a vertically integrated company:

> Never before [writes Davis] had the same individuals controlled the acquisition of prize goods through piracy or privateering, their delivery to the market vicinity, subsequent smuggling or transport of the goods to the waiting market, and then their wholesale and retail sale. The potential for profit in controlling every phase of the operation beckoned, and now the brothers resolved to do just that, taking advantage of the shortages caused by the war and the British blockade, and the distraction of the authorities thanks to the war.[6]

Barataria was a giant bargain store. You could go to the Grand Isle emporium to get good deals right off the ship, cash only, avoiding taxes and duties, not only on slaves, but on silk, linen, cloth, spices, precious woods, wine, pharmaceuticals, machinery, and anything else that could be plundered from a foreign merchant ship—a discount shoppers' paradise, with low, low prices. But if it wasn't convenient to travel over to Grand Isle, or if you needed to use credit instruments—with so much illicit trade draining away the region's coin, money was chronically tight—you could trade with Pierre Lafitte in New Orleans. It was all done quite openly.

Furious Spanish diplomats filed endless complaints about the Louisiana pirates. It was embarrassing for Claiborne, the first governor of the state of Louisiana, to have his principal city flagrantly thriving by snarling commerce throughout the Gulf and the Caribbean, and injuring legitimate trade upriver as well.

By late 1814, with the British coming to attack, New Orleans was in a panic. Admiral George Cockburn had burned the U.S. Capitol and the executive mansion in Washington; his assault on Baltimore created the famous rockets' red glare that inspired Francis Scott Key. The defenses of New Orleans seemed inadequate. General Andrew Jackson, though he loathed the privateers, was forced to accept their offer of help by the time the British were within sixty miles of the city.[7] The Lafittes had refused commissions in the British army—not because they were patriotic Americans, but because the British offered a sucker deal. The Lafittes had the right lawyer, as professional criminals must: Edward Livingston, the brother of the man who had made the treaty to acquire Louisiana from France. Livingston helped broker the deal by which perhaps four hundred Baratarians, many of them experienced soldiers who knew how to handle artillery, joined the U.S. militia.

The inclusion of the Lafittes into the force defending New Orleans signified the French Creole community's uniting with Jackson, and it gave Domingans a chance to prove their patriotism to the United States by fighting the hated British. A collection of forces under General Andrew Jackson routed the British troops at Chalmette on January 8, 1815, setting Jackson on the path to the presidency and bringing New Orleans glory for its role in defending the United States. Only about fifty of the Baratarians, not including Jean Lafitte, were present for the battle. Most of the rest were guarding Barataria Pass; the first warning of the impending invasion had come from the Baratarians.

The battle, a tremendous psychological event in the life of the new republic, marked Louisiana's integration into the United States; the heterogeneity of the troops might have suggested the benefits of an integrated U.S. society. Louisiana by this time had a distinguished military tradition among people of color, and the colored militias contributed soldiers to the battle, famously including the fifteen-year-old drummer boy Jordan Noble, who drummed out the orders for troop movement and subsequently became a musician in New Orleans. General Jackson's forces also included Choctaws and other Indians. In recognition of their service, the Lafitte brothers were pardoned for their previous activities and given a graceful exit from privateering. But they had lost most of their money, and by 1818, the Lafittes were back in business—this time on the island of Galveston, where Jean resold stolen slaves the pirate's way, for a dollar a pound, quick. Business was good: Cuba was at its peak of slave importation, so there were plenty of prizes to nab, and prices were strong in New Orleans.

Lafitte's most determined enemy was Beverly Chew, the customs collector, who had come to New Orleans from Virginia. One of the partners of Chew & Relf, he was a "legitimate" merchant of slaves and many other goods. The privateering days were coming to an end, and when the Lafittes' Galveston operation shut down, so did, it would appear, the clandestine pipeline that had been preying on slave shipments to Cuba. From then on, the interstate slave trade from the Upper South ruled unchallenged.

The name Jean Lafitte passed into the domain of romantic fiction, and became one of those names by which New Orleans conjures up its past and sells itself to visitors. After Carondelet's canal to the Bayou St. John was filled in and turned into a street, it was named Lafitte, and, adding insult to injury, Lafitte was the name given to the housing project for blacks that opened in 1941 near the site of the canal. The Chalmette Battlefield, where the so-called Battle of New Orleans was fought, is one of six sites in the area operated by the National Park Service today under the collective name of the Jean Lafitte Historical Park and Preserve. The NPS Web site contains this disclaimer:

> Why is this park named for Jean Lafitte? Although Jean Lafitte was a privateer who illegally traded in slaves and generally defied the law, his assistance during the British invasion that ended in the Battle of New Orleans in 1815 was invaluable to the Americans. In 1966 a state park was created at the present site of the Barataria Preserve and named after Lafitte because of his smuggling operations in the area. The name was kept when the state park was combined with the French Quarter Visitor Center and Chalmette Battlefield to form Jean Lafitte National Historical Park and Preserve.

We honor our crooks in Louisiana.

⁂

The British troops that General Jackson faced off against at Chalmette included Indians and blacks from Florida. Spain's hold on the Florida territory was weak; it was largely independent Indian territory, and a haven for black marronage. By the end of 1814, British general Edward Nicholls had armed and trained some three thousand Indians (Batons Rouges and Seminoles) and four hundred blacks in Florida.[8] After the defeat at Chalmette, many of the surviving black soldiers on the British side went back to Florida to live. They settled along the Apalachicola River, near a solidly built fort that Nicholls turned over to them upon his departure in 1815, which became known as the Negro Fort. By the following year, maroons, sometimes known as "Seminole Negroes," were cultivating crops for miles up and down the river.

It was no secret to plantation slaves in South Carolina and Georgia that the wildland of Florida was a place they could live well. They had been escaping there for over a century, allying themselves with the Seminoles (a composite people who had moved into the area from various other locations), and gradually intermarrying with them. The African Americans were nominally enslaved by the Seminoles, but in practice the arrangement was more like sharecropping, and with time the distinction seems to have eroded somewhat.

Planters in the region were unhappy about having a big maroon community close at hand, much less one with military training and a fort of its own. And, indeed, with the Negro Fort as their base, the maroons launched raids across the border into Georgia.

The Black Seminoles had already successfully resisted an 1813 attack from the United States. But in 1816, General Jackson sent General Edward P. Gaines with orders to destroy the fort and enslave the people, along with General Duncan Lamont Clinch and the allied Creeks, who had long been at war with the Seminoles. When gunboats flying the Stars and Stripes engaged in a firefight against the Negro Fort flying the Union Jack, a cannonball from one of the gunboats hit the Fort's powder magazine, blowing up the structure and killing some two hundred fifty Seminoles and Black Seminoles.

A war ensued, remembered as the First Seminole War, which pitted Seminoles and African Americans on the one side against Gaines's soldiers and Creek warriors on the other. For the United States, the war had two purposes: to acquire Spanish Florida for the United States, and to break up the maroon villages that had become a threat to slave owners. It was successful on both counts. Early in 1818, resplendent with glory from his victory at New Orleans, Andrew Jackson marched into Florida at the head of perhaps five thousand troops. Meeting no resistance from the Spanish, he destroyed Indian and black settlements, killed leaders, and executed two British citizens on the spot, never mind the diplomatic consequences.

There would be a Second Seminole War, beginning in 1835 when Jackson was president, turning on the Seminoles' refusal to leave their homes for Oklahoma under the provisions of the Indian Removal Act, and culminating in the removal of thousands of Seminoles, including Black Seminoles, from Florida. It was a seven-year guerrilla battle, much of it fought in the Florida swamp.

The United States had fought a war against an alliance of African Americans and Indians. Pensacola is only two hundred miles or so east of New Orleans. You can bet they heard about it in Louisiana, if only through the grapevine.

21

A Most Extraordinary Noise

A message could be conveyed from one end of the city to another in a single day without one white person's being aware of it.

—Robert Tallant[1]

When the British-born Benjamin Henry Latrobe was chartered in 1811 to build a waterworks for New Orleans, he was one of the most distinguished architects in the United States. Latrobe sent his son Henry to Louisiana to manage the enterprise, but the nation's finances became snarled during wartime, and the project stalled. Then Latrobe took on the work of rebuilding the U.S. Capitol, burned by the British in August 1814.

Henry Latrobe remained in New Orleans, but died suddenly from yellow fever on September 3, 1817. His demise revealed a not uncommon domestic arrangement, as described in a letter written by his mother: "Custom, in [New Orleans] tolerates these connections with colored women, but I cannot express to you how shocked I was to see three Mulatto children with their Mother call upon me and say they were the children of Henry. They are well provided for. He had purchased a house for them and they receive $40 a Month paid regularly."[2]

Benjamin Latrobe, now the grandfather of three free New Orleanians of color, traveled to New Orleans to supervise the waterworks project personally, arriving in December 1818. Because of his extensive technical knowledge, informed observations, and highly skilled drawing and even watercolor illustrations, the journals Latrobe kept are one of the most valuable documents of the place and time. His entry from January 19, 1819, describes the city's festive Sunday tradition, so unlike the weekly rhythm to which Anglo-Americans were accustomed:

> Americans are pouring in daily not in families but in large bodies. In a few Years therefore, this will be an American town. . . .
>
> At present, the most prominent, and to the Americans the most offensive feature of the French habits, is the manner in which they spend Sunday. For about 10 Years, the recoil of the French revolutionary principles has made religious profession fashionable, especially in England, from whence our American public mind always, more or less, receives its tone. . . .
>
> Sunday in New Orleans is distinguished only, 1. by the flags that are hoisted on all the ships, 2. by the attendance at Church (the Cathedral) of all the beautiful Girls in the place, and of 2 or 300 Quateroons, Negroes, and Mulattoes, and perhaps of 100 white Males, to hear high Mass, during which the two Bells of the Cathedral are ringing. 3. by the shutting up of the Majority of the Shops and warehouses kept by the Americans, and 4. By the firing of the Guns of most of the young Gentlemen in the neighboring swamps, to whom Sunday affords leisure for field sports. 5. The Presbyterian, Episcopal, and Methodist Churches are also open on that day, and are attended by a large Majority of the Ladies of their respective congregations.
>
> In other respects no difference between Sunday and any other day exists. The Shops are open, as well as the Theatre and the ball room.[3]

If the laxity of the sabbath was a perpetual topic for writers visiting New Orleans, so was the Creole Frenchwomen's reputation for cruelty. It became a stereotype of the class, much as the concubine was a stereotype of the free woman of color. Major Amos Stoddard wrote in 1812 that Creole women "possess ease, grace, and penetration; they are remarkably loquacious, and their manners are more polished than those of the men; they are hospitable, and manifest much pleasure in offering to their guests and visitors the best things they are able to furnish. They have one fault not easily extenuated; they are habitually cruel to their slaves."[4] Latrobe included in his journal stories of women (including the landlady of his hotel) brutally whipping slaves, to the point where it sickened him to attend the balls with the young women:

> At the ball on Washington's birthday, the 22d, the idea of these things destroyed all the pleasure I should otherwise have felt in seeing the brilliant assemblage of as many beautiful faces and forms as I ever saw collected in one room. All pale, languid, and mild. I fancied that I saw a cowskin in every pretty hand, gracefully waved in the dance; and admired the comparative awkwardness of look and motion of my countrywomen, whose arms had never been rendered pliant by the exercise of the whip upon the bound and screaming slaves.[5]

The "cowhide" Latrobe mentions was a whip of tightly plaited strands of hard leather that lacerated the skin everywhere it bit. "Servants who are slaves," Latrobe noted, "are always treated with more familiarity than hirelings . . . we find cruelty and confidence, cowhiding and caressing, perfectly in accord with one another among the creoles of this place and their slaves."[6]

Besides being cowhided and caressed, these enslaved women had plenty of opportunity to learn the *maitresse*'s secrets. In New Orleans, Christian Schultz observed in 1808, "you never see a coach with ladies in the inside but you will at the same time find an equal number of female slaves behind; no lady presuming even to cross a street or visit her next neighbor without her favorite female slave to attend her."[7] Whites often spoke carelessly in front of their omnipresent servants, so there was always something new for the grapevine.

Latrobe described two black funeral processions, something he had never seen before, and attended festivities. "As it is now the Carnival, every evening is closed with a ball, or a play, or a Concert. I have been to two of each," he wrote. He had a favorable impression of a ball he attended, but noted that "The only nuisance was a tall ill-dressed black, in the music Gallery, who played the tambourin standing up, and in a forced and vile voice called the figures as they changed."[8]

What was it about the sound of the black man's voice that so irritated Latrobe? Think how annoying the sound of a Jamaican dancehall DJ (e.g., Shabba Ranks) can be to Latrobe's social counterparts today.

In July 2007 I had the opportunity to attend a day of performances by folkloric groups in Guadeloupe dancing their traditional styles of *kadri*, or quadrille. Part of the contredanse complex, the quadrille was danced all over the globe, wherever armies went. By the standards of the day, it was lively and sexy, and it was the most popular dance in New Orleans during the time Latrobe was there. While admiring the time-capsule aspects of the Guadeloupe kadri I was immediately struck by the similarity of sound—timbre, rhythm, and flow—of the *commandeur*, or caller, to that peculiar Jamaican vocal style. When I mentioned this to musicologist Dominique Cyrille, a kadri specialist, she said, "I think that's one reason the Jamaican style caught on so easily here. It was already in people's ears." Nor is the resemblance coincidental. Quadrille was widely danced in Jamaica well into the twentieth century, and quadrille calling may well have been a source for Jamaican dancehall rapping. As Jamaican songwriter Willie Williams expressed in an interview: "In Jamaica . . . the original dancehall fashion was called quadrille."[9]

This style of figure-calling was influenced by military drill in which figures were called, and in which, especially in Louisiana, blacks participated.[10] The closeness of military drill and social dance was reinforced by the substantial presence in the ballroom of men from the ranks. The ballroom was the mating ground, where your fine marriageable daughter might meet her gallant lieutenant. And they were dancing to . . . *that?*

⁂

Latrobe might not have thought of the sounds black people made as musical, but he took careful notes. On February 21, 1819, he witnessed, and left the most extended description we have of, the Sunday afternoon dances at Congo Square. The energy at the site was dense: as of 1817, city law restricted the gatherings to that place, day, and time, so they could be carefully policed. Though Latrobe thought the whole thing barbaric, he described the dancing carefully, and sketched pictures of several of the instruments.

> [I accidentally stumbled] upon the Assembly of Negroes which I am told every Sunday afternoon meets on the Common in the rear of the city. . . .

In going up St. Peters Street and approaching the common I heard a most extraordinary noise, which I supposed to proceed from some horse Mill, the horses trampling on a wooden floor. I found however on emerging from the houses, onto the common, that it proceeded from a croud of 5 or 600 persons assembled in an open space or public square.

I went to the spot and crouded near enough to see the performance. All those who were engaged in the business seemed to be *blacks*. I did not observe a dozen yellow faces. They were formed into circular groups in the midst of four of which, which I examined (but there were more of them) was a ring, the largest not 10 feet in diameter.

In the first were two women dancing. They held each a coarse handkerchief extended by the corners in their hands, and *set* to each other in a miserably dull and slow figure, hardly moving their feet or bodies. The music consisted of two drums and a stringed instrument. An old man sat astride of a Cylindrical drum about a foot in diameter, and beat it with incredible quickness with the edge of his hand and fingers. The other drum was an open staved thing held between the knees and beaten in the same manner. They made an incredible noise. The most curious instrument however was a stringed instrument which no doubt was imported from Africa. On the top of the finger board was the rude figure of a Man in a sitting posture, and two pegs behind him to which the strings were fastened. The body was a Calabash. It was played upon by a very little old man, apparently 80 or 90 Years old. The women squalled out a burthen to the playing, at intervals, consisting of two notes, as the Negroes working in our cities respond to the Song of their leader.[11]

We'll never know how it sounded, but it appears that both ends of Louisiana's musical African duality—banjo-playing Senegambia and drumming Kongo—were making music together that day in 1819, as they had previously done in Saint-Domingue. In describing the plucked string instrument he saw played together with two drums at Congo Square, he echoes Moreau de St.-Méry's previously quoted description from Saint-Domingue, more than twenty years before: "These drums (the shorter of which is called the Bamboula . . .) resound under the fist blows and finger movements by *each player straddling his drum* [emphasis added] . . . The *Banzas*, a sort of primitive guitar with four strings, joins the concert."

Though he does not use the word, the stringed instrument Latrobe saw appears to be the first indication of a banjo in New Orleans. It's the most African-looking banjo to have been pictured in North America. Latrobe described other instruments as well:

Most of the circles contained the same sort of dancers. One was larger, in which a ring of a dozen women walked, by way of dancing, round the music in the Center. But the instruments were of different construction. One, which from the color of the wood seemed new, consisted of a block cut into something of the form of a cricket bat with a long and deep mortice down the Center. This thing made a considerable noise, being beaten lustily on the side by a short stick. In the same Orchestra was a square drum looking like a stool, which made an abominably loud noise: also a Calabash with a round hole in it, the hole studded with brass nails which was beaten by a woman with two short sticks.

A man sung an uncouth song to the dancing which I suppose was in some African language, for it was not french, and the Women screamed a detestable burthen on one single note. The allowed amusements of Sunday, have, it seems, perpetuated here, those of Africa among its inhabitants. I have never seen any thing more brutally savage, and at the same time dull and stupid than this whole exhibition. Continuing my walk about a mile along the Canal, and returning after Sunset near the same spot, the noise was still heard.

There was not the least disorder among the croud, nor do I learn on enquiry, that these weekly meetings of the negroes have ever produced any mischief. [paragraphing added]

Latrobe wrote this description the same year H. C. Knight described the "African slaves" of New Orleans who "rock the city with their Congo dances," as quoted at the beginning of this volume. Knight's description seems to be the earliest written appearance of the verb *rock* to refer to African American dancing and music. *Rock*, as Knight used it, meant not the action of the body while dancing, or some activity that called for euphemism, but referred instead to the effect of black dancing on the city. It also attested to the loudness of the music. Several hundred black people gathering around drums could make, as Latrobe put it, "a most extraordinary noise."

Here is Latrobe's picture of the "old man" sitting astride the "Cylindrical drum about a foot in diameter."

Why did Latrobe take the trouble to draw this picture? Because he had never seen such a thing before. There are no pictures of drums like this from Charleston. Or from Baltimore, Norfolk, Washington, D.C., or New York. To a Cuban or someone from the French Antilles, Congo Square would not have seemed remarkable,

except perhaps for the size of the gathering. Latrobe would have found an impressive variety of percussive forms and riggings to draw in Cuba, where Fernando Ortiz documented the existence of over a hundred different types of African drums. It was no accident that Congo Square was located next to the Creole part of town, not the Anglo-American, and that the Sunday gatherings endured roughly as long as Francophone dominance of the city.

As I have previously indicated, the uniqueness of New Orleans owes in no small part to its rapid succession of three distinct colonial eras, each with its own ruling European language and distinct associated African world. The city had superimposed on it in layers different identities that elsewhere remained separate.

These different identities continue today to distinguish neighbor from neighbor: the barriers of colonialism are as strong in the present-day Antilles as they ever were. With its mutually unintelligible languages and its political complexities, the region still struggles to connect adjacent islands that have always had natural ties but have been separated by language and the interests of large nations. The region remains frustratingly, resolutely disjunct.

Still, there are obvious links. One is the drum. And in particular, the drummer-who-sits-on-the-drum. With Latrobe's mounted drummer, we can trace an arc down the Antilles.

◦∞◦

In January 2007 I saw a performance by Alma Moyó, a Puerto Rican folkloric group in New York that devotes itself to *bomba*, the traditional Afro-Rican form that bears a substantial influence from Saint-Domingue.

One dance Alma Moyó performed that night in New York looked and sounded very much like something I'd seen in eastern Cuba. I wrote earlier

Photographed in 2003, the *tumba francesa* group La Caridad de Oriente, of Santiago de Cuba. The tumba francesa descends from the same Domingan diaspora in Cuba that subsequently went to New Orleans in 1809–10.

in this volume about the *tumba francesa* groups, who perform dances brought to Oriente (eastern Cuba) from Saint-Domingue by the refugees of 1803. In one of the tumba francesa dances, *frenté*, the drummer turns the *premier*, the big drum that plays solo improvisations, on its side and sits on it, reaching down between his knees to play. This is not a common move in Afro-Cuban music; it's something the tumba francesa is known for. In a display of mutual virtuosity, the drummer duets with the steps of a solo male dancer, who is festooned with kerchiefs. That's what the Alma Moyó performers did that night, the drummer following the dancer's steps and other gestures, mimicking his footwork and even his kerchief play with smacks and slaps.

Knowing that planters from Saint-Domingue also fled, in much smaller numbers, to Puerto Rico, I asked the group's director, Alex LaSalle, about it. He pointed out to me that his French name (pronounced Spanish-style, *la-SA-ye*) comes from the LaSalle sugar plantation in western Puerto Rico, from one of whose slaves he is descended. "In northwestern Puerto Rico," he said, "they called it *tumba*, not bomba." In bomba they call their kerchiefs not by the Spanish name of *pañuelos*, but by the same Hispanicized French term the tumba francesa uses—*tiñones*, or tignons, the same word used to apply to the turbans that women of color were required to wear in Saint-Domingue and New Orleans.

I asked LaSalle the name of the dance in which the drummer sits on the drum. "In western Puerto Rico," he said, "they call it wanga."

My jaw dropped open. I already knew that the *barriles*, the barrel drums of bomba, can sometimes have *fundamento*—a spirit that, in the manner of sacred African drums, is fed with the blood of a sacrificed animal. But Makandal was burned at the stake for making wanga, a word that might be translated as a charm, or perhaps, as the power that inhabits that charm. In Haitian vodou, the drummer sitting on the drum is associated with the branch of vodou called petro, which is in turn associated with strong action and violent movement (cf. the Dance of Don Pedro, in chapter 15). In Saint-Domingue, Boukman sang: *Eh! Eh! Bomba! Hen, hen!* Puerto Rican bomba today is often presented as something benignly folkloric, but I was getting a glimpse of what it was connected to.

The reader who has been with me this far will appreciate that Congo Square was a meeting ground that must have had a multiplicity of African musics going on in its adjacent circles. I suspect that one of them sounded something like the bomba of western Puerto Rico, or the frenté of Oriente's tumba francesa, or, for that matter, like drumming I have heard at Haitian vodou ceremonies in the New York region.

Filming in Haiti in the 1930s, Alan Lomax captured the (silent) image of a drummer sitting on his drum, altering the drum's tonality with foot pressure like the tumba francesa drummer does. He also filmed a group of peasants dancing contredanse (called in Haiti *matinik*, as in Martinique), looking very much like the tumba francesa.[12]

Unsurprisingly, the drummer-who-sits-on-the-drum turns up next door to Haiti, in the present-day music of the Congos of the Dominican Republic's Villa Mella, altering the pitch of his drum with foot pressure while he leans forward and plays with both hands. He's in Jamaica, doing the same thing in the Kongo-derived practice called *kumina*. Southeast of Puerto Rico, you can see him in Kreyol-speaking Guadeloupe, in what they call the *gwo ka* (literally, "big drum"), and that tradition traveled on down to Martinique. (One of the drums in gwo ka is called the *boula*, as it is in Cuban tumba francesa; the resemblance of the word to *bamboula* is not coincidental.) We can connect it all the way down to South America: on the coast of Venezuela, you can find the drummer-who-sits-on-the-drum, altering the drum's pitch with his foot.

Where doesn't the drummer-who-sits-on-the-drum turn up? In Havana, New Orleans's great partner city. If he was ever there, he disappeared. He's in eastern Cuba—Caribbean Cuba—but not in western, Gulf of Mexico Cuba. The drummer-who-sits-on-the-drum doesn't play in Havana's Regla de Ocha ceremonies, nor in Kongo palo, nor in Calabar-derived Abakuá. Maybe one of his descendants is sitting on the square box-drum called *cajón*, but that's already something different.

Ten years after the expulsion of Domingans from eastern Cuba flooded the newly acquired U.S. city of New Orleans with French speakers—which is to say, during the city's great Caribbean moment—the drummer-who-sits-on-the-drum was playing in Congo Square, where Benjamin Henry Latrobe sketched him. I don't know for sure how that drummer got to Congo Square, but my guess would be that he came to the Americas from Kongo, and that he arrived in New Orleans with the Domingans. In all those other parts of the hemisphere I named, he's still there, surviving into the age of video. But he turned up in New Orleans, then disappeared. As did hand drumming, which didn't survive the constraints of Anglo-American slavery; post-emancipation black drumming in New Orleans was based on military-derived stick technique. It may be that the idea of the laterally mounted drum played with the foot survived into John Robichaux's orchestra in the late 1880s, whose drummer, Dee Dee Chandler, became the first drummer we know of to play the bass drum with a foot pedal.[13] (And the persistence of the New Orleans tambourine tradition tells us that hand percussion survived the disappearance of the big drums.)

Someone like the drummer in Latrobe's drawing might still have been playing on Sundays at Congo Square when Louis Moreau Gottschalk was a child. In 1859, when the thirty-year-old Gottschalk was a world-famous pianist, composer, conductor, and producer of musical spectacles, he forged an important, if momentary, connection among New Orleans, Havana, and tumba francesa.

Gottschalk spent considerable time in Cuba, where he did something his Havana colleagues did not much do: he traveled to Oriente. In those days, it took fourteen uncomfortable days to go by land from one end of the island to the other, up and down mountains, across unbridged rivers, through bandit-infested territory. In the much smaller Dominican Republic, with similar terrain, "many citizens would make out their wills before beginning any trip."[14]

In Santiago de Cuba, Gottschalk found many people still speaking French. He concertized there, and briefly taught pupils. And he saw a tumba francesa group, performing in the street during Carnival. This was not exotica for Gottschalk; it was roots. He would have recognized it as a cognate of Congo Square. Inspired, Gottschalk brought the tumba francesa from Santiago to Havana, something no one had done, to perform in his spectacular concert work *La Nuit des Tropiques*, which involved a gargantuan ensemble of hundreds of players. Not the least shocking thing about it was Gottschalk's unprecedented placement of what the whites saw as *brujería* (witchcraft) from Santiago de Cuba out in front of the grandest orchestra anyone present had ever seen, in Havana's Teatro Tacón, the third largest theater in the world.[15]

Except on Día de Reyes (January 6), black habaneros played drums behind closed doors, not openly in the street. By exhibiting Santiago drum culture in Havana, where it was unknown, Gottschalk brought together for a moment the two geographically and culturally opposite sides of Cuba: the Caribbean (Santiago) and the Gulf of Mexico (Havana). He connected the dots I am connecting now—from Saint-Domingue, to Santiago de Cuba, to Havana, to Congo Square.

⸎

Christian Schultz, a traveler who witnessed the Congo Square dances in 1808, described

> Twenty different dancing groups of the wretched Africans, collected together to perform their *worship* after the manner of their country. They have their own national music, consisting for the most part of a long kind of narrow drum of various sizes, from two to eight feet in length, three or four of which makes a band. The principal dancers or leaders are dressed in a variety of wild and savage fashions, always ornamented with a number of tails of the smaller wild beasts. . . . These amusements continue until sunset, when one or two of the city patrol show themselves with their cutlasses, and the crowds immediately disperse.[16] [emphasis in original]

The last sentence would have been almost perfectly applicable in New Orleans as I knew it in 2004, when the Sunday afternoon second lines were closed down at five on the dot by squads of police, who were sometimes downright rude, even provocative, in doing so.

Schultz saw the dances at Congo Square as worship, correctly identifying the spiritual component of the music and dance, though I have never heard people in African religion speak of "worship." They communicate with the spirits, an activity in which the drum has a principal role. In Oriente and Puerto Rico, the tumba and the bomba had (and continue to have) spiritual significance. When we talk about Congo Square, we can assume that African religions were being practiced, or referenced, there—whether voodoo or something else—and that black New Orleans as a whole was buzzing with them, the way Cuba was (and is), the way Saint-Domingue had been.

The variety of sounds at Congo Square was commented on by James Creecy who, visiting fifteen years after Latrobe's description and more favorably disposed to the experience, saw "banjos, tom-toms, violins, jawbones, triangles and various other instruments." Harmony was present: he noted that the dancers "sing a second or counter to the music most sweetly," and observed that "in all [the dancers'] movements, gyrations, and attitudenizing exhibitions, the most perfect time is kept, making the beats with the feet, head, or hands, or all, as correctly as a well-regulated metronome! . . . Every stranger should visit Congo Square when in its glory."[17]

An African American music was coming into existence. Despite the African multinationality of the participants, Schultz identified what he heard the "Africans" play in 1808 as "their own national music." It was a crossroads moment, because the drums were still talking in the New Orleans of the early nineteenth century. They were literally, not metaphorically, language, which was one reason the British had been so assiduous about prohibiting them.

Congo Square may have looked like it was nothing but a party, but to play a hand drum in 1819 in the United States, where overt manifestations of Africanness had elsewhere been so thoroughly, deliberately erased, was a tremendous act of will, memory, and resistance. Thomas Nuttall, who visited the city in 1820, observed that on Sunday afternoon "the Negroes assemble in the suburbs of the city, and amuse themselves by dancing. When thus assembled by common friendship, if they have any reflection, they must be convinced of the efficient force which they possess to emancipate themselves; they are, however, strictly watched by the police, and the sole object of their meeting appears to be amusement."[18] Well, the sole object of their meeting had better appear to be amusement, or else. At every moment, the whites feared they might go up in flames the way Cap Français had.

The meetings at Congo Square must have been rich with all kinds of coded meaning. One could even read into them a kind of sonic marronage: the drums were a way slaves could escape, if only for a few hours.

∞

Benjamin Henry Latrobe died suddenly of yellow fever on September 3, 1820, three years to the day after the death of his son from the same disease.

In a city that saw waves of death every summer, voodoo was not afraid. If Congo Square was one system of underground communication, voodoo was another. The two crossed paths, but they operated differently. Voodoo was a distributed network that extended into the fine houses of the city. It had the taint of sedition and a city full of spies. The drummers at Congo Square were men, but voodoo was run by free women of color, who in New Orleans were more numerous, and had more property and power, than their male counterparts.

The voodoo of nineteenth-century New Orleans, often practiced at the Bayou St. John, at the lakeshore, or in the outlying swamps or in the countryside, was different from the vodou of Haiti. The Domingan migration of 1809–10 from Cuba to New Orleans was undoubtedly a milestone for the practice of voodoo in Louisiana, but was not its inception. Spirits had likely been traveling back and forth between Louisiana and Saint-Domingue all along. The newly arrived Domingans' vodou that came en masse from eastern Cuba had to coexist, and merge, with a solidly established Afro-Louisianan spiritual practice that had grown up with a distinct set of African roots as well as influences from the Choctaws, the Natchez, the Houmas, and other Indian groups, developing its own identity parallel to Saint-Domingue. Some vodou traditions would have arrived during Louisiana's earliest days on the first two slave ships to come to the territory, which were from Ouidah and presumably contained slaves from Ardra, the land of the *foddun* in Africa. But much stronger in French Louisiana was the element of Senegalese practice—a minority influence in Saint-Domingue—which contributed the charms called gris-gris.

Kongo people, meanwhile, had a centuries-old tradition employing the imagery and structures of Catholicism to express traditional African practice. They carried this practice of syncretization to the various Catholic territories of the New World. In Spanish New Orleans as in Cuba, the symbolic vocabulary of Catholicism was important. Blacks could enter the grand St.

Louis Cathedral, and it was an important point of communication. "Père Antoine"—Padre Antonio Sedella—welcomed them. Marie Laveau, the voodoo queen, a free colored child of the Spanish regime, born September 10, 1801, to the Creole planter Charles Laveau and his mistress Marguerite Henry, went to Père Antoine's early mass every morning before going out to work as a hairdresser.[19]

In African religion, women have one set of secrets and men another. This too was carried to the New World. In Cuba, where male laborers greatly outnumbered females on sugar plantations, the Abakuá secret society for men thrived, brought from the Calabar region of Africa. But in New Orleans, where the black component of the migration of Domingans from Cuba in 1809–10 was considerably female heavy, it is no surprise that, by one reckoning, followers of voodoo in New Orleans were 80 percent women. New Orleans had "voodoo queens," something unknown as such in Haiti, although in the excerpt cited in chapter 15, Moreau de St.-Méry speaks of a conjoined king-and-queen pair. But the kings had been left to die in the butchery of Saint-Domingue. The one famous male "voodoo priest," Doctor John (Jean Montanet), was not Domingan; after his death in 1885 at the age of "nearly a hundred," he was described by Lafcadio Hearn as a Bambara who had been kidnapped by Spanish slavers and shipped to Cuba, where he became a ship's cook and ultimately settled in New Orleans.[20] Montanet may have been more of a seller of charms—from which he is said to have made a lot of money—than a conductor of rituals. (In 1967, inspired by Hearn's description, the Irish-descended Mid-City pianist Mac Rebennack, whose grandfather was a minstrel, took the name "Dr. John" as his performing persona, and under that name became an important figure of American music in the last third of the twentieth century.)[21]

The free women of color in post-Domingan New Orleans were a skilled bunch: white men's mistresses (which required diplomacy and entrepreneurial savvy, as well as mastery of the amorous arts), domestics, tradeswomen, craftswomen, and businesswomen. Like the practice of love, voodoo in New Orleans was a good business. These women didn't have much power, but they had this power.

In the African religions as practiced in Cuba and Haiti today, women do not play the drums. That's for men. Women may not so much as touch a consecrated drum. Perhaps that has something to do with Ina Johanna Fandrich's observation that "New Orleans Voodoo practitioners work with a few

Catholic saints and the spirits of the dead but never seem to have developed an elaborate system of lwa or divinities."[22] The drums communicate with the gods, so it is possible that the dearth of men in the 1809–10 Domingan migration to Louisiana may have had something to do with the lack of the system of lwa in New Orleans. The men, whose job it was to call the lwa down to ride believers' heads, didn't come to New Orleans.

Especially in the years following the Haitian Revolution, when there was great tension in Louisiana, the practice of voodoo was underground. The women danced naked (at least in later years, as attested to in various accounts), in groups, with serpents, and they were feared. "The classical signature piece of Marie Laveau's Voodoo practices and New Orleans' 19th-century Voodoo ceremonies," writes Fandrich, "was the dance with a living serpent signifying the central deity of the religion. He/she/it was called *Li Grand Zombi* in New Orleans."[23] The centrality of the serpent—in a city that was, after all, sitting atop a snake-infested swamp—resonates with Moreau de St.-Méry's description of a ceremony with a live snake-god in Saint-Domingue. Vodouisants do not dance with live snakes in contemporary Haiti, but Damballah-Wedo, the lwa who bears the image of the snake, is ever-present there.

The religious tradition of the Domingans became susceptible in New Orleans not only to a further creolization with the Afro-Louisianan elements, but also to becoming crossed with a diversity of elements that began pouring into the city during the American years when it was both a magnet for all types of Americans and a primary immigration destination.

The peak of voodoo practice in New Orleans came well before the Civil War. By the early 1870s, voodoo had become a tourist attraction, with as many as twelve thousand people taking the train to the shores of Lake Pontchartrain on St. John's Eve (June 26), though by 1876 these large ceremonies had "deteriorated," as one writer put it.[24] A June 26, 1871, story in the *New Orleans Picayune* by an unimpressed journalist was headlined, "Voudou nonsense—a plain unvarnished account of the lake shore revels." But by then, New Orleans voodoo was world famous. When Marie Laveau died in 1881, her obituary ran in the *New York Times*.

One of the celebrated names of New Orleans voodoo lore is a figure about whom little hard information is known beyond a single account published in 1882 that purported to give an account of her initiation in the 1820s: Sanité Dédé, said to have come from Saint-Domingue.[25] What is popularly believed to be her tomb in St. Louis Cemetery #1, adjacent to old Congo Square, is a spot where people come to "do work." When I visited the tomb in 2004 I found triple-Xs scratched all over it, signifying favors granted. If voodoo is a force in the life of present-day New Orleans, it keeps very quiet. But various items left at the tomb—flowers, eggs, candles, handwritten notes, as well as other, odder things—bore witness that someone in New Orleans was practicing something, the same way unseen hands leave things at intersections in São Paulo or at crossroads in Guadeloupe, or drop wrapped-up packets by a tree in a park in Havana, or in all the other places where latter-day versions of traditional African religions continue to be practiced, sometimes openly, sometimes discreetly.

⟨∞⟩

Already wealthy from the commerce of its ports, New Orleans became a powerful city in the 1820s and experienced phenomenal growth in the 1830s, during the brief period after the rise of steamboat river traffic but before the emergence of the railroad as a freight-hauling competitor. In 1840, when the country was still in a depression from the Panic of 1837, New Orleans was the third-largest city in the U.S. census, barely edged out for second place by Baltimore.

New Orleans continued to be a money center. Its banks issued bilingual $10 notes that said *Dix* on them; according to an apocryphal but plausible story, the Anglo-Americans called the notes "Dixies." Dixieland was not only awash in paper money; the number-one slave market was also the best place to do business in silver, something that was in chronically short supply. "Spanish dollars" remained legal tender in the United States until 1857.

The jams at Congo Square were stopped in 1835, then apparently restarted for a time, but definitively shut down by 1851. That year, Congo Square—officially called Place Publique, for there was never any place officially called Congo Square—received the name of Place d'Armes, while the area formerly known as Place d'Armes was renamed Jackson Square, a name it retains to the present day. The former Congo Square became a site for military drill. Buildings have never been erected over it, and it remains an open commons.

It's an article of faith in New Orleans music that there is some kind of continuity from Congo Square to jazz. The only problem is, we don't know exactly what that continuity consists of. The music played there probably had little sonic resemblance to anything we know as jazz. For one thing, the characteristic instruments of jazz were not yet in wide use. What happened at

Congo Square wasn't considered music by whites, of course, and was thought unworthy of serious investigation.

But we know a few things about the music at Congo Square, and we can make some educated guesses. We know there was a diversity of rhythms, styles, timbres, costume, and drums. "As early as 1799 fifes and fiddles were used," writes Henry Kmen, "and in time banjos, triangles, jews harps, and tambourines were added."[26] We can be pretty sure the rhythm called habanera or tango was one of the rhythms being played. Probably something that sounded like the bomba in Puerto Rico and the tumba francesa in Oriente was going on. We can refer to the rich, understudied repository of information we can find today in contemporary Haitian vodou drumming. Maybe there was something like a backbeat, stamping on one and three and clapping on two and four. Maybe all of this was going on on the same Sunday.

I would bet that in Latrobe's day, the drummer-who-sits-on-the-drum marked the steps of a solo dancer as he does today all down the Antilles. There was likely some form of contredanse. Quite possibly, something like the pursuit-and-capture dance that in Cuba became *guaguancó* was going on. We can suppose that people sang to spirits, commented on their situation, and praised and insulted each other in verse.

There is evidence that with the passage of time, the direct participation of African-born people waned away and was replaced by a more creolized influence. Popular songs found their way into the jam. Kmen writes: "Observers tell of seeing jigs, fandangos, and Virginia breakdown in the square, and they speak of hearing melodies like "Old Virginia Never Tire," "Hey Jim Along Josey," and "Get Along Home You Yellow Gals."[27] Were those English-language songs sung together or in competition with songs in French, Spanish, or remnants of African languages? Did they stretch out on them? Add call and response choruses? Sing medleys? We don't know.

Everything we know about the unique, multilayered making of Afro-Louisiana—the Senegambian-majority French years, the Kongo-heavy Spanish period, the African American Protestants shipped from Upper to Lower South, the Domingan diaspora, and the pirate-trafficked Africans delivered en route to Cuba—suggests that from early on, there was a local style, peculiar to New Orleans, that sounded different from the style of music from anywhere else. Perhaps that is why today nothing else sounds quite like the still-evolving music of the groups of African American men known as Mardi Gras Indians. The Indians don't fall within the chronological purview of this book, and they demand a fuller treatment than I can provide, but they will be the subject of my final chapter.

Books about history end, but history doesn't ever come to a stop. Much is missing: Anglo-American slavery was designed to erase African American history. But African Americans made their own history, and in New Orleans, history parades down the street.

Sunpie (Bruce Barnes), leader of the North Side Skull and Bones Gang, surrounded by documentarians, challenges Big Chief Donald Harrison Jr., speaking in poetry as he incarnates an African American equivalent of Guédé, the Haitian lord of the dead, in the first light of the first Mardi Gras after the failure of the levees.

CODA

22

WE WON'T BOW DOWN

It is presumed that no apology will be required for presenting
to the public the life of a Hero. . . . In the following pages
he will be seen in the character of a Warrior, a Patriot and
a State prisoner; in every situation he is still the chief of
his Band, asserting their rights with dignity, firmness and
courage.

—*Introduction to* The Autobiography of Black Hawk (*1833*)

On a chilly Sunday night in New Orleans's Central City in January
2005, the cigarette smoke in the packed Blueprint Lounge was even
thicker than the fog outside. Big Chief Theodore Emile "Bo" Dollis
sat at the bar, nursing a drink. In an adjacent room, tambourines and drums
thumped, as a crowded circle of people sang, "Ho na naaaaaaae, hooo na
nae . . ."

Two men danced, gesticulating at each other from opposite sides of the
room. One brought his right arm down from high above his head to way
down low, in diagonal motion. The Wild Magnolias were running down the
signals they would use, and the songs they would sing, on Mardi Gras day.
These weekly "practices"—informal jams, really—were part of the prepara-
tion for that day, when they would go out on the street in their extravagant
hand-sewn costumes. All month long, similar events were going on in bars
all over town.

The only-in-New-Orleans art form of the Mardi Gras Indians (whom I will call the "Indians," in keeping with New Orleans custom) is not something for outsiders to penetrate, and it should be understood that I am speaking about their tradition from the outside. You can show up at a practice if someone tips you off where it'll be, and you can be there when they parade on Mardi Gras morning—if you can find them—but you don't become an Indian without being part of the community. And in that community, ghettoized since long before today's Indians were born, being an Indian is not something for white people to do (though I should qualify that statement by saying that there have been rare, and controversial, cases of white people joining Indian groups, but as far as I'm concerned, they've been the exception that proved the rule).

If you take what the Indians do simply as folk art, it's one of the great American cultural treasures. But it has overtly spiritual and social dimensions as well.

ᶜᐤᑯ

The Mardi Gras Indians are a product of black Carnival in black neighborhoods.

Outside of New Orleans, there's some confusion about this point. The Indians aren't part of the big Mardi Gras parades that pass down St. Charles, nor do they have anything to do with the "krewes" that put on those processions.

The Indians embody resistance. You can sum it up in four words: "We won't bow down." That's a line from their hymn "My Indian Red" (it's sometimes phrased as "We won't kneel down"). They're not Indians, although not a few of them have some Native American ancestry. They're small groups of working-class African American men who dress, or "mask" (the New Orleans word, though they don't as a rule wear masks), as American Indians, in highly stylized outfits that refer not to the Native Americans of Louisiana, but to the Plains Indians costumes of 1880s Wild West Show fame.

The most spectacular and recognizable feature of Mardi Gras Indian performance today is its members' lavish (and heavy) "suits"—wearable artworks that, with the headdress, or "crown," can be eight feet tall. Despite the allegorical patches sewed on the suits depicting mythical Native Americans, this is an African tradition, with beadwork that looks strikingly like examples from the Yoruba in Nigeria—or, closer to home, from Haiti.

New suits have to be designed and sewn from scratch, every year, by the individual men who wear them, often with the support of a sewing team. "Every year for Carnival time, we make a new suit," sings Bo Dollis. Another Indian song goes "Somebody gotta sew, sew, sew." A neophyte Indian gets sore hands from multiple needle sticks. You can't just go buy a flashy suit; you've got to create it, and no sloppy stitching allowed. A first-class suit can cost its working-class wearer thousands of dollars to make, so it's a tremendous commitment of money as well as time. The many hours spent sewing is an extended meditation, and when it's done, the suit is a power object. But there's more to the Indians' commitment than their suits.

An Indian "gang," or tribe, is a spiritual secret society, a social club, and a mutual aid organization all in one. Indians might appear in their suits for stage performance, but that's strictly lagniappe and is a comparatively recent development. The Indians' real performances are a kind of sacred theater that takes place on the streets of the black neighborhoods, uptown and downtown. Collectively, they're part of what knits New Orleans's black populace together.

Joseph Roach writes, "There is no agreed-upon explanation for the origins of present-day Mardi Gras Indians in New Orleans, and it would be surprising if one were ever established."[1] Perhaps that's part of the beauty of it, that you have to accept them as they are. The first known formally organized Mardi Gras Indian gang was the Creole Wild West, founded by a plasterer, Becate Batiste, in the mid-1880s. The form it took was apparently inspired by Buffalo Bill Cody's Wild West Show, which played New Orleans in the 1884–85 season, complete with a promotional parade through the uptown streets that featured fully costumed Plains warriors.[2] It must have been impressive: Indians parading through the streets displaying their culture, at a time of great repression for African Americans, to say nothing of the fact that Indians had drums. But Becate Batiste's Creole Wild West wasn't the beginning of something from scratch, any more than Boukman's uprising was the beginning of slave rebellion. It was a way of giving form to something that was already going on.

Black men wearing feathers and horns goes back to Africa, and Africans dressing as Indians at carnivals is as old as slavery in the hemisphere. From Brazil to Trinidad to Haiti to New Orleans, the image of the indigenous person turns up in black iconography. Dressing as Native Americans is not merely homage; it's a statement about how Africans survived and how cultures mixed, especially in Louisiana. Mardi Gras Indians I have talked to are emphatic that elements of their practice go back farther than Creole Wild West. Their oral tradition stresses the connection to Congo Square. If this is so, the tambourines that accompany their songs as they parade down the street might be a direct historical African American link to African hand-drumming tradition. Perhaps even more to the point, the Mardi Gras Indians provide a unique window into how a culture that is African in form but local in content grows, adapts, and serves the needs of its community.

An Indian gang is built around the central figure of the Big Chief, whom the tribe must protect and who in turn has chiefly obligations to them. To be a chief requires artistry, scholarship, strength, endurance, bravery, and consistency of action. There may be six members or more (or if circum-stances require, as in post-Katrina New Orleans, fewer), with well-defined roles. There's a Spy Boy, who is the number-two man in the tribe, and a Flag Boy, a Wild Man, a Trail Chief, and Scouts, plus tambourine players and other percussionists.

When they go out in the street, the gangs communicate using a private vocabulary. I can sing you the song called "Jockomo," but I don't know what the words "Jockomo fee-na-nay" mean, much less where they come from.

Few people outside of New Orleans had ever heard of the Mardi Gras Indians before the 1970s. They had a bad reputation locally, even among other African Americans, and were looked down on as low class, as "a kind of outsider, outlaw culture," in Felipe Smith's words.[3] "I was afraid to go near the Indians," recalled Big Chief Allison "Tootie" Montana's wife, Joyce.[4] The first systematic study of the Indians, an unpublished dissertation at Tulane, was completed only in 1973.[5] No one even knows for sure how many tribes there are—in 2005, I heard numbers as low as twenty-five and as high as forty-seven. Unlike the second lines of New Orleans, which can draw thousands to a Sunday strut, the Mardi Gras Indians have never been a tradition for mass participation. They have remained a semi-underground phenomenon all these years. There is no central Mardi Gras Indian organization; the groups are small and independent. They receive no official support and sometimes endure harassment. They divide into uptown and downtown Indians, each with their own suit-making traditions and their own spring holiday, Super Sunday, when all the Indians come out to parade together one day.

On Mardi Gras morning, when the town gets up in the early hours and many New Orleanians have stayed up all night, the Indians go out into their neighborhoods, where the float-riding, bead-throwing, white Mardi Gras krewes never venture. They walk their streets, flaunting their suits, playing their tambourines, and singing. There's no printed schedule, and it's not known in advance where they might go. As Cyril Neville sang it, "We're comin' out Mardi Gras mornin' / Ain't givin' no kind of warnin'." In New Orleans, where organizations are supposed to pay police fees when they have a parade, the Indians don't apply for a permit. In effect, they ask the question:

can a black man walk the streets of his own neighborhood—OK, in a seven-foot-tall feathered costume—without permission from anyone?

When one tribe encounters another in the street on Mardi Gras day, the Spy Boy, some distance in the vanguard, signals the Flag Boy, who alerts the Chief. There is a protocol which must be observed, or there could be trouble. If one were to insist that the other "bow down," there could be a fight, or, in Indian lingo, a "humbug." According to Tootie Montana and others, the act of bowing or kneeling in homage was called *humbah*, from which "humbug" presumably derives.[6]

Back in the day (the 1920s, say), grudges accumulated during the year turned into real fights that broke out between Indian gangs. Beefs were settled with real weapons, at a place called the Battlefield, in the tough South Rampart Street corridor of Back of Town, where Louis Armstrong grew up. Combatants would be hurt or even killed. The costumes weren't as elaborate then—decorated vests of dyed turkey feathers, beads, and bottle caps. But today, much of the competitive energy goes into making the suits, and conflict between the gangs is highly ritualized.

Indians today compete to be the "prettiest," but don't be misled. Prettiness, like sewing, is a manly attribute in Indian culture. The Indians still test each other when they go out, and an Indian is expected to back up his words with action if necessary. Though they might appear to be celebrating disunity by challenging each other as rivals, in the aggregate their tradition has come to mean the opposite: a statement of black unity.

Moreover, it is a living thing, in a state of growth and change. An experienced Indian may start his own group, as Victor Harris did in 1984 when he founded Fi-Yi-Yi, Spirit of the Mandingo Warrior. A former Spy Boy for Big Chief Tootie Montana's Yellow Pocahontas gang in the Seventh Ward, Harris was an innovator in masking African, eschewing Indian-themed images in order to invent costumes based on his researches into African design and, in doing so, demonstrating the flexibility of the tradition.

The Indians' deeply flavorful style of song has elements in common with the rumba of Matanzas and Havana—Cuban ports that were in constant communication with New Orleans, where the jobs on the docks were dominated by members of the Abakuá society (who derive from the still-extant Ekpe society in the Cross River region of Africa). There are points in common between Abakuá and the Indians—a secret society of men, with ritualized street theater, fantastical costume, esoteric language, and a voice-and-percussion music.

It is not unreasonable to postulate some Calabar (Cross River) influence, especially given that the peak of Calabar slaving to Cuba was during the Spanish period in Louisiana. But the Abakuá ritual is very specific, and doesn't look like what the Mardi Gras Indians do, and despite some features in common, their music is quite different.

The closest resemblance to the motifs of the Indians' suits might be in Trinidad, where the Carnival tradition derives largely from a French Creole population. There black men wear Indian headdresses and costumed figures like the Midnight Robber and Pierrot Grenade have boasting competitions and ambulatory musical street battles, complete with spies who run ahead. There are ambulatory battle dances in many places, like the *mayolé* cudgel-fighting tradition of Moule, Guadeloupe, which, like the Indians, transformed from bloody combat to symbolic fighting in the 1940s and '50s.

But there is no evidence for any direct influence of those traditions on New Orleans. Ultimately, though the Mardi Gras Indian tradition is part of a cultural continuum, it has its own distinct personality. As Cyril Neville put it at the start of "Big Chief Jolly," "They don't do this nowhere else but in New Orleans."

⌀

In the spiritual churches of New Orleans—nominally Protestant, very different even from Pentecostal churches, and a world all their own—there is the cult of Black Hawk. Claude Jacobs, who did extensive fieldwork in the New Orleans spiritual churches, writes

> Black Hawk services vary from one church to another, with the ritual
> ultimately depending on the leader. The only fixed elements are that it
> is always a night service, most or all of the church's electrical lights are
> turned off, and the music that is played has a strong steady beat that is
> said to be associated with Indian spirits.[7]

The historical Black Hawk was a Fox and Sauk Indian who sided with the British against the United States in the Upper Mississippi Valley during the War of 1812, then in 1832 crossed the Mississippi to reoccupy lands that had been taken from his people previously.[8] Abraham Lincoln, then a young man, served in the three-month Black Hawk War to suppress him, and Jefferson Davis was in charge of escorting Black Hawk to trial. Black Hawk dictated an autobiography (in his own language, to a U.S. government Indian agent, who translated it), a text of spirituality and resistance that was published in

1833, and though some skepticism has been expressed about its authenticity, it is apparently real.

In the spiritual church, the figure of Black Hawk acts as a "spirit guide." The photographer Michael P. Smith, who documented the activities of the Mardi Gras Indians and the spiritual churches of New Orleans, published a picture from a Black Hawk service at the Infant Jesus Spiritual Church of Prague (in New Orleans) in 1975 that shows a celebrant dressed very much like a Mardi Gras Indian.[9] Jason Berry quotes spiritual church reverend Jules Anderson on the resemblance between the two phenomena: "You could go on a Carnival day and see people full of Indian spirits [the Mardi Gras Indians]. You wouldn't know if you were in a Black Hawk service or an Indian rehearsal. These people experience a spirit take-over."[10]

The multiple subterranean lines of connection—the legacy of Congo Square, voodoo, the musical funeral procession, the Mardi Gras Indians, the spiritual churches, and other cultural phenomena—come together still in the contemporary music of New Orleans. If you've got ears, all those things are still there, oozing out of the city's funky music, sometimes only as points of reference, sometimes more profoundly.

The Indians' tradition predates the emergence of jazz. Jelly Roll Morton claimed to have been a Spy Boy (though he remembered the key phrase not as "bow down" but "bow wow").[11] In his 1938 Library of Congress interview, Morton sang a version of an old Mardi Gras Indian song—the first known recording of one—slapping out a rhythm behind it that is what in rock and roll became known as a backbeat.

The Mardi Gras Indians' call-and-response percussive chant is basic enough that it works perfectly when dressed up in the clothes of pretty much any style of African American music that came along after the 1880s. The Dixie Cups' 1965 pop hit "Iko Iko" is an Indian song, previously recorded by Sugar Boy Crawford in 1953 as "Jockomo," with a mambo-R&B feel. The Wild Magnolias' 1970s albums of Indian songs are among the greatest electric funk sides ever recorded. For that matter, the Neville Brothers first played together as a band in order to back up their uncle, Big Chief Jolly, in the Wild Tchoupitoulas. Indians have done hip-hop tracks that sound not like they're trying to rap, but like they've always been doing it.

Claude Trémé and Julie Moró's
tomb in St. Louis Cemetery #2.

ICI REPOSENT

CLAUDE TRÉMÉ

NÉ À SAVIGNY, COTE-D'OR, FRA

DÉCÉDÉ LE 17 MARS 1828

À L'ÂGE DE 69 ANS;

JULIE MORO,

VEUVE DE

CLAUDE TRÉMÉ,

NÉE À LA NOUVELLE ORLÉAN

LE 12 AVRIL 1775,

DÉCÉDÉE LE 8 AOUT 1843.

Vous qui les avez connus

ᕰᕰᕰ

On Mardi Gras day, February 8, 2005, we were in the Tremé, on St. Claude Avenue, at a block party put on by the Backstreet Cultural Museum. Formerly the Blandin Funeral Home, the Backstreet houses a collection of Mardi Gras Indian suits in the room where they used to lay the coffins out, and has hundreds of videos of jazz funerals made by the museum's founder, Sylvester Francis.

It's a spiritual block. Across the street is St. Augustine's (accent on the second syllable, *auGUSTin*). Built in the 1840s during New Orleans's period of grandeur, it's regarded as the oldest African American Catholic church in the country, though there is no such official distinction. At St. Augustine's, "free people of color bought two outer rows of pews for slaves to worship," as a plaque outside says. Its priest, Father Jerome Ledoux, officiates with a cypress stump as his pulpit. If you go one block to Rampart Street and walk uptown for ten minutes, you'll be at Congo Square.

Big Chief Alfred Doucette of the Flaming Arrow tribe was in the street, wearing a multicolored Indian suit dominated by enormous orange plumes. Then, from a couple of blocks uptown, I heard drums approaching. The first thing I noticed was how good they sounded. It wasn't only tambourines, but a small drum orchestra of various pitches and hefts, played with hands and sticks. Then I heard the chant:

Congooooo . . . Congo Nation.
Congoooo . . .

The drums slammed a wide-swinging two-bar rhythm, something that would fit with what we call the Bo Diddley beat. It was Congo Nation approaching, with Big Chief Donald Harrison Jr. looking regal in a tall suit of black and gray that extended several feet behind him in a buoyant tail. Harrison does not mask in the form of a Plains Indian; he is, to my knowledge, the only Mardi Gras Indian chief besides Fi-Yi-Yi to make an African-themed suit. As he approached Doucette, there was an elaborate protocol and greeting. The encounter between the two chiefs was brief, symbolic, and moving.

I've been around long enough to trust the feeling I get when I'm in the presence of something. I had that feeling in Cuba when I first saw an Abakuá ceremony. I had it that day in New Orleans.

ᕰᕰᕰ

As a young musician, Donald Harrison Jr. moved up to New York and stayed for years before relocating back to his hometown. I used to see him in New

York, sometimes playing alto sax with Eddie Palmieri. Though all Mardi Gras Indians are to some degree musicians, Harrison is the only Big Chief I know of who is also a highly trained, world-class jazz soloist, or, to flip it, the only jazz musician of his stature who can sew an Indian suit. His resume includes stints with bandleaders of the calibre of Palmieri and Art Blakey. Harrison has created hooks for radio hits, and he composed and conducted a Mardi Gras Indian mass. He's a scholar of deep bebop and an educator who coaches young players after school.

Everyone he teaches knows who his most famous student was. During his New York years, Harrison lived in Fort Greene, Brooklyn, where he was a musical mentor of sorts to his young neighbor, the teenaged Christopher Wallace, a.k.a. Biggie Smalls, a.k.a. the Notorious B.I.G., who would later become one of the most famous rappers of all time, and who was sensationally murdered in 1997.

"The first thing I told him was, 'You know, you would be a great rapper if I could understand what you were talking about,'" says Harrison. "'So you need to spend a lot of time really making the words where people can understand exactly what you're saying. . . . That's gonna put you on another level, right there—the enunciation.' Such a simple thing, but it's powerful." Sure enough, if you notice, Biggie on record has excellent diction. "One of the things I had him doing at one point, was learning solos, but learning how to scat 'em," Harrison recalls. "And he was a brilliant young person. . . . He would sing a Cannonball Adderly solo. I wish that he would have played jazz, but he went on the path that he deemed for himself, and it turned out that he became one of the best in his genre. Unfortunately, it led to his early demise. I still miss the young Chris. He had two sides. His mother was a devout Christian. He had a very loving and good side, and then he had his gangster side."

Biggie's murder, to the extent we know what it was about, seems to have had much to do with public disrespect between chiefs in the hip-hop world. The Mardi Gras Indians of today provide object lessons in how to resolve beefs. A few weeks after Mardi Gras, I asked Harrison about the encounter I'd seen with Alfred Doucette in front of the Backstreet. "It's like two heads of state meeting and going through a pomp and circumstance," he said, "and in order to greet each other, there's rituals that have to take place." In other words, it's not so much a theater of confrontation as it is a theater of diplomacy. It's a dramatization of what it takes to coexist: mutual respect.

Congo Nation, the name of Harrison's gang, recalls Congo Square, where, as Harrison put it, "the practices were held on Sunday—and they were called practices. We also know that the people gathered by their tribes and they would practice and then they would challenge each other, to see who was the best. . . . And when they met each other it was called being 'in the circle.' And you know that the Mardi Gras Indians still have practices on Sundays, and we know that when the Indians meet each other, that's 'in the circle,' and we know that they still challenge each other to see who's the best. So those are elements that are still alive."

Harrison can recite his lineage as an Indian, going back four generations to Big Chief Robbie. (I've seen *babalaos* of the Yoruba tradition in Cuba do much the same thing, reciting their string of teachers before divining.) He first masked Indian when he was two years old, alongside his father, the late Donald Harrison Sr., the celebrated Big Chief of the Guardians of the Flame. A Big Chief commonly has a boy at his side—a Little Chief—ensuring the community's survival by passing the tradition along to younger men. Harrison told me: "African Americans [have] been emasculated to such a large extent. So really, the underlying code of what the Indians do is to say, 'Today we're going to be men.'"

"Women never was in these masquerades at all," recalled Jelly Roll Morton.[12] There are female Indians today, but it's still a men's thing. Harrison's sister Cherice Harrison-Nelson, Big Queen of the Guardians of the Flame, says her father made women's standing in the Indians clear: "You are a *mere* embellishment to the Chief."

When I asked Harrison about the element of humbug, or confrontation, he said, "Everything that we [African Americans] have has been taken away from us. So another underlying element of that was because we believe in it so hard that we're willing to die for this, it would scare away people who would try to take it over."

So— extravagant new suits. Gangs beefing over territory and respect. A violent masculine image serving as a defense to keep control of the art form. It sounds like hip-hop, no? The Mardi Gras Indians have been holding it down for at least 120 years. That's called resistance.

❧

Indian history is still being written, most spectacularly in recent years with the death of Big Chief Tootie Montana. A grand-nephew of Becate Batiste, Montana is generally credited as the major figure in inspiring the change, a few decades ago, from physical to aesthetic combat. He worked for decades as a lathe operator, and his spectacular three-dimensionally constructed suits, which became the *ne plus ultra* of downtown Indian suit construction, were informed by his knowledge of the building trade.

On the night of June 27, 2005, the eighty-two-year-old Montana—Chief of Chiefs, some called him—showed up at a special city council meeting called to discuss mistreatment of Indians by New Orleans police at Uptown Super Sunday on March 19. With the other chiefs standing behind him—an unprecedented show of solidarity between uptown and downtown—he made an emotional, unscripted speech recounting years of harassment, ending with the words, "I want this to stop."

Then he fell over, stricken with a heart attack.[13] His son, Big Chief Darryl Montana, rushed to his side. There was no defibrillator available, and, as is typical in New Orleans, the ambulance was slow to arrive. A councilman led the room in prayer, and the assembled Indians began to sing their anthem, "My Indian Red"—with emphasis, I was told by someone who was there, on the words "we won't bow down."

Big Chief Tootie had, as a well-known Indian song had it, "died on the battlefield," fighting for the Indians, refusing to bow down. On Saturday, July 9, he had a jazz funeral, proceeding out of St. Augustine's, and was buried in St. Louis Cemetery #2. That day, New Orleanians were trying to decide whether to evacuate or take their chances with Hurricane Dennis, by then a Category Four hurricane that had killed fifty-six people in Haiti and sixteen in Cuba. In the end, Dennis weakened and made landfall in the Florida panhandle.

Less than two months later, Hurricane Katrina roared up the Gulf.

⁊◌⁊

On the first Mardi Gras after Hurricane Katrina, February 28, 2006, Big Chief Donald Harrison Jr. set out from St. Augustine's at seven in the morning.

St. Augustine's is on relatively high ground, right behind the French Quarter. The church suffered damage from wind and rain during the storm, but the block hadn't flooded when the levees failed. Despite the importance of the historic church to the Tremé community as it fought to reestablish itself, the archdiocese announced plans to merge St. Augustine's into another parish and transfer away its priest. (After a substantial public protest, during which activists locked themselves in the rectory, the archdiocese subsequently announced it would keep the church open.)

In the yard outside the church, I saw a young woman kneeling to pray at the Tomb of the Unknown Slave, an outdoor altar that honors the unknown num-

Big Chief Donald Harrison Jr., leader of Congo Nation, inside the historic black Catholic church St. Augustine's at sunrise, as he prepares to go out and receive a blessing on Mardi Gras morning, 2006.

ber of hastily buried dead African and Indian slaves. This well-executed piece of sacramental art is, says the plaque, "a constant reminder that we are walking on holy ground." Inside the church, between the stained glass windows depicting saints, there were smaller pictures on the wall of Mardi Gras Indians.

It had been the hardest year in memory. The year New Orleans was left to die. Most of the city's people hadn't come back. Some were finding better lives elsewhere, but many were simply stranded in exile, living next to strangers in a new *grand dérangement*, unable to get back to the communities that had been their lives. Black New Orleans had been insulted and humiliated by the days-long ordeal after the hurricane passed, when the Convention Center had turned into what more than one survivor called a modern-day slave ship, with no water, no toilets, and no rescuers. The entire world watched their community's degradation on television. Those who tried to escape across the only bridge out of town were turned back at gunpoint as they tried to enter Jefferson Parish.[14]

The entire community's finances had been devastated, all at one blow. The support networks built up slowly over the years—church groups, Social Aid and Pleasure Clubs, brass bands, Mardi Gras Indian tribes—were weakened at every point. Harrison lost his house, and spent months living with his family in a Baton Rouge motel. But that Mardi Gras morning, Big Chief Donald was wearing a spectacular new suit. It was a warm day, and the words "Congo Nation," spelled out in Swarovski rhinestones on his headdress, sparkled in the sun.

It wasn't possible to suit up all the members of Congo Nation, but there was a full complement of percussionists in civilian clothes. As they played, Big Chief Donald emerged from the front door of the church, carrying two crossed machetes. His wife, Mary, was there, slapping a tambourine. Herreast, his mother, was there.

So was sister Cherice, a public school teacher whose school, like the other public schools in New Orleans, had closed. People who wanted to come back had no public school for their children to go to. Some four thousand schoolteachers had been fired. New Orleans was largely built by black craftsmen, but migrant labor was being used for cleanup and rebuilding, because it could be exploited more. Undocumented laborers mostly don't come with families. You don't have to give them benefits or social services, just some money they can send home while they live in a camp or a squat. They'll work longer hours, doing more toxic jobs, for less money, than the law allows. You might even be able to get away with shafting them on payday. What recourse do they have? Better yet, they don't vote.

Cherice had lost her home and her job both, and FEMA was about to throw her out of the motel she was living in. Many others were in more or less the same bind. Everyone had been busted, with all their support networks destroyed at once.

Father Ledoux gave his blessing, and Harrison sang a prologue a cappella, ending with a line that kicked off the percussion. With the rhythm banging, the crowd picked up the refrain they all knew: *Shallow water, oh mama*, over and over, while Harrison sang lead against it. Then he began to sing the anthem "My Indian Red."

His flag was the hide of a mountain lion—*puma concolor coryi*, the only big cat native to Louisiana, also known as a "Florida panther." Mounted on a

Big Chief Donald's flag in 2006.

board cut to its shape, it took four men to carry it, flat, waist-high, so that as it approached you, you saw its snarling jaws and sharp teeth coming at you. Where he got it from, I have no idea. The dead are always present in African ritual, making sure the living do things right, and as the procession paraded down the street, a tribe member held aloft a large photograph of Donald Harrison Sr.—honoring the ancestor, who began masking Indian in 1949.

Rounding the corner, Harrison was challenged by Sunpie, a.k.a. Bruce Barnes, who is not an Indian, but a Skeleton. The Skeletons, also known as the Skull and Bones Gang, wear skeleton suits. They "come out of the coffin" early in the morning on Mardi Gras day, and run through the cemetery and the neighborhood, waking people up. They frighten the children so they'll be good. A reminder of the constant presence of death in life, they carry bloody joints of meat from the slaughterhouse. This is the same figure as the lwa Guédé, the skeletal lord of the dead who appears and multiplies among believers at Haitian vodou ceremonies. You can see Guédé in Port-au-Prince, in Brooklyn, in eastern Cuba—and at Mardi Gras in New Orleans, where he speaks English and romps through the Tremé.

Sunpie—in real life, a park ranger and an accordionist who leads a good zydeco band—taunted Harrison, chanting in a singsong melody that sounded much like a vendor's cry: "Skull and Bones Gang! This is the Northside Skull and Bones Gang! Dead man walkiiiin'! Dead man walkiiin'!" while Congo Nation sang "Let's go get 'em! . . . Let's go get 'em!"

The drums stopped. Harrison, as I know him, is a soft-spoken man, but Big Chief Donald is not. In the poetic duel that followed, he shouted:

> I'm the Big Chief of the Congo Nation!
> And on Mardi Gras day *I* cause a sensation!
> In the middle of a hurricane *I* made the sun come out!
> I said, jock-e-mo fee-na ma-hoo-na-rae!
> Do you know what I say? [transcription approximate]

The last line, challenging Sunpie on knowledge of Indian language, was said emphatically, in triplet rhythm. Sunpie jabbed back, reminding him of his mortality:

> I come where I come from and you live where I'm goin'!
> (*Crowd:* Oooh! *signifying that Sunpie's verbal punch landed*)
> That's a dead man walkiiin'!
> You gonna wake up in the mornin', find your own self dead!

Harrison in the street. On the left is a picture of the late Donald Harrison Sr. Next to it is the steeple of St. Augustine's, with storm damage still visible. To the right of Harrison is the sign of the Blandin Funeral Home, which now houses the Backstreet Cultural Museum. On the far right is the drum, which has both emblematic and musical importance.

Congo Nation's response was a volley of drums—the battery had been silent about a minute—that drowned Sunpie out as they launched back into their battle song: "Congooooo, Congo Nation . . ." The two groups, their sparring done, continued on their individual ways, Congo Nation singing "Shallow water, oh mama" and Sunpie chanting "Dead man walkiiin'!"[15]

Later in the afternoon, Victor Harris, Spirit of Fi-Yi-Yi, appeared on the block with a burst of energy in a storm of sparkling green suits and percussion as his crowd chanted "Fi-Yi-Yi! . . . Fi-Yi-Yi!" After his parading, he got on the mike—WWOZ was broadcasting live—and began an extended oration. Donald Harrison had emerged early that morning out of a Catholic church, with a priest at his back; now Victor Harris was in effect preaching a sermon, evoking the Protestant tradition. As he spoke from the Backstreet front porch, the drums continued pounding out in the street, a few yards away:

Fi-Yi-Yi! I'm a Big Chief! That's right!
No rain! No wind! No hail! No sto'm! [storm]
Could stop Fi-Yi-Yi from comin' back home!

Big Chief Fi-Yi-Yi (Victor Harris) moves through the crowd in front of St. Augustine's.

So I'm callin' all the people to come back home!
Where you belong! Down in New Orleans! Yeah!
I'm talking about—
Chicken and gumbo!
Red beans and rice!
Y'all know what I'm talkin' about!

New Orleanians had literally been given one-way tickets out of town, dispersed to every state in the union minus everything they owned. It was a blatantly partisan act of destruction of African American political power, part of the quest to create a permanent one-party Republican state. The way for Republicans to gain the Louisiana governorship and the Democratic-held Senate seat was for the black New Orleans voting bloc to go away and not come back. At both the federal and state level, they were happy to tie the city up in red tape, a process that was only just getting under way. The City of New Orleans was broke, and broken. The federal government had left the city hanging, forcing it to borrow the funds to repair basic infrastructure at a time when its treasury and credit rating had imploded. Vast areas of the city had no electricity. No stoplights were working. Fast-food joints were offering $9 an hour, but there was nowhere for workers to live.

Victor Harris and members of his gang were back in New Orleans by mid-October 2005, almost as soon as the city was pumped dry. At first they slept on the floor of the Backstreet, and on some nights pitched homemade tents in the yard of St. Augustine. As they tried to rebuild their lives and their community, they sewed their suits in the dark, empty city.

You don't go to those lengths for folklore. This was a sacramental act. These were men who had fought all their lives against the amnesia that is slavery's legacy. Now the survival of their community, and their history, and their identity, was on the line. Bo Dollis, Monk Boudreaux, Donald Harrison, Victor Harris, Larry Bannock, Alfred Doucette, Darryl Montana, all the other chiefs—they're Indians forever, and so are the younger men in their tribe. But if the communities they represent are dispersed, where will the next generations of Indians come from?

The Indians do not normally get a lot of attention from New Orleans media. But at that postcataclysmic Mardi Gras of 2006, they mattered. Cameras and microphones, including mine, swarmed around them as they affirmed with warrior spirit that the community was alive, though its ranks were thinned. There is no overall documentation of what happened across

New Orleans that day, but Indian actions were going on all over town. Any one observer could only be at one of them, or, with a little luck and lots of running around (bicycles are the preferred way to negotiate the city during Mardi Gras), two or three of them.

Uptown, Big Chief Bo Dollis led the Wild Magnolias out into the street with a brass band, something Indians don't normally do. The Ninth Ward Hunters brought bright, saturated color to a vista of deathly gray, parading across the St. Claude Avenue bridge, where flood victims had huddled when their homes were destroyed. They played tambourines and sang as they moved through the empty, twisted ghost town of the Lower Ninth Ward, where six months after the disaster the people were still gone and houses sat on top of upside-down cars.

They refused to cooperate in their own erasure. They were still men, and these were still their streets.

They wouldn't bow down.

They rocked the city with their Congo dances.

ACKNOWLEDGMENTS

No one who's serious about American music can turn down the opportunity to spend a year in New Orleans, so when I was offered a research fellowship at Tulane University, I jumped at the chance. Together with my wife, Constance Ash, a.k.a. Constance Sublette, we relocated our household from Lower Manhattan to spend from August 2004 to May 2005 in New Orleans, where I was a Tulane Rockefeller Humanities Fellow at the Stone Center for Latin American Studies.

I had lived in Louisiana until I was nine, in Natchitoches, so it was something of a homecoming for me. Constance, whom I consider my history teacher, came along for the ride, and what a ride. She read as much as I did, and we talked about it nonstop. We've been doing that since we met in 1975. New Orleans has a strongly pronounced annual rhythm, and as the calendar rolled around, we were pulled into its schedule of parades and festivals. We studied the history of the city in libraries and archives, and experienced the living culture in the street. We made dozens of new friends. It was an experience we wouldn't trade for anything.

Watermarking these pages is the indelible scum line of 2005, during what turned out to be the early stages of writing. Three months after we relocated back to New York at the end of my fellowship year, New Orleans was catastrophically flooded. We watched from a distance as the city was trashed, its people drowned, degraded, and dispersed, its vitality destroyed, and its viability severely compromised. Dozens of our new friends were displaced as New Orleanians became a modern-day diaspora. The little record collection I had put together from buying CDs at gigs and at the French Quarter store called Louisana Music Factory acquired a whole new significance. I could no longer listen to those records without shuddering, but I couldn't stop listening to them.

We lost the city that was the pride of American music. To lose any American city would have been unthinkable. But to lose New Orleans . . .

I was already well at work on this book by then—ha! I thought I was close to finishing it—as well as a parallel volume, a memoir of our year in New Orleans. For two months or so I stopped doing anything except for following the situation on the ground in Louisiana, then slowly took up my work again where I had left off. Many scholars in the area, including most of my Tulane colleagues, have not been as fortunate, and had their work badly interrupted.

Through all this, Constance was my collaborator. There are ideas in this book I got from her, sources she referred me to, and mutual experiences we shared perspectives on—the last chapter, for example, for which she was present at the scenes of action next to me. On occasion, she coined the perfect phrase to express something, which then found its way into my text. There are lots of ideas in it that we could truly say we had together. When you're married this long, you don't always know which half of your brain is your own anymore. I wrote this book, but it's very much our project, and the product of both our heads. I asked her if she wanted to say anything for this page, and her answer spoke for me as well: "Without living in New Orleans, there's so much I wouldn't know now about the past and about the present of our nation."

∽∞∾

This work would not have been possible without the pathbreaking research of Gwendolyn Midlo Hall.

Thanks go to Tom Reese (director) and Valerie McGinley Marshall of the Stone Center. A key factor in the success of our experience was the friendship of, as well as intellectual stimulation from, my erstwhile Tulane colleagues. In no particular order, I would like to shout out Christopher Dunn and family, Felipe Smith, Idelber Avelar, Marilyn Miller, Gayle Murchison, T. R. Johnson, Joel Dinerstein, Tatjana Pavlovic, Rosanne Adderley, Michael Cunningham, Vicki Mayer, Javier León, John Charles, and—there are many more, too many to name, but thank you all.

This book comes out of an ongoing conversation that involves many people. I found the New Orleans community to be rich with supporters of the city's culture. From administrators and lawyers to scholars of all sorts (both with and without academic credentials), radio DJs, journalists, and students, to say nothing of all the working artists and musicians, the city was teeming with people who knew why they were there, and though naming them all is impossible, I would like to acknowledge the friendship and hospitality of many people in New Orleans.

My appointment at the Stone Center was preceded by a trip I took to Santiago de Cuba in July 2003 with a team of New Orleanians, as a resource person for a group of several dozen listeners of New Orleans radio station WWOZ. The group was attending Carnival in Santiago—not as pleasure tourists, but on an educational, albeit enjoyable, mission to compare it with black Carnival traditions in New Orleans. It was an experience of enormous value, though this kind of travel to Cuba stopped being possible at the end of 2003, when the Bush administration put the hammer down. The trip was organized by the CubaNola Collective, whose visionary director, Ariana Hall, informed me about the availability of a fellowship at Tulane. On that trip, I spent time with David Freedman and the crew from WWOZ, a community radio station that has survived from a small wave of such stations in the 1960s to become a central fact in the music culture of New Orleans. It can be streamed at www.wwoz.org.

During my fellowship period, I had the pleasure of having an office on the fourth floor of the Howard-Tilton Memorial Library on Tulane's campus. Located on this floor is the Latin American Library, of which Tulane is rightfully proud. I would like to thank Hortensia Calvo and all the staff of the Latin American Library and Special Collections, Bruce Raeburn and Lynn Abbott at the Hogan Jazz Archive, the staff at the Louisiana Collection in Jones Hall, and the staff of Howard-Tilton. I had research and transcription assistance from Stephanie Clark.

At the Historic New Orleans Collection, thanks go to director Alfred Lemmon and to Pamela Arceneaux, Mary Lou Eichhorn, and Siva Blake. I would like to thank the librarians at the New Orleans Public Library, who were running with a skeleton crew under very hard circumstances in the months after Katrina but managed to make time to grant me access to the cabildo minutes. And thanks to Sylvester Francis and Donna Santiago of the Backstreet Cultural Museum and to the Department of Special Collections at the University of Notre Dame Libraries.

I had the honor of being a John Simon Guggenheim Fellow in 2005–06, and though the project I was working on is not yet finished, the fellowship sustained me through the catastrophe of New Orleans in 2005 and should be gratefully acknowledged as having contributed substantially to this volume. I also benefited in the writing of this book from research previously done at the New

York Public Library as a fellow at the Cullman Center for Scholars and Writers, and I would like to thank the staff of the library's Milstein Division as well.

In the course of researching and writing, I produced several installments of *Hip Deep*, heard on public radio as part of *Afropop Worldwide*. During that process I interviewed Donald Harrison, Gwendolyn Midlo Hall, Joseph Roach, and Helen Regis, among others, all of whose thoughts contributed to my understanding. (Transcripts of the interviews are posted at www.afropop .org.) I would like to thank my longtime Afropop colleagues Sean Barlow, Banning Eyre, Georges Collinet, Mike Jones, and Misha Turner.

The first week of August 2005, three weeks before you-know-what, I had the honor of returning to New Orleans to participate in the colloquium of jazz historians that is Satchmo Summerfest, and I would like to thank the organizers. Ideas expressed in this book were roughed out in the course of presentations made at Experience Music Project, the Center for Black Music Research conference (Chicago, 2006), the Bildner Center at City University of New York, Columbia University, George Mason University, the Ashé Cultural Center in New Orleans, and at Tulane.

In 2007, after the book was fully drafted but before editing was closed, I had the opportunity to present material from it at George Mason University, the Mission Cultural Center in San Francisco, the Experience Music Project Pop Conference, and a superb conference at Tulane sponsored by the Stone Center, and I attended the Fourth Seminar of Caribbean Ethnomusicology in St. Ann, Guadeloupe. I learned much about how to express my ideas in the process of presenting them to, and talking with, groups ranging from college freshmen to music writers to community activists to scholars of intimidating intellect. Thanks to Jim Lepore, Suzanne Carbonneau, Michael Nolan, Isabel Barraza, Eric Weisbard, Ann Powers, the Stone Center, George Lewis, Dominique Cyrille, and Felix Cotelet.

A very special thanks goes to Ben Socolov and the Westside Sound Foundation for the Arts and to Will Socolov. Thanks also to Garnette Cadogan, C. Daniel Dawson, Michael Zwack, Gage Averill, Michael Crutcher, David Rubinson, Elijah Wald, Laurent Dubois, John Garrigus, Peter Gordon, Ron Robboy, Ivor Miller, Mark Bingham, Lisa Katzman, and Kennedy Samuel. I must acknowledge the suggestions and esteemed friendship of Robert Farris Thompson.

It is gratifying to do a second book with Chicago Review Press. My editor, Yuval Taylor, put a great deal of effort into helping me shape this book, for which I am appreciative. Thanks go to Michelle Schoob, Allison Felus, Mary Kravenas, and Michelle Niebur. My agent, Sarah Lazin, made important suggestions. Portions of this material appeared in an earlier form in *American Legacy*, thanks to editor Audrey Peterson.

In closing, I would like to invoke the spirit of the late Robert Palmer, my friend and inadvertent mentor, who took me around his favorite town for some days in 1992, when I paid a visit to New Orleans to make an episode of *Afropop Worldwide*. Bob loved living in the Tremé, and he pointed me in all the right directions. I didn't know that fifteen years later I would do something with it, but I think he knew.

NOTES

Chapter 1: Rock the City

1. Knight, H. C., 127.
2. Stoddard, 151.
3. Pontchartrain, Dec. 21, 2002.

Chapter 2: The Gift of the River

1. Latrobe, 223.
2. Seed et al., 3–20.
3. Dokka et al.
4. Say *Mississippi*, *delta*, and *music*, and people may think you mean the "Mississippi Delta" of blues fame. That's not this delta. The Mississippi Delta of the blues is inland: it's the alluvial floodplain in northern Mississippi between the Mississippi and Yazoo Rivers, made habitable only after levees were constructed in the mid-1880s, which is one reason there are so many blues songs about floods.
5. Stoddard, 159.
6. Braudel 1972, 1:62.
7. Herodotus, 104.
8. Stoddard, 175.
9. Nuttall, 237.
10. Seed et al., 3–21.
11. Campanella, 49.

Chapter 3: Piety

1. Pond, 12–13.
2. Thomas, 92.
3. Braudel 1992, 2:198–99, 3:490–91.
4. MacCulloch, 164.
5. For an extended discussion of this idea, see my book *Cuba and Its Music*.
6. Thomas, 110.

7. MacCulloch, 241.
8. MacCulloch, 308.
9. Payne, 37.
10. Peguero and de los Santos, 77.

Chapter 4: Louis, Louis

1. Quoted in Allain 1995a, 90.
2. Though not the first slaves. A census shows that there were already thirty-two Africans in the Virginia colony in 1619, probably brought individually. Thornton, 421.
3. Thornton 1998, 421.
4. Robert Farris Thompson, private communication.
5. Wagman, 34, 40.
6. Curtin 1998, 90–91.
7. Linebaugh and Rediker, 127.
8. Scoville 1952, 296.
9. Scoville 1952, 296, 301, 305, 308.
10. Scoville 1952b, 393.

Chapter 5: Mardi Gras

1. McWilliams, 2.
2. Bannon, 5.
3. Le Moyne, 68–69.
4. Le Page du Pratz, 4.
5. Le Page du Pratz, 28–29. I am quoting from an English translation, published in 1774.
6. Le Page du Pratz, 17.
7. Le Moyne, 154.
8. Brasseaux 1995b, 526.
9. Brasseaux 1995b, 526.
10. Brasseaux 1995b, 526–27.

11. Hall 1992, 12.

12. Braudel 1992, 1:74.

13. Hall 1992, 12.

14. Hall 1992, 57–58. The words are Hall's.

15. Champlain described the site of Québec as *un détroit dans le fleuve.*

16. Allain 1995b, 110.

17. Baker, 480.

18. Potré-Bobinski and Smith, 8.

Chapter 6: The Duke of Arkansas

1. Quoted in Shennan, 118.

2. Pevitt, 13.

3. Quoted in Pevitt, 29–30.

4. Pevitt, 33n.

5. Pevitt, 74.

6. Saint-Simon, 63.

7. Gray, 29.

8. Pevitt, 187.

9. Pevitt, 175.

10. Braudel 1992, 1:206.

11. Saint-Simon, 63

12. Saint-Simon, 62.

13. Saint-Simon, 63.

14. Saint-Simon, 299.

15. Quoted in Shennan, 124.

16. Allain 1995b, 106.

17. Thomas, 242.

18. Hardy, James D., 116, Brasseaux 1995a, 156.

19. Dufour, 20.

20. Dufour, 20.

21. Le Page du Pratz, 12.

22. Le Page du Pratz, 13.

23. Le Page du Pratz, 13. His return to France from Louisiana, in 1734, took only forty-five days, going via the Bahamas and Newfoundland.

24. Quoted in Dufour, 24.

25. Brasseaux 1995b, 526–27.

26. Hardy, James D., 119–20.

27. Brasseaux 1995a, 158–59.

28. Conrad, 132.

29. Dawdy 2006a, 71.

30. Usner, 183.

31. Giraud, 142.

32. Horne, 175.

33. Schumpeter, 295.

34. Saint-Simon, 299.

Chapter 7: The Senegambian Period

1. Brasseaux 1995b, 533.

2. Hall 1992, 60.

3. Figures from Hall 1992, 60.

4. Hall 1992, 64.

5. Bénard de la Harpe, 167.

6. Usner, 185.

7. Thornton 1998b, 186–87.

8. Hall 1992, 132.

9. Hall 1992, 384–85.

10. This has a series of implications for the early development of black music in Louisiana, a topic I have written about in *Cuba and Its Music.*

11. Curtin 1998, 119.

12. Author's interview with Gwendolyn Midlo Hall.

13. Hall 1992, 124.

14. Hall 1992, 59.

15. Hall 2005, 90.

16. See *Cuba and Its Music*, Ch. 12.

17. Le Page du Pratz, 358.

18. Fandrich, 41.

19. Simmons, 55.

20. Levtzion, 208.

21. Usner, 192.

22. Le Page du Pratz, 18.

23. Le Page du Pratz, 44.

24. Le Page du Pratz, 19.

Chapter 8: An Ear for Musick

1. Bruce, 1:64.

2. Jefferson 1829, 39.

3. Isaac, 164.

4. "Memoir of President Davies," 313.

5. Bruce, 1:136.

6. Thompson 1983, 104–5.

7. Epstein 1977, 209.

8. Bénard de la Harpe, 190, 198.

9. Baron, 283; Lemmon 2002, 3.

10. Baron, 284.

11. Gayarré, 1:390.

12. Lemmon 2002, 3.

13. Baron, 283–84.

14. Goulet, 13.
15. Quoted in Goulet, 15.
16. Le Page du Pratz, 366.
17. Epstein 1977, 30.
18. Epstein 1975, 351ff; Sublette, Ch. 12.
19. Quoted in Isaac, 85.
20. Quoted in "Eighteenth century slaves," 176.
21. Hall 1992, 107.
22. Le Page du Pratz, 71–73.
23. Dawdy 2006a, 69.
24. Dawdy 2006a, 71.
25. Clark, 41.
26. Dawdy 2006b, 144.
27. Le Page du Pratz, 361–62.
28. Brasseaux 1995b, 533.
29. Thornton 1991, 1113.
30. Dawdy 2006b, 71.
31. Fortier, 131.
32. Dart, 578–79.

Chapter 9: The Cabildo

1. Quoted in Houck, 290–91.
2. See Anderson, 25–52, for a detailed account.
3. Gipson, 88.
4. Brasseaux 1995b, 532–33.
5. Brasseaux 1995b, 532.
6. Dawdy 2006a, 75.
7. See Anderson, 221–22.
8. Quoted in Dart, 581.
9. Lafargue, 109.
10. Garrigus, 33.
11. Dessens, 10.
12. Whitaker 1935, 158.
13. Whitaker 1935, 191.
14. Whitaker 1935, 177–82.
15. Holmes 1974, 522.
16. Ingersoll 1999b, 157.
17. Brasseaux 1995c, 437; Moore 1996, 70.
18. See Anderson, 83–87 for a summary of events.
19. Moore 1996, 63–70.
20. Quoted in Moore 1996, 67.
21. Hanger 1999a, 235.
22. Baron, 285.
23. Baron, 285.

24. Baade, 380.
25. Ingersoll 1999b, 161.
26. Din 1996a, 78.
27. Holmes 1974, 522.
28. Watson, 309.
29. Watson, 310.
30. Din 1996a, 78.
31. Kinnaird, 258–59; see also Andrew. The Mexican peso was even the model for the Japanese yen, in 1871.
32. Din 1996a, 77.
33. Whitaker 1962, 29.
34. Whitaker 1935, 185.
35. Hanger 1999a, 397.
36. Clark, 270.
37. Din and Harkins, 134.
38. Hanger 1998, 543.
39. Clark, 164.
40. Burson, 102.
41. Cale, 51. The quote is of Cale's wording, not the Affiches Américaines.
42. Houck, 244.
43. Houck, 245.
44. Lemmon 1996, 436.
45. Lemmon 1996, 437.
46. Burson, 242.

Chapter 10: The Kongo Period

1. Raynal, 178.
2. Curtin 1969, 84.
3. Hall 2005, 53.
4. Author's interview, 2005.
5. Blackburn, 117.
6. Franco, 96.
7. Author's interview, 2005.
8. Hall 2005, 176.
9. Hanger 1997, 76.
10. The best account of the San Maló gang is in Hall 1992, 213ff.
11. Burson, 113–17.
12. Burson, 199.
13. Burson, 199.
14. Hall 1992, 319–23, 331.
15. Scott, 274.
16. Hanger 1997, 12; Robinson, 404.
17. Dessens, 93.
18. Scott, 273.

19. Robert Farris Thompson, personal communication.

Chapter 11: The Eighteenth-Century Tango

1. Hall 2005, 99.
2. Cuming, 311.
3. For an extended discussion, see Gould.
4. Din and Harkins, 12.
5. Johnson, Jerah, 32.
6. I have not been able to find the original of this document. I am quoting from a translation in the Cabildo Museum of New Orleans.
7. Hanger 1997, 63.
8. Schöpf, 221–22.
9. Author's interview, 2005.
10. Díaz Fabelo, 96.
11. Thompson 2005a, 115.
12. Starr 2000, 39.
13. Scherman, 44.
14. Whitaker 1962, 136–37.
15. Baron, 287.
16. Chase, 105–11.
17. Vlach.

Chapter 12: Desire

1. Curtin 1998, 17.
2. Schöpf, 219.
3. Curtin 1998, 12.
4. Braudel 1992, 2:232.
5. Quoted in Dubois 2004a, 92.
6. Knight, Franklin, 108.
7. Moreau de St.-Méry 1958, 34.
8. Braudel 1992, 2:278–79.
9. Quoted in Ellis 1997, 163.
10. A particular account . . . , 28.
11. Moreau de St.-Méry 1958, 33–34.
12. Schöpf, 94.
13. Moreau de St.-Méry 1958, 35–36.
14. Cited in de Vaissière, 192.
15. Le Page du Pratz, 364.
16. Gray, 38.
17. Fick, 37.
18. Guédé, 26.
19. See Cuba and Its Music, Ch. 10, for an account of the development of the contradanza in Cuba.

20. Corvington, 115–17.
21. Dalmas, 10.
22. d'Auberteuil, 1:137n.
23. Eyma, 179–80.
24. Sublette, 109.
25. Porter, 252.
26. Porter, 252.
27. Geggus, 6.
28. Rosengarten, 168.
29. Mims, 245.

Chapter 13: The Sincerest Attachment

1. Curtin 1998, 158.
2. A tantalizing if utterly inconclusive counterpart to the mysterious Mardi Gras Indian word "Jockomo."
3. For a good account of this complex process, see Dubois 2004a.
4. Garrigus, 33.
5. Garrigus, 34.
6. King, xiii.
7. King, xii–xiii.
8. d'Auberteuil, 2:45.
9. Moreau de St.-Méry 1958, 104–5.
10. Hanger 1998, 555–56.
11. King, 84.
12. Dubois 2004a, 100.
13. Dalmas, 117–18.
14. Dubois 2004a, 32.
15. Fick, 97.
16. A particular account . . . , 3.
17. Drouin de Bercy, 10.
18. A particular account . . . , 5.
19. A particular account . . . , 10–11.
20. Fick, 110.
21. Dessens, 19.
22. Berquin-Duvallon 1803, 235.
23. Álvarez Estévez, 29.
24. Hobsbawm, 76.
25. Digital decimal clocks, displaying French revolutionary time, are available on the Internet.
26. Dubois 2004b, 163.

Chapter 14: Dance, Boatman, Dance

1. Pope, 41.
2. Campbell, 424.

3. Quoted in Reilly, 183.

4. Campbell, 424.

5. McCall, 21–22.

6. Schultz, 137.

7. Pope, 38.

8. Liljegren, 51.

9. Gayarré, 3:337–40.

10. Le Gardeur, 49.

11. Quoted as translated in Le Gardeur, 19. (Dollar sign in translated version of text.)

12. Freiberg, 301; Din and Harkins, 143.

13. Campanella, 106.

14. Liljegren, 62–63.

15. Holmes 1974, 204.

16. A letter from Whitney dated September 11, 1793, states: "The Secretary of State Mr. Jefferson agreed to send the Pattent to me as soon as it could be made out—so that I apprehended no difficulty in obtaining the Patent."

17. Gayarré, 3:349.

18. Campbell, 422.

19. Campbell, 422.

20. Hall 1992, 344.

21. Fiehrer 1999, 90.

22. Stoddard, 332–33.

23. Padgett, 601–2. (Translation in original.)

24. Whitaker 1962, 52.

25. Whitaker 1962, 42–44.

26. Clark, 44.

27. McDermott, 140–41.

28. Whitaker 1962, 152.

29. Le Gardeur, 27; Kmen 1966, 58.

30. Holmes 1974, 540.

31. Holmes 1965, 210.

32. Cuming, 333.

33. Baudry des Lozières, v.

Chapter 15: Not Only as a Dance

1. Raynal, 181–82.

2. Branson and Patrick, 197.

3. Dubois 2002, 299.

4. Moreau de St.-Méry 1796, 20–22.

5. Moreau de St.-Méry 1796, 43–47.

6. I am indebted to Robert Farris Thompson for pointing this out to me.

7. Moreau de St.-Méry 1796, 47–48.

8. The mention of vodou in the *Description* has sometimes wrongly been cited as the first mention of vodou in print, but Moreau had already published *Danse* when it came out.

9. Moreau de St.-Méry 1958, 64–68.

10. Fick, 265.

11. Fick, 57–58, 266.

12. Díaz Fabelo, 112.

13. Quoted in Fandrich, 133.

14. Métraux, 38.

15. Gunpowder is used in Cuba in divination ceremonies of *palo*, the Cuban version of the Kongo religion. Its use with tafia has echoes in blues lyrics, like Muddy Waters in "I'm Ready": "I'm drinkin' TNT and smokin' dynamite." He was ready, Kongo style.

16. Moreau de St.-Méry 1796, 48–50.

17. Moreau de St.-Méry 1796, 51–53.

18. Moreau de St.-Méry 1958, 68–69.

19. Epstein 1977, 84.

20. Gray, 348.

Chapter 16: Bonaparte's Retreat

1. Brady, 10.

2. Bellesiles, 79.

3. See Wills for an extended discussion of the election of 1800.

4. Egerton, 324.

5. Dubois undated, 17.

6. Dubois undated, 3.

7. Dubois 2004a, 404.

8. LaChance 1999, 135.

9. Hassall, 1.

10. Hassall, 18–19.

11. Hassall, 25.

12. Hassall, 29–33.

13. Laussat's number was about right; the 1800 census showed 386,000 people west of the Appalachians.

14. Weeks, 23.

15. Fiehrer 1999, 94.

16. Everett, 378.

17. McCall, 40–41.

18. Thiers, 6:74–76.

Chapter 17: An Addition to Capital

1. Dawdy 2006b, 142n, 153.
2. Jefferson, 1904, 150.
3. Stein, 425.
4. Stein, 40.
5. Stein, 40.
6. Bear, 4.
7. Lewis and Onuf, 256.
8. Stanton, 17.
9. Brown.
10. Rothman, 87.
11. Foster et al., 27.
12. Stanton, 17.
13. Letter to John Eppes, June 30, 1820. (Lowercase in original.)

Chapter 18: The Slave-Breeding Industry

1. Douglass, 411.
2. Davis, David Brion, 36.
3. Schöpf, 221.
4. Schöpf, 223.
5. Weeks, 33–34.
6. Quoted in Bancroft, 347.
7. Thomas, 570.
8. Quoted in Morgan, 50.
9. Quoted in Ellis 1993, 138.
10. See Follett.
11. Hall 2005, 160.
12. Fiehrer 1999, 88
13. Johnson, Walter, 83.
14. Sidbury, 207–8.
15. Deyle, 28.
16. Bernhard, 348.
17. Deyle, 215.
18. Quoted in Bancroft, 69.
19. Deyle, 60.
20. Sullivan, 199.
21. Bancroft, 69.
22. Johnson, Walter, 215.
23. Cited in Marx and Engels 1937, 67.
24. Harper.
25. Sutcliff, 52.
26. Johnson, Walter, 5–6.
27. Bancroft, 286.
28. Bruner, 11–12.
29. Northup, 181–82.

30. Lott, 212–12, 237–38.
31. Schöpf, 148.
32. Hamilton, 2:216.
33. Sullivan, 223.
34. I borrow the notion of "musical blackness" from Gaunt, 37ff.

Chapter 19: The French Quarter

1. Nuttall, 239.
2. Berquin-Duvallon 1803, 34–36.
3. Laussat, 146.
4. Laussat, 147–48.
5. Laussat, 150.
6. Le Gardeur, 39.
7. Quoted in Kmen, 3.
8. Paquette, 213–14.
9. Quoted in Paquette, 218.
10. LaChance 1996, 259.
11. Debien, 85–86.
12. Berquin-Duvallon 1803, 185–86.
13. Berquin-Duvallon 1803, 284.
14. Le Gardeur, 39.
15. Berquin-Duvallon 1803, 186.
16. Kmen, 44–45.
17. Kmen, 47.
18. Hanger 1998, 550n.
19. Kmen, 6–7.
20. Le Gardeur, 40.
21. Kmen, 203.
22. Kmen, 208.
23. Ingersoll 1999b, 172.
24. Sutcliff, 122–23.
25. Hanger 1997, 22.
26. Hanger 1997, 60–61.
27. Ingersoll 1999b, 170.
28. See Rousey.
29. Walton, 203.
30. Quoted in Marx and Engels 1939, 34.
31. Álvarez Estévez, 40.
32. LaChance 1996, 261.
33. LaChance 1996, 259.
34. LaChance 1996, 265.
35. Dessens, 128.
36. Dessens, 119.
37. Dessens, 74–76.
38. Gottschalk, 104–5.

39. See Starr 2001.

40. Pontchartrain, March 16, 2004.

41. Ashe, 341.

42. Creecy, 18–19.

43. Bancroft, 173. He was writing of the 1850s, but the comment is apposite to this period as well.

44. Gilmore, 390.

45. Nuttall, 243.

46. See De Grummond 1961a.

47. Ashe, 345–46.

48. Hall, unpublished.

49. Dormon, 289.

50. McCall, 153.

51. Jordan, Terry.

52. Campbell, 417.

Chapter 20: Bargainland

1. *Don Quixote*, Ch. 34.

2. Quoted in Davis, William C., 53.

3. Davis, William C., 2–5. I have drawn on Davis's work in various places in this chapter.

4. Raab, 18.

5. Adams, Margaret, 6–7; Asbury, 436; Smith, Tom, 59.

6. Davis, William C., 89.

7. Davis, William C., 209.

8. Wright, 567.

Chapter 21: A Most Extraordinary Noise

1. Tallant, 64.

2. Carter et al, 107n.

3. Carter et al, 185–85.

4. Stoddard, 324.

5. Latrobe, 184.

6. Latrobe, 204.

7. Schultz, 195.

8. Latrobe, 183.

9. www.reggae-vibes.com/concert/williams/williams.htm. Accessed July 2007.

10. For the relationship between social dance and military drill in the late eighteenth century, see Andrews. Thanks to Constance for pointing this source out to me.

11. Latrobe, 204.

12. Thanks to Gage Averill for pulling this clip out of his laptop while serving as a discussant to a talk I gave at Tulane.

13. See Thompson 2005b, 136–40.

14. Peguero and de los Santos, 269.

15. Starr 2000, 188–89.

16. Schultz, 197.

17. Creecy, 20–23.

18. Nuttall, 245.

19. Fandrich, 153.

20. Hearn, 77.

21. John, 4–5, 141.

22. Fandrich, 42.

23. Fandrich, 133.

24. Touchstone, 381.

25. Quoted in Ward, 32.

26. Kmen, 229.

27. Kmen, 229.

Chapter 22: We Won't Bow Down

1. Roach, 192.

2. See Roach, 203.

3. Author's interview, 2006.

4. In the film *Tootie's Last Suit*.

5. Draper.

6. There is a segment on this in *Tootie's Last Suit*.

7. Jacobs, 51.

8. Jacobs, 51; Wilentz, 426.

9. Smith, Michael P., 58, 59.

10. Berry, 20.

11. Jelly Roll Morton, Library of Congress interview with Alan Lomax, disc 1681A, June 8, 1938.

12. Jelly Roll Morton, Library of Congress interview with Alan Lomax, disc 1681A, June 8, 1938.

13. See Reckdahl for an account of the meeting.

14. Yes, named for Thomas Jefferson.

15. This is an abridged account of the exchange.

BIBLIOGRAPHY

Adair, Douglass. (1974). *Fame and the founding fathers.* W. W. Norton, New York.

Adams, John. (1851). *The words of John Adams, second president of the United States,* ed. Ch. F. Adams, v. 3, Boston.

Adams, Margaret. (1924). *Outline of Mafia riots in New Orleans.* Tulane University thesis.

Allain, Mathé. (1995a). "In search of a policy," in Conrad, Glenn R., ed., *The French experience in Louisiana.* Louisiana Purchase Bicentennial Series in Louisiana History, v. 1. Center for Louisiana Studies, Lafayette.

———. (1995b). "French emigration policies," in Conrad, Glenn R., ed., *The French experience in Louisiana.* Louisiana Purchase Bicentennial Series in Louisiana History, v. 1. Center for Louisiana Studies, Lafayette.

Álvarez-Estévez, Rolando. (2001). *Huellas francesas en el occidente de Cuba (siglos XVI-XIX).* Ediciones Boloña, Havana.

Anderson, Fred. (2005). *The war that made America: A short history of the French and Indian War.* Viking, New York.

Andrew, A. Piatt. (1904). "The End of the Mexican Dollar." *The Quarterly Journal of Economics,* 18:3, May.

Andrews, Melissa D. (2006). *Step in time: The ritual function of social dance and military drill in George Washington's Continental Army.* Master's thesis, Florida State University.

Asbury, Herbert. (1936). *The French Quarter: An informal history of the New Orleans underworld.* Knopf, New York.

Ashe, Thomas. (1811). *Travels in America, performed in 1806, for the purpose of exploring the rivers Alleghany, Monongahela, Ohio, and Mississippi, and ascertaining the produce and condition of their banks and vicinity.* New York.

Baker, Vaughan B. (1995). "Cherchez les femmes," in Conrad, Glenn R., ed., *The French experience in Louisiana.* Louisiana Purchase Bicentennial Series in Louisiana History, v. 1. Center for Louisiana Studies, Lafayette.

Bancroft, Frederic. (1959). *Slave trading in the old South.* Ungar, New York.

Bannon, John Francis. (1974). "The Spaniards in the Mississippi Valley—An introduction," in McDermott, John Francis, ed. (1974). *The Spanish in the Mississippi Valley 1762–1804.* University of Illinois Press, Urbana.

Baron, John H. (1987). "Music in New Orleans, 1718–1792." *American Music*, 5:3 Autumn.

Barras, John A. (2006). "Land area change in coastal Louisiana after the 2005 hurricanes: A series of three maps." U.S. Geological Survey Open-File Report 06-1274.

Baudry des Lozières, Louis-Narcisse. (1802). *Voyage a la Louisiane, et sur le continent d'Amerique septentrional, fait dans les années 1794 à 1798*. Dentu, Paris.

Bear, James A. Jr., ed. (1967). *Jefferson at Monticello*. University of Virginia Press, Charlottesville.

Bellesiles, Michael A. (2002). "'The soil will be soaked with blood': Taking the revolution of 1800 seriously," in Horn, James, Jan Ellen Lewis, and Peter S. Onuf, eds., *The revolution of 1800: Democracy, race and the new republic*. University of Virginia Press, Charlottesville.

Bénard de la Harpe, Jean-Baptiste. (1971). *The historical journal of the establishment of the French in Louisiana*. Trans. Joan Cain and Virginia Koening, ed., and annotated by Glenn R. Conrad.

Berquin-Duvallon, Pierre-Louis. (1806). *In Louisiana and the Floridas, in the year 1802, giving a correct picture of those countries*. Trans. John Davis. I. Riley, New York.

——. (1803). *Vue de la colonie espagnole du Mississippi*. Imprimerie Expeditive, Paris.

Berry, Jason. (1995). *The spirit of Black Hawk: A mystery of Africans and Indians*. University Press of Mississippi, Jackson.

Berry, Jason, Jonathan Foose, and Tad Jones. (2003). "In search of the Mardi Gras Indians," in Brennan, Jonathan, *When Brer Rabbit meets Coyote: African-Native American literature*. University of Illinois Press, Urbana.

Blackburn, Robin. (1997). *The making of New World slavery: From the baroque to the modern 1492–1800*. Verso, London.

Bodin, Rob. (1990). *Voodoo: Past and present*. Center for Louisiana Studies, Lafayette.

Brady, Patrick S. (1972). "The slave trade and sectionalism in South Carolina, 1787–1808." *Journal of Southern History*, 38:4, November.

Branson, Susan, and Leslie Patrick. (2001). "*Étrangers dans un pays étrange*: Saint-Domingan refugees of color in Philadelphia," in Geggus, David P., ed., *The impact of the Haitian Revolution in the Atlantic world*. University of South Carolina Press, Columbia.

Brasseaux, Carl A. (1995a). "The image of Louisiana," in Conrad, Glenn R., ed., *The French experience in Louisiana*. Louisiana Purchase Bicentennial Series in Louisiana History, v. 1. Center for Louisiana Studies, Lafayette.

——. (1995b). "The moral climate of French colonial Louisiana, 1699–1763," in Conrad, Glenn R., ed., *The French experience in Louisiana*. Louisiana Purchase Bicentennial Series in Louisiana History, v. 1. Center for Louisiana Studies, Lafayette.

——. (1995c). "Confusion, conflict, and currency," in Conrad, Glenn R., ed., *The French experience in Louisiana*. Louisiana Purchase Bicentennial Series in Louisiana History, v. 1. Center for Louisiana Studies, Lafayette.

——. (1996). "Acadian immigration, 1765–1769," in Brasseaux, Carl A., ed., *A refuge for all ages: Immigration in Louisiana history*. Louisiana Purchase Bicentennial Series in Louisiana History, v. 10. Center for Louisiana Studies, Lafayette.

Braudel, Fernand. (1972). *The Mediterranean and the Mediterranean world in the age of Philip II*. 2 v. Trans. by Siân Reynolds. Harper and Row, New York.

——. (1992). *Civilization and capitalism, 15th–18th century*. 3 v. Trans. by Siân Reynolds. University of California Press, Berkeley.

Broven, John. (1983). *Rhythm and blues in New Orleans*. Pelican, Gretna, LA.

Brown, William Wells. [n.d.] *Clotel: Electronic scholarly edition*. http://www.adam -matthew-publications.co.uk/online/Clothel/index.aspx. Accessed March 2007.

Bruce, Philip Alexander. (1896). *Economic history of Virginia in the seventeenth century*. 2 v. Macmillan, New York.

Bruner, Peter. (1919). *A slave's adventures toward freedom: Not fiction, but the true story of a struggle*. Oxford, OH.

Burson, Caroline Maude. (1940). *The stewardship of Don Esteban Miró*. American Printing Company, New Orleans.

Cale, John Gustav. (1971). *French secular music in Saint-Domingue (1750–1795) viewed as a factor in America's musical growth*. Ph.D. thesis, Louisiana State University.

Campanella, Richard. (2006). *Geographies of New Orleans: Urban fabrics before the storm*. Center for Louisiana Studies, Lafayette.

Campbell, Edna F. (1921). "New Orleans at the time of the Louisiana Purchase." *Geographical Review*, 11:3, July.

Chase, John. (1960). *Frenchmen, Desire, Good Children . . . and other streets in New Orleans*. Pelican, Gretna, LA.

Clark, John G. (1969). "New Orleans: Its first century of economic development." *Louisiana History* 10:1.

Conrad, Glenn R. (1995). "*Emigration forcée*: A French attempt to populate Louisiana 1716–1720," in Conrad, Glenn R., ed., *The French experience in Louisiana*. Louisiana Purchase Bicentennial Series in Louisiana History, v. 1. Center for Louisiana Studies, Lafayette.

Corvington, George Jr. (1970). *Port-au-Prince au cours des ans: La ville coloniale, 1743–1789*. Imprimerie Henri Deschamps, Port-au-Prince.

Creecy, Col. James R. (1860). *Scenes in the South, and other miscellaneous pieces*. Thomas McGill, Washington, DC.

Cripe, Helen. (1974). *Thomas Jefferson and music*. University Press of Virginia, Charlottesville.

Cuming, F. (1810). *Sketches of a tour to the western country through the states of Ohio and Kentucky, a voyage down the Ohio and Mississippi Rivers, and a trip through the Mississippi Territory, and part of West Florida*. Thos. W. Palmer, Philadelphia.

Curtin, Philip D. (1969). *The Atlantic slave trade: A census.* University of Wisconsin Press, Madison.

——. (1998). *The rise and fall of the plantation complex: Essays in Atlantic history.* 2d ed. Cambridge University Press, New York.

Cusset, Catherine. (1998). "Editor's preface: The lesson of libertinage." *Yale French Studies,* 94.

Dalmas, Antoine. (1814). *Histoire de la révolution de Saint-Domingue, depuis le commencemnt des troubles, jusqu'a la prise de Jérémie et du Mose S. Nicolas par les Angalis; suivie d'un mémoire sure le rétablissment de cette colonie. Tome premier.* Chez Mame Frères, Paris.

Dart, Henry P. (1936). "Cabarets of New Orleans in the French colonial period." *Louisiana Historical Quarterly,* 19:3, July.

d'Auberteuil, Hillard. (1776–77). *Considérations sur l'état present de la colonie française de Saint-Domingue, ouvrage politique et législatif.* 2 v. Chez Grangé, Paris.

Davis, David Brion. (2006). *Inhuman bondage: The rise and fall of slavery in the New World.* Oxford University Press, New York.

Davis, William C. (2005). *The pirates Laffite: The treacherous world of the corsairs of the Gulf.* Harcourt, Orlando.

Dawdy, Shannon Lee. (2006a). "The burden of Louis Congo and the evolution of savagery in colonial Louisiana," in Pierce, Steven, and Anupama Rao, eds., *Discipline and the other body: Correction, corporeality, colonialism.* Duke University Press, Durham.

——. (2006b). "Proper caresses and prudent distance: A how-to manual from colonial Louisiana," in Stoler, Ann Laura, ed., *Haunted by empire: Geographies of intimacy in North American history.* Duke University Press, Durham.

De Grummond, Jane Lucas. (1961a). "Lucinda Sparkle." *Louisiana History* 2:3, Summer.

——. (1961b). *The Baratarians and the Battle of New Orleans.* Legacy Publishing Company, Baton Rouge.

Debien, Gabriel. (1992). "The Saint-Domingue refugees in Cuba, 1793, 1815." Trans. by David Cheramie, in Brasseaux, Carl A., and Glenn Conrad, *The road to Louisiana: The Saint-Domingue refugees 1792–1809.* Center for Louisiana Studies, Lafayette.

Desmangles, Leslie G. (1992). *The faces of the gods: Vodou and Roman Catholicism in Haiti.* University of North Carolina Press, Chapel Hill.

Dessens, Nathalie. (2007). *From Saint-Domingue to New Orleans: Migration and influences.* University Press of Florida, Gainesville.

Deyle, Steven. (2005). *Carry me back: The domestic slave trade in American life.* Oxford University Press, New York.

Díaz Fabelo, Teodoro. (Undated). *Diccionario de la lengua conga residual en Cuba.* Casa del Caribe, Santiago de Cuba.

Din, Gilbert C. (1996a). "Bernardo de Gálvez: A reexamination of his governorship," in Din, Gilbert C., ed., *The Spanish presence in Louisiana 1763–1803*. Louisiana Purchase Bicentennial Series in Louisiana History. Center for Louisiana Studies, Lafayette.

——. (1996b). "The offices and functions of the New Orleans cabildo," in Din, Gilbert C., ed., *The Spanish presence in Louisiana 1763–1803*. Louisiana Purchase Bicentennial Series in Louisiana History. Center for Louisiana Studies, Lafayette.

Din, Gilbert C., and John E. Harkins. (1996). *The New Orleans cabildo: Colonial Louisiana's first city government, 1769–1803*. Louisiana State University Press, Baton Rouge.

Dokka, R. K., G. F. Sella, and T. H. Dixon. (2006). "Tectonic control of subsidence and southward displacement of southeast Louisiana with respect to stable North America." *Geophys. Res. Lett.*, 33, L23308, doi:10.1029/2006GL027250.

Dormon, James H., Jr. (1999). "The persistent specter: Slave rebellion in territorial Louisiana," in Vincent, Charles, ed. *The African American experience in Louisiana: Part A: From Africa to the Civil War*. Louisiana Purchase Bicentennial Series in Louisiana History. Center for Louisiana Studies, Lafayette.

Douglass, Frederick. (1855). *My bondage and my freedom*. Miller, Orton & Mulligan, New York.

Draper, David Elliott. (1973). *The Mardi Gras Indians: The ethnomusicology of black associations in New Orleans*. Ph.D. dissertation, Tulane University.

Drouin de Bercy. (1814). *De Saint-Domingue, de ses guerres, de ses révolutions, de ses resources, et des moyens a prendre pour y rétablir la paix et l'industrie*. Chez Hocquet, Paris.

Dubois, Laurent. (2004a). *Avengers of the New World: The story of the Haitian Revolution*. Belknap Press of Harvard University Press, Cambridge, MA.

——. (2004b). *A colony of citizens: Revolution and slave emancipation in the French Caribbean, 1787–1804*. University of North Carolina Press, Chapel Hill.

——. (2002). "'Troubled water': Rebellion and republicanism in the revolutionary French Caribbean," in Horn, James, Jan Ellen Lews, and Peter S. Onuf, eds., *The revolution of 1800: Democracy, race and the new republic*. University of Virginia Press, Charlottesville.

——. (Undated). "The Haitian Revolution and the sale of Louisiana; or, Thomas Jefferson's (unpaid) debt to Jean-Jacques Dessalines." Unpublished paper.

Dufour, Charles L. (1968). "The People of New Orleans," in Carter, Hodding, ed., *The past as prelude: New Orleans 1718–1968*. Tulane University, New Orleans.

Egerton, Douglas. (2002). "The empire of liberty reconsidered," in Horn, James, Jan Ellen Lewis, and Peter S. Onuf, eds., *The revolution of 1800: Democracy, race and the new republic*. University of Virginia Press, Charlottesville.

"Eighteenth century slaves as described by their masters." (1916). *The Journal of Negro History*, 1:2, April.

Ellis, Joseph J. (1993). *Passionate sage: The character and legacy of John Adams.* W. W. Norton, New Yok.

———. (1997). *American sphinx: The character of Thomas Jefferson.* Knopf, New York.

Epstein, Dena J. (1975). "The folk banjo: A documentary history." *Ethnomusicology,* 19.

———. (1977). *Sinful tunes and spirituals: Black folk music to the Civil War.* University of Illinois Press, Urbana.

Everett, Donald E. (1953). "Emigres and Militiamen: Free Persons of Color in New Orleans, 1803–1815." *The Journal of Negro History,* 38: 4, October.

Eyma, Xavier. (1857). *Les peaux noires: Scènes de la vie des esclaves.* Michel Lévy frères, Paris.

Fairclough, Adam. (2000). "Brutality and ballots, 1946–1956," in Vincent, Charles, ed. (2000). *The African American experience in Louisiana: Part C: From Jim Crow to civil rights.* Louisiana Purchase Bicentennial Series in Louisiana History. Center for Louisiana Studies, Lafayette.

Fandrich, Ina Johanna. (2005). *The mysterious voodoo queen, Marie Laveaux: A study of powerful female leadership in nineteenth-century New Orleans.* Routledge, New York.

Ferling, John. (2004). *Adams vs. Jefferson: The tumultuous election of 1800.* Oxford University Press, New York.

Fick, Carolyn E. (1990). *The making of Haiti: The Saint Domingue revolution from below.* University of Tennessee Press, Knoxville.

Fiehrer, Thomas. (1992). "From La Tortue to La Louisiane: An unfathomed legacy," in Brasseaux, Carl A. and Glenn Conrad, *The road to Louisiana: The Saint-Domingue refugees 1792–1809.* Center for Louisiana Studies, Lafayette.

———. (1999). "The African presence in colonial Louisiana: An essay on the continuity of Caribbean culture," in Vincent, Charles, ed. *The African American experience in Louisiana: Part A: From Africa to the Civil War.* Louisiana Purchase Bicentennial Series in Louisiana History. Center for Louisiana Studies, Lafayette.

Fischetti, Mark. (2001). "Drowning New Orleans." *Scientific American,* 285:4, October.

Follett, Richard. (2005). "'Lives of living death': The reproductive lives of slave women in the cane fields of Louisiana." *Slavery and Abolition,* 26:2, August.

Fortier, Alcée. (1966). *A history of Louisiana.* v. 1. 2d ed. Claitor's Book Store, Baton Rouge.

Foster, Eugene A., et al. (1998). "Jefferson fathered slave's last child." *Nature,* v. 396. November. 5.

Franco, José Luciano. (1996). *Comercio clandestino de esclavos.* 2d ed. Editorial de Ciencias Sociales, Havana.

Frégault, Guy. (1944). *Iberville le conquerant.* Societé des Editions Pascal, Montreal.

Freiberg, Edna B. (1980). *Bayou St. John in Colonial Louisiana: 1699–1803.* Harvey Press, New Orleans.

Garrigus, John. (2006). "History of St. Domingue, 1697–1791," in *Common routes: St. Domingue • Louisiana*. Somogy, Paris.

Gaspar, David Barry, and David Patrick Geggus, eds. (1997). *A turbulent time: the French Revolution and the greater Caribbean*. Indiana University Press, Bloomington.

Gaunt, Kyra. (2006). *The games black girls play: Learning the ropes from Double-dutch to hiphop*. New York University Press, New York.

Gayarré, Charles. (1866–67). *History of Louisiana*. 2d ed. 4 vol. W. J. Widdleton, New York.

Geggus, David Patrick. (1982). *Slavery, war, and revolution: The British occupation of Saint Domingue, 1793–1798*. Clarendon Press, Oxford.

Gilmore, H. W. (1944). "The old New Orleans and the new: A case for ecology." *American Sociological Review*, 9:4, August.

Gipson, Lawrence Henry. (1950). *The American Revolution as an aftermath of the Great War for the Empire, 1754–1763 and other essays in American colonial history*. Institute of Research, Lehigh University, Bethlehem, PA.

Giraud, Marcel. (1995). "German emigration." Translated by Glenn Conrad, in Conrad, Glenn R., ed., *The French experience in Louisiana*. Louisiana Purchase Bicentennial Series in Louisiana History, v. 1. Center for Louisiana Studies, Lafayette.

Goebel, Dorothy Burne. (1938). "British trade to the Spanish colonies, 1796–1823." *American Historical Review*, 43:2, January.

Gottschalk, Louis Moreau. (1881). *Notes of a Pianist*. J. B. Lippincott, Philadelphia.

Goudeau, D. A. and W. C. Conner. (1968). "Storm surge over the Mississippi River Delta, accompanying Hurricane Betsy, 1965." *Monthly Weather Review*, 96:2.

Gould, Virginia Meacham. (1999). "'If I can't have my rights, I can have my pleasures, and if they won't give me wages, I can take them': Gender and slave labor in antebellum New Orleans," in Vincent, Charles S., ed., *The African American experience in Louisiana: Part A: From Africa to the Civil War*. Louisiana Purchase Bicentennial Series in Louisiana History, v. 9. Center for Louisiana Studies, Lafayette.

Goulet, Anne-Madeleine. (2002). "Les méanders de la foi/The windings of faith." Liner notes to Le Concert Lorrain, *Manuscrit des Ursulines de la Nouvelle-Orléans*. K617 (Harmonia Mundi).

Gray, Francine du Plessix. (1998). *At home with the Marquis de Sade: A life*. Simon and Schuster, New York.

Guédé, Alain. (1999). *Monsieur de Saint-George: Le nègre des lumières*. Actes Sud, Arles.

Hall, Gwendolyn Midlo. (1992). *Africans in colonial Louisiana: The development of Afro-Creole culture in the eighteenth century*. Louisiana State Unviersity Press, Baton Rouge.

———. (2005). *Slavery and African ethnicities in the Americas: Restoring the links*. University of North Carolina Press, Chapel Hill.

———. (Unpublished). "The Franco-African peoples of Haiti and Louisiana: Population, language, culture, religion, and revolution."

Hamilton, Thomas. (1843). *Men and manners in America.* Edinburgh, W. Blackwood and Sons.

Hanger, Kimberly S. (1996). *A medley of cultures: Louisiana history at the cabildo.* Louisiana Museum Foundation, New Orleans.

———. (1997). *Bounded lives, bounded places: Free black society in colonial New Orleans, 1769–1803.* Duke University Press, Durham.

———. (1998). "'Desiring total tranquility'" and not getting it: Conflict involving free black women in Spanish New Orleans." *The Americas,* 54:4. (April).

———. (1999a). "A privilege and honor to serve: The free black militia of Spanish New Orleans," in Vincent, Charles S., ed., *The African American experience in Louisiana: Part A: From Africa to the Civil War.* Louisiana Purchase Bicentennial Series in Louisiana History, v. 9. Center for Louisiana Studies, Lafayette.

———. (1999b). "Avenues to freedom open to New Orleans' black population, 1769–1779," in Vincent, Charles S., ed., *The African American experience in Louisiana: Part A: From Africa to the Civil War.* Louisiana Purchase Bicentennial Series in Louisiana History, v. 9. Center for Louisiana Studies, Lafayette.

———. (1999c). "'Almost all have callings': Free blacks at work in Spanish New Orleans," in Vincent, Charles S., ed., *The African American experience in Louisiana: Part A: From Africa to the Civil War.* Louisiana Purchase Bicentennial Series in Louisiana History, v. 9. Center for Louisiana Studies, Lafayette.

Hardy, B. C. (1908). *The Princesse de Lamballe: A biography.* Archibald Constable and Company, London.

Hardy, James D., Jr. (1995). "The transportation of convicts to colonial Louisiana," in Conrad, Glenn R., ed., *The French experience in Louisiana.* Louisiana Purchase Bicentennial Series in Louisiana History, v. 1. Center for Louisiana Studies, Lafayette.

Harper, Chancellor. (1850). "Memoir on Slavery." *De Bow's Southern and Western Review,* November.

Hassall, Mary. (1808). *Secret history; or, The horrors of St. Domingo, in a series of letters, written by a lady at Cap François, to Colonel Burr, late vice-president of the United States, principally during the command of General Rochambeau.* R. Carr, Philadelphia. [pseud. of Leonora Sansay]

Hatfield, Joseph T. (1976). *William Claiborne: Jeffersonian centurion in the American Southwest.* University of Southwestern Louisiana, Lafayette.

Hearn, Lafcadio. (2001). *Inventing New Orleans: Writings of Lafcadio Hearn.* Ed. S. Frederick Starr. University Press of Mississippi, Jackson.

Hébert, A. Otis, Jr. (1974). "Resources in Louisiana depositories for the study of Spanish activities in Louisiana," in McDermott, John Francis, ed., *The Spanish in the Mississippi Valley 1762–1804.* University of Illinois Press, Urbana.

Herodotus. (1954). *The histories.* Trans. Aubrey de Sélincourt. Penguin, Baltimore.

Hobsbawm, Eric. (1962). *The age of revolution 1789–1848.* New American Library, New York.

Holmes, Jack D. L. (1965). *Gayoso: The life of a Spanish governor in the Mississippi Valley 1789–1799.* Louisiana State University Press, Baton Rouge.

——. (1974). "Spanish regulation of taverns and the liquor trade in the Mississippi Valley," in McDermott, John Francis, ed., *The Spanish in the Mississippi Valley.* University of Illinois Press, Urbana.

Horne, Alistair. (2005). *La belle France: A short history.* Knopf, New York.

Houck, Louis. (1909). *The Spanish regime in Missouri.* R. R. Donnelley & Sons, Chicago.

Ingersoll, Thomas N. (1999a). *Mammon and Manon in early New Orleans: The first slave society in the Deep South, 1718–1819.* University of Tennessee Press, Knoxville.

——. (1999b). "Free blacks in a slave society," in Vincent, Charles, ed., *The African American experience in Louisiana: Part A: From Africa to the Civil War.* Louisiana Purchase Bicentennial Series in Louisiana History. Center for Louisiana Studies, Lafayette.

Isaac, Rhys. (1982). *The transformation of Virginia: 1740–1790.* University of North Carolina Press, Chapel Hill.

Jacobs, Claude. (1989). "Spirit guides and possession in New Orleans black spiritual churches." *Journal of American Folklore,* 102:403, January–March.

James, C. L. R. (1989). *The black Jacobins: Toussaint 'Louverture and the San Domingo revolution.* 2d ed., rev. Vintage Books, New York.

Jefferson, Thomas. (1829). *Memoir, correspondence, and miscellanies, from the papers of Thomas Jefferson,* v.1, ed. Thomas Jefferson Randolph. F. Carr, Charlottesville.

——. (1904). *The writings of Thomas Jefferson,* v.1. The Thomas Jefferson Memorial Association, Washington, DC.

John, Dr. (1994). *Under a hoodoo moon: The life of Dr. John the Night Tripper.* St. Martin's Press, New York.

Johnson, Jerah. (1995). *Congo Square in New Orleans.* Louisiana Landmarks Society, New Orleans.

Johnson, Walter. (1999). *Soul by soul: Life inside the antebellum slave market.* Harvard University Press, Cambridge, MA.

Jordan, Louis. (Undated). "The Coins of Colonial and Early America." The Robert H. Gore Numismatic Endowment, University of Notre Dame, Department of Special Collections. http://www.coins.nd.edu/ColCoin/index.html. Accessed June 2007.

Jordan, Terry G. (1969). "The origin of Anglo-American cattle ranching in Texas: A documentation of diffusion from the Lower South." *Economic Geography,* 45:1, January.

Journal of Negro History. (1924). [unsigned article] 9:2, April.

Kemble, Frances A., and Frances A. Butler Leigh. (1995). *Principles and privilege: Two women's lives on a Georgia plantation.* University of Michigan Press, Ann Arbor.

King, Stewart R. (2001). *Blue coat or powdered wig: Free people of color in pre-revolutionary Saint-Domingue*. University of Georgia Press, Athens.

Kinnaird, Lawrence. (1976). "The western fringe of revolution." *The Western Historical Quarterly*, 7:3, July.

Kmen, Henry A. (1966). *Music in New Orleans: The formative years 1791–1841*. Louisiana State University Press, Baton Rouge.

Knight, Franklin. (2000). "The Haitian Revolution." *American Historical Review*, 105:1, February.

Knight, Henry C. (1824). *Letters from the south and west, by Arthur Singleton*. Richardson and Lord, Boston.

LaChance, Paul F. (1996). "The 1809 immigration of Saint-Domingue refugees to New Orleans: Reception, integration and impact," in Brasseaux, Carl A., ed., *A refuge for all ages: Immigration in Louisiana history*. Louisiana Purchase Bicentennial Series in Louisiana History, v. 10. Center for Louisiana Studies, Lafayette.

——. (1999). "The politics of fear: French Louisianans and the slave trade, 1706–1809," in Vincent, Charles, ed. *The African American experience in Louisiana: Part A: From Africa to the Civil War*. Louisiana Purchase Bicentennial Series in Louisiana History. Center for Louisiana Studies, Lafayette.

Lafargue, André. (1940). "The Louisiana Purchase: The French viewpoint." *Louisiana Historical Quarterly* 23:1, January.

Latrobe, Benjamin Henry. (1980). *The journals of Benjamin Henry Latrobe 1799–1820 from Philadelphia to New Orleans*. v. 3. Yale University Press, New Haven.

Laussat, Pierre-Clement. (1831). *Mémoires sur ma vie*. E. Vignancour, Pau.

Law, John. (1705). *Money and trade considered, with a proposal for supplying the nation with money*. Andrew Anderson, Edinburgh. 1966 facsimile edition, August M. Kelley, New York.

Le Gardeur, René J., Jr. (1963). *The first New Orleans theatre 1792–1803*. Leeward Books, New Orleans.

Le Moyne d'Iberville, Pierre. (1981). *Iberville's Gulf journals*. Trans. and ed. by Richebourg Gaillard McWilliams. University of Alabama Press, University.

Le Page du Pratz. (1774). *The history of Louisiana; or of the western parts of Virginia and Carolina*. Translated from the French. T. Becket, London.

Lemmon, Alfred E. (1996). "Music and art in Spanish colonial Louisiana," in Din, Gilbert C., ed., *The Spanish presence in Louisiana 1763–1803*. Louisiana Purchase Bicentennial Series in Louisiana History. Center for Louisiana Studies, Lafayette.

——. (2002). "Music in eighteenth-century New Orleans." Liner notes to Le Concert Lorrain, *Manuscrit des Ursulines de la Nouvelle-Orléans*. K617 (Harmonia Mundi).

Levtzion, Nehemia. (1994). *Islam in West Africa: Religion, Society and Politics to 1800*. Variorum, Aldershot, UK.

Lewis, Jan Ellen, and Peter S. Onuf, ed. (1999). *Sally Hemings and Thomas Jefferson: History, memory, and civic culture*. University Press of Virginia, Charlottesville.

Lewis, Peirce F. (2003). *New Orleans: The making of an urban landscape*. 2d ed. Center for American Places, Santa Fe.

Liljegren, Ernest R. (1939). "Jacobinism in Spanish Louisiana, 1792–1797." *Louisiana Historical Quarterly*, 22:1, January.

Linebaugh, Peter, and Marcus Rediker. (2000). *The many-headed hydra: Sailors, slaves, commoners, and the hidden history of the revolutionary Atlantic*. Beacon Press, Boston.

Lott, Eric. (1993). *Love and theft: Blackface minstrelsy and the American working class*. Oxford University Press, New York.

Louisiana Coastal Wetlands Conservation and Restoration Task Force and the Wetlands Conservation and Restoration Authority. (1998). *Coast 2050: Toward a sustainable coastal Louisiana*. Louisiana Department of Natural Resources, Baton Rouge. http://www.lca.gov/net_prod_download/public/lca_net_pub_products/doc/2050report.pdf. Accessed February 2005.

MacCulloch, Diarmid. (2003). *The Reformation: A history*. Penguin, New York.

Marx, Karl, and Frederick Engels. (1937). *The Civil War in the United States*. Ed. Richard Enmale. International Publishers, New York.

——. (1939). *Revolution in Spain*. Trans. anonymous. International Publishers, New York.

McCall, Edith. (1984). *Conquering the rivers: Henry Miller Shreve and the navigation of America's inland waterways*. Louisiana State University Press, Baton Rouge.

McDermott, John Francis, ed. (1974). *The Spanish in the Mississippi Valley 1762–1804*. University of Illinois Press, Urbana.

McWilliams, Tennant S. (1981). "Pierre LeMoyne d'Iberville and the competition for Empire," in Le Moyne d'Iberville, Pierre, *Iberville's Gulf journals*. University of Alabama Press, University.

"Memoirs of President Davies." (1987). *The quarterly register*. 9:4, May.

Métraux, Alfred. (1972). *Voodoo in Haiti*. Trans. Hugo Charteris. Schocken Books, NY.

Mims, Stewart L. (1912). "The diary of a voyage to the United States, by Moreau de Saint-Mery." *Proc. American Philosophical Society*, 51:205, July.

Moore, John Preston. (1974). "Anglo-Spanish rivalry on the Louisiana frontier, 1763–68," in McDermott, John Francis, ed., *The Spanish in the Mississippi Valley 1762–1804*. University of Illinois Press, Urbana.

——. (1996). "'The good wine of Bordeaux': Antonio de Ulloa," in Din, Gilbert C., ed., *The Spanish presence in Louisiana 1763–1803*. Louisiana Purchase Bicentennial Series in Louisiana History. Center for Louisiana Studies, Lafayette.

Moreau de St.-Méry, M. L. E. (1796). *Danse. Article extrait d'un ouvrage*. Imprimé par l'Auteur, Philadelphia.

———. (1958). *Description topographique, physique, civile, politique et historique de la partie française de l'isle Saint-Domingue.* New ed., vol. 1. Société de l'Historie des Colonies Françaises, Paris.

Morgan, Kenneth. (2001). "Slavery and the debate over ratification of the United States constitution." *Slavery & Abolition,* 22:3, December.

Morrison, Betty L. (1977). *A guide to voodoo in New Orleans 1820–1940.* Her Publishing, Gretna LA.

Nuttall, Thomas. (1821). *A journal of travels into the Arkansa Territory, during the year 1819. With occasional observations on the manners of the aborigines.* Thos. W. Palmer, Philadelphia.

Padgett, James A. (1937). "A decree for Louisiana issued by the Baron of Carondelet, June 1, 1795." *Louisiana Historical Quarterly,* 20:3, July.

Paquette, Robert. (1997). "Revolutionary Saint Domingue in the making of territorial Louisiana," in Gaspar, David Barry, and David Patrick Geggus, *A turbulent time: The French Revolution and the greater Caribbean.* Indiana University Press, Bloomington.

A particular account of the insurrection of the negroes of St. Domingo, begun in August, 1791. (1792). Tr. from French. London.

Payne, Stanley G. (1984). *Spanish Catholicism: An historical overview.* University of Wisconsin Press, Madison.

Peguero, Valentina, and Danilo de los Santos. (1978). *Visión general de la historia dominicana.* William Lawlor Publications, Stevens Point, WI.

Perrin du Lac, François Marie. (1807). *Travel through the two Louisianas, and among the savage nations of the Missouri; also, in the United States, along the Ohio, and the adjacent provinces, in 1801, 1802, & 1803.* Trans. anonymous. Richard Phillips, London.

Pevitt, Christine. (1997). *Philippe Duc d'Orléans, Regent of France.* Atlantic Monthly Press, New York.

Pichardo, Esteban. (1985). *Diccionario provincial de voces cubanas (1835).* Editorial de Ciencias Sociales, Havana.

Pond, Shephard. (1941). "The Spanish dollar: The world's most famous silver coin." *Bulletin of the Business Historical Society,* 15:1, February.

Pontchartrain, Blake. Untitled articles of various dates in *Gambit Weekly,* New Orleans.

Pope, John. (1792). *A tour through the southern and western territories of the United States of North-America; the Spanish dominions on the river Mississippi, and the Floridas; the countries of the Creek nations; and many uninhabited parts.* Printed by John Dixon, Richmond, VA.

Porteous, Laura L. (1934). "The gri-gri case." *Louisiana Historical Quarterly,* 17:1.

Porter, Kenneth Wiggins. (1951). "Negroes and the Seminole War, 1817–1818." *The Journal of Negro History,* 36:3, July.

Potré-Bobinskí, Germaine, and Clara Mildred Smith. (1936). *Natchitoches: The up-to-date oldest town in Louisiana.* Dameron-Pierson, New Orleans.

Raab, Selwyn. (2005). *Five families: The rise, decline, and resurgence of America's most powerful Mafia empires.* Thomas Dunne, New York.

Raynal, Guillaume-Thomas. (1780). *Histoire philosophique et politique des établissemens et du commerce des Européens dans les deux Indes.* v. 6. Geneva.

Reckdahl, Katy. (2005). "Chief of Chiefs." *Gambit Weekly* (New Orleans), July 5.

Rediker, Marcus. (2004). *Villains of all nations: Atlantic pirates in the Golden Age.* Beacon Press, Boston.

Reilly, Robin. (1974). *The British at the gates: The New Orleans campaign in the War of 1812.* G. P. Putnam's Sons, New York.

Roach, Joseph. (1996). *Cities of the dead: Circum-Atlantic performance.* Columbia University Press, New York.

Robertson, James Alexander. (1911). *Louisiana under the rule of Spain, France and the United States 1785–1807.* 2 v. Arthur H. Clark, Cleveland.

Robinson, Donald L. (1971). *Slavery in the structure of American politics, 1765–1820.* Harcourt Brace Jovanovich, New York.

Rosengarten, Joseph G. (1911). "Moreau de Saint Mery and his French friends in the American Philosophical Society." *Proc. American Philosophical Society,* 50:199, May–August.

Rothman, Joshua D. (1999). "James Callender and social knowledge of interracial sex in antebellum Virginia," in Lewis, Jan Ellen, and Peter S. Onuf, eds., *Sally Hemings and Thomas Jefferson: History, memory, and civic culture.* University Press of Virginia, Charlottesville.

Rousey, Dennis Charles (1996). *Policing the southern city: New Orleans, 1805–1889.* Louisiana State University Press, Baton Rouge.

Saint-Simon, Louis de Rouvroy, Duc de. (1972). *Historical memoirs of the Duc de Saint-Simon. Volume III: 1715–1723.* Ed. and trans. Lucy Norton. Hamish Hamilton, London.

Schama, Simon. (1987). *The embarrassment of riches: An interpretation of Dutch culture in the Golden Age.* Knopf, New York.

Scherman, Tony. (1999). *Backbeat: Earl Palmer's story.* Smithsonian Institution Press, Washington, DC.

Schöpf, Johann D. (1911). *Travels in the confederation, 1783–84.* Vol. 2. Trans. Alfred J. Morrison. Campbell, Philadelphia.

Schultz, Christian. (1810). *Travels on an inland voyage through the states of New York, Pennsylvania, Virginia, Ohio, Kentucky and Tennessee, and through the territories of Indiana, Louisiana, Mississippi and New-Orleans.* 2 v. Isaac Riley, New York.

Schumpeter, Joseph. (1954). *Economic doctrine and method: An historical sketch.* Trans. R. Aris. George Allen & Unwin, London.

Scott, Rebecca. (2005). *Degrees of freedom: Louisiana and Cuba after slavery.* Belknap Press, Cambridge, MA.

Scoville, Warren C. (1952a). "The Huguenots and the diffusion of technology I." *Journal of Political Economy*, 60:4, August.

——. (1952b). "The Huguenots and the diffusion of technology II." *Journal of Political Economy*, 60:5, October.

Seed, R. B., et al. (2005). *Preliminary report on the performance of the New Orleans levee systems in Hurricane Katrina on August 29, 2005.* American Society of Civil Engineers Report No. USB/CITRIS—05/01, November 17.

Shennan, J. H. (1979). *Philippe, Duke of Orléans: Regent of France 1715–1723.* Thames and Hudson, London.

Sidbury, James. (2002). "Thomas Jefferson in Gabriel's Virginia," in Horn, James, Jan Ellen Lewis, and Peter S. Onuf, eds., *The revolution of 1800: Democracy, race and the new republic.* University of Virginia Press, Charlottesville.

Simmons, William S. (1971). *Eyes of the night: Witchcraft among a Senegalese people.* Little, Brown, Boston.

Smith, Michael P. (1989). "Portfolio: New Orleans spiritual churches." *Journal of American Folklore*, 102:403 January–March.

Smith, Tom. (2007). *The Crescent City lynchings: The murder of Chief Hennessy, the New Orleans "Mafia" trials, and the Parish Prison mob.* Lyons Press, Guilford, CT.

Sonneck, O. G. (1915). *Early opera in America.* G. Schirmer, New York.

Stanton, Lucia. (2000). *Free some day: The African-American families of Monticello.* Thomas Jefferson Foundation Monticello Monograph Series n.p.

Starr, S. Frederick. (2000). *Louis Moreau Gottschalk.* University of Illinois Press, Urbana.

——. (2001). Introduction to Hearn, Lafcadio. (2001). *Inventing New Orleans: Writings of Lafcadio Hearn.* Ed. S. Frederick Starr. University Press of Mississippi, Jackson.

Stein, Susan R. (1993). *The worlds of Thomas Jefferson at Monticello.* Harry N. Abrams, New York.

Stinchcombe, Arthur L. (1995). *Sugar island slavery in the age of enlightenment: The political economy of the Caribbean world.* Princeton University Press, Princeton.

Stoddard, Maj. Amos. (1812). *Sketches, historical and descriptive, of Louisiana.* Mathew Carey, Philadelphia.

Sublette, Ned. (2004). *Cuba and its music: From the first drums to the mambo.* Chicago Review Press, Chicago.

Sullivan, Edward. (1852). *Rambles and scrambles in North and South America.* Richard Bentley, London.

Sutcliff, Robert. (1812). *Travels in some parts of North America in the years 1804, 1805, and 1806.* B. & T. Kite, Philadelphia.

Tallant, Robert. (1946). *Voodoo in New Orleans.* Macmillan, New York.

Taylor, Joe G. (1960). "The foreign slave trade in Louisiana After 1808." *Louisiana History* 1:1, Winter.

Thiers, M. A. (1965). *Histoire de la révolution française.* 10 v. Treizième Edition. Furne et Cie., Paris.

Thomas, Hugh. (1997). *The slave trade.* Simon and Schuster, New York.

Thompson, Robert Farris. (1983). *Flash of the spirit: African and Afro-American art and philosophy.* Vintage Books, New York.

———. (2005a). *Tango: An art history of love.* Pantheon, New York.

———. (2005b). "When saints go marching in: Kongo Louisiana, Kongo New Orleans," in *Resonance from the past: African sculpture from the New Orleans Museum of Art.* Museum for African Art, New York.

Thornton, John. (1991). "African dimensions of the Stono rebellion." *The American Historical Review,* 96:4, October.

———. (1998a). "The African experience of the '20. and odd Negroes' arriving in Virginia in 1619." *William and Mary Quarterly,* 55:3, July.

———. (1998b). *Africa and Africans in the making of the New World.* 2d ed. Cambridge University Press, Cambridge.

Tootie's last suit. (2007). Documentary film directed by Lisa Katzman.

Touchstone, Blake. (1972). "Voodoo in New Orleans." *Louisiana History* 13:4.

Tuckey, Captain J. K. (1818). *Narrative of an expedition to explore the River Zaire, usually called the Congo.* William B. Gilley, New York.

Usner, Daniel H. Jr. (1995). "From African Captivity to American Slavery," in Conrad, Glenn R., *The French Experience in Louisiana.* Louisiana Purchase Bicentennial Series in Louisiana History, v. 1. Center for Louisiana Studies, Lafayette.

de Vaissière, Pierre. (1909). *Saint-Domingue: La société et la vie créoles sous l'ancien régime (1629–1789).* Perrin et Cie., Paris.

Vlach, John. (1975). *Sources of the shotgun house: African and Caribbean antecedents for Afro-American architecture.* Ph.D. thesis, Indiana University.

Wagman, Morton. (1980). "Corporate Slavery in New Netherland." *The Journal of Negro History,* 65:1, Winter.

Walton, William. (1810). *Present state of the Spanish colonies; including a particular report of Hispañola, or the Spanish part of Santo Domingo; with a general survey of the settlements on the south continent of America, as relates to history, trade, population, customs, manners, &c. with a concise statement of the sentiments of the people on their relative situation to the mother country, &c.* Longman, Hurst, Rees, Orme, and Brown, London.

Ward, Martha. (2004). *Voodoo queen: The spirited lives of Marie Laveau.* University Press of Mississippi, Jackson.

Weeks, William Earl. (1992). *John Quincy Adams and American global empire.* University Press of Kentucky, Lexington.

Whitaker, Arthur P. (1935). "Antonio de Ulloa." *The Hispanic American Historical Review*, 15:2, May.

——. (1962). *The Mississippi question 1795–1803: A study in trade, politics, and diplomacy.* Peter Smith, Gloucester, MA.

Wilentz, Sean. (2005). *The rise of American democracy: Jefferson to Lincoln.* W. W. Norton, New York.

Wills, Garry. (2003). *"Negro President": Jefferson and the slave power.* Houghton Mifflin, Boston.

Wright, J. Leitch Jr. (1968). "A Note on the First Seminole War as Seen by the Indians, Negroes, and Their British Advisers." *Journal of Southern History*, 34:4, November.

INDEX